International Trade:
Selected Readings

W9-AWG-937

International Trade:
Selected Readings

Edited by
Jagdish N. Bhagwati

The MIT Press
Cambridge, Massachusetts,
and London, England

© 1981 by
The Massachusetts Institute of Technology

All rights reserved. No part of this book may be reproduced in any form or by any means, electronic or mechanical, including photocopying, recording, or by any information storage and retrieval system, without permission in writing from the publisher.

This book was set in Times New Roman by Asco Trade Typesetting Ltd., Hong Kong, and printed and bound by The Alpine Press Incorporated in the United States of America.

Library of Congress Cataloging in Publication Data

Main entry under title:

International trade.

Bibliography: p.
Includes index.
1. Commerce—Addresses, essays, lectures. 2. Commercial policy—Addresses, essays, lectures. I. Bhagwati, Jagdish N., 1934–
HF1411.I56   1981   382   80-20366
ISBN 0-262-02160-9 (hard)
ISBN 0-262-52060-5 (paper)

Contents

21

22

23

24

25

26

27

28

Editor's Introduction

This selection of readings in the theory of international trade has been designed to supplement courses at both undergraduate levels at the better universities and the graduate levels at all universities.

It was originally conceived as a re-issue of the highly successful Penguin Modern Economics Readings, which, having gone into several printings, was allowed to go out of print, leaving me the recipient of many letters requesting that I arrange for a reprinting of these readings by another publisher. When The MIT Press agreed to my suggestion to do this, it became clear to me, however, that a great number of interesting developments had taken place in the theory of international trade in the decade since I chose the papers for the Penguin readings in 1969 and that the interests of the teachers and students would be better served if the collection was substantially altered to reflect these new developments. The MIT Press also agreed to a larger selection of papers than the Penguin constraints had permitted, enabling me to put together a far more satisfactory group of papers, representative of nearly all the important areas of recent research in the theory of international trade.

The papers in this volume are, as before, not necessarily the pioneering papers on their subject. At times, I have deliberately selected reviews or restatements of important literature when they do a better job of conveying the subject matter than more obscure, pioneering papers. Such lucid and insightful surveys include especially Johnson's well-known piece on domestic distortions (chapter 11), Lipsey's excellent review of the orthodox literature on customs union theory (chapter 18), and Smith's splendid synthesis of the theoretical work on growth and trade (chapter 25).

Part I: General Equilibrium

The volume is divided into six parts, spanning the major areas of international trade theory. Part I contains four papers on general equilibrium theory and tools. Chapter 1 is Paul Samuelson's classic paper on factor price equalization, which, with its earlier companion paper on the same subject (June 1948), laid the foundation of the modern theory of international trade by casting the Heckscher-Ohlin ideas into a well-defined analytical model. Its precise subject of factor price equalization in this model, now called the Heckscher-Ohlin-Samuelson model, has led to a great body of work on the precise conditions under which factor price equalization will follow from goods price equalization under free trade, with extensions to the many factors and many goods models by McKenzie, Gale, Nikaido, and others (summarized in Samuelson's October 1967 article).

Chapter 2, however, which consists of a classic paper by Robert Mundell, turns the problem around and asks whether factor price equalization in a world of international mobility of one of the factors will restore goods price equalization when a tariff has destroyed the goods price equalization directly, and it demonstrates elegantly that indeed the factor price equalization theorem can be turned on its head.

Chapter 3 is another celebrated paper, by Ronald Jones, which brings together the basic theorems of the 2×2 Heckscher-Ohlin-Samuelson model into one, unified algebraic treatment of considerable simplicity and elegance. The resulting "Jones algebra" is now beginning to be widely used, as is evident from chapters 14 and 25.

Finally, chapter 4 is a beautiful piece by Michael Mussa, which may be viewed as a geometric companion piece to the Samuelson paper insofar as it develops the geometry of the 2×2 model in terms of its dual, thus adding to our pedagogic repertoire. This geometry is particularly helpful in analyzing factor market distortions, and it should be of considerable value insofar as the use of duality theory is likely to get more popular in trade theory as it has in the theory of public finance and elsewhere. (The reader is also referred to the complementary paper of Woodland (*Canadian Journal of Economics*, February 1977).

Part II: Trade-Pattern Theories

The theory of international trade has addressed, among many "positive" questions, the problem of what determines the pattern of trade of nation-states. The traditional, one-factor Ricardian theory has long given way to the Heckscher-Ohlin theory, starting with the Samuelsonian formulation noted earlier. The latter explains the trade pattern by reference to factor endowment differences among countries; that is, a labor-abundant country would export labor-intensive goods. Two important questions are raised by this theory. First, what about the accumulation of capital? If factor endowments change, what happens to comparative advantage a la Heckscher-Ohlin? This is the question most elegantly addressed by Ronald Findlay's piece reprinted in chapter 5. The paper is an important contribution that must be taught as soon as the static Heckscher-Ohlin version has been explained in the classroom. Second, if there are many commodities introduced into the Heckscher-Ohlin model, can we sustain a Ricardian-type chain proposition; namely, that all of the labor-abundant country's exports will be labor-intensive compared to all of its imports? Jones, in a classic paper (*Review of Economic Studies*, 1956–1957), said yes. I pointed out (*Journal of Political Economy*, September/October 1972) that when factor prices were equalized this need not be so. Alan Deardorff, in chapter 6, has nicely restated these results, proving the Jones proposition carefully for the case when factor prices are not equalized. He also extends the argument to include traded intermediates, thus providing the student with an analytical glimpse into a more realistic model.

Paul Krugman's paper, reprinted in chapter 7, provides a contrasting, new approach. Utilizing a modified version of the Dixit-Stiglitz model of product differentiation with scale economies, he produces trade between identical economies where "comparative advantage" is *not* the cause of trade, whether that comparative advantage comes from Ricardian or Heckscher-Ohlin factors. Gains from trade also follow. This "new" model of trade is better suited to explain trade in "similar" products between advanced countries, trade which is now called "intra-industry" trade. It also has different implications than the Heckscher-Ohlin model for issues such as the effect of trade policy changes on income distribution. Krugman's work in this area is paralleled by that of Dixit and Norman and also by that of Lancaster, who has indeed pioneered the economic analysis of product quality differences that must lie at the heart of any serious analysis of so-called intra-industry trade. The basic focus on mutual trade in "similar" products, which Lancaster, Krugman, et al. seek to model, was essentially provided by Linder in a classic volume in 1961, whose importance was foreseen in my 1964 *Economic Journal* survey of trade theory.

Part III: Tariffs and Quotas

While many of the papers in this volume address the theory of tariffs as it borders on the theory of commercial policy in its various aspects, such as customs union theory (chapters 18 and 19), the suitability of tariffs under alternative forms of market distortions (chapters 11 and 12), and their implications for cost-benefit analysis (chapter 17), part III addresses two important areas of the "positive" theory of tariffs that have engaged much attention recently.

The first area concerns the question of whether tariffs and quotas are equivalent. This question was opened up by my Haberler *Festschrift* paper (in R. Caves, H. G. Johnson, and P. B. Kenen, editors, *Trade, Growth and the Balance of Payments*, Rand McNally, 1965), where I noted that when competitive market-structure assumptions were dropped in a partial-equilibrium framework, the replacement of a tariff by a quota at the level of imports generated by the tariff would not necessarily create an implicit tariff identical to the (explicit) tariff that had been replaced by the quota. The voluminous literature that has followed this paper has then focused on two questions. First, if tariffs and quotas *are* equivalent in the sense defined by me, then the real equilibrium and welfare implications of tariffs and (equivalent) quotas are also identical. But suppose that they are *not* equivalent. Then the analyst could well go further and ask which instrument will produce higher welfare, holding *some* target variable (for example, domestic, import-competing production) constant. This opens up therefore a differently-oriented "equivalence" literature. Among important contributions to this type of analysis are the papers of McCulloch and Johnson (*American Economic Review*, September 1973), Fishelson and Flatters (*Journal of International Economics*, November 1975), and Pelcovits (*Journal of International Economics*, November 1976). Next, analysis has proceeded in the direction of exploring equivalence in a general-equilibrium framework. Carlos Rodriguez's paper in chapter 8 asks if the Cournot-Johnson analysis of optimum tariffs and retaliation is re-examined by substituting optimum quotas for the optimum tariffs, will the outcome be different? Johnson's analysis allows for the possibility that, despite retaliation, a country exercising its monopoly power could wind up better off than under free trade. By contrast, Rodriguez (and Tower in an independent analysis with similar results in *Review of Economic Studies*, 1975) shows that the optimum quota retaliation relentlessly restricts trade, asymptotically approaching autarky. The differential outcome under tariff and quota retaliation reflects the fact that, although a quota and a tariff are equivalent at any *one* point in the process, they change differently a country's offer curve that the *other* country faces, hence its response, and hence the path characterizing the retaliatory process.

The second area of extensive theoretical contributions in part III has been triggered off by the search for a suitable way of looking at tariffs when intermediate goods are traded. From this has arisen the theory of effective protection, which seeks to develop an index of protection on "value added" and relate it to gross output or primary factor allocation changes in the economy. Chapter 9 is an important paper by Corden that sets out the concept of effective protection and the issues it addresses and raises. A substantial body of literature examining the concept of effective protection in general equilibrium models has subsequently emerged. The interested student is best referred to a symposium on the subject in the *Journal of International Economics* (August 1973). There, Bruno, Bhagwati and Srinivasan, and others synthesize and extend the earlier work of Corden, Jones, Ramaswami and Srinivasan, etc.; later papers of Uekawa (*Journal of International Economics*, May 1979) and Wegge (*Journal of International Economics*, May 1979) build, in turn, on the work of Bruno and Bhagwati and Srinivasan.

Finally, the reader may note the use of the concept/index of effective protection as a guide in making socially correct project-choice decisions in cost-benefit analysis, a purpose quite distinct from the "positive" purpose of making inferences about resource allocational or output effects of a tariff structure (as in the foregoing literature and in chapter 9). This distinct, "normative" use of the concept is discussed in the contribution of Srinivasan and Bhagwati in chapter 17.

Part IV: Gains From Trade, Distortions, and Recent Extensions

The bulk of the rest of this volume relates to normative questions that indeed occupy the central attention of international economists. Chapter 10 reprints Samuelson's recent restatement of his classic proof that "some trade is superior to no trade," whether the country is atomistic or "large." Chapter 11, on the other hand, consists of Johnson's influential restatement of the Bhagwati-Ramaswami (*Journal of Political Economy*, February 1963) propositions that, for domestic distortions, a tariff is not the appropriate first-best policy intervention and a tariff that fully offsets such a domestic distortion may, in replacing suboptimal laissez faire by another suboptimal situation, be immiserizing. Chapter 12 reprints my Kindleberger *Festschrift* generalization of the theory of distortions and welfare. It goes well beyond the Bhagwati-Ramaswami-Johnson results and synthesizes a substantial body of literature on different types of distortions and ranking of alternative policy interventions designed to deal with them. Chapters 11 and 12 therefore ought to be read in conjunction to get a comprehensive view of the modern theory of commercial policy as it has emerged in the last fifteen years since the 1963 Bhagwati-Ramaswami paper, which, it should be emphasized, was in turn stimulated by the earlier work of Haberler (*Economic Journal*, June 1950) and Hagen (*Quarterly Journal of Economics*, November 1958).

Chapters 13 and 14 treat two alternative types of distortions, both relating to factor markets, providing a more intensive analysis that feeds into the preceding two chapters on distortions. Brecher's paper (chapter 13) considers the problems created by a *generalized* sticky wage, which leads to unemployment, a problem dealt with by many before him, including Haberler and Johnson (chapter 11), but solved elegantly by him in this paper. Brecher's analysis extends to ranking alternative policies in the presence of this sticky-wage distortion and thus extends and complements the analysis in chapters 11 and 12.

Neary's analysis in chapter 14, on the other hand, relates to the factor market distortion when the wage is flexible but there is a wage differential between sectors, in total contrast to the Brecher analysis of when the wage is identical between sectors but inflexible below a floor. The earlier analyses by Bhagwati and Srinivasan (*Journal of International Economics*, February 1971), Jones (*Journal of Political Economy*, May/June 1971), Kemp and Herberg (Kindleberger *Festschrift*), Magee, and others had highlighted many pathologies that would arise in the presence of such a wage differential; the corresponding policy interventions had been analyzed by Hagen and Bhagwati and Ramaswami and are reviewed in chapters 11 and 12. Neary's major contribution is to consider plausible adjustment mechanisms under which the move from one equilibrium to another will occur and then show that many of the pathologies will then not be observed. Neary's paper is of great interest also insofar as it is a beautiful specimen of his important work on short-run specific-factor models, synthesized in his September 1978 *Economic Journal* paper. It should be mentioned that the interest in sector-specific factor models was stimulated by Jones's important paper in the Kindleberger *Festschrift*, whereas the idea (as most ideas) of such a model can be traced to earlier writings by Haberler and Harrod, among others.

Chapter 15 reprints a paper by Bhagwati and Srinivasan on market disruption and the appropriate policy intervention when foreign quotas may be invoked with a probability that increases (endogenously) with the level of domestic exports. This paper is of importance not merely because it deals with a phenomenon of increasing policy concern but also because it incorporates uncertainty into the analysis (thus giving the reader a glimpse into an area of growing theoretical concern by Bardhan, Batra, Kemp, Liviatan, Helpman and Razin (1979) and other trade theorists comprehensively surveyed in Pomery (1979)) and links the results with the theory of distortions. For it is shown that the country facing such a market disruption possibility, where the threat of quota invocation is endogenous to its exports, should utilize an optimal tariff; if there is additionally a putty-clay problem, *that* should be taken care of by a production tax-cum-subsidy instead. All this is consonant with the conclusions of the theory of noneconomic objectives, as reviewed in chapter 12, and in fact illustrates how a (first-period) noneconomic objective may be turned into an economic objective by linking up second-period outcomes to first-period decisions in a many-period analysis.

Chapters 16 and 17 are papers on two other recent subjects that have attracted much theoretical and policy attention. Sheikh's paper (chapter 16) is an elegant analysis of the illegal trade that circumvents tariffs in the real world. This area was opened up by Bhagwati and Hansen (*Quarterly Journal of Economics*, May 1973), who used the 2 × 2 framework where the increased real costs of illegal trade were modeled, as in Samuelson's classic analysis of transport costs, as constituted by the traded goods themselves; this is the so-called "melting ice" assumption. Sheikh, however, models them as requiring primary factors directly via a fictional "non-traded" good, thus utilizing a variant of the Komiya nontraded goods model, where the 2 × 2 structure on the 2 traded goods determines the prices of the 2 primary factors and hence the price of the nontraded good as well.

A substantial body of theoretical work has grown around this theme of illegal trade, by Johnson, Cooper, Ray, Falvey, etc., much of which has been reprinted (in Bhagwati, editor, *Illegal Transactions in International Trade: Theory and Measurement*, North Holland, 1973).

Moreover, tariff theory is being brought closer to reality in two other respects, which are not reflected in the present volume, as important work in these areas is still emerging. First, Brock and Magee (*American Economic Review*, May 1978) have drawn attention to the problem of tariff-seeking or tariff-making; that is, how should one model the lobbying process for tariffs? A great deal of empirical discussion of this matter is now available, but the theoretical work is still scarce. An important exception is an unpublished paper of Findlay and Wellisz that addresses the problem in a general equilibrium, trade-theoretic framework. Second, when tariff-seeking, that is, lobbying for protection, is successful, the economy gets a tariff that, if not prohibitive, will result in tariff revenue. But revenues themselves will then be "sought," as lobbies indeed exist for getting a share of the revenues that flow out from the government. Trade theorists have generally assumed a Meade-type lump-sum transfer of tariff revenues to consumers, but this assumption makes little sense in reality. The theory of tariffs thus needs to be generalized to include the revenue-seeking activities as well; this analysis has been initiated by Bhagwati and Srinivasan (*Journal of Political Economy*, November/December 1980).

Finally, chapter 17 addresses yet another area of considerable research in recent years; namely, how should one evaluate projects in cost-benefit analysis when the economy is characterized by trade distortions? This is evidently a second-best problem and one that is of policy relevance to many governments. A number of cost-benefit analysts such as Little, Mirrlees, and Bruno have suggested that the social cost of projects in this situation be measured by evaluating output foregone, thanks to the project, at world prices when the economy is atomistic. Again, trade economists such as Krueger have proposed the use of "domestic resource costs" (DRC) as the relevant criterion, whereas some have proposed using effective rates of protection (ERP) toward this end. Chapter 17 reprints a paper by Srinivasan and Bhagwati that addresses this issue and sorts out the correct criterion and its relationship to the DRC and ERP criteria. It also extends the project-choice analysis to cases where the distortion is not from trade policies but from several factor market distortions, including those treated in chapters 13 and 14. Among the important conclusions in chapter 17 is the possibility that the social cost of a project under trade (and, for that matter, under other) distortions may be negative, a possibility that illuminates many paradoxes such as the possibility of welfare-improving diversion of resources to "wasteful" lobbying for tariff-imposition or for revenue seeking. An important earlier paper in this area is by Findlay and Wellisz (*Journal of Political Economy*, June 1976), and further extensions of interest for students of development-cum-trade theory and policy may be found in Bhagwati, Srinivasan, and Wan (*Economic Journal*, March 1979) and Bhagwati and Srinivasan (*Indian Economic Review*, October 1979, and *Quarterly Journal of Economics*, February 1980).

Part V: Tariff Discrimination: Customs Unions et al.

This part singles out two important papers that represent divergent analytical approaches to the theory of preferential tariff reduction. Chapter 18, a paper by Lipsey, represents a review of the major analytical contributions, beginning with Viner's classic work and then encompassing the important contributions of Lipsey, Lancaster, Meade, and others, where the analysis is predicated on a country reducing its tariff down to zero for another member country but retaining it at the initial level for the "outside," nonmember country. Following Viner, the analysis then distinguishes between unions that will then lead to reduced and those that will lead to increased welfare for the country and establishes conditions for these differential outcomes.

Kemp and Wan, on the other hand, in their paper presented in chapter 19, take an altogether different approach. They argue that it is always possible for any subset of countries in the world economy to abolish tariffs on one another, choose an external tariff that maintains trade with the outside world (and hence the outside world's welfare as well) unchanged, and improve the welfare of some member(s) of the union without hurting any other member's welfare by using lump-sum transfers. In short, their approach, by making the common external tariff a policy variable, enables them to resurrect the pre-Vinerian intuition that a *partial* move to free trade by any subset of countries could be made welfare improving for them and for the world as a whole. I expect future research to develop further this alternative, interesting approach to customs union theory.

Part VI: Growth, Foreign Investment, and Bottlenecks

The final section of this volume addresses questions raised by growth of resources, whether domestic or foreign-owned, and by technical progress. Chapter 20 is a classic paper of Findlay and Grubert in which they discuss the effect of different types of technical change on the output elasticity of supply at constant goods prices, thus complementing the corresponding Rybczynski analysis of the effects of factor supply change on the output elasticity of supply.

Chapters 21 and 22, on the other hand, analyze the consequences of growth on welfare under alternative distortions and demonstrate how the paradox of immiserizing growth can arise. Chapter 21 is my paper, which showed how a decline in the growth-induced terms of trade may lead to a secondary loss that outweighs the primary gain from growth, whereas chapter 22 by Johnson shows immiserization as a possibility when growth takes place subject to a tariff in a small economy. Both paradoxes can be explained, of course, as arising because growth is taking place subject to a distortion whose cost is accentuated by the growth sufficiently to outweigh the gain that would arise if growth were to occur with optimal policies in place, as I subsequently noted (*Review of Economic Studies*, November 1968, and later in the paper presented in chapter 12). Thus, in chapter 21 the distortion arises from the failure to use an optimal tariff when the country is large, and in chapter 22 it arises from the fact that a tariff is distortionary for a small country.

Chapter 23 utilizes the approach of chapter 22 to analyze the question of whether the inflow of *foreign* capital is immiserizing if a small economy is tariff-distorted, a question of great interest, as many countries have used tariffs to *induce* capital inflow. Brecher and Alejandro, as Uzawa had done previously and independently in Japanese, show that if the importable good is capital-intensive, foreign capital inflow will be *necessarily* immiserizing. Their analysis is then extended to embrace the earlier analyses of the welfare impact of foreign inflows in the presence of tariffs, including the classic Mundell analysis in chapter 2.

Chapter 24 turns the Brecher-Alejandro-Uzawa analysis on its head and asks what would happen to national welfare if, instead of varying the foreign capital inflow with a given tariff, the tariff is varied with given capital inflow. This is a novel problem, raised originally by Tironi in the context of Latin American worries that the benefits of their intra–Latin-American trade liberalization might accrue wholly to foreign multinationals rather than to the countries. In terms of trade-theoretic analysis, one has therefore to reckon with the fact that redistribution of income toward foreign-owned factors of production may outweigh the primary gain from liberalized trade, thus creating the "paradox" that free trade may be immiserizing, relative to autarky, even for a small country. The Bhagwati-Brecher paper, reprinted as chapter 24, analyzes this problem for the general case when the foreign-owned factors include *both* capital and labor and establishes geometrically the conditions under which the paradox just described will arise. Their analysis, and that of related unpublished theoretical contributions by Ricardo Martin and others, also has bearing on the welfare-impact analysis of member-country welfare in customs unions with full internal factor mobility and a common external tariff, so that chapter 24 has a legitimate claim to have been included in part V and represents a yet third approach to the analysis of customs union theory.

Whereas chapters 20 through 24 are contributions that are essentially comparative-static in nature, chapter 25 contains a comprehensive survey by Smith of recent contributions to the dynamic theory of growth and trade. It should help the student to get a quick and firm grasp of the central findings of this area of research and then be better prepared to confront the welfare-theoretic issues that have been raised by Emmanuel, Steedman, and others, in one way or another, alleging the possible suboptimality of free trade vis-à-vis autarky in growing economies. The student who wishes to pursue these questions, as he should and indeed cannot avoid if he lives in England or France, is advised to consult Smith (*Journal of International Economics*, May 1979), Samuelson (*Journal of*

International Economics, November 1975 and February 1978), Emmanuel versus Samuelson (*Journal of International Economics*, February 1978), and Srinivasan and Bhagwati (in Chipman and Kindleberger, eds., *Essays in International Economics*, Memorial Volume for Sohmen, North-Holland, 1980).

A further topic in this volume relates to the notion of foreign exchange "bottlenecks", an ex ante planning concept that has led to such considerable and persistent confusion in the trade-and-developmental, cost-benefit, and related literature on foreign exchange difficulties that I have decided to include two brief readings on the subject that should suffice to destroy any lack of clarity on the concept. Chapter 26 reprints the first section of a well-known paper of McKinnon's that develops the bottleneck concept in the Harrod-Domar, growth-theoretic framework very elegantly and relates it to the notion of the marginal productivity of foreign capital inflow as well. Chapter 27, a paper by Desai and Bhagwati, on the other hand, develops the concept in a state framework, utilizing the geometric tools of conventional trade theory, and contrasts it sharply with the ex post concepts of payments deficits, open and suppressed. Students who are interested in further theoretical analysis of the bottleneck concept should consult Findlay (in the Kindleberger *Festschrift*); an excellent computable-model application of the concept is by Chenery and Bruno (*Economic Journal*, March 1962).

The readings conclude with a relatively different approach to growth-theoretic issues, associated with the work of Frenkel, Onitsuka, and Fischer. Chapter 28 is an abbreviated version of a paper by Fischer and Frenkel, which presents a two-sector model of a small growing economy that trades in both investment goods and securities as well as consumption goods. While the two-sector model had frequently been used in analyzing the growth process of open economies, it was usually assumed that there was trade in consumption goods and in either securities or investment goods but not both. The main difficulty in modeling trade in both investment goods and securities when the terms of trade are fixed is that a country's income will be the same whether it acquires income streams from abroad by buying securities paying the world interest rate or whether it obtains income by investing in capital that yields the same rate of return. By specifying a demand function for investment goods, based on an adjustment cost formulation in which more rapid rates of investment reduce the rate of return to capital, the authors allow for trade in both investment goods and securities and are also able to break the familiar link between the stability of the two-sector model and relative factor intensities in production. The model is used to study the dynamics of capital accumulation and the various trade accounts for a small open economy.

In conclusion, I would like to thank Richard Brecher, Ronald Findlay, Peter Neary, Paul Krugman, Ronald McKinnon, Jacob Frenkel, Alasdair Smith, and T. N. Srinivasan for many helpful suggestions that have assisted me in finalizing the selection of readings, and Robert Feenstra for research assistance.

References

Bhagwati, J. N. "The Pure Theory of International Trade: A Survey." *Economic Journal*, March 1964.

Bhagwati, J. N. "On the Equivalence of Tariffs and Quotas." In R. E. Caves, H. G. Johnson, P. B. Kenen, eds., *Trade, Growth, and the Balance of Payments: Essays in Honor of Gottfried Haberler*, pp. 53–67. Chicago: Rand McNally, 1965.

Bhagwati, J. N., ed. *International Trade: Selected Readings*. Baltimore: Penguin.

Bhagwati, J. N. "The Heckscher-Ohlin Theorem in the Multi-Commodity Case." *Journal of Political Economy* 80, no. 5 (September/October 1972): 1052–1055.

Bhagwati, J. N., ed. *Illegal Transactions in International Trade: Theory and Measurement*. Amsterdam: North-Holland, 1973.

Bhagwati, J. N., and B. Hansen. "A Theoretical Analysis of Smuggling." *Quarterly Journal of Economics*, 83 (May 1973): 172–187.

Bhagwati, J. N., and V. K. Ramaswami. "Domestic Distortions, Tariffs, and the Theory of Optimum Subsidy." *Journal of Political Economy* 71, no. 1 (February 1963): 44–50.

Bhagwati, J. N., and T. N. Srinivasan. "The Theory of Wage Differentials: Production Response and Factor Price Equalization." *Journal of International Economics* 1, no. 1 (February 1971): 19–35.

Bhagwati, J. N., and T. N. Srinivasan. "Revenue-Seeking: A Generalization of the Theory of Tariffs." Forthcoming in the *Journal of Political Economy*, 1980.

Brock, W. A., and S. P. Magee. "The Economics of Special Interest Politics: The Case of the Tariff." *American Economic Review Papers and Proceedings* 68, no. 2 (May 1978): 250.

Chenery, H. B., and M. Bruno. "Development Alternatives in an Open Economy." *Economic Journal* 72 (March 1962): 79–103.

Dixit, A., and J. Stiglitz. "Monopolistic Competition and Optimum Product Diversity." *American Economic Review* 67, no. 3 (June 1977): 297–308.

Emmanuel, A. "A Note on 'Trade Pattern Reversals,'" *Journal of International Economics* 8, no. 1 (February 1978): 143–145.

Findlay, R. "The 'Foreign Exchange Gap' and Growth in Developing Economies." In J. N. Bhagwati, R. W. Jones, R. A. Mundell, J. Vanek, eds., *Trade, Balance of Payments and Growth: Papers in International Economics in Honor of Charles P. Kindleberger*, pp. 168–182. Amsterdam: North-Holland, 1971.

Findlay, R., and S. Wellisz. "Project Evaluation, Shadow Prices, and Trade Policy." *Journal of Political Economy* 84, no. 3 (June 1976): 543–552.

Findlay, R., and S. Wellisz. "Rent-Seeking, Welfare, and the Political Economy of Trade Restriction." Unpublished paper, Columbia University, September 1979.

Fishelson, G., and F. Flatters. "The (Non) equivalence of Optimal Tariffs and Quotas Under Uncertainty." *Journal of International Economics* 5, no. 4 (November 1975): 385–393.

Haberler, G. "Some Problems in the Pure Theory of International Trade." *Economic Journal* 60 (June 1950): 223–240.

Hagen, E. "An Economic Justification of Protectionism." *Quarterly Journal of Economics* 72 (November 1958): 496–514.

Helpman, E., and A. Razin. *A Theory of International Trade Under Uncertainty.* New York: Academic Press, 1979.

Herberg, H., and M. C. Kemp. "Factor Market Distortions, The Shape of the Locus of Competitive Outputs, and the Relation Between Product Prices and Equilibrium Outputs." In J. N. Bhagwati *et al.*, eds., *Trade, Balance of Payments and Growth: Papers in International Economics in Honor of Charles P. Kindleberger*, pp. 22–48. Amsterdam: North-Holland, 1971.

Jones, R. W. "Factor Proportions and the Heckscher-Ohlin Theorem." *Review of Economic Studies* 24, no. 63 (1956–1957): 1–10.

Jones, R. W. "Distortions in Factor Markets and the General Equilibrium Model of Production." *Journal of Political Economy* 79, no. 3 (May/June 1971a): 437–459.

Jones, R. W. "A Three Factor Model in Theory, Trade and History." In J. N. Bhagwati *et al.*, eds., *Trade, Balance of Payments and Growth: Papers in International Economics in Honor of Charles P. Kindleberger*, pp. 3–21. Amsterdam: North-Holland, 1971b.

Lancaster, K. "A Theory of Trade Between Identical Economies," Discussion Paper No. 75-7604 (unpublished), Columbia University, June 1975.

Linder, S. *An Essay on Trade and Transformation.* John Wiley & Sons, 1961.

Magee, S. P. *International Trade and Distortions in Factor Markets.* New York: Marcell Dekker, 1976.

McCulloch, R., and H. G. Johnson. "A Note on Proportionally-Distributed Quotas." *American Economic Review* 63 (September 1973): 726–732.

Neary, J. P. "Short-Run Capital Specificity and the Pure Theory of International Trade." *Economic Journal* 88 (September 1978): 488–510.

Pelcovits, M. D. "Quotas Versus Tariffs." *Journal of International Economics* 6, no. 4 (November 1976): 363–370.

Pomery, J. "Uncertainty and International Trade." In R. Dornbusch and J. A. Frenkel, eds., *International Economic Policy: Theory and Evidence*, pp. 112–157. Baltimore: Johns Hopkins University Press, 1979.

Samuelson, P. A. "International Trade and Equalization of Factor Prices." *Economic Journal* 58, no. 230 (June 1948): 163–184. Reproduced as chapter 67 in *Collected Scientific Papers of Paul A. Samuelson*, Vol. II. Cambridge, Massachusetts: MIT Press, 1966.

Samuelson, P. A. "Summary on Factor-Price Equalization." *International Economic Review* 8, no. 3 (October 1967): 286–295. Reproduced as chapter 161 in: *Collected Scientific Papers of Paul A. Samuelson*, Vol. III. Cambridge, Massachusetts: MIT Press, 1972.

Samuelson, P. A. "Trade Pattern Reversals in Time-Phased Ricardian Systems and Intertemporal Efficiency." *Journal of International Economics* 5, no. 9 (November 1975): 309–363. Reproduced as chapter 251 in *Collected Scientific Papers of Paul A. Samuelson*, Vol. IV. Cambridge, Massachusetts: MIT Press, 1977.

Samuelson, P. A. "Free Trade's Intertemporal Pareto-Optimality." *Journal of International Economics* 8, no. 1 (February 1978a): 147–149.

Samuelson, P. A. "Interest Rate Equalization and Nonequalization by Trade in Leontief-Sraffa Models." *Journal of International Economics* 8, no. 1 (February 1978b): 21–27.

Smith, M. A. M. "Intertemporal Gains from Trade." *Journal of International Economics* 9, no. 2 (May 1979): 239–248.

Srinivasan, T. N., and J. N. Bhagwati. "Trade and Welfare in a Steady State." In J. S. Chipman and C. P. Kindleberger, eds., *Essays in International Economics: Memorial Volume for Sohmen*, Amsterdam: North-Holland, 1980.

"Symposium on Effective Protection." *Journal of International Economics* 3, no. 3 (August 1973).

Tironi, E. *Foreign Direct Investment and Economic Integration Policies: The Andean Case.* Unpublished doctoral dissertation, MIT, Cambridge, Massachusetts, 1976.

Tower, E. "The Optimum Quota and Retaliation." *Review of Economic Studies* 42 (1975): 623–630.

Uekawa, Y. "The Theory of Effective Protection, Resource Allocation and the Stolper-Samuelson Theorem: The Many-Industry Case." *Journal of International Economics* 9, no. 2 (May 1979): 151–171.

Wegge, L. L. "Conjugate Small Country Production Equilibrium Concepts." *Journal of International Economics* 9, no. 2 (May 1979): 173–196.

Woodland, A. D. "A Dual Approach to Equilibrium in the Production Sector in International Trade." *Canadian Journal of Economics* 10, no. 1 (February 1977): 50–68.

I
General Equilibrium

1
International Factor-Price Equalisation Once Again

Paul A. Samuelson

1. Introduction

My recent paper attempting to show that free commodity trade will, under certain specified conditions, inevitably lead to complete factor-price equalisation appears to be in need of further amplification.[1] I propose therefore (1) to restate the principal theorem, (2) to expand upon its intuitive demonstration, (3) to settle the matter definitively by a brief but rigorous mathematical demonstration, (4) to make a few extensions to the case of many commodities and factors, and finally (5) to comment briefly upon some realistic qualifications to its simplified assumptions.

I cannot pretend to present a balanced appraisal of the bearing of this analysis upon interpreting the actual world, because my own mind is not made up on this question: on the one hand, I think it would be folly to come to any startling conclusions on the basis of so simplified a model and such abstract reasoning; but on the other hand, strong simple cases often point the way to an element of truth present in a complex situation. Still, at the least, we ought to be clear in our deductive reasoning; and the elucidation of this side of the problem plus the qualifying discussion may contribute towards an ultimate appraisal of the theorem's realism and relevance.

2. Statement of the Theorem

My hypotheses are as follows:

1. There are but two countries, America and Europe.
2. They produce but two commodities, food and clothing.

This paper was originally published in *The Economic Journal*, June 1949, pp. 181–197.

3. Each commodity is produced with two factors of production, land and labour. The production functions of each commodity show "constant returns to scale," in the sense that changing all inputs in the same proportion changes output in that same proportion, leaving all "productivities" essentially unchanged. In short, all production functions are mathematically "homogeneous of the first order" and subject to Euler's theorem.
4. The law of diminishing marginal productivity holds: as any one input is increased relative to other inputs, its marginal productivity diminishes.
5. The commodities differ in their "labour and land intensities." Thus, food is relatively "land using" or "land-intensive," while clothing is relatively "labour-intensive." This means that whatever the prevailing ratio of wages to rents, the optimal proportion of labour to land is greater in clothing than in food.
6. Land and labour are assumed to be qualitatively identical inputs in the two countries and the technological production functions are assumed to be the same in the two countries.
7. All commodities move perfectly freely in international trade, without encountering tariffs or transport costs, and with competition effectively equalising the market price-ratio of food and clothing. No factors of production can move between the countries.
8. Something is being produced in both countries of both commodities with both factors of production. Each country may have moved in the direction of specialising on the commodity for which it has a comparative advantage, but it has not moved so far as to be specialising completely on one commodity.[2]

All of this constitutes the hypothesis of the theorem. The conclusion states:

Under these conditions, real factor prices must be exactly the same in both countries (and indeed the proportion of inputs used in food production in America must equal that in Europe, and similarly for clothing production).

Our problem is from now on a purely logical one. Is "If H, then inevitably C" a correct statement? The issue is not whether C (factor-price equalisation) will actually hold; nor even whether H (the hypothesis) is a valid empirical generalisation. It is whether C can fail to be true when H is assumed true. Being a logical question, it admits of only one answer: either the theorem is true or it is false.

One may wonder why such a definite problem could have given rise to misunderstanding. The answer perhaps lies in the fact that even so simple a set-up as this one involves more than a dozen economic variables: at least four inputs for each country, four marginal productivities for each country (marginal productivity of American labour in food, of American land in food ...), two outputs for each country, the prices of the two commodities, the price in each country of the two inputs, the proportions of the inputs in different lines of production, and so forth. It is not always easy for the intellect to move purposefully in a hyperspace of many dimensions.

And the problem is made worse by the fact, insufficiently realised, that constant returns to scale is a very serious limitation on the production functions. A soon as one knows a single "curve" on such a surface, all other magnitudes are frozen into exact quantitative shapes and cannot be chosen at will. Thus, if one knows the returns of total product to labour working on one acre of land, then one already knows everything: the marginal productivity schedule of land, all the iso-product curves, the marginal-rate-of-substitution schedules, etc. This means one must use a carefully graduated ruler in drawing the different economic functions, making sure that they are numerically consistent in addition to their having plausible qualitative shapes.

3. Intuitive Proof

In each country there is assumed to be given totals of labour and land. If all resources are devoted to clothing, we get a certain maximum amount of clothing. If all are devoted to food production, we get a certain maximum amount of food. But what will happen if we are willing to devote only part of all land and part of total labour to the production of food, the rest being used in clothing production? Obviously, then we are in effect sacrificing some food in order to get some clothing. The iron law of scarcity tells us that we cannot have all we want of both goods, but must ultimately give up something of one good in getting some of another.

In short there is a best "production-possibility," or "transformation" curve showing us the maximum obtainable amount of one commodity for each amount of the other. Such a production-possibility schedule was drawn up for each country in figure 1 of my earlier article. And in each case it was made to be a curve *convex* from above, so that the more you want of any good the greater is the cost, at the margin, in terms of the other good. This convexity property is very important and is related to the law of diminishing marginal productivity. Few readers had any qualms about accepting convexity, but perhaps some did not realise its far-reaching implications in showing why the factor-price equalisation theorem had

CLOTHING

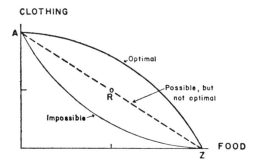

Figure 1

to be true. I propose, therefore, to show why the production-possibility curve must obviously be convex (looked at from above).[3]

To show that convexity, or increasing relative marginal costs must hold, it is sufficient for the present purpose to show that concavity, or decreasing marginal costs, involves an impossible contradiction. Now at the very worst, it is easily shown we can move along a straight-line opportunity cost line between the two axes. For suppose we agree to give up half of the maximum obtainable amount of food. How much clothing can we be sure of getting? If we send out the crudest type of order: "Half of all labour and half of all land is to be shifted to clothing production," we will (because of the assumption of constant returns to scale) *exactly halve* food production; and we will acquire *exactly half* of the maximum amount of clothing produceable with all resources. Therefore, we end up at a point, R, exactly half-way between the limiting points A and Z. Similarly, if we decide to give up 10, 20, 30 or 90% of the maximum amount of food produceable, we can give out crude orders to transfer exactly 10, 20, 30 or 90% of *both* inputs from food to clothing. Because of constant returns to scale, it follows that we can be sure of getting 90, 80, 70 or 10% of maximum clothing.

In short, by giving such crude down-the-line orders that transfer both resources *always in the same proportion*, we can at worst travel along a straight line between the two limiting intercepts. Any concave curve would necessarily lie inside such a constant-cost straight line and can therefore be ruled out: hence decreasing (marginal, opportunity) costs are incompatible with the assumption of constant returns to scale.

But of course we can usually do even better than the straight-line case. A neophyte bureaucrat might be satisfied to give crude down-the-line orders, but there exist more efficient ways of giving up food for clothing. This is where social-economist (or "welfare economist") can supplement the talents of the mere technician who knows how best to use inputs in the production of any one good and nothing else. There are an infinity of ways of giving up, say, 50% of food: we may simply give up labour, or simply give up land, or give up constant percentages of labour and land, or still other proportions. But there will be only one best way to do so, only one best combination of labour and land that is to be transferred. Best in what sense? Best in the sense of getting for us the maximum obtainable amount of clothing, compatible with our pre-assigned decision to sacrifice a given amount of food.

Intuition tells us that, qualitatively, we should transfer a larger proportion of labour than of land to clothing production. This is because clothing is the labour-intensive commodity, by our original hypothesis. This means that the proportion of labour to land is actually declining in the food line as its production declines. What about the proportion of labour to land in clothing production? At first we were able to be generous in sparing labour, which after all was not "too well adapted" for food production. But now, when we come to give up still more food, there is less labour left in food production relative to land; hence, we cannot contrive to be quite so generous in transferring further labour to clothing production. As we expand clothing production further, the proportion of labour to land must also be falling in that line; but the labour-land ratio never falls to as low as the level appropriate for food, the land-intensive commodity.[4]

Intuition tells us that by following an optimal pattern which recognises the difference in factor intensities of the two goods, we can end up on a production possibility curve that is bloated out beyond a constant-cost straight line: in short, on a production possibility curve that is convex, obeying the law of increasing marginal costs of one good as it is expanded at the expense of the other good. Or to put the same thing in the language of the market-place: as the production of clothing expands, upward pressure is put on the price of the factor it uses most intensively, on wages relative to land rent. An increase in the ratio of wages to rent must in a competitive market press up the price of the labour-intensive commodity relative to the land-intensive commodity.

This one-directional relationship between relative factor prices and relative commodity prices is an absolute necessity, and it is vital for the recognition of the truth in the main theorem. Let me elaborate therefore upon the market mechanism bringing it about. Under perfect competition, everywhere within a domestic market there will be set up a uniform ratio of wages to rents. In the food industry, there will be one, and only one, optimal proportion of labour to land; any attempt to combine productive factors in proportions that deviate from the optimum will be penalised by losses, and there will be set up a process of corrective adaptation. The same competitive forces will force an adaptation of the input proportion in clothing production, with equilibrium being attained only when the input proportions are such as to equate exactly the ratio of the physical marginal productivities of the factors (the "marginal rate of substitution" of labour for land in clothing production) to the ratio of factor prices prevailing in the market. The price mechanism has an unconscious wisdom. As if led by an invisible hand, it causes the economic system to move out to the optimal production-possibility curve. Through the intermediary of a common market factor-price ratio, the marginal rates of substitution of the factors become the same in both industries. And it is this marginal condition which intuition (as well as geometry and mathematics) tells us prescribes the optimal allocation of resources so as to yield maximum output. Not only does expanding clothing production result in the earlier described qualitative pattern of dilution of the ratio of labour to land in both occupations; more than that, a price system is one way of achieving the exactly optimal quantitative degree of change in proportions.

I have established unequivocally the following facts:

Within any country: (a) an increase in the ratio of wages to rents will cause a definite decrease in the proportion of labour to land in both industries; (b) to each determinate state of factor proportion in the two industries there will correspond one, and only one, commodity price ratio and a unique configuration of wages and rent; and (c) the change in factor proportions incident to an increase in wages/rents must be followed by a one-directional increase in clothing prices relative to food prices.

An acute reader may try to run ahead of the argument and may be tempted to assert: "But all this holds for one country, as of a given total factor endowment. Your established chain of causation is only from factor prices (and factor proportions) to commodity prices. Are you entitled to reverse the causation and to argue that the same commodity-price ratio must—even in countries of quite different total factor endowments—lead back to a common unique factor-price ratio, a common unique way of combining the inputs in the food and clothing industries, and a common set of absolute factor prices and marginal productivities?"

My answer is yes. This line of reasoning is absolutely rigorous. It is only proportions that matter, not scale. In such a perfectly competitive market each small association of factors (or firms, if one prefers that word) feels free to hire as many or as few extra factors as it likes. It neither knows nor cares anything about the totals for society. It is like a group

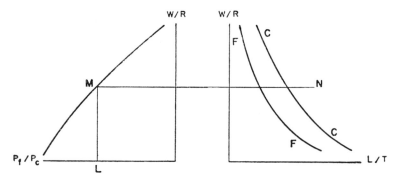

Figure 2

of molecules in a perfect gas which is everywhere in thermal equilibrium. The molecules in any one small region behave in the same way regardless of the size of the room around them. A sample observed in the middle of a huge spherical room would act in the same way as a similar sample observed within a small rectangular room. Similarly, if we observe the behaviour of a representative firm in one country it will be exactly the same in all essentials as a representative firm taken from some other country—regardless of the difference in total factor amounts and relative industrial concentration—provided only that factor-price ratios are really the same in the two markets.[5]

All this follows from the italicised conclusion reached just above, especially from (c) taken in conjunction with (a) and (b).

This really completes the intuitive demonstration of the theorem. The same international commodity price ratio, must—so long as both commodities are being produced and priced at marginal costs—enable us to infer backwards a unique factor-price ratio, a unique set of factor proportions, and even a unique set of absolute wages and rents.

All this is summarised in the accompanying chart. On the right-hand side I have simply duplicated figure 2 of my earlier paper. On the left-hand side I have added a chart showing the one-directional relation of commodity prices to factor prices.[6] As wages fall relative to rents the price of food is shown to rise relative to clothing in a monotonic fashion. The accompanying chart applies to either country and—so long as neither country is specialising completely—its validity is independent of their differing factor endowments. It follows that when we specify a common price ratio (say at L), we can move backward unambiguously (from M to N, etc.) to a common factor-price ratio and to a common factor proportion set-up in the two countries.

4. Mathematical Proof

Now that the theorem has been demonstrated by common-sense reasoning, let me confirm it by more rigorous mathematical proof. The condition of equilibrium can be written in a variety of ways, and can be framed so as to involve more than a dozen equations. For example, let me call America's four marginal physical productivities—of labour in food, of land in food, of labour in clothing, of land in clothing—a, b, c and d. I use Greek letters—α, β, γ, δ—to designate the corresponding marginal productivities in Europe. Then we can end up with a number of equilibrium expressions of the form

$$\frac{a}{b} = \frac{c}{d}, \frac{\alpha}{\beta} = \frac{\gamma}{\delta}, \frac{a}{c} = \frac{\alpha}{\gamma}, \ldots \text{ etc.}$$

A number of economists have tortured themselves trying to manipulate these expressions so as to result in $a = \alpha$, etc., or at least in $\frac{a}{b} = \frac{\alpha}{\beta}$, etc. No proof of this kind is possible. The essential thing is that these numerous marginal productivities are by no means independent. Because proportions rather than scale are important, knowledge of the behaviour of the marginal productivity of labour tells us exactly what to expect of the marginal-productivity schedule of land. This is because increasing the amount of labour with land held constant is equivalent to reducing land with labour held constant.[7]

Mathematically, instead of writing food production, F, as any joint function of labour devoted to it, L_f, and of land, T_f, we can write it as

$$F = F(L_f, T_f) = T_f f\left(\frac{L_f}{T_f}\right), \tag{1}$$

where the function f can be thought of as the returns of food on one unit of land, and where the number of units of land enters as a scale factor. The form of this function is the same for both countries; and there is, of course, a similar type of function holding for cloth production, C, in terms of L_c and T_c namely

$$C = C(L_c, T_c) = T_c c\left(\frac{L_c}{T_c}\right). \tag{2}$$

It is easy to show mathematically, by simple partial differentiation of (1), the following relations among marginal physical productivities:

M.P.P. labour in food $= \dfrac{\partial F}{\partial L_f} = f'\left(\dfrac{L_f}{T_f}\right),$

where f' represents the derivative of f and depicts the schedule of marginal product of labour (working on one unit of land). This must be a declining schedule according to our hypothesis of diminishing returns, so that we must have

$$f''\left(\frac{L_f}{T_f}\right) < 0.$$

By direct differentiation of (1), or by use of Euler's theorem, or by use of the fact that the marginal product of land can also be identified as a rent residual, we easily find that

M.P.P. land in food $= \dfrac{\partial F}{\partial T_f} = f\left(\dfrac{L_f}{T_f}\right) - \dfrac{L_f}{T_f}f'\left(\dfrac{L_f}{T_f}\right) = g\left(\dfrac{L_f}{T_f}\right),$

where g is the name for the rent residual. It is easy to show that

$$g'\left(\frac{L_f}{T_f}\right) = -\frac{L_f}{T_f}f''\left(\frac{L_f}{T_f}\right)$$

By similar reasoning, we may write the marginal productivity of land in clothing production in its proper relation to that of labour:

M.P.P. labour in clothing $= \dfrac{\partial C}{\partial L_c} = c'\left(\dfrac{L_c}{T_c}\right)$

M.P.P. land in clothing $= \dfrac{\partial C}{\partial T_c} = c\left(\dfrac{L_c}{T_c}\right) - \dfrac{L_c}{T_c}c'\left(\dfrac{L_c}{T_c}\right) = h\left(\dfrac{L_c}{T_c}\right)$

$$h'\left(\frac{L_c}{T_c}\right) = -\frac{L_c}{T_c}c''\left(\frac{L_c}{T_c}\right)$$

The art of analysis in these problems is to select out the essential variables so as to reduce our equilibrium equations to the simplest form. Without specifying which country we are talking about, we certainly can infer from the fact that something of both goods is being produced with both factors the following conditions:

Real wages (or labour marginal "value" productivities) must be the same in food and clothing production when expressed in terms of a common *measure*, such as clothing; the same is true of real rents (or land marginal "value" productivities). Or

(food price) (M.P.P. labour in food) = (clothing price) (M.P.P. labour in clothing) (food price) (M.P.P. land in food) = (clothing price) (M.P.P. land in clothing),

which can be written in terms of previous notation as

$$\left(\frac{P_f}{P_c}\right) f'\left(\frac{L_f}{T_f}\right) - c'\left(\frac{L_c}{T_c}\right) = 0$$

$$\left(\frac{P_f}{P_c}\right)\left[f\left(\frac{L_f}{T_f}\right) - \frac{L_f}{T_f}f'\left(\frac{L_f}{T_f}\right)\right] - \left[c\left(\frac{L_c}{T_c}\right) - \frac{L_c}{T_c}c'\left(\frac{L_c}{T_c}\right)\right] = 0.^8$$

Now these are two equations in the three variables $\frac{L_f}{T_f}$, $\frac{L_c}{T_c}$, and $\frac{P_f}{P_c}$. If we take the latter price ratio as given to us by international-demand conditions, we are left with *two* equations to determine the *two* unknown factor proportions. This is a solvent situation, and we should normally expect the result to be determinate.

But a purist might still have doubts: "How do you know that these two equations or schedules might not twist around and intersect in multiple equilibria?" Fortunately, the answer is simple and definite. On our hypothesis, any equilibrium configuration turns out to be absolutely unique. We may leave to a technical footnote the detailed mathematical proof of this fact.[9]

5. Multiple Commodities and Factors

Adding a third or further commodities does not alter our analysis much. If anything, it increases the likelihood of complete factor-price equalisation. For all that we require is that at least *two* commodities are simultaneously being produced in both countries and then our previous conclusion follows. If we add a third commodity which is very much like either of our present commodities, we are not changing the situation materially. But if we add new commodities which are more extreme in their labour-land intensities, then we greatly increase the chance that two regions with very different factor endowments can still come into complete factor-price equalisation. A "queer" region is not penalised for being queer if there is queer work that needs doing.

I do not wish at this time to go into the technical mathematics of the n commodity, and r factor case. But it can be said that: (1) so long as the two regions are sufficiently close together in factor proportions, (2) so long as the goods differ in factor intensities, and (3) so long as the number of goods, n, is greater than the number of factors, r, we can hope to experience complete factor-price equalisation. On the other hand, if complete specialisation takes place it will do so for a whole collection of goods, the dividing line between exports and imports being a variable one depending upon reciprocal international demand (acting on factor prices) as in the classical theory of comparative advantage with multiple commodities.[10]

When we add a third productive factor and retain but two commodities, then the whole presumption towards factor-price equalisation disappears. Suppose American labour and American land have more capital to work with than does European labour and land. It is then quite possible that the marginal physical productivities of labour and land might be double that of Europe in both commodities. Obviously, commodity-price *ratios* would still be equal, production of both commodities will be taking place, but nonetheless absolute factor prices (or relative for that matter) need not be moved towards equality. This is our general expectation wherever the number of factors exceeds the number of commodities.

6. The Conditions of Complete Specialisation

If complete specialisation takes place in one country, then our hypothesis is not fulfilled and the conclusion does not follow. How important is this empirically, and when can we expect complete specialisation to take place? As discussed earlier, the answer depends upon how disparate are the initial factor endowments of the two regions—how disparate in comparison with the differences in factor intensities of the two commodities.[11]

Unless the two commodities differ extraordinarily in factor intensities, the production-possibility curve will be by no means so convex as it is usually drawn in the neoclassical literature of international trade, where it usually resembles a quarter circle whose slope ranges the spectrum from zero to infinity. It should rather have the crescentlike shape of the new moon. Opportunity costs tend to be more nearly constant than I had previously realised. This is a step in the direction of the older classical theory of comparative advantage. But with this important difference: the same causes that tend to produce *constant* costs also tend to produce *uniform* cost ratios between nations, which is not at all in the spirit of classical theory. (Undoubtedly much of the specialisation observed in the real world is due to something different from all this, namely decreasing-cost indivisibilities, tempered and counteracted by the existence of localised resources specifically adapted to particular lines of production.)

A parable may serve the double purpose of showing the range of factor endowment incompatible with complete specialisation and of removing any lingering element of paradox surrounding the view that commodity mobility may be a perfect substitute for factor mobility.

Let us suppose that in the beginning all factors were perfectly mobile, and nationalism had not yet reared its ugly head. Spatial transport costs being of no importance, there would be one world price of food and clothing, one real wage, one real rent, and the world's land and labour would be divided between food and clothing production in a determinate way, with uniform proportions of labour to land being used everywhere in clothing production, and with a much smaller—but uniform— proportion of labour to land being used in production of food.

Now suppose that an angel came down from heaven and notified some fraction of all the labour and land units producing clothing that they were to be called Americans, the rest to be called Europeans; and some different fraction of the food industry that henceforth they were to carry American passports. Obviously, just giving people and areas national labels does not alter anything: it does not change commodity or factor prices or production patterns.

But now turn a recording geographer loose, and what will he report? Two countries with quite different factor proportions, but with identical real wages and rents and identical modes of commodity production (but with different relative importances of food and clothing industries). Depending upon whether the angel makes up America by concentrating primarily on clothing units or on food units, the geographer will report a very high or a very low ratio of labour to land in the newly synthesised "country." But this he will never find: that the ratio of labour to land should ever exceed the proportions characteristic of the most labour-intensive industry (clothing) or ever fall short of the proportions of the least labour-intensive industry. Both countries *must* have factor proportions intermediate between the proportions in the two industries.

The angel can create a country with proportions *not* intermediate between the factor intensities of food and clothing. But he cannot do so by following the above-described procedure, which was calculated to leave prices and production unchanged. If he wrests some labour in food production away from the land it has been working with, "sending" this labour to Europe and keeping it from working with the American land, then a substantive change in production and prices will have been introduced. Unless there are abnormal repercussions on the pattern of effective demand, we can expect one or both of the countries to specialise completely and real wages to fall in Europe relative to America in one or both commodities, with European real rents behaving in an opposite fashion.

The extension of this parable to the many-commodities case may be left to the interested reader.

7. Some Qualifications

A number of qualifications to this theoretical argument are in order. In the first place, goods do not move without transport costs, and to the extent that commodity prices are not equalised it of course follows that factor prices will not tend to be fully equalised. Also, as I indicated in my earlier article, there are many reasons to doubt the usefulness of assuming identical production functions and categories of inputs in the two countries; and consequently, it is dangerous to draw sweeping practical conclusions concerning factor-price equalisation.

What about the propriety of assuming constant returns to scale? In justice to Ohlin, it should be pointed out that he, more than almost any other writer, has followed up the lead of Adam Smith and made *increasing returns* an important cause for trade. It is true that increasing returns *may* at the same time create difficulties for the survival of perfect competition, difficulties which cannot always be sidestepped by pretending that the increasing returns are due primarily to *external* rather than internal economies. But these difficulties do not give us the right to deny or neglect the importance of scale factors.[12] Where scale is important it is obviously possible for real wages to differ greatly between large free-trade areas and small ones, even with the same relative endowments of productive factors. And while it may have been rash of me to draw a moral concerning the worth of emigration from Europe out of an abstract simplified model, I must still record the view that the more realistic deviations from constant returns to scale and the actual production functions encountered in practice are likely to reinforce rather than oppose the view that high standards of life are possible in densely populated areas such as the island of Manhattan or the United Kingdom.

There is no iron-clad a priori necessity for the law of diminishing marginal productivity to be valid for either or both commodities.[13] In such cases the usual marginal conditions of equilibrium are replaced by inequalities, and we have a boundary maximum in which we go the limit and use zero of one of the inputs in one industry. If it still could be shown that one commodity is always more labour intensive than the other, then the main theorem would probably still be true. But it is precisely in these pathological cases that factor intensities may become alike or reverse themselves, giving rise to the difficulties discussed in footnote 6.

In conclusion, some of these qualifications help us to reconcile results of abstract analysis with the obvious facts of life concerning the extreme diversity of productivity and factor prices in different regions of the world. Men receive lower wages in some countries than in others for a variety of reasons: because they are different by birth or training; because their effective know-how is limited and the manner of their being combined with other productive factors is not optimal; because they are confined to areas too small to develop the full economies of scale; because some goods and materials cannot be brought to them freely from other parts of the world, as a result of natural or man-made obstacles; and finally because the technological diversity of commodities with respect to factor intensities is not so great in comparison with the diversity of regional factor endowments to emancipate labourers from the penalty of being confined to regions lacking in natural resources. In the face of these hard facts it would be rash to consider the existing distribution of population to be optimal in any sense, or to regard free trade as a panacea for the present geographical inequalities.

2

International Trade and Factor Mobility

Robert A. Mundell

Commodity movements and factor movements are substitutes. The absence of trade impediments implies *commodity*-price equalization and, even when factors are immobile, a tendency toward *factor*-price equalization. It is equally true that perfect factor mobility results in *factor*-price equalization and, even when commodity movements cannot take place, in a tendency toward *commodity*-price equalization.

There are two extreme cases between which are to be found the conditions in the real world: There may be perfect factor mobility but no trade, or factor immobility with unrestricted trade. The classical economists generally chose the special case where factors of production were internationally immobile.

This paper will describe some of the effects of relaxing the latter assumption, allowing not only commodity movements but also some degree of factor mobility. Specifically it will show that an increase in trade impediments stimulates factor movements and that an increase in restrictions to factor movements stimulates trade.[1] It will also make more specific an old argument for protection.

Trade Impediments and Factor Movements

Under certain rigorous assumptions the substitution of commodity for factor movements will be complete. In a two-country two-commodity two-factor model, commodity-price equalization is sufficient to ensure factor-price equalization and factor-price equalization is sufficient to ensure commodity-price equalization if (1) production functions are homogeneous of the first degree (that is, if marginal productivities, relatively and absolutely, depend only on the proportions in which factors

This paper was originally published in *American Economic Review* 47 (June 1957): 321–335.

are combined) and are identical in both countries; (2) one commodity requires a greater proportion of one factor than the other commodity at any factor prices at all points on any production function; and (3) factor endowments are such as to exclude specialization.[2]

These assumptions permit us to isolate some important influences determining the pattern of international trade and factor flows and for present purposes will be adhered to. Our first task is to show that an increase in trade impediments encourages factor movements.

Assume two countries, A and B, producing two final commodities, cotton and steel, by means of two factors, labor and capital.[3] Country A is well endowed with labor but poorly endowed with capital relative to country B; cotton is labor-intensive relative to steel. For expositional convenience we shall use community indifference curves.

For the moment we shall assume that country B represents the "rest of the world" and that country A is so small in relation to B that its production conditions and factor endowments can have no effect on prices in B.[4]

Let us begin with a situation where factors are immobile between A and B but where impediments to trade are absent. This results in com- modity- and factor-price equalization. Country A exports its labor- intensive product, cotton, in exchange for steel. Equilibrium is represented in figure 1: TT is A's transformation function (production-possibility

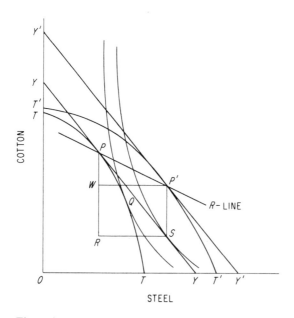

Figure 1

curve), production is at *P*, and consumption is at *S*. Country *A* is exporting *PR* of cotton and importing *RS* of steel. Her income in terms of steel or cotton is *OY*.

Suppose now that some exogenous factor removes all impediments to the movement of capital. Clearly, since the marginal product of capital is the same in both *A* and *B*, no capital movement will take place and equilibrium will remain where it is. But now assume that *A* imposes a tariff on steel and for simplicity make it prohibitive.[5] Initially the price of steel will rise relative to the price of cotton in *A* and both production and consumption will move to *Q*, the autarky (economic self-sufficiency) point. Factors will move out of the cotton into the steel industry, but since cotton is labor-intensive and steel is capital-intensive, at constant factor prices the production shift creates an excess supply of labor and an excess demand for capital. Consequently the marginal product of labor must fall and the marginal product of capital must rise. This is the familiar *Stolper-Samuelson tariff argument.*[6]

But since capital is mobile, its higher marginal product in *A* induces a capital movement into *A* from *B*, changing factor endowments so as to make *A* more capital-abundant. With more capital, *A*'s transformation curve expands until a new equilibrium is reached.

Some help in determining where this new equilibrium will be is provided by figure 2. Country *A* initially has *OC* of capital and *OL* of labor; *OO'* is the efficiency locus along which marginal products of labor and capital

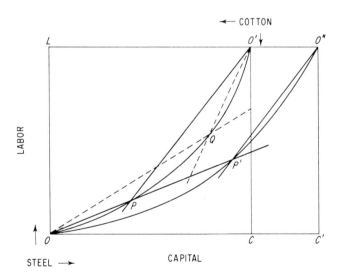

Figure 2

are equalized in steel and cotton. Equilibrium is initially at P, which corresponds to P on the production block in figure 1. Factor proportions in steel and cotton are given by the slopes of OP and $O'P$, respectively.

After the tariff is imposed, production moves along the efficiency locus to Q, corresponding to the autarky point Q in figure 1. The slopes of OQ and $O'Q$ indicate that the ratios of labor to capital in both cotton and steel have risen (that is, the marginal product of capital has risen and the marginal product of labor has fallen). Capital flows in and the cotton origin O' shifts to the right.

With perfect mobility of capital the marginal products of both labor and capital must be equalized in A and B. This follows from the assumption that the production functions are linear, homogeneous, and identical in both countries. Because marginal products in the rest of the world are assumed to be constant, the returns to factors in A will not change. Factor proportions in both steel and cotton in A then must be the same as before the tariff was imposed—so equilibrium must lie along OP-extended at the point where it is cut by a line $O''P'$ parallel to $O'P$, where O'' is the new cotton origin. But this is not yet sufficient to tell us exactly where along OP-extended the point P' will be.

Because marginal products in the new equilibrium are the same as before the tariff, commodity prices in A will not have changed; but if both incomes earned by domestic factors and commodity prices are unchanged, consumption will remain at S (in figure 1). Production, however, must be greater than S, because interest payments must be made to country B equal in value to the marginal product of the capital inflow. In figure 1, then, production equilibrium must be at some point above or to the northeast of S.

To find the exact point we must show the effects of a change in capital endowments on production block. Because steel is capital-intensive we should expect the production block after the capital movement has taken place to be biased in favor of steel at any given price ratio; that this is so has been recently proved by Rybczynski [87].[7]

Because the same price ratio as at P will prevail, the locus of all tangents to larger and larger production blocks based on larger and larger endowments of capital must have a negative slope. Such a line, which I shall call the R line, is drawn in figure 1.

Capital will flow in until its marginal product is equalized in A and B, which will be at the point where A can produce enough steel and cotton for consumption equilibrium at S without trade, and at the same time make the required interest payment abroad. This point is clearly reached at P' directly above S. At any point along the R line to the northwest of P', country A would have to import steel in order to consume at S (that is, demand conditions in A cannot be satisfied to the northwest of P'). At P' demand conditions in A are satisfied and the interest payment can be made abroad at the same price ratio as before the tariff was levied. Thus the capital movement need not continue past this point, although any point to the southeast of P' would be consistent with equilibrium.

Production takes place in A at P', consumption is at S, and the transfer of interest payments is the excess of production over consumption in A, SP' of cotton.[8] The value of A's production has increased from OY to OY' in terms of steel, but YY' (which equals in value SP' of cotton) must be transferred abroad, so income is unchanged.

We initially assumed a prohibitive tariff; in fact, even the smallest tariff is prohibitive in this model! A small tariff would not prohibit trade immediately: Because of the price change some capital would move in and some trade would take place. But as long as trade continues, there must be a difference in prices in A and B equal to the ad valorem rate of tariff—hence a difference in marginal products—so capital imports must continue. Marginal products and prices can only be equalized in A and B when A's imports cease.

The tariff is now no longer necessary! Because marginal products and prices are again equalized, the tariff can be removed without reversing the capital movement. The tariff has eliminated trade, but after the capital movement there is no longer any need for trade.

This is not really such a surprising result when we refer back to the assumptions. Before the tariff was imposed we assumed both unimpeded trade and perfect capital mobility. We have then two assumptions each of which is sufficient for the equalization of commodity and factor prices. The effect of the tariff is simply to eliminate one of these assumptions— unimpeded trade; the other is still operative.

However, one qualification must be made. If impediments to trade exist in both countries (tariffs in both countries or transport costs on both goods) and it is assumed that capital owners do not move with their capital, the interest payments on foreign-owned capital will be subject to these impediments; this will prevent complete equalization of factor and commodity prices. (This question could have been avoided had we allowed the capitalist to consume his returns in the country where his capital was invested.) The proposition that capital mobility is a perfect substitute for trade still stands however, if one is willing to accept the qualification as an imperfection to capital mobility.

Effect of Relative Size

The previous section assumed that country A was very small in relation to country B. It turns out, however, that the relative sizes of the two countries make no difference in the model provided complete specialization does not result.

Suppose as before that country A is exporting cotton in exchange for steel. There are no impediments to trade and capital is mobile. But we no longer assume that A is small relative to B. Now A imposes a tariff on steel raising the internal price of steel in relation to cotton, shifting resources out of cotton into steel, raising the marginal product of capital, and lowering the marginal product of labor. A's demand for imports and her supply of exports fall. This decline in demand for B's steel exports and supply of B's cotton imports raises the price of cotton relative to steel in B; labor and capital in B shift out of steel into cotton raising the marginal product of labor and lowering the marginal product of capital in B. Relative factor returns in A and B move in opposite directions, so the price changes in A which stimulate a capital movement are reinforced by the price changes in B. The marginal product of capital rises in A falls in B; capital moves from B to A, contracting B's and expanding A's production block.

The assumption that capital is perfectly mobile means that factor and commodity prices must be equalized after the tariff. It is necessary now to show that they also will be unchanged. The price of cotton relative to steel is determined by world demand and supply curves. To prove that prices remain unchanged it is sufficient to show that these demand and supply curves are unchanged—or that at the pretariff price ratio demand equals supply after the capital movement has taken place. But we know that at the old price ratio marginal products, hence incomes, are unchanged—thus demand is unchanged. All that remains then is to show that at constant prices production changes in one country cancel out production changes in the other country.

This proposition can be proved in the following way: If commodity and factor prices are to be unchanged after the capital movement has taken place, then factor proportions in each industry must be the same as before; then the increment to the capital stock used in A will, at constant prices, increase the output of steel and decrease the output of cotton in A, and the decrement to the capital stock in B will decrease the output of steel and increase the output of cotton in B. But the increase in A's capital is equal to the decrease in B's capital, and since production expands at constant prices and with the same factor proportions in each

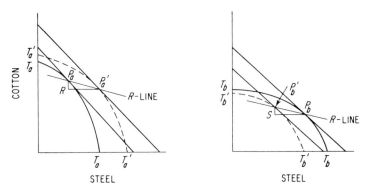

Figure 3a   Figure 3b

country, the increase in resources used in producing steel in A must be exactly equal to the decrease in resources devoted to the production of steel in B. Similarly, the decrease in resources used in producing cotton in A is the same as the increase in resources devoted to cotton production in B. Then, since production functions are linear and homogeneous, the equal changes in resources applied to each industry (in opposite directions) imply equal changes in output. Therefore, the increase in steel output in A is equal to the decrease in steel output in B, and the decrease in cotton output in A is equal to the increase in cotton output in B (that is, world production is not changed, at constant prices, by a movement of capital from one country to another). In the world we are considering it makes no difference in which country a commodity is produced if commodity prices are equalized.

This proposition can perhaps be made clearer by a geometric proof. In figure 3a, $T_a T_a$ is A's transformation curve before the tariff, and $T_a' T_a'$ is the transformation curve after the tariff has been imposed and the capital movement has taken place. At constant prices equilibrium moves along A's R line from P_a to P_a', increasing the output of steel by RP_a' and decreasing the output of cotton by RP_a. Similarly, in figure 3b, $T_b T_b$ is country B's transformation curve before the capital movement and $T_b' T_b'$ is the transformation curve after capital has left B. At constant prices production in B moves along B's R line to P_b', steel production decreasing by SP_b and cotton production increasing by SP_b'.

To demonstrate the proposition that world supply curves are unchanged, it is necessary to prove that RP_a' equals SP_b and that RP_a equals SP_b'. The proof is given in figure 4. OL_a and OC_a are, respectively, A's initial endowments of labor and capital; OL_b and OC_b are the endowments of B. OO_a and OO_b are the efficiency loci of A and B with production

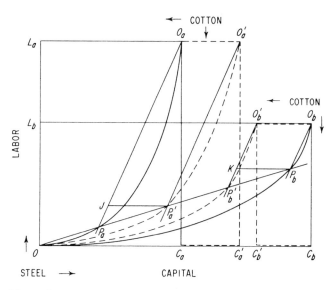

Figure 4

taking place along these loci at P_a and P_b, corresponding to the same letters in figures 3a and 3b.

Now when A imposes a tariff on steel, suppose that $C_b C_b'$ of capital leaves B, shifting B's cotton origin from O_b to O_b'. At constant prices labor-capital ratios in each industry must be the same as before, so equilibrium must move to P_b', corresponding to P_b' in figure 3b. Because the capital outflow from B must equal the capital inflow to A, A's cotton origin must move to the right by just the same amount as B's cotton origin moves to the left (that is, from O_a to O_a'; and A's production equilibrium at constant prices must move from P_a to P_a'). The proof that world supply is unchanged at constant prices is now obvious, since JP_aP_a' and $KP_b'P_b$ are identical triangles. P_aP_a', representing the increase in steel output in A, equals P_bP_b', the decrease in steel output in B, and the decrease in cotton output in A, JP_a, equals the increase in cotton output in B, KP_b'.[9]

This relationship holds at all combinations of commodity and factor prices provided some of each good is produced in both countries. It means that world supply functions are independent of the distribution of factor endowments. More simply it means that it makes no difference to world supply where goods are produced if commodity and factor prices are equalized. Because world supply and demand functions are not changed by the capital movements, so that the new equilibrium must be established at the same prices as before, our earlier assumption that A is very small in relation to B is an unnecessary one.[10]

The general conclusion of this and the preceding is that tariffs will stimulate factor movements. Which factor moves depends, of course, on which factor is more mobile. The assumption used here, that capital is perfectly mobile and that labor is completely immobile, is an extreme one which would have to be relaxed before the argument could be made useful. But a great deal can be learned qualitatively from extreme cases and the rest of the paper will retain this assumption. When only capital is mobile, a labor-abundant country can attract capital by tariffs and a capital-abundant country can encourage foreign investment by tariffs. The same is true for an export tax, because in this model the effect of an export tax is the same as that of a tariff.

The analysis is not restricted to tariffs; it applies as well to changes in transport costs. An increase of transport costs (of commodities) will raise the real return of and thus attract the scarce factor, and lower the real return and thus encourage the export of the abundant factor. The effect of any trade impediment is to increase the scarcity of the scarce factor and hence make more profitable an international redistribution of factors. Later we shall consider, under somewhat more realistic assumptions than those used above, the applicability of this proposition as an argument for protection.

Factor Mobility Impediments and Trade

To show that an increase in impediments to factor movements stimulates trade, we shall assume that some capital is foreign-owned and illustrate the effects on trade of taxing this capital. Strictly speaking, this is not an impediment to a capital *movement*; but if it were assumed that a steady capital flow was taking place, the tax on foreign-owned capital would operate as an impediment.

We shall use figures 1 and 2. Begin with equilibrium initially at P' in figure 1. No impediments to trade exist, but because factor and commodity prices are already equalized no trade takes place. We assume that $O'O''$ of capital in figure 2 is foreign-owned, so a transfer equal in value to YY' in figure 1 is made. Consumption equilibrium in A is at S.

If a tax is now levied on all foreign capital its net return will be decreased, and since factor prices must be equalized in A and B, all of it ($O'O''$) must leave A. As capital leaves A, her production block contracts. At constant prices more cotton and less steel are produced. The price of steel relative to cotton tends to rise but, because there are no impediments to trade, it is prevented from doing so by steel imports and cotton exports.

As all foreign capital leaves A, the final size of A's transformation function is TT, that consistent with domestically owned capital. Production equilibrium moves from P' to P, but consumption equilibrium remains at S because interest payments are no longer made abroad. PR is now exported in exchange for steel imports of RS. The effect of the tax has been to repatriate foreign capital and increase trade. By similar reasoning it could be shown that a subsidy will attract capital and decrease trade, although in the latter case the capital movement will only stop when factor prices change (that is, specialization takes place).

To achieve efficiency in world production it is unnecessary that both commodities and factors move freely. As long as the production conditions are satisfied, it is sufficient that *either* commodities *or* factors move freely. But if some restrictions, however small, exist to both commodity and factor movements, factor- and commodity-price equalization cannot take place (except in the trivial case where trade is unnecessary because prices are already equal). This principle applies only to those restrictions that are operative—obviously it does not apply to import tariffs on goods which are exported, transport costs for factors that are immobile anyway, or quotas larger than those required for equalization to take place.

If it were not for the problem of transporting interest payments, referred to earlier, one mobile factor would be sufficient to ensure price equalization. When the labor-abundant country imposes the tariff, equalization will take place as long as the other country continues a free-trade policy and there are no transport costs involved. But if the capital-abundant country imposes a tariff, inducing the export of capital, prices cannot be equalized even if the labor-abundant country maintains free trade unless the transfer of goods constituting interest payments is also tariff-free.[11]

An Argument for Protection?

The proposition that an increase in trade impediments stimulates factor movements and an increase in impediments to factor movements stimulates trade has implications as an argument for protection. To examine these implications we shall relax some of the assumptions previously made—first, by introducing trade impediments, then by decreasing the degree of factor mobility, and finally by relaxing the assumption that constant returns to scale apply by taking account of external economies.

We shall begin with a model similar to that used earlier except that we shall assume country A to be considerably smaller than country B.[12]

Take as a starting point the absence of trade impediments; trade is sufficient to ensure commodity- and factor-price equalization. Suppose that, overnight, transport costs come into existence; this raises the price of importables relative to exportables, shifts resources into importables, raises the marginal product of the scarce factor, and lowers that of the abundant factor in each country. Incomes of A-capitalists and B-workers increase while incomes of A-workers and B-capitalists decrease. These changes in factor returns create the incentive for a capital movement from B to A, a labor movement from A to B, or a combination of both movements. Where the final equilibrium will be depends on the degree of factor mobility. I shall assume that labor is immobile between countries but that capital is at least partially mobile.

If we assume that capital is perfectly mobile, but that capitalists do not move with their capital, the latter will move from B to A until the return from capital invested in A is the same as from that invested in B; but this implies that marginal physical products cannot be equalized, since transport costs must be paid on the goods constituting interest payments.[13] The introduction of transport costs would, then, reduce world income even if capital were perfectly mobile unless capitalists are willing to consume their income in the country in which their capital is invested.

But we shall not assume that capital is perfectly mobile. Instead suppose that B-capitalists insist on receiving a higher return on any capital they invest in A than on that which they invest in B, perhaps because of political instability, patriotism, risk, or economic uncertainty. Let us assume that B-capitalists require a 10 per cent higher return on capital invested in A than on that invested in B, but that if this interest differential rises above 10 per cent, capital is perfectly mobile. Suppose further that the return to capital in both countries before introducing transport costs was 12 per cent, and that the effect of introducing transport costs is to lower the marginal product of capital in B to 11 per cent and to raise it in A to 17 per cent. Since the interest differential is less than 10 per cent, no capital movement will take place.

It is at this point that we shall consider the argument for a tariff in A. Let A impose a tariff, further increasing her relative scarcity of capital and B's relative scarcity of labor. Rates of return on capital change to, let us say, 25 per cent in A and 9 per cent in B, creating an interest differential of 16 per cent. Capital will now move from B to A until this differential is reduced to 10 per cent. Obviously the rates of return cannot return to the pretariff rates of 17 per cent for A and 11 per cent for B: (1) because part of the tariff will be "used up" in bringing the marginal products of capital in A and B to the point where B has an incentive to export capital; and (2) because transport costs must be paid on the interest returns.

If capital moves until the return in A falls to 20 per cent and in B rises to 10 per cent, what can be said about the economic effects of the tariff as far as country A is concerned?

1. A-capitalists are better-off; the tariff increases and the capital inflow decreases capital scarcity, but the net effect is a higher return than before the tariff.

2. A-workers are worse off in spite of the fact that the total ratio of capital to labor in A has increased. Marginal products are determined not by the total ratio of capital to labor in a country, but by the ratio of capital to labor in each industry. The capital from B is largely absorbed by increasing the output of capital-intensive importables in A; it can never succeed in raising the capital-labor ratio in each industry to its pretariff level. Real wages must be lower than before the tariff.

3. Real national income in A is less than before the tariff; the tariff makes A's scarce factor relatively more scarce, and her abundant factor relatively more abundant, reducing her potential gains from international trade. Even under the most favorable assumptions, with capital perfectly mobile and capitalists moving with their capital, A's income would remain the same; it could not improve.

So far no valid tariff argument has been produced.[14] Capital can be attracted to a capital-scarce country by a tariff, but the capital movement can only alleviate some of the unfavorable effects of the tariff; it cannot eliminate them.

The argument can be rescued if we assume the appropriate nonlinearities of scale.[15] If external economies of scale exist in the production of A-importables,[16] the tariff will encourage more capital to enter than would otherwise be attracted, as the marginal product of capital entering A will not fall as rapidly as it would fall in the absence of economies of scale. The new equilibrium will be established with a higher marginal product of labor, factor returns now being dependent not only on the proportions in which factors are combined but also on the total output of importables. Real wages will be higher in A than without economies of scale, although it is not certain that they will be higher than before the tariff; to demonstrate the latter it would have to be established that the economies of scale are sufficient to make up for the transport costs which must be paid on the interest returns. If they are sufficient, the tariff would be unequivocally beneficial.[17]

It is easy to see that economies of scale in importables or diseconomies of scale in exportables increase the likelihood that the net effect of the tariff in a labor-abundant country is favorable, and vice versa. To justify an argument for protection on the above grounds, it would have to be established that capital-intensive industries are subject to external economies of scale and/or that labor-intensive industries are subject to external diseconomies of scale; and these nonlinearities are of the required size.[18]

Concluding Remarks

A number of questions present themselves. Did increased protection in the late-nineteenth century in North America stimulate the large labor and capital inflows of that period (assuming land to have been the abundant factor)? Did the increased protection in Britain in this century stimulate capital export? Did the breakdown in international factor movements in the interwar period stimulate trade? And to what extent have the high tariff barriers between Canada and the United States contributed to the stimulus of American investment in Canada? It would be interesting to see what help this model offers in finding answers to these questions.

This paper was originally presented to Professor Meade's seminary at L.S.E. in 1956. I am indebted for helpful comments to W. M. Corden, M. Friedman, A. Harberger, H. G. Johnson, R. Lipsey, J. E. Meade, S. A. Ozga, and T. Rybczynski.

3

The Structure of
Simple General
Equilibrium Models

Ronald W. Jones

1. Introduction

It is difficult to find any major branch of applied economics that has not made some use of the simple general equilibrium model of production. For years this model has served as the work-horse for most of the developments in the pure theory of international trade. It has been used to study the effects of taxation on the distribution of income and the impact of technological change on the composition of outputs and the structure of prices. Perhaps the most prominent of its recent uses is to be found in the neoclassical theory of economic growth.

Such intensive use of the simple two-sector model of production suggests that a few properties are being retranslated in such diverse areas as public finance, international trade, and economic growth. The unity provided by a common theoretical structure is further emphasized by the dual relationship that exists between sets of variables in the model itself. Traditional formulations of the model tend to obscure this feature. My purpose in this chapter is to analyze the structure of the simple competitive model of production in a manner designed to highlight both the dual relationship and the similarity that exists among a number of traditional problems in comparative statics and economic growth.

The model is described in sections 2 and 3. In section 4 I discuss the dual nature of two theorems in the theory of international trade associated with the names of Stolper and Samuelson on the one hand and Rybczynski on the other. A simple demand relationship is added in section 5, and a problem in public finance is analyzed—the effect of excise subsidies or taxes on relative commodity and factor prices. The static model of production is then reinterpreted as a neo-classical model of economic

This paper was originally published in *Journal of Political Economy* 73 (December 1965): 557–572.

growth by letting one of the outputs serve as the capital good. The dual of the "incidence" problem in public finance in the static model is shown to have direct relevance to the problem of the stability of the balanced growth path in the neoclassical growth model. In the concluding section of the chapter I show how these results can be applied to the analysis of technological progress. Any improvement in technology or in the quality of factors of production can be simply viewed as a composite of two effects, which I shall term the "differential industry" effect and the "differential factor" effect. Each effect has its counterpart in the dual problems discussed in the earlier part of the paper.

2. The Model

Assume a perfectly competitive economy in which firms (indefinite in number) maximize profits, which are driven to the zero level in equilibrium. Consistent with this, technology in each of two sectors exhibits constant returns to scale. Two primary factors, labor (L) and land (T), are used in producing two distinct commodities, manufactured goods (M) and food (F). Wages (w) and rents (r) denote the returns earned by the factors for use of services, whereas p_M and p_F denote the competitive market prices of the two commodities.

If technology is given and factor endowments and commodity prices are treated as parameters, the model serves to determine eight unknowns: the level of commodity outputs (two), the factor allocations to each industry (four), and factor prices (two). The equations of the model could be given by the production functions (two), the requirement that each factor receive the value of its marginal product (four), and that each factor be fully employed (two). This is the format most frequently used in the theory of international trade and the neoclassical theory of growth.[1] I consider, instead, the formulation of the model suggested by activity analysis.

The technology is described by the columns of the A matrix,

$$A = \begin{pmatrix} a_{LM} & a_{LF} \\ a_{TM} & a_{TF} \end{pmatrix},$$

where a_{ij} denotes the quantity of factor i required to produce a unit of commodity j. With constant returns to scale total factor demands are given by the product of the a's and the levels of output. The requirement that both factors be fully employed is thus given by equations (1) and (2). Similarly, unit costs of production in each industry are given by the columns of A multiplied by the factor prices. In a competitive equilibrium with both goods being produced, these unit costs must reflect market prices, as in equations (3) and (4).[2]

$$a_{LM}M + a_{LF}F = L, \tag{1}$$

$$a_{TM}M + a_{TF}F = T, \tag{2}$$

$$a_{LM}w + a_{TM}r = p_M, \tag{3}$$

$$a_{LF}w + a_{TF}r = p_F. \tag{4}$$

This formulation serves to emphasize the dual relationship between factor endowments and commodity outputs on the one hand (equations (1) and (2)) and commodity prices and factor prices on the other (equations (3) and (4)).

In the general case of variable coefficients the relationships shown in equations (1)–(4) must be supplemented by four additional relationships determining the input coefficients. These are provided by the requirement that in a competitive equilibrium each a_{ij} depends solely upon the ratio of factor prices.

3. The Equations of Change

The comparative statics properties of the model described in section 2 are developed by considering the effect of a change in the parameters on the unknowns of the problem. With unchanged technology the parameters are the factor endowments (L and T) and the commodity prices (p_M and p_F), the right-hand side of equations (1)–(4).

Let a hat ($\hat{}$) indicate the relative change in a variable or parameter. Thus, $\hat{p}_F$ denotes dp_F/p_F and $\hat{L}$ denotes dL/L.[3] The four equations in the rates of change are shown in (1a)–(4a):

$$\lambda_{LM}\hat{M} + \lambda_{LF}\hat{F} = \hat{L} - [\lambda_{LM}\hat{a}_{LM} + \lambda_{LF}\hat{a}_{LF}]. \tag{1a}$$

$$\lambda_{TM}\hat{M} + \lambda_{TF}\hat{F} = \hat{T} - [\lambda_{TM}\hat{a}_{TM} + \lambda_{TF}\hat{a}_{TF}], \tag{2a}$$

$$\theta_{LM}\hat{w} + \theta_{TM}\hat{r} = \hat{p}_M - [\theta_{LM}\hat{a}_{LM} + \theta_{TM}\hat{a}_{TM}], \tag{3a}$$

$$\theta_{LF}\hat{w} + \theta_{TF}\hat{r} = \hat{p}_F - [\theta_{LF}\hat{a}_{LF} + \theta_{TF}\hat{a}_{TF}]. \tag{4a}$$

The λ's and θ's are the transforms of the a's that appear when relative changes are shown. A fraction of the labor force is used in manufacturing (λ_{LM}), and this plus the fraction of the labor force used in food production (λ_{LF}) must add to unity by the full-employment assumption (shown by equation (1)). Similarly for λ_{TM} and λ_{TF}. The θ's, by contrast, refer to the factor shares in each industry. Thus, θ_{LM}, labor's share in manufacturing, is given by $a_{LM}w/p_M$. By the zero profit conditions, θ_{Lj} and θ_{Tj} must add to unity.

In this section I assume that manufacturing is labor-intensive. It follows that labor's share in manufacturing must be greater than labor's share in food, and that the percentage of the labor force used in manufacturing must exceed the percentage of total land that is used in manufacturing. Let λ and θ be the notations for the matrices of coefficients shown in (1a), (2a) and (3a), (4a):

$$\lambda = \begin{pmatrix} \lambda_{LM} & \lambda_{LF} \\ \lambda_{TM} & \lambda_{TF} \end{pmatrix} ; \quad \theta = \begin{pmatrix} \theta_{LM} & \theta_{TM} \\ \theta_{LF} & \theta_{TF} \end{pmatrix} .$$

Since each row sum in λ and θ is unity, the determinants $|\lambda|$ and $|\theta|$ are given by

$$|\lambda| = \lambda_{LM} - \lambda_{TM} \quad and \quad |\theta| = \theta_{LM} - \theta_{LF},$$

and both $|\lambda|$ and $|\theta|$ are positive by the factor-intensity assumption.[4]

If coefficients of production are fixed, equations (1a)–(4a) are greatly simplified as every $\hat{a}_{ij}$ and, therefore, the λ and θ weighted sums of the $\hat{a}_{ij}$ reduce to zero. In the case of variable coefficients, sufficient extra conditions to determine the $\hat{a}$'s are easily derived. Consider, first, the maximizing role of the typical competitive entrepreneur. For any given level of output he attempts to minimize costs; that is, he minimizes unit costs. In the manufacturing industry these are given by $(a_{LM}w + a_{TM}r)$. The entrepreneur treats factor prices as fixed, and varies the a's so as to set the derivative of costs equal to zero. Dividing by p_M and expressing changes in relative terms leads to equation (6). Equation (7) shows the corresponding relationship for the food industry:

$$\theta_{LM}\hat{a}_{LM} + \theta_{TM}\hat{a}_{TM} = 0, \tag{6}$$

$$\theta_{LF}\hat{a}_{LF} + \theta_{TF}\hat{a}_{TF} = 0. \tag{7}$$

With no technological change, alterations in factor proportions must balance out such that the θ-weighted average of the changes in input coefficients in each industry is zero.

This implies directly that the relationship between changes in factor prices and changes in commodity prices is *identical* in the variable and fixed coefficients cases, an example of the Wong-Viner envelope theorem. With costs per unit of output being minimized, the change in costs resulting from a small change in factor prices is the same whether or not factor proportions are altered. The saving in cost from such alterations is a second-order small.[5]

A similar kind of argument definitely does *not* apply to the λ-weighted average of the $\hat{a}$'s for each factor that appears in the factor market-clearing relationships. For example $(\lambda_{LM}\hat{a}_{LM} + \lambda_{LF}\hat{a}_{LF})$ shows the percentage change in the total quantity of labor required by the economy as a result of changing factor proportions in each industry at unchanged outputs. The crucial feature here is that if factor prices change, factor proportions alter in the same direction in both industries. The extent of this change obviously depends upon the elasticities of substitution between factors in each industry. In a competitive equilibrium (and with the internal tangencies implicit in earlier assumptions), the slope of the isoquant in each industry is equal to the ratio of factor prices. Therefore the elasticities of substitution can be defined as in (8) and (9):

$$\sigma_M = \frac{\hat{a}_{TM} - \hat{a}_{LM}}{\hat{w} - \hat{r}}, \tag{8}$$

$$\sigma_F = \frac{\hat{a}_{TF} - \hat{a}_{LF}}{\hat{w} - \hat{r}}. \tag{9}$$

Together with (6) and (7) a subset of four equations relating the $\hat{a}$'s to the change in the relative factor prices is obtained. They can be solved in pairs; for example (6) and (8) yield solutions for the $\hat{a}$'s of the M industry. In general,

$$\hat{a}_{Lj} = -\theta_{Tj}\sigma_j(\hat{w} - \hat{r}), \qquad j = M, F;$$

$$\hat{a}_{Tj} = \theta_{Lj}\sigma_j(\hat{w} - \hat{r}), \qquad j = M, F.$$

These solutions for the $\hat{a}$'s can then be substituted into equations (1a)–(4a) to obtain:

$$\lambda_{LM}\hat{M} + \lambda_{LF}\hat{F} = \hat{L} + \delta_L(\hat{w} - \hat{r}), \tag{1b}$$

$$\lambda_{TM}\hat{M} + \lambda_{TF}\hat{F} = \hat{T} - \delta_T(\hat{w} - \hat{r}), \tag{2b}$$

$$\theta_{LM}\hat{w} + \theta_{TM}\hat{r} = \hat{p}_M, \tag{3b}$$

$$\theta_{LF}\hat{w} + \theta_{TF}\hat{r} = \hat{p}_F, \tag{4b}$$

where

$$\delta_L = \lambda_{LM}\theta_{TM}\sigma_M + \lambda_{LF}\theta_{TF}\sigma_F,$$

$$\delta_T = \lambda_{TM}\theta_{LM}\sigma_M + \lambda_{TF}\theta_{LF}\sigma_F.$$

In the fixed-coefficients case, δ_L and δ_T are zero. In general, δ_L is the aggregate percentage saving in labor inputs at unchanged outputs associated with a 1% rise in the relative wage rate, the saving resulting from the adjustment to less labor-intensive techniques in both industries as relative wages rise.

The structure of the production model with variable coefficients is exhibited in equations (1b)–(4b). The latter pair states that factor prices are dependent only upon commodity prices, which is the factor-price equalization theorem.[6] If commodity prices are unchanged, factor prices are constant and equations (1b) and (2b) state that changes in commodity outputs are linked to changes in factor endowments via the λ matrix in precisely the same way as θ links factor price changes. This is the basic duality feature of the production model.[7]

4. The Magnification Effect

The nature of the link provided by λ or θ is revealed by examining the solution for $\hat{M}$ and $\hat{F}$ at constant commodity prices in (1b) and (2b) and for $\hat{w}$ and $\hat{r}$ in equations (3b) and (4b).[8] If both endowments expand at the same rate, both commodity outputs expand at identical rates. But if factor endowments expand at different rates, the commodity intensive in the use of the fastest growing factor expands at a greater rate than either factor, and the other commodity grows (if at all) at a slower rate than either factor. For example, suppose labor expands more rapidly than land. With M labor-intensive,

$$\hat{M} > \hat{L} > \hat{T} > \hat{F}.$$

This *magnification effect* of factor endowments on commodity outputs at unchanged commodity prices is also a feature of the dual link between commodity and factor prices. In the absence of technological change or excise taxes or subsidies, if the price of M grows more rapidly than the price of F,

$$\hat{w} > \hat{p}_M > \hat{p}_F > \hat{r}.$$

Turned the other way around, the source of magnification effect is easy to detect. For example, since the relative change in the price of either commodity is a positive weighted average of factor-price changes, it must be bounded by these changes. Similarly, if input coefficients are fixed (as a consequence of assuming constant factor and commodity prices), any disparity in the growth of outputs is reduced when considering the consequent changes in the economy's demand for factors. The reason, of course, is that each good requires both factors of production.

Two special cases have been especially significant in the theory of international trade. Suppose the endowment of only one factor (say labor) rises. With $\hat{L}$ positive and $\hat{T}$ zero, $\hat{M}$ exceeds $\hat{L}$ and $\hat{F}$ is negative. This is the Rybczynzki theorem in the theory of international trade: at unchanged commodity prices an expansion in one factor results in an absolute decline in the commodity intensive in the use of the other factor. (See Rybczynski [17] and also Jones [13a], chapter 1.) Its dual underlies the Stolper-Samuelson [21] tariff theorem.[9] Suppose $\hat{p}_F$ is zero (for example, F could be taken as numeraire). Then an increase in the price of M (brought about, say, by a tariff on imports of M) raises the return to the factor used intensively in M by an even greater relative amount (and lowers the return to the other factor). In the case illustrated, the *real* return to labor has unambiguously risen.

For some purposes it is convenient to consider a slight variation of the Stolper-Samuelson theorem. Let p_j stand for the *market* price of j as before, but introduce a set of domestic excise taxes or subsidies so that $s_j p_j$ represents the price received by producers in industry j; s_j is one plus the *ad valorem* rate of subsidy to the industry.[10] The effect on factor prices of an imposition of subsidies on commodities is derived from equations (3c) and (4c):

$$\theta_{LM}\hat{w} + \theta_{TM}\hat{r} = \hat{p}_M + \hat{s}_M , \tag{3c}$$

$$\theta_{LF}\hat{w} + \theta_{TF}\hat{r} = \hat{p}_F + \hat{s}_F . \tag{4c}$$

At fixed commodity prices, what impact does a set of subsidies have on factor prices? The answer is that all the subsidies are "shifted backward" to affect returns to factors in a *magnified* fashion. Thus, if M is labor-intensive and if the M industry should be especially favored by the subsidy,

$$\hat{w} > \hat{s}_M > \hat{s}_F > \hat{r}.$$

The *magnification* effect in this problem and its dual reflects the basic structure of the model with fixed commodity prices. However, if a demand relationship is introduced, prices are determined within the model and can be expected to adjust to a change in factor endowments or, in the dual problem, to a change in excise subsidies (or taxes). In the next section I discuss the feedback effect of these induced price changes on the composition of output and relative factor prices. The crucial question to be considered concerns the extent to which commodity price changes can dampen the initial magnification effects that are produced at constant prices.

5. The Extended Model: Demand Endogenous

To close the production model I assume that community taste patterns are homothetic and ignore any differences between the taste patterns of laborers and landlords. Thus, the ratio of the quantities consumed of M and F depends only upon the relative commodity price ratio, as in equation (5):

$$\frac{M}{F} = f\left(\frac{p_M}{p_F}\right). \tag{5}$$

In terms of the rates of change, (5a) serves to define the elasticity of substitution between the two commodities on the demand side, σ_D:

$$(\hat{M} - \hat{F}) = -\sigma_D(\hat{p}_M - \hat{p}_F). \tag{5a}$$

The effect of a change in factor endowments at constant commodity prices was considered in the previous section. With the model closed by the demand relationship, commodity prices adjust so as to clear the commodity markets. Equation (5a) shows directly the change in the ratio of outputs consumed. Subtracting (2b) from (1b) yields the change in the ratio of outputs produced:

$$(\hat{M} - \hat{F}) = \frac{1}{|\lambda|}(\hat{L} - \hat{T}) + \frac{\delta_L + \delta_T}{|\lambda|}(\hat{w} - \hat{r}).$$

The change in the factor-price ratio (with no subsidies or taxes) is given by

$$(\hat{w} - \hat{r}) = \frac{1}{|\theta|}(\hat{p}_M - \hat{p}_F),$$

so that, by substitution,

$$(\hat{M} - \hat{F}) = \frac{1}{|\lambda|}(\hat{L} - \hat{T}) + \sigma_S(\hat{p}_M - \hat{p}_F),$$

where

$$\sigma_S \equiv \frac{1}{|\lambda| |\theta|}(\delta_L + \delta_T).$$

σ_S represents the elasticity of substitution between commodities on the *supply* side (along the transformation schedule).[11] The change in the commodity-price ratio is then given by the mutual interaction of demand and supply:

$$(\hat{p}_M - \hat{p}_F) = -\frac{1}{|\lambda|\,(\sigma_S + \sigma_D)}(\hat{L} - \hat{T}). \tag{10}$$

Therefore the resulting change in the ratio of commodities produced is

$$(\hat{M} - \hat{F}) = \frac{1}{|\lambda|}\frac{\sigma_D}{\sigma_S + \sigma_D}(\hat{L} - \hat{T}). \tag{11}$$

With commodity prices adjusting to the initial output changes brought about by the change in factor endowments, the composition of outputs may, in the end, not change by as much, relatively, as the factor endowments. This clearly depends upon whether the "elasticity" expression, $\sigma_D/(\sigma_S + \sigma_D)$, is smaller than the "factor-intensity" expression, $|\lambda|$. Although it is *large* values of σ_S (and the underlying elasticities of factor substitution in each industry, σ_M and σ_F) that serve to dampen the spread of outputs, it is *small* values of σ_D that accomplish the same end. This comparison between elasticities on the demand and supply side is familiar to students of public finance concerned with questions of tax (or subsidy) incidence and shifting. I turn now to this problem.

The relationship between the change in factor prices and subsidies is given by (3c) and (4c). Solving for the change in the ratio of factor prices,

$$(\hat{w} - \hat{r}) = \frac{1}{|\theta|}\{(\hat{p}_M - \hat{p}_F) + (\hat{s}_M - \hat{s}_F)\}. \tag{12}$$

Consider factor endowments to be fixed. Any change in factor prices will nonetheless induce a readjustment of commodity outputs. On the supply side,

$$(\hat{M} - \hat{F}) = \sigma_S\{(\hat{p}_M + \hat{p}_F) + (\hat{s}_M - \hat{s}_F)\}.$$

The relative commodity price change that equates supply and demand is

$$(\hat{p}_M - \hat{p}_F) = -\frac{\sigma_S}{\sigma_S + \sigma_D}(\hat{s}_M - \hat{s}_F). \tag{13}$$

Substituting back into the expression for the change in the factor-price ratio yields

$$(\hat{w} - \hat{r}) = \frac{1}{|\theta|}\frac{\sigma_D}{\sigma_S + \sigma_D}(\hat{s}_M - \hat{s}_F). \tag{14}$$

This is a familiar result. Suppose M is subsidized more heavily than F. Part of the subsidy is shifted backward, affecting relatively favorably the factor used intensively in the M-industry (labor). Whether labor's relative return expands by a greater proportion than the spread in subsidies depends upon how much of the subsidy has been passed forward to consumers in the form of a relatively lower price for M. And this, of course, depends upon the relative sizes of σ_S and σ_D.

Notice the similarity between expressions (11) and (14). Factors produce commodities, and a change in endowments must result in an altered composition of production, by a magnified amount at unchanged prices. By analogy, subsidies "produce" returns to factors, and a change in the pattern of subsidies alters the distribution of income. In each case, of course, the extent of readjustment required is eased if commodity prices change, by a factor depending upon the relative sizes of demand and supply elasticities of substitution.

6. The Aggregate Elasticity of Substitution

The analysis of a change in factor endowments leading up to equation (11) has a direct bearing on a recent issue in the neoclassical theory of economic growth. Before describing this issue it is useful to introduce yet another elasticity concept—that of an economy-wide elasticity of substitution between factors.[12] With no subsidies, the relationship between the change in the factor price ratio and the change in endowments can be derived from (10). Thus,

$$(\hat{w} - \hat{r}) = -\frac{1}{|\lambda|\,|\theta|\,(\sigma_S + \sigma_D)}(\hat{L} - \hat{T}). \tag{15}$$

By analogy with the elasticity of substitution in a particular sector, define σ as the percentage rise in the land/labor endowment ratio required to raise the wage/rent ratio by 1%. Directly from (15),

$$\sigma = |\lambda|\,|\theta|\,(\sigma_S + \sigma_D).$$

But recall that σ_S is itself a composite of the two elasticities of substitution in each industry, σ_M and σ_F. Thus, σ can be expressed in terms of the three *primary* elasticities of substitution in this model:

$$\sigma = Q_M\sigma_M + Q_F\sigma_F + Q_D\sigma_D,$$

where

$$Q_M = \theta_{LM}\lambda_{TM} + \theta_{TM}\lambda_{LM},$$

$$Q_F = \theta_{LF}\lambda_{TF} + \theta_{TF}\lambda_{LF},$$

$$Q_D = |\lambda| \cdot |\theta|.$$

Note that σ is not just a linear expression in σ_M, σ_F, and σ_D—it is a weighted average of these three elasticities as $\Sigma Q_i = 1$. Note also that σ can be positive even if the elasticity of substitution in each industry is zero, for it incorporates the effect of intercommodity substitution by consumers as well as direct intracommodity substitution between factors.

Finally, introduce the concept, σ, into expression (11) for output changes:

$$(\hat{M} - \hat{F}) = \frac{|\theta|\sigma_D}{\sigma}(\hat{L} - \hat{T}), \tag{11a}$$

and into expression (14) for the change in factor prices in the subsidy case:

$$(\hat{w} - \hat{r}) = \frac{|\lambda|\sigma_D}{\sigma}(\hat{s}_M - \hat{s}_F). \tag{14a}$$

One consequence is immediately apparent: if the elasticity of substitution between commodities on the part of consumers is no greater than the overall elasticity of substitution between factors, the *magnification* effects discussed in section 4 are more than compensated for by the dampening effect of price changes.

7. Convergence to Balanced Growth

The two-sector model of production described in sections 1–6 can be used to analyze the process of economic growth. Already I have spoken of increases in factor endowments and the consequent "growth" of outputs. But a more satisfactory growth model would allow for the growth of at least one factor of production to be determined by the system rather than given parametrically. Let the factor "capital" replace "land" as the second factor in the two-sector model (replace T by K). And let M stand for machines rather than manufacturing goods. To simplify, I assume capital does not depreciate. The new feedback element in the system is that the rate of increase of the capital stock, $\hat{K}$, depends on the current output of machines, M. Thus $\hat{K} = M/K$. The "demand" for M now represents savings.

Suppose the rate of growth of the labor force, $\hat{L}$, is constant. At any moment of time the rate of capital accumulation, $\hat{K}$, either exceeds, equals, or falls short of $\hat{L}$. Of special interest in the neoclassical theory of growth (with no technological progress) is the case of balanced growth where $\hat{L} = \hat{K}$. Balance in the growth of factors will, as we have seen, result in balanced growth as between the two commodities (at the same rate). But if $\hat{L}$ and $\hat{K}$ are not equal, it becomes necessary to inquire whether they tend toward equality (balanced growth) asymptotically or tend to diverge even further.

If machines are produced by labor-intensive techniques, the rate of growth of machines exceeds that of capital if labor is growing faster than capital, or falls short of capital if capital is growing faster than labor. (This is the result in section 4, which is dampened, but not reversed, by the price changes discussed in section 5.) Thus, the rate of capital accumulation, if different from the rate of growth of the labor supply, falls or rises toward it. The economy tends toward the balanced-growth path.

The difficulty arises if machines are capital intensive. If there is no price change, the change in the composition of outputs must be a magnified reflection of the spread in the growth rates of factors. Thus, if capital is growing more rapidly than labor, machine output will expand at a greater rate than either factor, and this only serves to widen the spread between the rates of growth of capital and labor even further.[13] Once account is taken of price changes, however, the change in the composition of outputs may be sufficiently dampened to allow convergence to balanced growth despite the fact that machines are capital intensive.

Re-examine equation (11a), replacing $\hat{T}$ by $\hat{K}$ and recognizing that $|\theta|$ is negative if machines are capital intensive. If σ exceeds $-|\theta|\sigma_D$, on balance a dampening of the ratio of outputs as compared to factor endowments takes place. This suggests the critical condition that must be satisfied by σ, as compared with σ_D and $|\theta|$, in order to insure stability. But this is not precisely the condition required. Rather, stability hinges upon the *sign* of $(\hat{M} - \hat{K})$ being opposite to that of $(\hat{K} - \hat{L})$. There is a presumption that when $(\hat{M} - \hat{F})$ is smaller than $(\hat{K} - \hat{L})$ (assuming both are positive) the output of the machine sector is growing less rapidly than is the capital stock. But the corresponding is not exact.

To derive the relationship between $(\hat{M} - \hat{K})$ and $(\hat{M} - \hat{F})$ consider the two ways of expressing changes in the national income (Y). It can be viewed as the sum of returns to factors or the sum of the values of output in the two sectors. Let θ_i refer to the share of factor i or commodity i in the national income. In terms of rates of change,

$$\hat{Y} = \theta_L(\hat{w} + \hat{L}) + \theta_K(\hat{r} + \hat{K}) = \theta_M(\hat{p}_M + \hat{M}) + \theta_F(\hat{p}_F + \hat{F}).$$

But the share of a factor in the national income must be an average of its share in each sector, with the weights given by the share of that sector in the national income. This, and equations (3b) and (4b), guarantee that

$$\theta_L \hat{w} + \theta_K \hat{r} = \theta_M \hat{p}_M + \theta_F \hat{p}_F.$$

That is, the rates of change of the financial components in the two expressions for $\hat{Y}$ balance, leaving an equality between the physical terms:

$$\theta_L \hat{L} + \theta_K \hat{K} = \theta_M \hat{M} + \theta_F \hat{F}.$$

The desired relationship is obtained by observing that θ_K equals $(1 - \theta_L)$ and θ_M is $(1 - \theta_F)$. Thus,

$$(\hat{M} - \hat{K}) = \theta_F(\hat{M} - \hat{F}) - \theta_L(\hat{K} - \hat{L}).$$

With this in hand it is easy to see that (from (11a)) $(\hat{M} - \hat{K})$ is given by

$$(\hat{M} - \hat{K}) = \frac{\theta_L}{\sigma} \left\{ -\frac{\theta_F |\theta|}{\theta_L} \sigma_D - \sigma \right\} (\hat{K} - \hat{L}). \tag{16}$$

It is not enough for σ to exceed—$|\theta|\sigma_D$, it must exceed—$(\theta_F/\theta_L)|\theta|\sigma_D$ for convergence to balanced growth.[14] It nonetheless remains the case that σ greater than σ_D is sufficient to insure that the expression in brackets in (16) is negative. For (16) can be rewritten as (16a):

$$(\hat{M} - \hat{K}) = -\frac{\theta_L}{\sigma} \left\{ \sigma - \left[1 - \frac{\theta_{LM}}{\theta_L} \right] \sigma_D \right\} (\hat{K} - \hat{L}). \tag{16a}$$

Thus, it is overly strong to require that σ exceed σ_D.[15]

8. Savings Behavior

A popular assumption about savings behavior in the literature on growth theory is that aggregate savings form a constant percentage of the national income. (See, for example, Solow [20].) This, of course, implies that σ_D is unity. In this case it becomes legitimate to inquire as to the values of σ or σ_M and σ_F as compared with unity. For example, if each sector's production function is Cobb-Douglas (σ_M and σ_F each unity), stability is guaranteed. But the value "unity" that has a crucial role in this comparison only serves as a proxy for σ_D. With high σ_D even greater values for σ_M and σ_F (and σ) would be required.

If σ_D is unity when the savings ratio is constant, is its value higher or lower than unity when the savings ratio depends positively on the rate of profit? It turns out that this depends upon the technology in such a way as to encourage convergence to balanced growth precisely in those cases where factor intensities are such as to leave it in doubt.

The capital goods, machines, are demanded not for the utility they yield directly, but for the stream of additional future consumption they allow. This is represented by the rate of return (or profit), which is linked by the technology to the relative price of machines according to the magnification effects implicit in the Stolper-Samuelson theorem. The assumption that the savings ratio (the fraction of income devoted to new machines) rises as the rate of profit rises implies that the savings ratio rises as the relative price of machines rises (and thus that σ_D is less than unity) if and only if machines are capital intensive. Of course the savings assumption also implies that σ_D exceeds unity (that is, that the savings ratio falls as the relative price of machines rises) if machines are labor intensive, but convergence to balanced growth is already assured in this case.[16]

9. The Analysis of Technological Change

The preceding sections have dealt with the structure of the two-sector model of production with a given technology. They nonetheless contain the ingredients necessary for an analysis of the effects of technological progress. In this concluding section I examine this problem and simplify by assuming that factor endowments remain unchanged and subsidies are zero. I concentrate on the impact of a change in production conditions on relative prices. The effect on outputs is considered implicitly in deriving the price changes.

Consider a typical input coefficient, a_{ij}, as depending both upon relative factor prices and the state of technology:

$$a_{ij} = a_{ij}(w/r, t).$$

In terms of the relative rates of change, $\hat{a}_{ij}$ may be decomposed as

$$\hat{a}_{ij} = \hat{c}_{ij} - \hat{b}_{ij}.$$

$\hat{c}_{ij}$ denotes the relative change in the input–output coefficient that is called forth by a change in factor prices as of a given technology. The $\hat{b}_{ij}$ is a measure of technological change that shows the alteration in a_{ij} that would take place at constant factor prices. Since technological progress usually involves a *reduction* in the input requirements, I define $\hat{b}_{ij}$ as $-(1/a_{ij})\partial a_{ij}/\partial t$.

The $\tilde{b}_{ij}$ are the basic expressions of technological change. After the discussion in section 3 it is not surprising that it is the λ and θ weighted averages of the $\hat{b}_{ij}$ that turn out to be important. These are defined by the following set of π's:

$$\pi_j = \theta_{Lj}\hat{b}_{Lj} + \theta_{Tj}\hat{b}_{Tj}, \qquad j = M, F;$$

$$\pi_i = \lambda_{iM}\hat{b}_{iM} + \lambda_{iF}\hat{b}_{iF}, \qquad i = L, T.$$

If a $\hat{B}$ matrix is defined in a manner similar to the original A matrix, π_M and π_F are the sums of the elements in each column weighted by the relative factor shares, and π_L and π_T are sums of the elements in each row of $\hat{B}$ weighted by the fractions of the total factor supplies used in each industry. Thus, π_M, assumed non-negative, is a measure of the rate of technological advance in the M-industry and π_L, also assumed non-negative, reflects the overall labor-saving feature of technological change.

Turn now to the equations of change. The $\hat{c}_{ij}$ are precisely the $\hat{a}_{ij}$ used in equations (6)–(9) of the model without technological change. This subset can be solved, just as before, for the response of input coefficients to factor price changes. After substitution, the first four equations of change (equations (1a)–(4a)) become

$$\lambda_{LM}\hat{M} + \lambda_{LF}\hat{F} = \pi_L + \delta_L(\hat{w} - \hat{r}), \tag{1d}$$

$$\lambda_{TM}\hat{M} + \lambda_{TF}\hat{F} = \pi_T - \delta_T(\hat{w} - \hat{r}), \tag{2d}$$

$$\theta_{LM}\hat{w} + \theta_{TM}\hat{r} = \hat{p}_M + \pi_M, \tag{3d}$$

$$\theta_{LF}\hat{w} + \theta_{TF}\hat{r} = \hat{p}_F + \pi_F. \tag{4d}$$

The parameters of technological change appear only in the first four relationships and enter there in a particularly simple form. In the first two equations it is readily seen that, in part, technological change, through its impact in reducing input coefficients, has precisely the same effects on the system as would a change in factor endowments. π_L and π_T replace $\hat{L}$ and $\hat{T}$, respectively. In the second pair of equations the improvements in industry outputs attributable to technological progress enter the model precisely as do industry subsidies in equations (3c) and (4c) of section 4. Any general change in technology or in the quality of factors (that gets translated into a change in input coefficiencies) has an impact on prices and outputs that can be decomposed into the two kinds of parametric changes analyzed in the preceding sections.

Consider the effect of progress upon relative commodity and factor prices. The relationship between the changes in the two sets of prices is the same as in the subsidy case (see equation (12)):

$$(\hat{w} - \hat{r}) = \frac{1}{|\theta|}\{(\hat{p}_M - \hat{p}_F) + (\pi_M - \pi_F)\}. \tag{17}$$

Solving separately for each relative price change,

$$(\hat{p}_M - \hat{p}_F) = -\frac{|\theta|}{\sigma}\{(\pi_L - \pi_T) + |\lambda|\sigma_S(\pi_M - \pi_F)\}, \tag{18}$$

$$(\hat{w} - \hat{r}) = -\frac{1}{\sigma}\{(\pi_L - \pi_T) - |\lambda|\sigma_D(\pi_M - \pi_F)\}. \tag{19}$$

For convenience I refer to $(\pi_L - \pi_T)$ as the "differential factor effect" and $(\pi_M - \pi_F)$ as the "differential industry effect".[17]

Define a change in technology as "regular" if the differential factor and industry effects have the same sign.[18] For example, a change in technology that is relatively "labor-saving" for the economy as a whole ($\pi_L - \pi_T$ positive) is considered "regular" if it also reflects a relatively greater improvement in productivity in the labor-intensive industry. Suppose this to be the case. Both effects tend to depress the relative price of commodity M: the "labor-saving" feature of the change works exactly as would a relative increase in the labor endowment to reduce the relative price of the labor-intensive commodity (M). And part of the differential industry effect, like a relative subsidy to M, is shifted forward in a lower price for M.

Whereas the two components of "regular" technological change reinforce each other in their effect on the commodity price ratio, they pull the factor price ratio in opposite directions. The differential factor effect in the above case serves to depress the wage/rent ratio. But part of the relatively greater improvement in the labor-intensive M industry is shifted backward to increase, relatively, the return to labor. This "backward" shift is more pronounced the greater is the elasticity of substitution on the demand side. There will be some "critical" value of σ_D, above which relative wages will rise despite the downward pull of the differential factor effect:

$$(\hat{w} - \hat{r}) > 0 \text{ if and only if } \sigma_D > \frac{(\pi_L - \pi_T)}{|\lambda|\,(\pi_M - \pi_F)}.$$

If technological progress is not "regular" these conclusions are reversed. Suppose $(\pi_L - \pi_T) > 0$, but nonetheless $(\pi_M - \pi_F) < 0$. This might be the result, say, of technological change where the primary impact is to reduce labor requirements in food production. Labor is now affected relatively adversely on both counts, the differential factor effect serving to depress wages as before, and the differential industry effect working to the relative advantage of the factor used intensively in food production—land. On the other hand, the change in relative commodity prices is now less predictable. The differential factor effect, in tending to reduce M's relative price, is working counter to the differential industry effect, whereby the F industry is experiencing more rapid technological advance. The differential industry effect will, in this case, dominate if the elasticity of substitution between goods on the supply side is high enough:

$$(\hat{p}_M - \hat{p}_F) > 0 \text{ if and only if } \sigma_S > -\frac{\pi_L - \pi_T}{|\lambda| (\pi_M - \pi_F)}.$$

The differential factor and industry effects are not independent of each other. Some insight into the nature of the relationship between the two can be obtained by considering two special cases of "neutrality".

Suppose, first, that technological change is "Hicksian neutral" in each industry, implying that, at unchanged factor prices, factor proportions used in that industry do not change (see Hicks [8]). In terms of the $\hat{B}$ matrix, the rows are identical ($\hat{b}_{Lj} = \hat{b}_{Tj}$). As can easily be verified from the definition of the π, in this case

$$(\pi_L - \pi_T) = |\lambda| (\pi_M - \pi_F),$$

and technological change must be "regular". If, overall, technological change is "labor-saving" (and note that this can happen even if it is Hicksian neutral in each industry), the price of the relatively labor-intensive commodity must fall. Relative wages will, nonetheless, rise if σ_D exceeds the critical value shown earlier, which in this case reduces to unity.

The symmetrical nature of this approach to technological change suggests an alternative definition of neutrality, in which the columns of the $\hat{B}$ matrix are equal. This type of neutrality indicates that input requirements for any factor, i, have been reduced by the same relative amount in every industry. The relationship between the differential factor and industry effects is given by

$$(\pi_M - \pi_F) = |\theta| (\pi_L - \pi_T).$$

Again, technological change must be "regular". If the reduction in labor coefficients in each industry exceeds the reduction in land coefficients, this must filter through (in dampened form unless each industry uses just one factor) to affect relatively favorably the labor-intensive industry. The remarks made in the case of Hicksian neutrality carry over to this case, except for the fact that the critical value which σ_D must exceed in order for the differential industry effect to outweigh the factor effect on relative wages now becomes higher. Specifically, σ_D must exceed $1/|\lambda| |\theta|$, which may be considerably greater than unity. This reflects the fact that in the case of Hicksian neutrality $(\pi_L - \pi_T)$ is smaller than $(\pi_M - \pi_F)$, whereas the reverse is true in the present case.

With Hicksian neutrality the paramount feature is the difference between rates of technological advance in each industry. This spills over into a differential factor effect only because the industries require the two factors in differing proportions. With the other kind of neutrality the basic change is that the input requirements of one factor are cut more than for the other factor. As we have just seen, this is transformed into a differential industry effect only in dampened form.

These cases of neutrality are special cases of "regular" technological progress. The general relationship between the differential factor and industry effects can be derived from the definitions to yield

$$(\pi_L - \pi_T) = Q_M \beta_M + Q_F \beta_F + |\lambda| (\pi_M - \pi_F) \tag{20}$$

and

$$(\pi_M - \pi_F) = Q_L \beta_L + Q_T \beta_T + |\theta| (\pi_L - \pi_T). \tag{21}$$

In the first equation the differential factor effect is broken down into three components; the labor-saving bias of technical change in each industry (β_j is defined as $\hat{b}_{Lj} - \hat{b}_{Tj}$) and the differential industry effect.[19] In the second expression the differential industry effect is shown as a combination of the relatively greater saving in each factor in the M industry (β_L, for example, is $\hat{b}_{LM} - \hat{b}_{LF}$) and the differential factor effect.[20] With these relationships at hand it is easy to see how it is the possible asymmetry between the row elements and/or the column elements of the $\hat{B}$ matrix that could disrupt the "regularity" feature of technical progress.[21]

For some purposes it is useful to make the substitution from either (20) or (21) into the expressions for the changes in relative factor and commodity prices shown by (17)–(19). For example, if technological change is 'neutral' in the sense described earlier, where the reduction in the input coefficient is the same in each industry (although different for each factor), β_L and β_T are zero in (21) and the relationship in (17) can be rewritten as

$$(\hat{w} - \hat{r}) = \frac{1}{|\theta|} (\hat{p}_M - \hat{p}_F) + (\pi_L - \pi_T).$$

To make things simple, suppose π_T is zero. The uniform reduction in labor input coefficients across industries might reflect, say, an improvement in labor quality attributable to education. Aside from the effect of any change in commodity prices on factor prices (of the Stolper-Samuelson variety), relative wages are directly increased by the improvement in labor quality.

Alternatively, consider substituting (20) into (19), to yield (19a):

$$(\hat{w} - \hat{r}) = -\frac{1}{\sigma}\left\{Q_M\beta_M + Q_F\beta_F + Q_D(1 - \sigma_D)\frac{\pi_M - \pi_F}{|\theta|}\right\}. \tag{19a}$$

Will technological change that is Hicks neutral in every industry leave the factor-price ratio unaltered at a given ratio of factor endowments? Equation (19a) suggests a negative answer to this query unless progress is at the same rate in the two industries ($\pi_M = \pi_F$) or unless σ_D is unity.[22]

There exists an extensive literature in the theory of international trade concerned with (a) the effects of differences in production functions on pre-trade factor and commodity price ratios (and thus on positions of comparative advantage), and (b) the impact of growth (in factor supplies) or changes in technological knowledge in one or more countries on the world terms of trade.[23] The analysis of this paper is well suited to the discussion of these problems. The connection between (a) and expressions (17)–(19) is obvious. For (b) it is helpful to observe that the impact of any of these changes on world terms of trade depends upon the effect in each country separately of these changes on production and consumption at constant commodity prices. The production effects can be derived from the four equations of change for the production sector (equations (1a)–(4a) or later versions) and the consumption changes from equation (5a).[24] The purpose of this paper is not to reproduce the results in detail but rather to expose those features of the model which bear upon all of these questions.

I am indebted to the National Science Foundation for support of this research in 1962–1964. I have benefited from discussions with Hugh Rose, Robert Fogel, Rudolph Penner, and Emmanuel Drandakis. My greatest debt is to Akihiro Amano [1], whose dissertation was a stimulus to my own work.

References

[1] Amano, A., *Neo-Classical Models of International Trade and Economic Growth* (University of Rochester, New York, 1963).

[2] Amano, A., "Determinants of Comparative Costs: A Theoretic Approach", *Oxford Economic Papers* (November 1964).

[3] Amano, A., "A Two-Sector Model of Economic Growth Involving Technical Progress" (unpublished).

[4] Bhagwati, J. and H. Johnson, "Notes on Some Controversies in the Theory of International Trade", *Economic Journal* (March 1960).

[5] Dorfman, R., P. A. Samuelson and R. M. Solow, *Linear Programming and Economic Analysis* (McGraw-Hill, New York, 1958).

[6] Drandakis, E., "Factor Substitution in the Two-Sector Growth Model", *Review of Economic Studies* (October 1963).

[7] Findlay, R. and H. Grubert, "Factor Intensities, Technological Progress and the Terms of Trade", *Oxford Economic Papers* (February 1959).

[8] Hicks, J. R., *The Theory of Wages* (Macmillan, New York, 1932).

[9] Hicks, J. R., "Linear Theory", *Economic Journal* (December 1960).

[10] Inada, Ken-ichi, "On Neoclassical Models of Economic Growth", *Review of Economic Studies* (April 1965).

[11] Johnson, H., "Economic Expansion and International Trade", *Manchester School of Economic and Social Studies* (May 1955).

[12] Johnson, H., "Economic Development and International Trade", in: *Money, Trade, and Economic Growth* (George Allen & Unwin, London, 1962) ch. 4.

[13] Jones, R. W., "Stability Condition in International Trade: A General Equilibrium Analysis", *International Economic Review* (May 1961).

[13a] Jones, R. W., *International Trade: Essays in Theory* (North-Holland, 1979) ch. 1.

[14] Kemp, C. M., *The Pure Theory of International Trade* (Prentice-Hall, Englewood Cliffs, 1964) pp. 10–11.

[15] Meade, J. E., *A Neo-Classical Theory of Economic Growth* (Allen & Unwin, London, 1961) pp. 84–86.

[16] Meier, G. M., *International Trade and Development* (Harper & Row, New York, 1963) ch. 1.

[17] Rybczynski, T. M., "Factor Endowments and Relative Commodity Prices", *Economica* (November 1955).

[18] Samuelson, P. A., "Prices of Factors and Goods in General Equilibrium", *Review of Economic Studies*, 21 (1) (1953–1954).

[19] Shinkai, Y., "On Equilibrium Growth of Capital and Labor", *International Economic Review* (May 1960).

[20] Solow, R., 'A Contribution to the Theory of Economic Growth', *Quarterly Journal of Economics* (February 1956).

[21] Stolper, W. F., and P. A. Samuelson, "Protection and Real Wages", *Review of Economic Studies* (November 1941).

[22] Takayama, A., "On a Two-Sector Model of Economic Growth: A Comparative Statics Analysis", *Review of Economic Studies* (June 1963).

[23] Takayama, A., "Economic Growth and International Trade", *Review of Economic Studies* (June 1964).

[24] Uzawa, H., "On a Two-Sector Model of Economic Growth", *Review of Economic Studies* (October 1961).

[25] Uzawa, H., "On a Two-Sector Model of Economic Growth—II", *Review of Economic Studies* (June 1963).

4

The Two-Sector Model in Terms of Its Dual: A Geometric Exposition

Michael Mussa

1. Introduction

The two-sector model is usually described in terms of the production functions for the economy's two outputs. It is the purpose of this paper to show that for many purposes, particularly for analyzing factor market distortions, it is more convenient to work with the duals of the production functions.[1] This is so because many of the essential features of the two-sector model (e.g. the Stolper-Samuelson theorem and the factor price equalization theorem) deal with relationships between prices. Production functions, however, focus directly on quantities and only indirectly on prices. In contrast, the duals of the production functions deal directly with prices.

The analysis in this paper is conducted in terms of a simple diagram that is developed in section 2. Sections 3, 4, 5, and 6 show how this diagram may be used to establish the essential properties of the two-sector model: the factor price equalization theorem, the Rybczynski theorem, the Stolper-Samuelson theorem, and the effects of technological change. Sections 7, 8, and 9 are devoted to the analysis of factor market distortions. Specifically, section 7 shows how to determine the effects of factor market distortions of any degree of complexity on factor prices and factor intensities. This analysis provides a convenient demonstration of the seemingly paradoxical result that a *tax* on a factor in the industry that does not use that factor intensively *increases* the return to that factor in terms of both goods. Section 8 introduces the concept of the 'shadow price' of a factor of production [see Diamond and Mirrlees (1976), Findlay and Wellisz (1976), Bhagwati, Srinivasan and Wan (1978), and Srinivasan and Bhagwati (1978)] and shows how these shadow prices may be used to

This paper was originally published in *Journal of International Economics* 9, no. 4 (November 1979): 513–526.

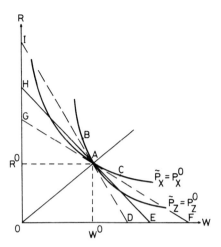

Figure 1

compare the total distortionary effect of widely divergent factor market distortions. Finally, section 9 considers an economy that is so highly distorted that the shadow price of one factor of production is actually negative, and examines some of the peculiar characteristics of such an economy.[2]

2. The Dual of the Lerner-Pearce Diagram

The basic diagram is shown in figure 1.[3] The dual of the production function for commodity X, $\tilde{P}_X(W, R)$, determines the isoprice curve labeled '$\tilde{P}_X = P_X^0$' which indicates the combinations of the wage rate of labor, W, and the rental rate of capital, R, which are consistent with zero profits in producing X, given the price P_X^0. A higher (lower) price of X shifts this curve proportionately outward (inward) along every ray through the origin. The dual of the production function for commodity Z, $\tilde{P}_Z(W, R)$, determines the isoprice curve labeled '$\tilde{P}_Z = P_Z^0$' which indicates the combinations of W and R which are consistent with a given price P_Z^0, for commodity Z. The absolute values of the slopes of the isoprice curves indicate the ratios of labor to capital which will be used in the respective industries.[4] The isoprice curves are convex as viewed from the origin because the labor-capital ratio in each industry is an increasing function of the rental-wage ratio. The curvature of the isoprice curves reflects the elasticity of substitution between labor and capital in the respective industries.[5]

The two isoprice curves shown in figure 1 intersect once and only once.

This point of intersection, A, determines the wage rate, W^0, and the rental rate, R^0, which are consistent with the production of both commodities at the given output prices, P_X^0 and P_Z^0. At this wage-rental combination, the labor-capital ratio in X, l_X^A, is equal to minus the slope of the line FAG; and the labor-capital ratio in Z, l_Z^A, is equal to minus the slope of the line DAI. To indicate the ratio of labor to capital determined by the economy's endowments of these factors (L and K), the line EAH has been constructed with a slope of $-l = -L/K$. In figure 1 this line lies between the tangents to the two isoprice curves at A. In this situation, production of both commodities is consistent with full employment of the economy's factors of production since the labor-intensive industry, Z, uses a labor-capital ratio which is greater than the endowment ratio and the capital intensive industry, X, uses a labor-capital ratio which is less than the endowment ratio. If l were greater than l_Z^A, the economy would have to specialize in producing Z in order to maintain full employment of both labor and capital. In this situation, factor prices would not be determined by the point A, but rather by some point B at which the slope of the isoprice curve for Z is equal to $-l$. At these factor prices, production of X would be unprofitable since the $\tilde{P}_X = P_X^0$ curve lies below B. Conversely, if l were less than l_X^A, the economy would specialize in X and factor prices would be determined by some point such as C.

If, for given prices of X and Z the isoprice curves failed to intersect, the economy would produce only the commodity with the higher isoprice curve. Factor prices would be determined by the point at which the slope of this isoprice curve equaled $-l$. If the isoprice curves intersect more than once, then the relevant point of intersection is the one (there cannot be more than one) at which the slope of the line indicating the endowment ratio lies between the tangents to the two isoprice curves. If no point of intersection satisfies this condition, then the economy will specialize in the commodity which has the higher tangent to its isoprice with a slope of $-l$, and factor prices will be determined by this point of tangency.

3. Factor Price Equalization

In discussing factor price equalization, we are concerned with two economies which have identical technologies and face the same *relative* price for their outputs. An equiproportionate change in the nominal prices of X and Z has no effect on the relationships shown in figure 1, other than a homogeneous outward or inward shift of the two isoprice curves. Therefore, without loss of generality, we may assume that both countries face the same nominal output prices. Hence, figure 1 applies equally to both economies. The only difference between the diagrams for the two countries is that the lines which indicate the endowment ratios will, in general, have different slopes. However, provided both of these lines lie between the tangents to the two isoprice curves at A, both economies will produce both commodities and will have the same factor prices. It follows that the ratios of the two factor prices to each other and to the two commodity prices must be the same for both economies.

This demonstration of factor price equalization breaks down if the isoprice curves fail to intersect, or if the endowment ratio for either of the economies is such that it specializes. The only circumstance in which factor price equalization can fail when both economies produce both commodities is if the isoprice curves intersect more than once and if the endowment ratios of the two countries place them at different points of intersection. To preclude this possibility, it is sufficient to impose the "strong factor intensity assumption" which implies that the isoprice curve which is steeper at one wage-rental ratio must be steeper at every other wage-rental ratio.

4. The Rybczynski Effect

From figure 1 we may determine the distribution of the economy's capital stock and labor force between X and Z. Adopting Jones's (1965) notation, $\lambda_{KX} = K_X/K$, $\lambda_{KZ} = K_Z/K$, $\lambda_{LX} = L_X/L$, and $\lambda_{LZ} = L_Z/L$ indicate the fractions of the capital stock and the labor force which are used in the production of X and the production of Z. The condition for full employment of the labor force requires that

$$l_X^A \lambda_{KX} + l_Z^A \lambda_{KZ} = l. \tag{1}$$

Using the fact that $\lambda_{KX} + \lambda_{KZ} = 1$, it follows that

$$\lambda_{KX} = (l_Z^A - l)/(l_Z^A - l_X^A); \qquad \lambda_{KZ} = (l - l_X^A)/(l_Z^A - l_X^A). \tag{2}$$

In figure 1 the right triangles $AR^0 G$, $AR^0 H$, and $AR^0 I$ share a common base and have angles at A for which the tangents are, respectively, l_X^A, l, and l_Z^A. It follows that λ_{KX} is shown by the ratio of the distance HI to the distance GI and that λ_{KZ} is shown by the ratio of the distance GH to the distance GI. A symmetric argument applied to the full employment condition for the capital stock and the right triangles $AW^0 D$, $AW^0 E$, and $AW^0 F$ allow us to conclude that

$$\lambda_{KX} = HI/GI, \qquad \lambda_{KZ} = GH/GI, \qquad \lambda_{LX} = DE/DF,$$

$$\lambda_{LX} = EF/DF. \tag{3}$$

Using (3) we can determine the effect of a change in the economy's endowment of labor or capital on its outputs of X and Z. An increase in L increases the slope of the line EAH; in particular, the distance $R^0 H$ increases proportionately with the increase in L. It follows that $\lambda_{KZ} = GH/GI$ rises more than proportionately with the increase in L and that $\lambda_{KX} = HI/GI$ falls. Since the capital stock is fixed and since the factor ratios in the two industries remain unchanged, it follows that the output of Z is proportional to λ_{KZ} and the output of X is proportional to λ_{KX}. Hence, the output of Z, the labor-intensive commodity, rises more than proportionately with an increase in L, and the output of X, the capital-intensive commodity, falls. Similarly, by looking at the effect of an increase in the capital stock on the distances DE and EF, we may conclude that the output of X will rise more than proportionately with an increase in K and that the output of Z will fall.

5. The Stolper-Samuelson Theorem

The effects of a change in relative commodity prices may be analyzed with the aid of figure 2. An increase in the relative price of X is indicated by a shift of the isoprice curve for X from $\tilde{P}_X = P_X^0$ to $\tilde{P}_X = P_X^1$. This moves the point of intersection between the two isoprice curves from A to B. The wage rate consistent with the production of both commodities falls

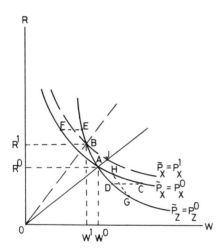

Figure 2

from W^0 to W^1 and the rental rate rises from R^0 to R^1. Since P_X has risen and P_Z has been held constant, it is clear that the wage rate has fallen relative to the prices of both commodities. Furthermore, since the rental rate associated with the point J is the rental rate which is consistent with a constant ratio of R to P_X, it is clear that the rental rate rises relative to the prices of both commodities. This establishes half of the Stolper-Samuelson theorem: an increase in the price of the capital-intensive commodity increases the return to capital in terms of both commodities and reduces the return to labor in terms of both commodities. Moreover, since both isoprice curves are steeper at B than they are at A, it follows that an increase in the relative price of the capital intensive commodity induces production of both commodities to become more labor intensive. Combining this fact with the previous analysis of the distribution of the economy's endowments of labor and capital, it can be shown that λ_{KX} and λ_{LX} both rise as a result of an increase in the relative price of X. This, in turn, implies that the output of X rises and the output of Z declines.

To determine the effects of an increase in the relative price of the labor intensive commodity, consider the move from B back to A. We immediately obtain the other half of the Stolper-Samuelson theorem: the wage rate rises in terms of both commodities and the rental rate falls in terms of both commodities. Moreover, production in both industries becomes more capital intensive and the output of Z rises while the output of X declines.

6. Technological Advance

In terms of the production function, technological advance means that there is an inward shift of the isoquant; a given level of output can be produced with lower levels of input. In terms of the dual of the production function, technological advance means an outward shift of the isoprice curve; at a given output price, a firm can afford to pay more for its factor inputs and still maintain zero profits. Specifically, Hicks neutral technological advance causes a homogeneous outward shift of the isoprice curve associated with any given output price. In fact, the effect of such a Hicks neutral technological advance in the X industry is precisely what is illustrated by the outward shift of the $\tilde{P}_X$ curve from $\tilde{P}_X = P_X^0$ to $\tilde{P}_X = P_X^1$ in figure 2, except that it is necessary to reinterpret the $\tilde{P}_X = P_X^1$ curve as the isoprice curve corresponding to a higher level of technical efficiency in X, rather than to a higher price of X. With this reinterpretation, it is apparent from figure 2 that the effect of a 10 percent, Hicks neutral technological advance in X (the capital-intensive industry), at constant output prices, is to increase the rental rate on capital in terms of both goods by more than 10 percent and to reduce the wage of labor in terms of both goods. Similarly, a 10 percent, Hicks neutral technological advance in Z (the labor intensive industry) would shift the $\tilde{P}_Z$ curve homogeneously outward by 10 percent. The effect of such a technological advance in Z would be to increase the wage rate by more than 10 percent and to reduce the rental rate. Moreover, it is apparent that this analysis of the effects of technological advance extends to cases where the advance is not Hicks neutral. Any technological advance in X results in a generally nonhomogeneous outward shift of the $\tilde{P}_X$ curve and, hence, reduces the wage rate and increases the rental rate. In contrast, any technological advance in Z increases the wage rate and reduces the rental rate.

7. Factor Market Distortions

Figure 2 may also be used to determine many of the effects of factor market distortions. Suppose, for instance, that a subsidy is paid to labor used in the production of Z.[6] Given the output prices, P_X^0 and P_Z^0, the equilibrium of the economy must lie at a pair of points like D and C in figure 2 for which the rental rate is the same in both industries and for which the wage rate paid by firms in Z (exclusive of subsidy) is below the wage rate paid by firms in X. We see immediately the somewhat paradoxical results that a subsidy to labor in the labor intensive industry makes both industries become more *capital* intensive and increases the wage paid by firms (exclusive of subsidy) in the subsidized industry. Furthermore, since all workers receive the wage paid in the X industry, all workers gain by more than the rate of subsidy and, hence, the total gain is far in excess of the total subsidy paid.

Next, consider a tax on labor used in the production of X, the capital intensive commodity. This tax also results in an equilibrium at a pair of points like D and C in figure 2. The only difference from the previous case is that workers now receive the wage rate indicated by the point D, rather than the wage rate indicated by the point C. Thus a *tax* on labor in the capital intensive industry benefits workers, even though it does not benefit them as much as a subsidy to labor in the labor intensive industry.

A subsidy to labor in X or a tax on labor in Z results in an equilibrium at a pair of points like E and F in figure 2. Both the subsidy and the tax benefit the owners of capital by raising the rental rate. The tax on labor in the labor intensive industry has the most deleterious effect on wages, since under this tax all workers are paid the wage associated with the point F. The more paradoxical result, however, is that a subsidy to labor in the capital intensive industry actually makes workers worse off than if no subsidy were paid.

Taxes and subsidies on capital used in X or Z can also be analyzed in terms of the diagram. The effect of such distortions is to induce vertical gaps between the two isoprice curves. The whole analysis is completely symmetric with that for wage distortions. Furthermore, the apparatus deals easily with simultaneous distortions of different factor prices. For instance, the pair of points G and H in figure 2 represent the equilibrium which would result from any of the following four combinations of distortions: a tax on labor in Z and a subsidy to capital in Z; a tax on labor in Z and a tax on capital in X; a subsidy to labor in X and a subsidy to capital in Z; or a subsidy to labor in X and a tax on capital in X. In each of these four cases the wage rate received by workers is determined by the wage paid in the industry in which labor is not taxed or subsidized and the rental rate received by capital owners is determined by the rental rate paid in the industry in which capital is not taxed or subsidized. For instance, for the case of a tax on labor in Z and a tax on capital in X, the wage rate received by workers is that associated with the point H, and the rental rate received by capital owners is that associated with the point G. Finally, since a tax (subsidy) on an output is equivalent to an equal percentage tax (subsidy) on both inputs used in producing that output, the apparatus of figure 2 may be used to analyze the effects of distortions of output prices.

8. Shadow Prices in a Distorted Economy

In an economy free of distortions, the prices of factors measure the marginal social values of these factors. Specifically, the wage rate and the rental rate associated with the undistorted equilibrium point A indicate the amount by which the value of the economy's output would rise if the endowment of labor or capital, respectively, were increased by a unit. The question of what would happen to the value of output, at given output prices, if the supply of a factor were increased remains a meaningful question in a distorted economy. But the answer to this question is not provided by the prices received by factor owners or by the prices paid by factor users. To determine the marginal social values of labor and capital, it is necessary to calculate a shadow wage rate, W^S, and a shadow rental rate, R^S.[7]

Given the prices of the two outputs and the distortions prevailing in the economy, the amounts of labor and capital used to produce a unit of

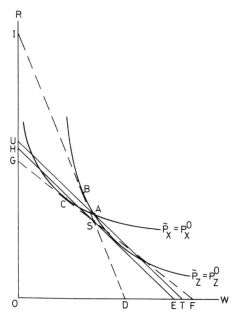

Figure 3

X, a_{LX} and a_{KX}, and the amounts of labor and capital used to produce a unit of Z, a_{LZ} and a_{KZ}, are fixed by the wage rates and rental rates facing the two industries. Given these factor requirements, the appropriate procedure for determining W^S and R^S is to calculate the equilibrium wage rate and rental rate for this fixed-coefficients technology. Specifically, from Jones (1965) it follows that W^S and R^S must satisfy

$$a_{LX} W^S + a_{KX} R^S = P_X^0, \tag{4}$$

$$a_{LZ} W^S + a_{KZ} R^S = P_Z^0. \tag{5}$$

For the set of distortions indicated by the points B and C in figure 3, the combinations of W and R which are consistent with (4) are shown by the tangent to the $\tilde{P}_X = P_X^0$ curve at C, and the combinations of W and R which are consistent with (5) are shown by the tangent to the $\tilde{P}_Z = P_Z^0$ curve at B. The point of intersection of these two tangents, S, determines the values of W^S and R^S which jointly satisfy (4) and (5). It is convenient to construct a line through S with a slope equal to $-l$. The argument of section 4 may be modified to show that the intercepts of this line, relative to the intercepts of the tangents to the two isoprice curves, indicate the distribution of labor and capital between X and Z. Specifically, figure 3 has been labeled so that (3) continues to hold. By rotating the line which shows the endowment ratio around the point S, it is easily shown that the Rybczynski effect continues to hold in a distorted economy.

One important use for the shadow factor prices is that suggested by Diamond and Mirrlees (1976) and Findlay and Wellisz (1976) and further developed by Bhagwati, Srinivasan and Wan (1978), Srinivasan and Bhagwati (1978), and Bhagwati and Wan (1979). Suppose that a planning agency is considering the desirability of producing a new commodity and is concerned with how to induce firms to produce it if it is desirable from a social point of view. Given the existing set of distortions, the appropriate social criterion is to produce at least a small amount of a new commodity if the cost of diverting labor and capital (in an optimal fashion) from X and Z is smaller than the value of the new commodity.[8] Graphically, this criterion is satisfied if the isoprice curve for the new commodity lies above the shadow price point, S. From figure 3 it is apparent that a commodity could satisfy this criterion and yet not be profitable at the factor prices associated with any of the three points, A, B, or C. It follows that in a distorted economy it may be socially desirable to produce some new commodities which would not be socially desirable in an undistorted economy. Furthermore, to ensure that a new commodity which is socially desirable is also privately profitable, and vice versa, it is necessary to tax or subsidize inputs used by producers of new products. The appropriate set of taxes and subsidies is that which makes the factor prices paid by producers of new products equal to the shadow factor prices.

A further use for the shadow factor prices is in determining the total damage done by a given set of distortions and in comparing the damage done by different sets of distortions. The measure of damage is the reduction in the value of the economy's final output, at given output prices. The value of output is given by

$$V = W^S L + R^S K. \tag{6}$$

Dividing V by the economy's labor force yields

$$V/L = W^S + R^S/l. \tag{7}$$

Graphically, V/L is measured by the horizontal intercept of the line through S with a slope of $-l$. Thus, for the distortion analyzed in figure 3, V/L is indicated by the distance OE. In comparison, for the nondistorted economy, with shadow factor prices determined by the point A, V/L is indicated by the distance OT. Hence, the loss generated by the distortions shown in figure 3, relative to the nondistorted situation, is indicated by

ET/OT. This loss could be compared with the loss generated by an entirely different set of distortions to determine which set of distortions generates the greatest loss. Finally, it should be noted that the loss measured by the reduction in V/L is the sum of two components. First, as a result of distortions in the factor market, the output transformation curve is generally inside the transformation curve for the undistorted economy; and second, the production point on the new transformation curve does not, in general, correspond to the point at which the value of output is maximized (at given output prices) on the new transformation curve.[9]

9. Negative Shadow Prices and Highly Distorted Economies

When an economy is "highly distorted" by large divergences between required factor returns in different industries, the possibility exists that the shadow price of one of the factors of production (but not both) may be negative. This phenomenon has been explored in recent papers by Srinivasan and Bhagwati (1978) and Bhagwati, Srinivasan and Wan (1978). For present purposes it is interesting to note that this phenomenon of negative shadow prices is related to other peculiarities that arise in the context of highly distorted economies. Specifically, consider the situation, illustrated in figure 4, that arises from either a high tax on the use of capital in Z (the labor intensive industry) or a high subsidy on the use of capital in X (the capital intensive industry).

One peculiar aspect of the situation depicted in figure 4 is that an increase in the *percentage* rate of tax on capital in Z makes the economy *less* distorted. This is because the ratio of the distance QC to the slope of the line $SFCG$ is greater than the ratio of the distance QB to the slope of the line $SDBI$. As we move a small distance along the two isoprice curves (approximated by their tangents) in the direction of A, the ratio of distance between the curves to the height of the $\tilde{P}_X = P_X^0$ curve rises. Therefore, an *increase* in the percentage distortion between the rental rate on capital used in the two industries is associated with a movement *toward* the point A and hence toward a *less* distorted economy. This fact is the source of many counter-intuitive results. Normally, we would not expect that an increase in the percentage tax on capital employed in Z (or subsidy on capital employed in X) would increase the capital-labor ratios in both industries, increase the wage rate, reduce the return received by capital owners and the rental paid by capital users, and generally reduce the level of distortion in the economy; but rather produce the exact opposite of all these results. All of these results make sense once

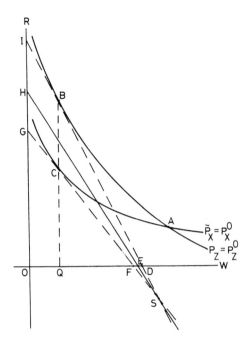

Figure 4

it is recognized that an increase in percentage distortion means a reduction in the absolute distortion and a move toward the point A.

A second peculiarity of the situation shown in figure 4 is that relative factor intensities indicated by physical factor ratios do not correspond to relative factor intensities indicated by relative value shares. This is because the rental rate paid in Z is so much above the rental rate paid in X that it outweighs the fact that X is physically capital intensive, and makes the share of capital in the value of Z output greater than the share of capital in the value of X output. Graphically, this fact may be seen by noting that the share of capital in X is measured by QF/OF, while the share of capital in Z is measured by $QD/OD > QF/OF$. It is apparent, geometrically, that this situation will arise if and only if the tangents to the two isoprice curves intersect below the W-axis.[10]

A third peculiarity associated with figure 4 is that an increase in the economy's endowment of capital *reduces* the value of total output. In other words, even holding output prices constant, "growth" that results from capital accumulation is immiserizing.[11] This result may be proved by appealing to equation (6) or by noting that the distance OE in figure 4 that measures V/L becomes shorter as K is increased. Initially, the finding that an increase in the capital stock reduces the value of output may appear paradoxical. It makes perfect sense once it is recognized that in this highly distorted economy, capital has a negative marginal social value.

A final peculiarity arises in connection with the evaluation of the social benefits of producing new commodities. In a "highly distorted" economy, it is socially beneficial to produce any new commodity with a positive price, provided that it can be produced with a sufficiently high ratio of the factor with a negative shadow price. Since throwing away units of a factor with a negative shadow price improves social welfare, using them to produce something of positive value is exceedingly attractive.

10. Conclusion

The dual of a production function represents technology as a relationship between output price and input prices. For this reason, the diagrammatic technique developed in this paper is particularly useful in illustrating the properties of the two-sector model which are essentially concerned with prices: the factor price equalization theorem, the Stolper-Samuelson theorem, the effects of distortions of factor prices and product prices, and the determination of shadow prices. The behavior of factor ratios is also easily analyzed since these ratios are indicated by the slopes of the respective isoprice curves. It is also possible to use the present diagrammatic technique to ascertain the behavior of quantities of outputs and inputs; however, for this purpose it is probably more convenient to use a diagrammatic technique which is based on the production function representation of technology.

The initial version of this paper was written while visiting the Center for Monetary and Banking Studies at the Graduate Institute of International Studies in Geneva in the fall of 1976. Financial support for that visit was provided by a grant from the Ford Foundation.

References

Amano, A., 1963, Neo-classical models of international trade and economic growth, Ph.D. dissertation, University of Rochester.

Bertrand, T. and F. Flatters, 1971, Tariffs, capital accumulation, and immiserising growth, *Journal of International Economics* 1, 453–460.

Bhagwati, J., 1968, Distortions and immiserising growth: A generalization, *Review of Economic Studies* 35, 481–485.

Bhagwati, J. and T. N. Srinivasan, 1971, The theory of wage differentials: Production response and factor price equalization, *Journal of International Economics* 1, 19–35.

Bhagwati, J. and H. Wan, 1979, The stationarity of shadow prices of factors in project evaluation, with and without distortions, American Economic Review 69, 261–273.

Bhagwati, J., T. N. Srinivasan and H. Wan, 1978, Value subtracted, negative shadow prices of factors in project evaluation, and immiserising growth: Three paradoxes in the presence of trade distortions, *Economic Journal* 88, 121–125.

Burgess, D., 1976, Tariffs and income distribution: Some empirical evidence for the United States, *Journal of Political Economy* 84, 17–46.

Diamond, P. and J. Mirrlees, 1976, Private constant returns and public shadow prices, *Review of Economic Studies* 43, 41–48.

Findlay, R. and S. Wellisz, 1976, Project evaluation, shadow prices, and trade policy, *Journal of Political Economy* 84, 543–552.

Herberg, H. and M. Kemp, 1971, Factor market distortions, the shape of the locus of competitive outputs, and the relation between product prices and equilibrium outputs, in: Bhagwati et al., eds., *Trade, Balance of Payments and Growth* (North-Holland, Amsterdam).

Johnson, H. G., 1966, Factor market distortions and the shape of the transformation curve, *Econometrica* 34, 686–698.

Jones, R. W., 1965, The structure of simple general equilibrium models, *Journal of Political Economy* 73, 557–572.

Jones, R. W., 1971, Distortions in factor markets and the general equilibrium model of production, *Journal of Political Economy* 79, 437–459.

Little, I. and J. Mirrlees, 1969, *Manual for Industrial Project Analysis in Developing Countries*, vol. 2 (OECD, Paris).

Magee, S. P., 1973, Factor market distortions, production, and trade: A survey, *Oxford Economic Papers* 25, 1–43.

McFadden, D. L. et al., 1975, *An Econometric Approach to Production Theory* (North-Holland, Amsterdam).

Neary, P., 1978, Short-run capital specificity and the pure theory of international trade, *Economic Journal* 88, 488–510.

Shepard, R. W., 1953, *Cost and Production Functions* (Princeton University Press, Princeton).

Srinivasan, T. and J. Bhagwati, 1978, Shadow prices for project selection in the presence of distortions: Effective rates of protection and domestic resource costs, *Journal of Political Economy* 86, 97–116.

Woodland, A., 1977, A dual approach to equilibrium in the production sector in international trade theory, *Canadian Journal of Economics* 10, 50–68.

II
Trade-Pattern Theories

5

Factor Proportions and Comparative Advantage in the Long Run

Ronald Findlay

The basic model of comparative advantage in the theory of international trade has been that associated with the names of Heckscher and Ohlin. The form in which this model has been analyzed over the last few decades has been in terms of the two-factor, two-good geometry developed by Lerner and Samuelson. All the six papers in the new *Readings in International Economics* (1967) under the section headed "The Theory of Comparative Advantage" are of this type. Recently the model has been extended in some interesting directions. Oniki and Uzawa (1965) have made one of the goods a capital good and studied the effect of accumulation and labor force growth on international equilibrium over time. Komiya (1967) has introduced a third nontraded good into the system and examined the consequences of this for various standard propositions of trade theory within the usual static context. Kenen (1965) has produced an ingenious model in which capital takes the form of augmenting the productivity of labor and land instead of being a separate "factor" in its own right.

The present paper examines a model which combines the Oniki-Uzawa and Komiya features by making the third nontraded good a capital good. The main result is to show how factor proportions, and hence the pattern of comparative advantage, in the long run depend ultimately upon the values of two parameters, the propensity to save and the growth rate of the labor force.

I

The economy produces three types of goods denoted X, Y, and Z. Let X and Y be consumer goods and Z a capital good. Each of the three goods is produced by the services of labor, which is exogenously given, and

This paper was originally published in *The Journal of Political Economy* 78, no. 1 (January/February 1970): 27–34.

capital, which is the stock of goods of type Z available to the economy. The production function for each good is taken to be of the usual neo-classical type with constant returns to scale. The growth rate of labor is also exogenously fixed, and for simplicity it is assumed that capital goods do not depreciate. Capital goods are assumed not to move in international trade, but the consumer goods X and Y can be bought and sold in the world market at fixed prices.

The fixed prices of X and Y in world trade means that the domestic production costs of amounts of X and Y that have the same value at these prices must be the same, assuming perfect competition and the absence of transport costs and tariffs. If the "strong factor-intensity assumption" that one commodity is always more capital intensive than the other at any factor price-ratio is also made, then it is a well-established result that factor prices will be uniquely determined. The capital-labor ratio in the nontraded capital goods sector will hence be determined, along with those for the two consumer goods sectors. The fixed international terms of trade for X and Y therefore fix the capital and labor input coefficients for all three commodities. Physical units can be chosen in such a way that the prices per unit of each commodity are all equal to unity. Taking the initial endowment of capital and labor as given, we have two equations in three unknowns (X, Y, and Z) by the balance conditions that the amount of each factor used in all three sectors must add up to the amount available, the capital and labor input coefficients per unit of each output in these equations being determined by the fixed terms of trade and the production functions. One more equation is needed to close the system, and this is provided by the condition that the proportion of national income saved and invested is a constant. Since investment is nothing but the output of Z, this condition implies that the ratio of the output of Z to the combined output of all three sectors is equal to a constant, which is the average propensity to save.

We, therefore, have the following system of equations:

$$a_{11}X + a_{12}Y + a_{13}Z = L, \tag{1}$$

$$a_{21}X + a_{22}Y + a_{23}Z = K, \tag{2}$$

$$-sX - sY + (1 - s)Z = O, \tag{3}$$

in which L and K are the initial endowments of labor and capital, the a_{ij} are the technical coefficients determined in the manner explained, and s is the average propensity to save. This system is readily solved for X, Y, and Z, given L and K. For the analysis of growth, however, it is necessary to adjust (1), (2), and (3) by dividing both sides of each equation by K to obtain

$$a_{11}\frac{X}{K} + a_{12}\frac{Y}{K} + a_{13}k = \lambda, \tag{1'}$$

$$a_{21}\frac{X}{K} + a_{22}\frac{Y}{K} + a_{23}k = 1, \tag{2'}$$

$$-s\frac{X}{K} - s\frac{Y}{K} + (1 - s)k = 0, \tag{3'}$$

where $k = Z/K$ and $\lambda = L/K$. Therefore, k is the rate of growth of capital since Z represents additions to the capital stock. The solution of this system can give us k, the rate of growth of capital as a function of λ, the labor-capital ratio.

By Cramer's Rule we have

$$k = \frac{\lambda s(a_{22} - a_{21}) - s(a_{12} - a_{11})}{\Delta}, \tag{4}$$

where

$$\Delta = (1 - s)(a_{11}a_{22} - a_{21}a_{12}) - s(a_{12}a_{23} - a_{22}a_{13})$$
$$+ s(a_{11}a_{23} - a_{21}a_{13}).$$

The problem that now arises is whether k will converge to the constant growth rate of the labor force, n. If $k > n$ then λ will be falling, and convergence requires $dk/d\lambda > 0$. That is, if the growth rate of capital is faster than labor, the system operates to reduce it and vice versa, so that the two rates are equal in the limit. Differentiating (4) with respect to λ we obtain

$$\frac{dk}{d\lambda} = \frac{s(a_{22} - a_{21})}{\Delta}. \tag{5}$$

We now investigate the sign of this derivative. A sufficient condition for this derivative to be positive, and hence for the two rates to converge, is easily obtained. If the capital good Z is more capital intensive than X but less capital intensive than Y, it follows that the determinant Δ will be positive. Figure 1 shows that under these conditions we must have $a_{22} > a_{21}$. Reversing the relative capital intensities of X and Y will make Δ negative and $a_{22} < a_{21}$, so that the sign of (5) is again positive. Hence a sufficient condition for the convergence of the capital growth rate to

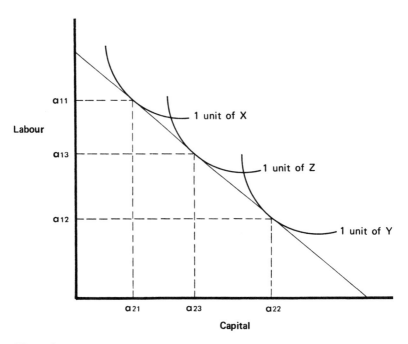

Figure 1

that of the labor force is for the capital intensity in the nontraded capital goods sector Z to be between those of the traded consumer goods sectors X and Y.

If Z is either more or less capital intensive than both X and Y, the sign of (5) is indeterminate. With the problem of convergence to long-run equilibrium factor proportions settled, the next section analyzes the pattern of comparative advantage under given demand conditions.

II

The system can also be solved for X/K and Y/K. Division of one by the other will give us the ratio of the outputs of the two consumer goods,

$$\alpha = \frac{X}{Y} = \frac{[(1 - s)a_{22} + sa_{23}]\lambda - [(1 - s)a_{12} + sa_{13}]}{[(1 - s)a_{11} + sa_{13}] - [(1 - s)a_{21} + sa_{23}]\lambda}, \tag{6}$$

which gives us the output proportions α as a function of the factor proportions λ.

Demand conditions for X and Y have now to be introduced. As shown by Robinson (1956) and Jones (1956–59), the Heckscher-Ohlin theory requires "homothetic" demand patterns for its logical validity, that is, the proportions of the goods purchased at any price ratio must be independent of the level of income. We thus have:

$$\beta = \frac{X}{Y} = f\left(\frac{Px}{Py}\right), \tag{7}$$

where Px/Py is the relative prices or terms of trade and β is the proportion in which the two goods are demanded. Equation (6) can be written as $\alpha = g(\lambda, s, Px/Py)$.

Hence, whether a country exports X or Y, that is to say whether it has a comparative advantage in X or Y, depends on whether

$$\alpha \gtrless \beta. \tag{8}$$

at the given value of the terms of trade. Since α, depends on λ, which varies over time, there is the possibility that the inequality in (8) can reverse itself in the course of time. The comparative advantage of a country in international trade is thus not something fixed but something changing with the evolution of its factor proportions.

The analysis of relative stability can now be combined with the definition of comparative advantage given in (8), to form the concept of comparative advantage *in the long run*. If the factor-intensity condition is met, we have seen that the system tends to balanced growth of capital and labor at the fixed rate n. Since $k = n$ in the limit, we can solve (4) for the value of λ to which the system tends in terms of x, n, and the technical coefficients.

Denoting the value of λ in the limit by λ^*, this gives

$$\lambda^* = \frac{\Delta n + s(a_{12} - a_{11})}{s(a_{22} - a_{21})}. \tag{9}$$

If α^* denotes the value of α corresponding to λ^*, whether the country has a comparative advantage in the long run in X or Y depends on whether

$$\alpha^* \gtrless \beta. \tag{10}$$

Since α^*, unlike α, is a constant, comparative advantage in the long run does not shift over time at given terms of trade.

The dynamic version of comparative advantage developed above can now be related to the familiar static Heckscher-Ohlin theorem. Equation (6) gives us α^* as a function of λ^*. Differentiating, we obtain

$$\frac{\partial \alpha^*}{\partial \lambda^*} = \frac{(1 - s)\Delta}{D^2}, \tag{11}$$

where D is the denominator of the right-hand side of (6). The sign of this derivative clearly depends on the sign of Δ. If X is more labor intensive than Y, Δ will be positive, meaning that the more labor abundant the country, the greater will be the proportion of the labor-intensive good in production at given terms of trade. If demand conditions are homothetic and the same in all countries, this implies that the labor (capital)-abundant country will have a comparative advantage in the labor (capital)-intensive good. The same result would follow if Y is the labor-intensive good and Δ is negative. The familiar Heckscher-Ohlin theorem is thus derived in a more general setting, including the production of a nontraded capital good. The above analysis can be adapted to the usual case simply by putting Z equal to zero.

III

The Heckscher-Ohlin theorem stops at factor proportions as the fundamental determinant of trade. However, we have shown in (9) that the factor proportion λ ultimately depends on the "dynamic determinants" s and n. The effect of these variables on comparative advantage can be analyzed by differentiation of (9) with respect to each of them:

$$\frac{d\lambda^*}{dn} = \frac{\Delta}{s(a_{22} - a_{21})}. \tag{12}$$

The sign of this expression is positive since both numerator and denominator will be positive if X is more labor intensive, or negative if the opposite is the case. From (11) we have seen that α varies directly with λ so it follows that the greater the rate of growth of labor the greater will be the proportion of the labor-intensive commodity in production in the long run and, therefore, the greater the likelihood that the country will have a comparative advantage in the labor-intensive commodity.

Differentiating (9) with respect to s we obtain

$$\frac{d\lambda^*}{ds} = \frac{-(a_{22} - a_{21})(a_{11}a_{22} - a_{21}a_{12})n}{[s(a_{22} - a_{21})]^2}. \tag{13}$$

From the factor-intensity assumptions the two terms in the numerator of (13) are either both positive or both negative, so that in either case the effect of a higher propensity to save is to reduce the labor-capital ratio toward which the system tends in the long run.

The effect of the propensity to save on comparative advantage is given by differentiating (6) totally with respect to s to obtain:

$$\frac{d\alpha^*}{ds} = \frac{\partial\alpha^*}{\partial s}\bigg|_{\lambda^*} + \frac{\partial\alpha^*}{\partial\lambda^*}\frac{d\lambda^*}{ds}. \tag{14}$$

The last two terms have already been obtained in (11) and (13). The first term is given as:

$$\frac{\partial \alpha^*}{\partial s}\bigg|_{\lambda^*} = \text{constant} = \frac{(a_{22} - a_{21})a_{23}\lambda^{*2} + (a_{11} - a_{12})a_{23}\lambda^*}{D^2}$$

$$+ \frac{-(a_{22} - a_{21})a_{13}\lambda^* + (a_{12} - a_{11})a_{13}}{D^2}, \qquad (15)$$

where D is the denominator of the right-hand side of (6). What (15) shows is the direct effect of the variation in s on α^* through the shift in resources toward the capital goods sector and away from the consumer goods sectors. Obviously, if the resources are withdrawn in the same proportion, α^* will not change directly as a result of the variation in s. This will be the case if the labor-capital ratio in the Z sector is exactly equal to that of the whole economy, so that $\lambda^* = a_{13}/a_{23}$. Inserting this value of λ^* into (15), we observe that the numerator becomes zero, confirming our intuition. If the labor-capital ratio in the Z sector is higher than λ^*, an increase in the output of Z due to a higher s will reduce the labor-capital ratio in the combined X and Y sector, and hence shift α^* in favor of the relatively capital-intensive consumer good, and vice versa in the case where the labor-capital ratio in Z is lower than λ^*. This can again be checked against (15) by differentiating the numerator of this expression with respect to λ^* and evaluating this derivative at the point $\lambda^* = a_{13}/a_{23}$ to obtain:

$$\frac{dN}{d\lambda^*} = (a_{22} - a_{21})a_{13} + (a_{11} - a_{12})a_{23}, \qquad (16)$$

where N is the numerator of the right-hand side of (15). Each of the expressions in parenthese will be positive if X is more labor intensive than Y, and negative in the opposite case. Thus, if $\lambda^* < a_{13}/a_{23}$ and X is more labor intensive than Y, the sign of (15) will be negative so an increase in s reduces α^* (the output of the capital-intensive good X), and vice versa when $\lambda^* > a_{13}/a_{23}$. If Y is more labor intensive than X, these results will be reversed. If we call the first term of (14) the "direct effect" and the second term the "indirect effect," we observe that both terms either move in the same direction to shift α^* in favor of the capital-intensive good or the direct effect works in the opposite direction, so the result depends on which of the two effects is stronger. If the direct effect were to predominate, a higher s and therefore a lower λ^* or labor-capital ratio, would be associated with a higher ratio of the output of the labor-intensive commodity to that of the capital-intensive one; in other words the Leontief Paradox. It would therefore be of some interest to see whether this case can arise since it would provide another possible explanation of the famous paradox.

If we substitute the right-hand side of (9) for λ^* in (15) and combine the result with the right-hand sides of (11) and (13), we obtain

$$\frac{d\alpha^*}{ds} = \frac{\Delta^2(a_{22} - a_{21})(a_{23}n - 1)n}{[s(a_{22} - a_{21})]^2 D^2}. \tag{17}$$

The term $(a_{23}n - 1)$ must be negative, since $1/a_{23} = Z/K_Z > n = Z/(K_x + K_y + K_z)$, where the K refer to the total capital input in each of the sectors. The last equality holds because the capital growth rate converges to n in the limit. The sign of $(a_{22} - a_{21})$ is positive or negative depending upon whether X or Y is the more labor intensive. Hence the result in either case is that a higher s must be associated with a higher relative output of the capital-intensive good. The Leontief Paradox thus cannot arise as the result of the introduction of a nontraded capital goods sector, but only in the long run. A higher s can cause a lower labor-capital ratio to be associated with a higher relative output of the labor-intensive good as a result of the direct effect, but if sufficient time is allowed the higher s will reduce the labor capital ratio further until the opposite is the case, if n is the same in both cases.

References

Caves, R., and H. G. Johnson, eds. *Readings in International Economics.* Irwin, 1967.

Jones, R. "Factor Endowment and the Heckscher-Ohlin Theorem." *Rev. Econ. Studies* 24 (1956–57): 1–10.

Kenen, P. B. "Nature, Capital, and Trade," *J.P.E.* 73, no. 5 (October 1965): 437–60.

Komiya, R. "Non-Traded Goods and the Pure Theory of International Trade." *Internat. Econ. Rev.* 8 (June 1967): 132–52.

Oniki, H., and H. Uzawa. "Patterns of Trade and Investment in a Dynamic Model of International Trade." *Rev. Econ. Studies* 32 (1), no. 89 (January 1965): 15–38.

Robinson, R. "Factor Proportions and Comparative Advantage Part I." *Q.J.E.* 70, no. 2 (May 1956): 169–92.

Editor's Note

Attention of the reader should be drawn to a valuable comment by Professor Alan V. Deardorff of the University of Michigan, appearing in the *Journal of Political Economy*, vol. 82, no. 4 (July/August 1974): 829–833. He shows that the sign of the determinant Δ depends only on the relative factor intensities of X and Y. My assumption that the factor-intensity of Z is in between those of X and Y is therefore unnecessarily restrictive. He also examines the consequences of relaxing my implicit assumption that both X and Y have positive levels of production.

6

Weak Links in the Chain of Comparative Advantage

Alan V. Deardorff

1. Introduction

My purpose in this paper is to investigate the proposition that trade in many commodities can be understood by first ranking the goods in order of factor intensities, then showing that all of a country's exports must lie higher on this list than all of its imports. A similar idea of a chain of comparative advantage was shown by Haberler (1936, p. 137) to be valid in a many-commodity extension of the classical theory of trade, the rankings there being of course in terms of comparative costs. The proposition was also stated for a two-factor, two-country version of the Heckscher-Ohlin model by Jones (1956–57), but was shown by Bhagwati (1972) to be incorrect if factor prices are equalized. Jones and Bhagwati apparently concurred, however, that the proposition would be valid whenever factor prices are not equalized, though neither provided a proof. Since a prime cause of unequal factor prices is the existence of tariffs, and since Travis (1964, 1972) has claimed that protection can account for the Leontief paradox, presumably by altering the pattern of trade, it seems that a concensus has not yet been reached as to just how general the chain-of-comparative-advantage idea is.[1] In what follows, I explore the matter further and show that these differences of opinion can be reconciled.

Specifically, I show first that Jones and Bhagwati were right, so long as we remain in the model that they were considering, which excludes the possibility of produced goods being used as intermediate factors of production. That is, I will demonstrate the chain proposition in such a model whenever factor prices are unequal, whether that inequality is the result of complete specialization with no impediments to trade (section 2) or of tariffs and transport costs (section 3). Then I will introduce intermediate

This paper was originally published in *Journal of International Economics* 9, no. 2 (May 1979): 197–209.

goods. This modification, it turns out, does not invalidate the chain proposition so long as there are unequal factor prices and free trade (section 4). But when impediments to trade are added as well, the chain proposition collapses. For I show, in section 5, that an increase in a tariff can cause a good that was previously exported to become imported and, at the same time, a good that was previously imported to become exported. It follows that no ranking of the goods is possible, on the basis of factor intensities, autarky prices, or anything else, that will permit separation of exports and imports via a single break in the chain.

It is ironic that Jones, Bhagwati, and others have found comfort in the presence of transport costs and other impediments to trade, which prevent factor-price equalization and thus remove the indeterminacy of production and trade. For the example in section 5 shows that, when there are intermediate goods, these same impediments to trade can invalidate the chain proposition when it would otherwise hold.

In the two-factor world considered here, the chain proposition is related to, but not identical to, the Heckscher-Ohlin theorem. The former merely says that some ranking of goods exists which suffices to determine trade. The latter says that the appropriate ranking is by factor intensities and, furthermore, that relative factor endowments determine which end of the chain contains a country's exports. However, in the cases considered here, the two propositions stand or fall together, so long as the price definition of factor abundance is used in stating the Heckscher-Ohlin theorem. For I will show in sections 2–4 that a country in which capital is relatively cheap, with trade, must export more capital intensive goods than it imports. And it can be shown, if there are only two countries, that relative factor prices must bear the same relationship with trade as without, so long as trade impediments are non-negative.[2] Thus, these sections also demonstrate the Heckscher-Ohlin theorem: that a country in which capital is relatively cheap in autarky must export relatively capital intensive goods. Also, of course, the counter example of section 5 shows that both propositions fail when there are both trade impediments and intermediate goods.

While most of the argument will be confined to a two-country world, it is of some interest also to show how the chain idea may extend to a world of many countries. This is not difficult, with the tools available, and, in section 6, I show that the chain of comparative advantage can be broken into several segments, one for each country. With the countries arranged along the chain in the same order as their relative factor endowments, each country will then export only goods within its segment of the chain and will import all others. That is true, however, only if trade is free and factor prices are unequal. Without the need, in this case, for intermediate goods, I will also show that tariffs can cause a rather dramatic rearrangement of the pattern of trade.

Considering the obvious importance, in the real world, of both trade impediments and intermediate goods, the results of this paper may seem to cast doubt on both the Heckscher-Ohlin theory and on the concept of comparative advantage itself. I therefore conclude in section 7 with a discussion of these more fundamental problems.

2. Free Trade

Consider two countries, A and B, producing and trading n goods with no impediments to trade between them, so that the prices of the goods, $p_1, \ldots, p_n$, are the same in both countries. Production of each good requires the use of only two factors of production, capital (K) and labor (L), which are nontraded and available in each country in fixed supply. Production functions are identical between countries, and have the usual properties of concavity and homogeneity. Assume further that the goods can be ranked unambiguously in terms of capital intensity, X_1 being the most capital intensive and X_n, the least. Thus, there are no factor-intensity reversals between any pair of goods, and isoquants of different goods can intersect only once. Assume finally that perfect competition prevails in both countries, so that price equals average cost for any good that is produced and is less than or equal to average cost for any good that is not produced.

Suppose now that all that is known about a free trade equilibrium is that particular and unequal factor prices prevail in the two countries. What does this imply about the pattern of trade?

Begin by drawing the unit isocost lines for the two countries. These are shown in figure 1 as the lines AA' for country A and BB' for country B, and represent the combinations of capital and labor which would cost, say, one dollar (or other international numeraire) in each of the two countries. They are shown as intersecting at a point M, with country A depicted as having a higher ratio of wage to rental (ω) than country B.[3]

From these isocost lines one can conclude what the free trade prices of each good must be. That is, the price of each good must be such as to place its unit-value isoquant exactly tangent to the outermost of the two unit-isocost lines, as shown by the (solid) isoquants drawn in figure 1. For if a unit-value isoquant were to lie wholly outside both AA' and BB', the good would not be produced in either country, while if it lay anywhere inside either one of the lines, its production would yield a positive profit

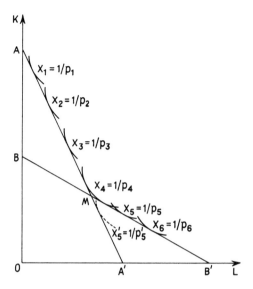

Figure 1

in the corresponding country. Furthermore, while it is possible for an isoquant to be tangent to both isocost lines (as good 4 in figure 1), this need not happen for any good and, without factor intensity reversals, cannot happen for more than one.

It is now immediately evident from figure 1 that the pattern of trade must agree with the ranking of the goods by factor intensity. The most capital intensive goods (1, 2, and 3 in figure 1) can only be produced in the high wage country, A, and must therefore be exported by A, while the most labor intensive (5 and 6) must be produced and exported by B. Good 4, in this case, may be produced in both countries and may be exported by either. It therefore constitutes the division of the chain of comparative advantage.

We have already noted that the high relative wage in A implies that it is capital abundant by the price definition.[4] It is also true in this case that A must be capital abundant by the physical definition as well. For we can see in fig. 1 that all production in A requires a higher ratio of capital to labor than all production in B. Thus, our result implies that every export of the capital abundant country, by either definition, must be more capital intensive than every one of its imports.[5]

Before extending this analysis to include tariffs, transport costs, and intermediate goods, it should be pointed out that the technique used here does not derive the trade equilibrium. Rather, it assumes that an equilibrium exists and merely examines a particular property of that equilibrium.

Much more information would be needed to determine, for example, what the equilibrium factor prices should be and where, in the chain of comparative advantage, the division between the two countries should be located.

3. Impeded Trade

If tariffs or transport costs permit different prices in the two countries, then the argument as given above is no longer valid, for there will be different unit-value isoquants in the two countries. But the argument can easily be salvaged if direct *subsidies* to trade are not permitted. For then a good will be exported only if its price is at least as high abroad as at home, and imported only if its price is at least as low abroad as at home, to compensate exporters and importers for the additional cost of tariffs and transport.[6]

To see how this works, consider again the two countries whose unit isocost lines, with trade, are those shown in figure 1. Suppose that some good, X_i, is exported by country A. To be exported it must be produced, and thus the unit-value isoquant of X_i in A must be tangent to AA'. Suppose it were tangent below the intersection M, like the dotted isoquant X_5' in figure 1. For the good to be exported from A, it must also fetch at least as high a price in B (to cover any transport cost or tariff) and this would place B's unit-value isoquant for the same good still closer to the origin than X_5' and certainly inside the line BB'. The good would then yield a positive profit in B, and this is impossible. Thus, the unit-value isoquants of all of A's exports must be tangent to AA' above its intersection with BB' exactly as was the case with free trade. Applying a similar argument to exports from B, it follows as before that all of A's exports must be more capital intensive than all of A's imports.

This then validates the Bhagwati-Jones conjecture that a capital abundant country (using the price definition of abundance) will export only goods which are more capital intensive than any of its imports, if there are impediments to trade and unequal factor prices.[7,8]

4. Intermediate Goods and Free Trade

Now suppose that any or all of goods $1, \ldots, n$ can be used as intermediate inputs in production. The argument of section 2 with free trade remains intact if unit-value isoquants are replaced by unit-value-*added* isoquants.

For any good X_i, let the production function be given by

$$X_i = F^i(K_i, L_i, X_{1i}, \ldots, X_{ni}),$$

where X_{ji} are the inputs of goods j into production of good i. Let

$$V_i(K_i, L_i, p_1, \ldots, p_n) = \max_{X_i, X_{ji}} \left[p_i X_i - \sum_{j=1}^{n} p_j X_{ji} \right]$$

$$\text{s.t. } X_i = F^i(K_i, L_i, X_{1i}, \ldots, X_{ni}).$$

For given values of all prices, the functions $V_i(K_i, L_i, \cdot)$ describe, in nominal terms, the maximum net revenue that can be earned and allocated to payment of the primary factors, capital and labor. They can therefore be used to determine the pattern of specialization, in exactly the same way that we earlier used production functions multiplied by prices.[9] That is, unit-value-added isoquants can be defined by setting $V_i = 1$, and production will require tangency between these and the unit-isocost lines.[10]

With free trade, all prices are the same in the two countries, which therefore share identical unit-value-added isoquants. The argument of section 2 can be repeated and the same result obtained. Thus, the chain of comparative advantage can still be used when there are intermediate goods, so long as trade is free and the prices of primary factors are not equalized. The factor intensities used in constructing the chain represent only direct capital and labor requirements, and do not include factors that are used indirectly by being embodied in intermediate inputs. For, as long as intermediate inputs are traded freely, they need not be produced within the country in which they are used.

5. Intermediate Goods and Impeded Trade

If trade is not free, however, there is a problem. It arises because the position of a unit-value-added isoquant depends on all prices and not just on the price of the corresponding final good. Thus, when a tariff on, say, good 5 in figure 1 raises its price in A above that in B, it does, as before, pull A's isoquant toward the origin to a position like X'_5. But it also pushes A's isoquants of other goods that use good 5 as an input out further from the origin than they are in country B. And this makes it impossible to infer individual relative prices from the positions of individual isoquants in the two countries as was done before. The same problem arises if prices differ due to·transport costs, though for ease of exposition we will limit attention here to a tariff.

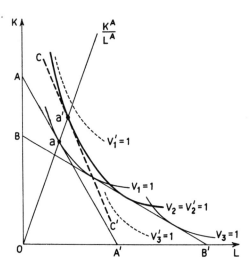

Figure 2

To see what can happen consider the following special case which will suffice to provide a counterexample to the chain proposition. Suppose there are only three goods, with goods 1 and 2 acting solely as final goods and with good 3 acting only as an intermediate input to production of good 1. Suppose further that country B is so large that we can take its prices as independent of trade with country A and that A is so capital abundant that it produces, in *free* trade, only the most capital intensive good 1. The free trade situation is depicted as the solid unit-value-added isoquants and isocost lines in figure 2. The line AA' represents free trade factor prices in country A, which employs its entire endowment of capital and labor, K^A and L^A, in the production of good 1 at point a. Country B, with factor prices given by BB', produces all three goods using the unit-value-added isoquants, $V_1 = 1$, $V_2 = 1$, and $V_3 = 1$. Country A exports good 1 and imports goods 2 and 3.

Now suppose that country A levies a tariff on imports of good 3, raising its domestic price. This will pull A's unit-value-added isoquant for good 3 in toward the origin, to a position like $V_3' = 1$. The isoquant for good 2 will not be affected (since good 2 does not use good 3 as an input), but the unit-value-added isoquant of good 1 will be pushed out away from the origin, as additional production is required to cover the increased cost of the input of good 3 and leave a unit left over for value added.[11] If the tariff is large enough and if good 3 is a sufficiently important input into production of good 1, the new unit-value-added isoquant will be $V_1' = 1$ in figure 2.[12]

It can now be seen from the figure that country A will specialize completely in production of good 2, at point a', with factor prices given by the line CC', since this is the only pattern of production and factor prices that can both yield zero profits and employ the factors in the ratio K^A/L^A. If both countries consume something of both goods 1 and 2, it follows that country A, with the tariff, will export good 2 and import good 1. The pattern of trade in these two goods has therefore been completely reversed by the tariff on good 3.[13]

The intuition behind this result is straightforward and is reflected in the diagram. When a tariff raises the price of the intermediate good, it also makes the final good more costly to produce, and since the intermediate good is itself very labor intensive, country A cannot reduce that cost by producing it itself. Instead, all production switches to good 2 which does not require the labor intensive, and now expensive, input of good 3.

Another way of seeing what is going on in this example is to look at effective rates of protection. With a tariff on the intermediate good and none on either final good, the effective rate of protection of industry 1 is negative. Thus, while the explicit effects of tariffs are only to tax trade, the tariff on the intermediate good has the implicit effect of subsidizing imports of, in this case, the capital intensive good.

The counterexample of this section shows that a ranking by capital intensities cannot suffice to determine trade.[14] But more importantly, it shows that a ranking by *any other criterion* must fail as well. In the example, any ranking that places all of A's exports above all of A's imports with free trade will fail to do so when a tariff is applied. For good 1 has changed from an export to an import and good 2 has done just the reverse.

6. Many Countries

Analysis of the free trade cases, both with and without intermediate goods, extends readily to the case of many countries, though naturally one cannot expect a single division of the chain of comparative advantage to delineate correctly the trade of all countries. Since the analysis is similar to what has gone before, it will be left to the reader to imagine or draw the appropriate diagrams. Simply insert, as in figure 1, the unit isocost lines for all countries. World prices—common to all countries—must then give rise to unit-value (-added) isoquants that are tangent to the outer envelope of all of these isocost lines. Each country will then produce and export only those goods with isoquants tangent to its own isocost line, the intersections of which with adjacent cost lines therefore provide upper and lower limits on the factor intensities of its exports.

Thus, the chain of goods ranked by capital intensity is broken into segments, one for each country, and the segments are ordered identically with the relative capital abundance of the countries. As in the two-country case, adjacent segments may contain one good in common, if the isoquant for such a borderline good happens to touch two countries' isocost lines in the manner of good 4 in figure 1. Otherwise the division between segments of the chain occurs between goods. Each country must export all goods which appear only in its segment of the chain and must import all goods which do not appear in its segment. Borderline goods may be exported by either or both of the countries in whose segments they appear. It follows that each of a country's exports must be at least as capital intensive as each of the exports of all less capital abundant countries and at least as labor intensive as each of the exports of all less labor abundant countries.

This conclusion, however, is extremely sensitive to the assumption of free trade. Even without intermediate goods, impediments to trade can drastically alter the pattern of trade.

To see this, return to the two-country configuration of figure 1 and add a tiny third country, C, with a factor endowment ratio lying between the ratios employed by A and B in industry 4. With free trade, such a country will specialize completely in production of good 4, exporting it in exchange for imports of all other goods. Now suppose, however, that it levies a large tariff on imports of the most capital intensive good, 1. The tariff will raise the price of good 1 in C, pulling its unit value isoquant in towards—and past—C's unit isocost line. Country C will begin production of good 1 and the relative wage in C will fall. However, good 1 is so capital intensive that much of it cannot be produced with the factors available in C and, if demand is also fairly inelastic, imports of good 1 will continue. Thus, there is nothing to prevent a further increase in the tariff from raising its price still more, to bring its unit-value isoquant inside BB'. When that happens, a new isocost line must appear in C, tangent only to isoquants of goods 1 and 6. Production of good 4 (C's original export good) ceases entirely and production of good 6 begins instead. And good 6 must also be exported, since good 1 cannot be, and imports of goods 2, 3, 4, and 5 must continue. Thus, country C, because of a tariff, has changed from being an exporter of a good of intermediate factor intensity to become an exporter of the most labor intensive good that there is.

It should perhaps be noted that this extreme response of the trade pattern to a tariff is only possible for a country whose factor abundance is intermediate between those of other countries. This explains why this result was not possible in the two-country case.

7. Conclusion

It would indeed be useful if we could construct some ranking of commodities, by some criterion, which would enable us to predict the pattern of trade, even if only in the sense of saying that each of a country's exports must lie higher on this list than each of its imports. I have shown that such a ranking is possible in certain cases. But it is impossible both in Bhagwati's "not unimportant" case of factor price equalization and in the obviously important case of positive trade impediments and intermediate goods. This does not mean, however, that trade theorists should abandon the Heckscher-Ohlin theorem or the Law of Comparative Advantage. What it does mean is that we should search for alternative statements of these propositions that will retain their validity and still tell us something useful about the pattern of trade in the real world.

One such formulation has been developed, as a statement about the "factor content" of trade. Vanek (1968) showed that, under certain assumptions, the factor content of a country's trade can be inferred from a chain of factor endowment rankings, very much like the chain of comparative advantage in trade of goods discussed here.[15] The assumptions used to prove this result, however, include factor price equalization. It is therefore not known, yet, whether the factor content version of the Heckscher-Ohlin theorem can be extended to the troublesome case considered here of trade impediments and intermediate goods.[16] This is an important issue, since it was implicitly the factor content of trade that was the focus of Leontief's (1954) famous calculations.

The result in section 5, in which an export good and an import good exchange roles, is as critical for the theory of comparative advantages as it is for the Heckscher-Ohlin theory. For it implies that no ranking of goods can suffice to determine trade, not even one based on relative autarky prices. Yet this does not mean that comparative advantage plays no role in determining the pattern of trade. Rather, the role that it does play is not as strong as the chain proposition would suggest. I have shown elsewhere that relative autarky prices must be negatively correlated with net exports [Deardorff (1980)]. The result of section 5 is consistent with such a correlation, so long as the relative autarky price of good 1 is higher than that of good 2.

Finally, I would like to point out a use that has been made of the Bhagwati-Jones proposition of section 3, a use which turns out to be inappropriate in view of the result of section 5. Harkness and Kyle (1975) motivated their use of logit analysis in an empirical test of the Heckscher-Ohlin theorem on the grounds that the theorem predicts only the direction, not the extent, of trade. They acknowledged Bhagwati's (1972) observation that even the prediction of direction fails if factor prices are equalized, but argued that transportation costs are such a fact of life that Bhagwati's counterexample cannot arise in the real world. Yet intermediate goods are just as much a fact of life as transportation costs. The counterexample which the two together permit can therefore not be dismissed so easily.

I would like to thank Jagdish Bhagwati, Ronald Jones, Richard Porter, Robert Stern and members of the Research Seminar in International Economics, University of Michigan, for their helpful comments.

References

Baldwin, Robert E., 1971, Determinants of the commodity structure of U.S. trade, *American Economic Review* 61, 126–146.

Batra, Raveendra N. and Francisco R. Casas, 1973, Intermediate products and the pure theory of international trade: A neo-Heckscher-Ohlin framework, *American Economic Review* 63, 297–311.

Bhagwati, Jagdish H., 1972, The Heckscher-Ohlin theorem in the multi-commodity case, *Journal of Political Economy* 80, 1052–1055.

Bhagwati, Jagdish H. and T. N. Srinivasan, 1973, The general equilibrium theory of effective protection and resource allocation, *Journal of International Economics* 3, 259–281.

Bruno, M., 1973, Protection and tariff change under general equilibrium, *Journal of International Economics* 3, 205–226.

Deardorff, Alan V., 1980, The general validity of the law of comparative advantage, *Journal of Political Economy*, forthcoming.

Diewert, W. E., 1973, Functional forms for profit and transformation functions, *Journal of Economic Theory* 6, 284–316.

Haberler, Gottfried von, 1936, *The Theory of International Trade with its Applications to Commercial Policy* (William Hodge & Co., London).

Harkness, Jon and John F. Kyle, 1975, Factors influencing United States comparative advantage, *Journal of International Economics* 5, 153–165.

Horiba, Y., 1974, General equilibrium and the Heckscher-Ohlin theory of trade: The multicountry case, *International Economic Review* 15, 440–449.

Jones, Ronald W., 1956–57, Factor proportions and the Heckscher-Ohlin theorem, *Review of Economic Studies* 24, 1–10.

Leontief, Wassily, 1954, Domestic production and foreign trade: The American capital position re-examined, *Economia Internazionale* 7, 3–32.

Melvin, James, 1968, Production and trade with two factors and three goods, *American Economic Review* 58, 1249–1268.

Samuelson, Paul A., 1954, The transfer problem and transport costs: Analysis of the effects of trade impediments, *Economic Journal*, 264–289.

Travis, William P., 1964, *The Theory of Trade and Protection* (Harvard University Press, Cambridge, Mass.).

Travis, William P., 1972, Production, trade, and protection when there are many commodities and two factors, *American Economic Review* 62, 87–106.

Vanek, Jaroslav, 1968, The factor proportions theory: The n-factor case, *Kyklos* 4, 749–756.

7

Increasing Returns, Monopolistic Competition, and International Trade

Paul R. Krugman

1. Introduction

It has been widely recognized that economies of scale provide an alternative to differences in technology or factor endowments as an explanation of international specialization and trade. The role of "economies of large scale production" is a major subtheme in the work of Ohlin (1933); while some authors, especially Balassa (1967) and Kravis (1971), have argued that scale economies play a crucial role in explaining the postwar growth in trade among the industrial countries. Nonetheless, increasing returns as a cause of trade has received relatively little attention from formal trade theory. The main reason for this neglect seems to be that it has appeared difficult to deal with the implications of increasing returns for market structure.

This paper develops a simple formal model in which trade is caused by economies of scale instead of differences in factor endowments or technology. The approach differs from that of most other formal treatments of trade under increasing returns, which assume that scale economies are external to firms, so that markets remain perfectly competitive.[1] Instead, scale economies are here assumed to be internal to firms, with the market structure that emerges being one of Chamberlinian monopolistic competition.[2] The formal treatment of monopolistic competition is borrowed with slight modifications from recent work by Dixit and Stiglitz (1977). A Chamberlinian formulation of the problem turns out to have several advantages. First, it yields a very simple model; the analysis of increasing returns and trade is hardly more complicated than the two-good Ricardian model. Second, the model is free from the multiple equilibria which are the rule when scale economies are external to firms,

This paper was originally published in *Journal of International Economics* 9, no. 4 (November 1979): 469–479.

and which can detract from the main point. Finally, the model's picture of trade in a large number of differentiated products fits in well with the empirical literature on "intra-industry" trade [e.g. Grubel and Lloyd (1975)].

The paper is organized as follows. Section 2 develops the basic modified Dixit-Stiglitz model of monopolistic competition for a closed economy. Section 3 then examines the effects of opening trade as well as the essentially equivalent effects of population growth and factor mobility. Finally, section 4 summarizes the results and suggests some conclusions.

2. Monopolistic Competition in a Closed Economy

This section develops the basic model of monopolistic competition with which I will work in the next sections. The model is a simplified version of the model developed by Dixit and Stiglitz. Instead of trying to develop a general model, this paper will assume particular forms for utility and cost functions. The functional forms chosen give the model a simplified structure which makes the analysis easier.

Consider, then, an economy with only one scarce factor of production, labor. The economy is assumed able to produce any of a large number of goods, with the goods indexed by i. We order the goods so that those actually produced range from 1 to n, where n is also assumed to be a large number, although small relative to the number of potential products.

All residents are assumed to share the same utility function, into which all goods enter symmetrically,

$$U = \sum_{i=1}^{n} v(c_i), \qquad v' > 0, \qquad v'' < 0, \tag{1}$$

where c_i is the consumption of the ith good.

It will be useful to define a variable, ε, where

$$\varepsilon_i = -\frac{v'}{v'' c_i}, \tag{2}$$

and where we assume $\partial \varepsilon_i / \partial c_i < 0$. The variable ε_i will turn out to be the elasticity of demand facing an individual producer; the reasons for assuming that is is decreasing in c_i will become apparent later.

All goods are also assumed to be produced with the same cost function. The labor used in producing each good is a linear function of output,

$$l_i = \alpha + \beta x_i, \qquad \alpha, \beta > 0, \tag{3}$$

where l_i is labor used in producing good i, x_i is the output of good i, and α is a fixed cost. In other words, there are decreasing average costs and constant marginal costs.

Production of a good must equal the sum of individual consumptions of the good. If we identify individuals with workers, production must equal the consumption of a representative individual times the labor force:

$$x_i = Lc_i. \tag{4}$$

Finally, we assume full employment, so that the total labor force L must be exhausted by employment in production of individual goods:

$$L = \sum_{i=1}^{n} l_i = \sum_{i=1}^{n} [\alpha + \beta x_i]. \tag{5}$$

Now there are three variables we want to determine: the price of each good relative to wages, p_i/w; the output of each good, x_i; and the number of goods produced, n. The symmetry of the problem will ensure that all goods actually produced will be produced in the same quantity and at the same price, so that we can use the shorthand notation

$$\left. \begin{array}{l} p = p_i \\ x = x_i \end{array} \right\}, \quad \text{for all } i. \tag{6}$$

We can proceed in three stages. First, we analyze the demand curve facing an individual firm; then we derive the pricing policy of firms and relate profitability to output; finally, we use an analysis of profitability and entry to determine the number of firms.

To analyze the demand curve facing the firm producing some particular product, consider the behavior of a representative individual. He will maximize his utility (1) subject to a budget constraint. The first-order conditions from that maximization problem have the form

$$v'(c_i) = \lambda p_i, \quad i = 1, \ldots, n, \tag{7}$$

where λ is the shadow price on the budget constraint, which can be interpreted as the marginal utility of income.

We can substitute the relationship between individual consumption and output into (7) to turn it into an expression for the demand facing an individual firm,

$$p_i = \lambda^{-1} v'(x_i/L). \tag{8}$$

If the number of goods produced is large, each firm's pricing policy will have a negligible effect on the marginal utility of income, so that it can take λ as fixed. In that case the elasticity of demand facing the ith firm will, as already noted, be $\varepsilon_i = -v'/v''c_i$.

Now let us consider profit-maximizing pricing behavior. Each individual firm, being small relative to the economy, can ignore the effects of its decisions on the decisions of other firms. Thus, the ith firm will choose its price to maximize its profits,

$$\Pi_i = p_i x_i - (\alpha + \beta x_i)w. \tag{9}$$

The profit-maximizing price will depend on marginal cost and on the elasticity of demand:

$$p_i = \frac{\varepsilon}{\varepsilon - 1}\beta w \tag{10}$$

or $p/w = \beta\varepsilon/(\varepsilon - 1)$.

Now this does not determine the price, since the elasticity of demand depends on output; thus, to find the profit-maximizing price we would have to derive profit-maximizing output as well. It will be easier, however, to determine output and prices by combining (10) with the condition that profits be zero in equilibrium.

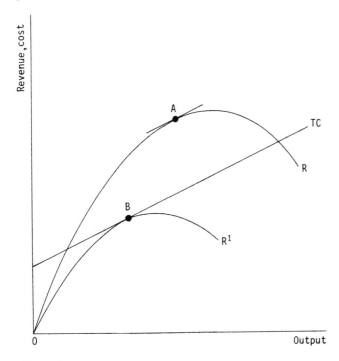

Figure 1

Profits will be driven to zero by entry of new firms. The process is illustrated in figure 1. The horizontal axis measures output of a representative firm; the vertical axis revenue and cost expressed in wage units. Total cost is shown by TC, while OR and OR' represent revenue functions. Suppose that given the initial number of firms, the revenue function facing each firm is given by OR. The firm will then choose its output so as to set marginal revenue equal to marginal cost, at A. At that point, since price (average revenue) exceeds average cost, firms will make profits. But this will lead entrepreneurs to start new firms. As they do so, the marginal utility of income will rise, and the revenue function will shrink in. Eventually equilibrium will be reached at a point such as B, where it is true both that marginal revenue equals marginal cost and that average revenue equals average cost. This is, of course, Chamberlin's famous tangency solution [Chamberlin (1962)].

To characterize this equilibrium more carefully, we need to show how the price and output of a representative firm can be derived from cost and utility functions. In figure 2 the horizontal axis shows *per-capita* con-

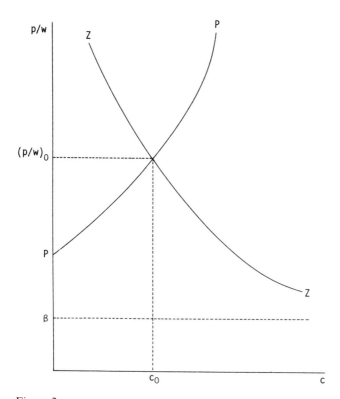

Figure 2

sumption of a representative good, while the vertical axis shows the price of a representative good in wage units. We have one relationship between c and p/w in the pricing condition (10), which is shown as the curve PP. Price lies everywhere above marginal cost, and increases with c because, by assumption, the elasticity of demand falls with c.

A second relationship between p/w and c can be derived from the condition of zero profits in equilibrium. From (9), we have

$$O = px - (\alpha + \beta x)w, \tag{11}$$

which can be rewritten

$$p/w = \beta + \alpha/x = \beta + \alpha/Lc. \tag{12}$$

This is a rectangular hyperbola above the line $p/w = \beta$, and is shown in figure 2 as ZZ.

The intersection of the PP and ZZ schedules determines individual consumption of each good and the price of each good. From the consumption of each good we have output per firm, since $x = Lc$. And the assumption of full employment lets us determine the number of goods produced:

$$n = \frac{L}{\alpha + \beta x}. \tag{13}$$

We now have a complete description of equilibrium in the economy. It is indeterminate *which n* goods are produced, but it is also unimportant, since the goods enter into utility and cost symmetrically. We can now use the model to analyze the related questions of the effects of growth, trade, and factor mobility.

3. Growth, Trade, and Factor Mobility

The model developed in the last section was a one-factor model, but one in which there were economies of scale in the use of that factor, so that in a real sense the division of labor was limited by the extent of the market. In this section we consider three ways in which the extent of the market might increase: growth in the labor force, trade, and migration.

3.1. Effects of Labor Force Growth

Suppose that an economy of the kind analyzed in the last section were to experience an increase in its labor force. What effect would this have? We can analyze some of the effects by examining figure 3. The PP and ZZ schedules have the same definitions as in figure 2; before the increase

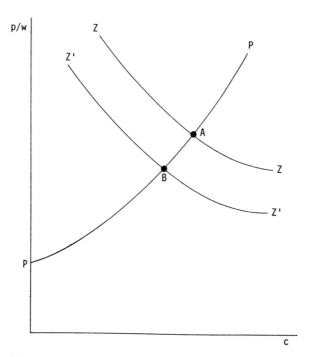

Figure 3

in the labor force equilibrium is at A. By referring back to equations (10) and (11) we can see that an increase in L has no effect on PP, but that it causes ZZ to shift left. The new equilibrium is at B: c falls, and so does p/w. We can show, however, that both the output of each good and the number of goods produced rise. By rearranging (12) we have

$$x = \alpha/(p/w - \beta), \tag{14}$$

which shows that output must rise, while since $n = L/(\alpha + \beta Lc)$, a rise in L and a fall in c imply a rise in n.

Notice that these results depend on the fact that the PP curve slopes upward, which in turn depends on the assumption that the elasticity of demand falls with c. This assumption, which might alternatively be stated as an assumption that the elasticity of demand rises when the price of a good is increased, seems plausible. In any case, it seems to be necessary if this model is to yield reasonable results, and I make the assumption without apology.

We can also consider the welfare implications of growth. Comparisons of overall welfare would be illegitimate, but we can look at the welfare of representative individuals. This rises for two reasons: there is a rise in the "real wage" w/p, and there is also a gain from increased choice, as the number of available products increases.

I have considered the case of growth at some length, even though our principal concern is with trade, because the results of the analysis of growth will be useful next, when we turn to the analysis of trade.

3.2. Effects of Trade

Suppose there exist two economies of the kind analyzed in section 2, and that they are initially unable to trade. To make the point most strongly, assume that the countries have identical tastes and technologies. (Since this is a one-factor model, we have already ruled out differences in factor endowments.) In a conventional model, there would be no reason for trade to occur between these economies, and no potential gains from trade. In this model, however, there will be both trade and gains from trade.

To see this, suppose that trade is opened between these two economies at zero transportation cost. Symmetry will ensure that wage rates in the two countries will be equal, and that the price of any good produced in either country will be the same. The effect will be the same as if *each* country had experienced an increase in its labor force. As in the case of growth in a closed economy, there will be an increase both in the scale of production and in the range of goods available for consumption. Welfare in both countries will increase, both because of higher w/p and because of increased choice.

The direction of trade—which country exports which goods—is indeterminate; all that we can say is that each good will be produced only in one country, because there is (in this model) no reason for firms to compete for markets. The *volume* of trade, however, is determinate. Each individual will be maximizing his utility function, which may be written

$$U = \sum_{i=1}^{n} v(c_i) + \sum_{i=n+1}^{n+n^*} v(c_i),\tag{15}$$

where goods $1, \ldots, n$ are produced in the home country and $n + 1,$ $\ldots, n + n^*$ in the foreign country. The number of goods produced in each country will be proportional to the labor forces:

$$n = \frac{L}{\alpha + \beta x},$$

$$n^* = \frac{L^*}{\alpha + \beta x}.\tag{16}$$

Since all goods will have the same price, expenditures on each country's goods will be proportional to the country's labor force. The share of imports in home country expenditures, for instance, will be $L^*/(L + L^*)$; the values of imports of each country will be national income times the import share, i.e.

$$M = wL \cdot L^*/(L + L^*)$$

$$= wLL^*/(L + L^*) \tag{17}$$

$$= M^*.$$

Trade is balanced, as it must be, since each individual agent's budget constraint is satisfied. The volume of trade as a fraction of world income is maximized when the economies are of equal size.

We might note that the result that the volume of trade is determinate but the direction of trade is not is very similar to the well-known argument of Linder (1961). This suggests an affinity between this model and Linder's views, although Linder does not explicitly mention economies of scale.

The important point to be gained from this analysis is that economies of scale can be shown to give rise to trade and to gains from trade even when there are no international differences in tastes, technology, or factor endowments.

3.3. Effects of Factor Mobility [3]

An interesting extension of the model results when we allow for movement of labor between countries or regions. There is a parallel here with Heckscher-Ohlin theory. Mundell (1957) has shown that in a Heckscher-Ohlin world trade and factor mobility would be substitutes for one another, and that factor movements would be induced by impediments to trade such as tariffs or transportation costs. The same kinds of results emerge from this model.

To see this, suppose that there are two regions of the kind we have been discussing, and that they have the same tastes and technologies. There is room for mutual gains from trade, because the combined market would allow both greater variety of goods and a greater scale of production. The same gains could be obtained without trade, however, if the population of one region were to migrate to the other. In this model, trade and growth in the labor force are essentially equivalent.

If there are impediments to trade, there will be an incentive for workers to move to the region which already has the larger labor force. This is clearest if we consider the extreme case where no trade in goods is possible, but labor is perfectly mobile. Then the more populous region will offer both a greater real wage w/p and a greater variety of goods, inducing immigration. In equilibrium all workers will have concentrated in one region or the other. Which region ends up with the population depends on initial conditions; in the presence of increasing returns history matters.

Before proceeding further we should ask what aspect of reality, if any, is captured by the story we have just told. In the presence of increasing returns factor mobility appears to produce a process of agglomeration. If we had considered a many-region model the population would still have tended to accumulate in only one region, which we may as well label a city; for this analysis seems to make most sense as an account of the growth of metropolitan areas. The theory of urban growth suggested by this model is of the "city lights" variety: people migrate to the city in part because of the greater variety of consumption goods it offers.

Let us return now to the two-region case to make a final point. We have seen that which region ends up with the population depends on the initial distribution of population. As long as labor productivity is the same in both regions, though, there is no difference in welfare between the two possible outcomes. If there is any difference in the conditions of production between the two regions, however, it does matter which gets the population—and the process of migration can lead to the wrong outcome.

Consider, for example, a case in which both fixed and variable labor costs are higher in one region. Then it is clearly desirable that all labor should move to the other region. But if the inferior region starts with a large enough share of the population, migration may move in the wrong direction.

To summarize: in the model of this paper, as in some more conventional trade models, factor mobility can substitute for trade. If there are impediments to trade, labor will concentrate in a single region; which region depends on the initial distribution of population. Finally, the process of agglomeration may lead population to concentrate in the wrong place.

4. Summary and Conclusions

This paper adapts a Chamberlinian approach to the analysis of trade under conditions of increasing returns to scale. It shows that trade need not be a result of international differences in technology or factor endowments. Instead, trade may simply be a way of extending the market and allowing exploitation of scale economies, with the effects of trade being similar to those of labor force growth and regional agglomeration. This is a view of trade which appears to be useful in understanding trade among the industrial countries.

What is surprising about this analysis is that it is extremely simple. While the role of economies of scale in causing trade has been known for some time, it has been underemphasized in formal trade theory (and in textbooks). This paper shows that a clear, rigorous, and one hopes persuasive model of trade under conditions of increasing returns can be constructed. Perhaps this will help give economies of scale a more prominent place in trade theory.

References

Balassa, Bela, 1967, *Trade Liberalization among Industrial Countries* (McGraw-Hill, New York).

Barker, Terry, 1977, International trade and economic growth: An alternative to the neoclassical approach, *Cambridge Journal of Economics* 1, no. 2, 153–172.

Chacoliades, Miltiades, 1970, Increasing returns and the theory of comparative advantage, *Southern Economic Journal* 37, no. 2, 157–162.

Chamberlin, Edward, 1962, *The Theory of Monopolistic Competition*.

Dixit, Avinash and Joseph Stiglitz, 1977, Monopolistic competition and optimum product diversity, *American Economic Review*, June, 297–308.

Gray, Peter, 1973, Two-way international trade in manufactures: A theoretical underpinning, *Weltwirtschaftliches Archiv* 109, 19–39.

Grubel, Herbert, 1970, The theory of intra-industry trade, in. I. A. McDougall and R. H. Snape, eds., *Studies in International Economics* (North-Holland, Amsterdam).

Grubel, Herbert and Peter Lloyd, 1975, *Intra-Industry Trade* (MacMillan, London).

Hufbauer, Gary and John Chilas, 1974, Specialization by industrial countries: Extent and consequences, in H. Giersch, ed., *The International Division of Labour* (Institut für Weltwirtschaft, Kiel).

Kemp, Murray, 1964, *The Pure Theory of International Trade* (Prentice-Hall).

Kindleberger, Charles, 1973, *International Economics* (Irwin).

Kravis, Irving, 1971, The current case for import limitations, in: Commission on International Trade and Investment Policy. *United States Economic Policy in an Interdependent World* (U.S. Government Printing Office, Washington).

Linder, Staffan Burenstam, 1961, *An Essay on Trade and Transformation* (John Wiley and Sons).

Melvin, James, 1969, Increasing returns to scale as a determinant of trade, *Canadian Journal of Economics and Political Science* 2, no. 3, 389–402.

Mundell, Robert, 1957, International trade and factor mobility, *American Economic Review* 47, 321–335.

Negishi, Takashi, 1969, Marshallian external economies and gains from trade between similar countries, *Review of Economic Studies* 36, 131–135.

Negishi, Takashi, 1972, *General Equilibrium Theory and International Trade* (North-Holland, Amsterdam).

Ohlin, Bertil, 1933, *Interregional and International Trade* (Harvard University Press).

III
Tariffs and Quotas

8

The Non-Equivalence
of Tariffs and Quotas
under Retaliation

Carlos Alfredo
Rodriguez

The standard Marshallian demonstration that, except for revenue effects, tariffs and quotas are equivalent has been reexamined in recent theoretical contributions. Bhagwati (1965) reopened the issue by demonstrating the possibility of non-equivalence in the presence of monopoly, with subsequent contributions by Shibata (1968) and him (1968) distinguishing between alternative ways of defining equivalence but underlining the same basic conclusion that the equivalence proposition could break down in the presence of monopoly. Subsequently, the theoretical analysis of non-equivalence has been extended to the case of U.S. oil-type quotas by McCulloch and Johnson (1973).[1] Yet another theoretical contribution by Fishelson and Flatters (1973) has examined the non-equivalence that would arise under uncertainty.[2]

In this note we extend the theoretical analysis of non-equivalence of tariffs and quotas by introducing the possibility of retaliation. By using a Cournot-Johnson type of retaliation mechanism (such that each country in a two-country system chooses an optimal quota in light of the quota-shifted foreign offer curve facing it and ignoring the consequences of its choice on the quota-level that the foreign country would choose in retaliation), we show that a protective warfare which uses quotas will lead, in general, to a different outcome than when tariffs are the weapons chosen. We also show that, contrary to the case of optimum-tariff retaliation analyzed by Johnson (1953) where the tariff warfare may none-the-less improve the welfare of the country which initiated the war, the case of optimal-quota retaliation inexorably leads to elimination of trade and the consequent loss of welfare to each of the trading countries.

We assume two countries, I and II, each producing two goods, X and Y, under competitive conditions, Y being exported by country I. When

This paper was originally published in *Journal of International Economics* 4 (1974): 295–298.

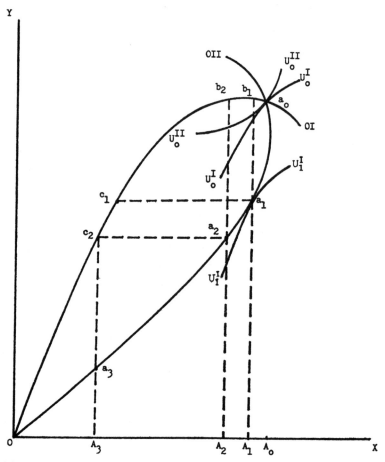

Figure 1

quotas are applied, quota holders are assumed to behave competitively. In figure 1, OI and OII represent the offer curves of countries I and II, respectively. Competitive equilibrium in the absence of trade restrictions is attained at point a_0 where OA_0 of good X is imported by country I, a_0A_0 of good Y is imported by country II and the terms of trade are the ratio OA_0/a_0A_0. Following the assumptions and methodology employed by Meade (1952) we can define indifference curves from trade along which each country remains at the same level of utility. $U_0^IU_0^I$ and $U_0^{II}U_0^{II}$ represent the pair of those curves corresponding to the utility levels enjoyed by each country at the unrestricted competitive equilibrium. Since at a_0 both offer curves are less than infinitely elastic, either country could gain by imposing some degree of trade restriction. As is well known, a country will maximize its utility when trading at a point where the foreign offer curve is tangent to an indifference curve from trade.

Assume that country I starts the process and sets an optimal import quota of OA_1 units of good X—it must be $OA_1 < OA_0$ for the quota to be binding—such that the new equilibrium is at point a_1 on OII where the welfare of country I is maximized since the indifference curve $U_1^IU_1^I$ is tangent to the foreign offer curve. The new offer curve of country I which country II is facing becomes the locus $Ob_1a_1A_1$ which is the same as the original offer curve until point b_1 where it becomes a vertical line since more imports are not feasible due to the import quota. The response of country II will depend on whether her optimal level of trade falls in the region Oc_1 (on OI) or in the region c_1b_1. If the optimal level of trade for country II falls in the region Oc_1, either an export or an import quota can be used to attain it; if it falls in the region c_1b_1 only an export quota can be used since any point in that region implies more imports and less exports than at the initial equilibrium at a_1. The reader can easily verify that, whatever the initial position, the final result of the retaliation process will be the same; we will thus only illustrate the case where the level of trade that maximizes the utility of country II falls at the kink, b_1, of the new offer curve of country I. To reach point b_1, an export quota in the amount OA_1, equal to the import quota on the same good imposed by country I seems to be necessary. If this quota is imposed, however, the imports of country II are undetermined at any level between A_1a_1 and A_1b_1 and, as such, there is no presumption that trade at b_1 will be reached given the competitive behavior of both suppliers and demanders. It is then reasonable to assume that country II will fix an export quota marginally smaller than OA_1—OA_2 in the figure—which will allow for trade to occur at b_2 (arbitrarily close to b_1). The offer curve of country II now becomes Oa_2b_2 which coincides with the original OII only in the region

Oa_2. The optimal level of trade for country I must now be at the kink a_2 of the new offer curve of country II. This new level of trade can be unambiguously attained through an export quota in the amount A_3c_2 (the reader can verify that if an import quota slightly smaller than OA_2 is used our final results will be unchanged). To the export quota A_3c_2 of country I, country II now responds with an export quota of OA_3 which shifts trade from point a_2 to point c_2, more favorably to country II. This, however, will bring as response a still smaller export quota by country I in the amount A_3a_3 which shifts trade to point a_3. To this country II responds with a still smaller export quota and, as the reader can easily verify, the process will continue until all trade is completely eliminated.

Conclusions

We can therefore conclude that, even in the absence of monopoly, revenue effects or uncertainty, tariffs and quotas are not equivalent when foreign retaliation is allowed for. Furthermore, we have shown that optimal quota retaliation will lead to the elimination of international trade between the countries involved. Our analysis would seem to strengthen the policy presumption that tariffs are preferable to quotas.

The author is indebted to Jagdish Bhagwati for his comments and suggestions.

References

Bhagwati, J., 1968, More on the equivalence of tariffs and quotas, *American Economic Review* 58, 142–146.

Fishelson, G. and F. Flatters, 1973, *The (Non) Equivalence of Tariffs and Quotas under Uncertainty*, unpublished manuscript (University of Chicago).

Johnson, H. G., 1953, Optimum tariffs and retaliation, *The Review of Economic Studies* 21, 142–153.

Meade, J. E., 1952, *A Geometry of International Trade* (Allen & Unwin, London).

McCulloch, R. and H. G. Johnson, 1973, A note on proportionally distributed quotas, *American Economic Review* 63, 726–732.

Shibata, H., 1968, Note on the equivalence of tariffs and quotas, *American Economic Review* 58, 137–142.

Postscript

After this paper reached proof stage, Harry G. Johnson pointed out to me that although the retaliation process seems to lead asymptotically to the elimination of trade, it can never logically eliminate trade completely. It will never pay either country to impose a zero trade quota since this step would always imply a reduction in welfare as compared with some positive amount of trade, however small (see H. G. Johnson, "Quotas and Retaliation: A note," unpublished manuscript, University of Chicago, 1974). Consequently, the proposition that trade is eliminated should be modified to read that the volume of trade tends asymptotically to zero (although in fact, never reaches it). It has also been called to my attention that Edward Tower has independently arrived at results which are similar to those presented in this paper.

9

The Structure of a Tariff System and the Effective Protective Rate

W. Max Corden

The theory of tariff structure is concerned with the effects of tariffs and other trade taxes in a system with many traded goods. It allows for the vertical relationships between tariff rates derived from the input–output relationships between products, an aspect until recently completely neglected in the literature of international trade theory. Early contributions to the theory of tariff structure, developing the idea of the effective protective rate with respect to the policies of particular countries, have come from Barber (1955) for Canada, Humphrey (1962) for the United States, and Corden (1963) for Australia.[1] Johnson's (1965) exposition is the fullest available so far and also explores many implications. Empirical contributions in which calculations of effective rates have been made on a large scale are by Balassa (1965) and Basevi (1966).[2] The present paper builds on this earlier work. In particular, in part I the general equilibrium implications of the effective-protective-rate concept are spelled out, its relation to equilibrating exchange-rate adjustment is shown, and nontraded goods are introduced explicitly into the model. Part II suggests a variety of applications and extensions of the concept. The effective protective rate is a new measure which has considerable possibilities for the study of systems of protection. I have attempted here to show what it means, how it can be used, and how calculations of it must be interpreted when there is substitution between inputs.

It will be assumed in most of this paper that,

(i) The physical input–output coefficients are all fixed.
(ii) The elasticities of demand for all exports and supply of all imports are infinite.

This paper was originally published in *Journal of Political Economy* 74 (1966): 221–237. Also published in Jagdish Bhagwati, editor, *International Trade: Selected Readings*, Penguin Books, 1969.

(iii) All tradable goods remain traded even after tariffs and other taxes and subsidies have been imposed, so that the internal price of each importable is given by the foreign price plus tariff.

(iv) Appropriate fiscal and monetary policies maintain total expenditure equal to full employment income.

(v) All tariffs and other trade taxes and subsidies are non-discriminatory as between countries of supply or demand.

Assumption (i) is reconsidered in part II, section h, and assumptions (ii) and (iii) in part II, section j.

I. The Basic Theory of Tariff Structure and Effective Protective Rates

a. The Effective Protective Rate

Ordinary *nominal* tariffs apply to commodities, but resources move as between economic activities. Therefore, to discover the resource-allocation effects of a tariff structure one must calculate the protective rate for each activity, that is, the *effective* protective rate. This is the main message of the new theory of tariff structures. The effective protective rate is the percentage increase in value added per unit in an economic activity which is made possible by the tariff structure relative to the situation in the absence of tariffs but with the same exchange rate. It depends not only on the tariff on the commodity produced by the activity but also on the input coefficients and the tariffs on the inputs.

Consider the simple case of an importable product, j, which has only a single input, also an importable, i. There are no taxes and subsidies affecting j and i other than the import tariffs. The formula for the effective protective rate for the activity producing j can be derived as follows:
Let

$v_j = $ value added per unit of j in activity j in absence of tariffs;
$v_j' = $ value added per unit of j in activity j made possible by the tariff structure;
$g_j = $ effective protective rate for activity j;
$p_j = $ price of a unit of j in absence of tariffs;
$a_{ij} = $ share of i in cost of j in absence of tariffs;
$t_j = $ tariff rate on j;
$t_i = $ tariff rate on i.

Then

$$v_j = p_j(1 - a_{ij}),\qquad(1)$$

$$v'_j = p_j[(1 + t_j) - a_{ij}(1 + t_i)], \tag{2}$$

$$g_j \equiv \frac{v'_j - v_j}{v_j}. \tag{3}$$

From equations (1), (2), and (3),

$$g_j = \frac{t_j - a_{ij}t_i}{1 - a_{ij}}. \tag{4}$$

This is the key formula, the implications of which can really be summarized as follows:

If $t_j = t_i$, then $g_j = t_j = t_i$.

If $t_j > t_i$, then $g_j > t_j > t_i$.

If $t_j < t_i$, then $g_j < t_j < t_i$.

If $t_j < a_{ij}t_i$, then $g_j < 0$.

If $t_j = 0$, then $g_j = -t_i \dfrac{a_{ij}}{1 - a_{ij}}$.

If $t_i = 0$, then $g_j = \dfrac{t_j}{1 - a_{ij}}$.

$$\frac{\partial g_j}{\partial t_j} = \frac{1}{1 - a_{ij}},$$

$$\frac{\partial g_j}{\partial t_i} = -\frac{a_{ij}}{1 - a_{ij}},$$

$$\frac{\partial g_j}{\partial a_{ij}} = \frac{t_j - t_i}{(1 - a_{ij})^2}.$$

Furthermore, equation (4) can be rewritten as

$$t_j = (1 - a_{ij})g_j + a_{ij}t_i. \tag{4.1}$$

This means that the nominal rate on the final good is a weighted average of its own effective rate and the tariff rate on its input.

For many importable inputs into the jth product (inputs $1, 2, \ldots, n$), but with no exportable or non-traded inputs, it can similarly be shown (Johnson, 1965; Basevi, 1966) that

$$g_j = \frac{t_j - \sum\limits_{i=1}^{n} a_{ij} t_i}{1 - \sum\limits_{i=1}^{n} a_{ij}}. \tag{4.2}$$

The implications are the same as above, except that in place of the single input tariff, t_i, it is necessary to write the weighted average of input tariffs

$$\frac{\sum\limits_{i=1}^{n} a_{ij} t_i}{\sum\limits_{i=1}^{n} a_{ij}}.$$

It is important to note that the effective protective rate for a product is not influenced by tariffs on inputs into its inputs. One need go only one step downward in the input–output structure. For example, a tariff on raw cotton, while it reduces effective protection for spinning, has no effect on the effective rate for weaving. To the weavers only the cost of yarn matters, and that is determined by the given world yarn price plus tariff.

b. Introducing Exportables
So far we have been concerned with the effective protection for an importable where the only inputs are importables. It is easy to encompass the discussion to include exportables. We can calculate the effective protection for an importable where some or all inputs are exportables, or for an exportable where the inputs are importables or other exportables. It needs only to be remembered that an export subsidy raises the internal price of a product and is the equivalent of a tariff, while an export tax is the equivalent of an import subsidy. In formula (4.2), g_j could be defined as the effective protective rate for any traded good, and the i would include all inputs, whether importables or exportables. We continue to assume absence of non-traded inputs. Two examples can be given of how this method works. Suppose we have an exportable not subject to an export tax or subsidy. Its input is an importable paying a 10 per cent tariff. If the free-trade share of this input in the exportable's cost is 50 per cent, then effective protection for the exportable is negative, namely, -10 per cent. Alternatively, consider an importable which does not benefit from a tariff but which uses as an input an exportable paying a 25 per cent export tax (expressed as a percentage of the tax-free price). If the free-trade share of the exportable in the cost of the importable is 60 per cent, then the effective protection of the importable is 37.5 per cent.

c. Production and Consumption Taxes on Tradables

So far we have allowed only for taxes and subsidies on trade. But effective protective rates are also affected by taxes and subsidies on domestic production or on domestic consumption of tradable goods—in the case of importables, taxes and subsidies which apply either to domestically produced import-competing goods alone or uniformly to these and to equivalent imports. We are concerned here only with taxes and subsidies levied specifically on tradable goods. Consumption taxes on finished goods do not affect effective protective rates. Consumption taxes on inputs have the same effect as tariffs on inputs—they raise the costs of the inputs to the using industries and therefore reduce effective protective rates for users. A production tax on any product has the same effect as an import subsidy or an export tax for that product, it reduces its effective rate. A production tax on an input, while it reduces the protection for the input, has no effect on effective protection for the using industry. Thus in our formula, t_j should be redefined to represent the net effect of the tariff or export subsidy and any production tax on industry j, while t_i nets the tariff or export subsidy on input i with any consumption tax on it.

d. The Scale of Effective Rates

Assume that the effective protective rate for each activity producing a tradable product has been calculated, taking into account tariffs, export taxes, export and import subsidies, consumption taxes, and production taxes. The next step is to order all these effective rates on a continuous scale through zero. The order is likely to be quite different from a similar scale based on nominal tariff rates and nominal export subsidies and taxes. It is quite possible that the nominal rates consist wholly of tariffs and export subsidies and hence are all *positive* nominal protective rates, and yet the scale of effective rates may include many negative rates. But whether a rate is positive or negative does not really matter for the present: all that matters is the order on the scale. The scale summarizes the total protective-rate structure. Assuming normal non-zero substitution elasticities in production, it tells us the *direction* in which this structure causes resources to be pulled as between activities producing traded goods. Domestic production will shift from low to high effective-protective-rate activities. Leaving aside for the moment a complication to be discussed below, namely, substitution between traded and non-traded goods, if four activities producing traded goods can be ordered along a scale A, B, C, D in ascending order of effective rates, we can say that output of A must fall and of D must rise and that resources will be pulled from

A to *B* and from *A* and *B* to *C*; but without more precise information about production–substitution elasticities, we cannot say whether the outputs of *B* and *C* will rise or fall.

This is the production effect of the protective-rate structure and depends, thus, on the scale of effective rates and on production–substitution elasticities. In addition, the pattern of consumption will be affected by the protective-rate structure; consumption will shift from final goods with high nominal tariffs toward goods with low nominal tariffs. Thus the consumption effect still depends on the nominal tariffs of final goods as well as on consumption–(or expenditure–) substitution elasticities. Since fixed input coefficients and continued imports of all importables are assumed (assumptions (i) and (iii) above), no consumption or usage effect results from tariffs on inputs.

e. The Exchange-Rate Adjustment
Now introduce into the analysis a single and only non-traded good, *N*. Assume that it is not an input into any tradable good, and no tradable good is an input into it. If the price of *N* remained constant, some resources would move from *N* into activities which obtain positive effective rates and toward *N* from activities with negative effective rates. Similarly, some consumption would be diverted toward *N* from products with positive nominal rates and in the reverse direction where nominal rates are negative (for example, export taxes). Assumption (iv) was that aggregate expenditure is maintained equal to full employment income, so that this change in the production and expenditure patterns must lead to excess demand for or excess supply of *N* (internal imbalance) and a balance-of-payments surplus or deficit (external imbalance). To restore internal and external balance, a change in the price of *N* relative to the general internal price level of traded goods is then necessary. This could be brought about by flexible factor prices or by exchange-rate adjustment. If we assume a constant price of *N*, the exchange rate must alter; the function of exchange-rate adjustment in the model is to alter the price relationship between *N* and traded goods. This can clearly be generalized for the case where there are many non-traded goods; one must then hold constant not the price of each separate non-traded good but, rather, some kind of average price level. It should be noted that if the activities producing traded goods did not have significant production–substitution relationships with non-traded goods and if consumption–substitution relationships among traded and non-traded goods were also low, then the exchange-rate adjustment needed to maintain internal and external balance would also not be significant.

Suppose that in the first instance the protective-rate structure leads to balance-of-payments surplus and excess demand for non-traded goods as a whole.[3] Exchange-rate appreciation is then required to restore internal and external balance. In relation to non-traded goods, the exchange-rate appreciation is the equivalent of a uniform *ad valorem* import subsidy (negative tariff) and export tax, applying to all tradables including, of course, tradable inputs. Thus it provides a uniform rate of negative effective protection for all tradables. This exchange-rate adjustment must be regarded as an integral part of the effect of a protective structure. If the appreciation were, for example, 20 per cent, all tradables with an effective rate of less than 20 per cent will, in a sense, have been taxed in relation to non-tradables, and only effective rates over 20 per cent mean protection in relation to non-tradables. If we subtract 20 per cent from all effective protective rates as previously calculated, we obtain a scale of *net effective protective rates*. Only when the net rate is positive is an activity protected relative to non-tradables. Clearly the exchange-rate adjustment implied by a protective structure must be estimated if the full effects of such a structure on resource allocation are to be understood.

f. Four Concepts of Protection

There emerge from this analysis four distinct concepts of when an industry is really protected.

First, there is the old-fashioned approach that an industry is protected if its nominal tariff is positive. But it is the message of this article that, while the nominal tariff is relevant to the consumption effect, in itself it can tell us nothing about the production effect.

Second, there is the more sophisticated approach which emerges from the new theory of tariff structure that an industry is protected if its effective tariff is positive. It is true that, if the prices of non-traded goods are given and the exchange rate does not alter, any industry with a positive effective rate will tend to attract resources into it from non-traded goods and is thus protected relative to non-traded goods. But it clearly may not be protected relative to non-traded goods once exchange-rate adjustment is permitted.

Third, one might take into account the exchange-rate effects of a protective structure and consider an industry to be protected only when its *net* effective rate is positive, for only then is it protected relative to non-traded goods.

Fourth, one might argue that an activity is only truly protected if the net result of the protective structure combined with the appropriate exchange-rate adjustment is to raise value added in that activity. This is the concept of *total protection*. The direction of change in output or value added depends not only on protection relative to non-traded goods but also on protection relative to other traded goods. Even if we find that a particular tradable activity has a positive net protective rate and its production-substitution elasticity with the non-traded sector is positive so that there is a movement of resources into that activity from the non-traded sector, it does not follow that output of that activity must increase. For there may be substitution against it because some other tradable activities have higher effective rates. Whether an industry is protected in this fourth sense (that is, is *totally* protected) depends not only on substitution relative to non-tradables (the direction of which is indicated by the sign of the *net* rate) but also on substitution relative to other tradables (which is influenced by its position in the scale of effective rates).

g. Non-Traded Inputs
So far it has been assumed that there are no non-traded inputs (for example, electricity or services) in traded goods. If there are, then the non-traded sector is affected in three ways by a protective structure, the first effect not having entered so far. First, positive total protection of traded goods leads to additional demand for non-traded inputs; those non-traded inputs intensive in the protected industries will rise in price relatively to the general price level in the non-traded sector. Second, positive nominal tariffs or export subsidies on finished traded goods will divert demand from these goods on to substitute non-traded goods. Third, primary factors will move from the non-traded sector in general into protected traded-goods industries (and also into industries producing those non-traded inputs which are indirectly protected).

Now the important question arises whether, to calculate effective protective rates of tradables, non-traded inputs should be treated in the same way as tradable inputs or whether they should be treated like primary factors. Balassa (1965) and Basevi (1966) treat a non-tradable input just like any tradable input with a zero tariff or export-tax subsidy. In defense it could be argued that the effective protective rate refers to the effect of the tariff structure on value added per unit in the industry under consideration; and to obtain value added all inputs, whether traded or non-traded, must be excluded. The alternative approach is to treat non-traded inputs in the same way as primary factors. Value added per unit in a tradable industry would then be defined as value added by primary factors plus value added by non-traded inputs. The intuitive defense is that protection for an activity producing a traded product represents not only protection for those primary factors intensive in that activity but also protection for those industries producing non-traded inputs in which that activity is intensive and thus, indirectly, protection for the primary factors intensive in these non-traded input industries. There appears, thus, to be a complete identity between primary factors and non-traded input industries.

To resolve the issue, one must ask what the purpose of the effective-protective-rate concept is. The answer is that it should shed light on the direction of the resource-allocation effects of a protective structure. If we have calculated that tradable industry X has 10 per cent effective protection and tradable industry Y has 20 per cent, we should be able to conclude that resources will be drawn from X to Y and into both from non-protected tradable industries and from those non-traded industries where prices have stayed constant.

Consider a simple model so constructed as to isolate the first of our three effects of a protective structure on the non-traded sector and, thus, to focus on the essentials of the problem. Let there be three industries producing M (importables), X (exportables), and N (non-traded goods). There are two primary factors: L, which is an input into M and X but cannot be used in N; and L_n, which is an input specific to N. Both M and X are final consumption goods, while N is an input into M and X and is not consumed directly. All three production functions are constant returns to scale, and (departing from the fixed coefficient assumption) in M and X there is continuous substitutability between the two inputs L and N. Internal and external balance are maintained with a flexible exchange rate and appropriate monetary policy. Equilibrium can be represented in a familiar manner with a box diagram, the dimensions of which are the stock of L and the output of N (depending on the stock of L_n), and a production-possibility curve in a quadrant with axes showing outputs of M and X. In free trade, the price ratio between M and X is given, and from this can be deduced outputs of M and X and inputs of L and N into each industry. Now suppose that a 10 per cent nominal tariff is imposed on M and a 10 per cent export subsidy on X, so that the price ratio remains unchanged. Our simple model tells us that outputs and resource allocation also will not change. Now suppose that we use the first method in calculating the effective rates and so treat N as we would a traded input. Assume that M is L-intensive relative to X; therefore the share of value added (defined as the cost of L) in the price of M will be greater than in the price of X. Thus the nominal protective rates of 10 per cent would yield an effective rate for M less than that for X (in both cases greater than 10 per cent). We would then conclude wrongly that resources will move from M to X. On the other hand, if non-traded inputs were treated as primary factors, we would calculate both effective rates at 10 per cent (as there are no traded inputs). Since relative effective rates would not have changed, we would conclude correctly that resources will not move as between X and M. While this model is very simple, it seems to prove conclusively that non-traded inputs should ideally be treated like primary factors and not like traded inputs.

The essence of the distinction between traded and non-traded inputs stems from our assumptions (ii) and (iii) (infinite foreign-trade elasticities; trade in tradable products remains after protection). Thus a tradable input is in infinite supply to an industry, and the price of each individual traded good is given (apart from the effects of taxes and subsidies). If non-traded inputs were also in infinitely elastic supply, they could indeed be treated like traded inputs. But in the absence of unemployment and excess capacity a user industry can obtain extra non-traded inputs only at increased cost, and some part of the increment in the price of the final good on account of the tariff will not increase value added per unit but will raise the price of the input. The tariff protects not only those primary factors but also those non-traded inputs (and hence their factors) which are intensive in the using industries. But the effects on the primary factors and the non-traded inputs cannot be separated out. Unless there are two inputs only and one is in infinitely elastic supply so that its price does not rise when the price of the output rises, it is impossible to distinguish the effective protective rate for different inputs. For each product one can talk only about a single effective rate for all those inputs combined which are not in infinitely elastic supply to the industry.[4]

In section e, it was argued that if the net effective rate is positive an activity is protected relative to non-traded goods. This must now be qualified. It is protected relative to the non-traded sector as a whole, assuming that the average price level of non-traded goods stays constant. But it will not be protected relative to all non-traded goods, since the protective structure will have led to increases in the relative prices and so resource movements into those non-traded industries which produce inputs primarily for highly protected traded industries.

II. Applications and Extensions of the New Concept

a. Escalation of the Tariff Structure
By translating a set of nominal rates into a set of effective rates, one can understand more clearly the general characteristics of a tariff structure and of changes in it. For example, a widely noted characteristic of the

tariff structures of many countries is that nominal rates tend to be low or even zero for raw materials and to rise or "escalate" with the degree of processing.[5] In an escalated structure, the nominal rate on made-up clothing is higher than that on cloth, the cloth rate is higher than the yarn rate, and at the bottom is the raw-cotton rate. Two distinct implications follow.

i. Except for the basic material which has no other tradable product as an input, the effective rate is always higher than the nominal rate. This indeed is the attraction of escalated structures to protectionists: the degree of protection provided to industries is not so obvious.

ii. It means low or zero protection for the raw material at the bottom of the chain. This is not significant when, as often, there is no potential domestic production of the material; but when there is, then an escalated structure biases trade in favor of raw materials against processed products. It is then correct to say that the escalated structures of the advanced countries encourage underdeveloped countries to export raw materials rather than to export processed products. If an advanced country replaced an escalated structure with a uniform tariff leading to the same value of imports, its production mix would include a higher proportion and its import mix a lower proportion of raw materials. On the other hand, when there is no potential production of raw materials in the advanced country, replacing the escalated structure with the uniform tariff would not raise the import of processed products. In that case, the criticism of the escalated structure is not a criticism of its effect on the pattern of protection but, rather, of the level of protection.

b. Effect of Reduction in Tariff on an Intermediate Good
Another application of the new concept concerns a country which offers to reduce the tariff on an intermediate good at international tariff negotiations and so appears to be making a "concession" that will reduce protection and increase trade. In fact, the extra imports and lower domestic production of the intermediate good which may result must be set against the consequences of the higher effective rate for the user industry. A change in the nominal rate for an intermediate good alters at least two effective rates in opposite directions. On balance, total protected production may rise or fall, with trade moving in the opposite direction. This is clearest in the special case where the elasticity of supply of the intermediate good is zero, so that the only consequences of the tariff reduction result from the rise in the effective rate for the user industry.

c. Infant Industries Growing Up

The following example suggests that historians of commercial policies and of industrialization should calculate effective rates. In a normal process of industrial development by import replacement, a country starts with importing nearly finished products free of duty, carrying out final processing or assembly behind a tariff wall, and gradually moves backward into earlier productive stages, extending the tariff at the same time. The number of nominal tariffs increases, and no nominal tariff may ever be reduced. While the historian naturally reports a growth in the tariff, effective rates are falling and infant industries are growing up. In the first stage, for example, cotton cloth pays a duty of 40 per cent, while yarn enters duty-free, the effective rate for weaving being (say) 100 per cent. In the second stage, the 40 per cent tariff is extended to yarn. So the effective rate for cloth now drops from 100 per cent to 40 per cent. Therefore, weaving has at least partially grown up. In the third stage, the effective rate for spinning might fall. It should be noted, incidentally, that an industry would be regarded as having "grown up" in the sense of the fourth meaning of protection above (total protection) not when its effective rate falls to zero but, rather, when it falls to the level when a restoration of free trade in all goods associated with the appropriate exchange-rate adjustment would leave output in this industry unchanged.

d. Multiple Exchange Rates

Our concept and technique of analysis can be used to analyse multiple exchange-rate systems. The first step is arbitrarily to choose any rate, say the official or the free market rate, and define it as the "base" rate. Then all rates charged on imports and paid on exports can be converted into nominal tariff rates, import subsidies, export taxes, or export subsidies. For example, if the rate applying to capital-goods imports is 9 pesos to the dollar, and 10 pesos has been chosen as the base rate, then there is an import subsidy of 10 per cent. The set of nominal rates is next converted into a set of effective rates using the procedure already described. This set is then ordered so that it can be seen in which direction resources are pulled by the multiple rate system as between traded-goods producers. Next, from the set of effective rates and a similar set of nominal tariffs and consumption taxes and from guesses or estimates of elasticities, must be estimated the single exchange rate which would achieve the same balance of payments result as the multiple rate system.[6] Finally, the set of effective rates must be restated in relation to this equilibrium rate. If the resulting net effective rate is negative, the multiple system has exerted a pull of resources out of that activity into the non-traded sector; while if it is positive, it is likely to have attracted resources into it. Any rate can serve as a base to start the calculation off; the vital subsequent step is to estimate correctly the equilibrium rate in relation to which all the effective rates must finally be restated to yield the net effective rates.

e. Analysing the Effects of Foreign Tariffs

Let "our" country be Canada and the "foreign" country the United States. Assume that the U.S. demand curves for Canadian exports and the U.S. supply curves to Canada of U.S. exports are all infinitely elastic. Now the tariffs and other taxes and subsidies imposed by the United States provide protection or "anti-protection" for the industries of Canada, and their effect on the allocation of resources in Canada can be analysed in the same manner as the effects of Canada's own tariffs and other taxes. For example, a U.S. tariff on furniture lowers the demand curve facing Canadian exporters and has the same effect on the allocation of resources in Canada as a Canadian export tax on furniture. The concern here is only with resource-allocation effects. The fiscal effects obviously depend on which country taxes and subsidizes.

A scale of effective rates can then be constructed which represents the protection or antiprotection imposed by the U.S. tax-subsidy structure on Canadian industry. The effects of this structure can be analysed alone, holding constant Canada's own structure; the effects of the Canadian structure could be analysed alone, this being the approach expounded in this paper so far; or the combined effects of the two structures could be analysed, constructing a scale of combined effective rates. In any particular case, the two components of a combined effective rate (say a Canadian export subsidy combined with a U.S. import tariff) could cancel each other. The exchange-rate adjustment must again be taken into account. Even in the simple case when both the Canadian and the U.S. tax-subsidy structures consist mainly of tariffs on finished goods, the required exchange-rate adjustment could go either way and would, in any case, be less than when the effects of one of the structures alone is considered.[7]

f. Labor as an Input

So far we have distinguished between traded inputs, assumed to be in infinitely elastic supply, and non-traded inputs plus the primary factors of production (labor, capital, etc.) where extra quantities are likely to come forth only at higher cost. The argument was that a tariff on a final good raises the returns per unit only to the non-traded inputs and primary factors and, therefore, should be related to the sum of their shares in total cost. If any non-traded input were in infinitely elastic supply it could be grouped with the traded inputs [it would be counted among the i in formula (4.2)]. The effective rate would then describe the degree of protection (percentage increment in returns per unit) to the primary factors and any remaining non-traded inputs.

Now this principle could also be applied to any primary factors which are in infinitely elastic supply. Suppose that there are no non-traded inputs but only traded inputs and three factors of production: labor, capital, and land. If labor were in infinitely elastic supply, it could be grouped with the traded inputs; and the effective rate would be calculated in relation to the shares of capital and land, being then the effective protective rate for these two factors only. Alternatively, capital might be in infinitely elastic supply, in which case capital cost would be treated as just another input (another i in the formula); the result would be an effective rate of protection for labor and land. If labor and capital were in infinitely elastic supply, the effective rate to land would be calculated. To extend our previous method in this way, fixed physical input coefficients must be assumed for all those factors in infinitely elastic supply which are to be grouped with the tradable materials. Our earlier assumption of fixed input coefficients was necessary only for the tradable materials and not for other inputs or each primary factor separately.

The case where labor, or some types of labor, are in infinitely elastic supply may be relevant for some underdeveloped countries. While the cause is likely to be a given income or wage level in the subsistence hinterland, or perhaps in a neighboring country which supplies immigrants, the given money wage facing the protected industry need not be at the same level as that in the hinterland, the margin between them being the equivalent of the difference between the f.o.b. and the c.i.f. price of an import. Now, when labor is treated as just another input, what is the equivalent of a tariff on the input? All such "tariffs" will of course reduce the effective protection for the employing industries. One such "tariff" is a payroll tax on the use of labor, another is any tax which raises costs of transport of immigrants or costs of transfer from the hinterland. If it is the real wage rather than the money wage which is fixed, then anything which raises labor's cost of living is like a tariff on this input. To give a very Ricardian example, a tariff on corn will raise money wages and reduce effective protection for labor-using weavers. In fact, corn is an input into labor, and labor is an input into cloth; we are back to the case where a tariff on a tradable input reduces effective protection for the using industry. If it is the real wage after tax which is fixed, then an income tax levied on labor employed in industry reduces effective protection. On the other hand, state provision of urban facilities which raise the real value of a given money wage spent in the city increases the effective protective rate for the employing industries.

g. Capital as an Input

All calculations which treat labor as an input yield in fact effective protective rates for capital (plus land and other factors). Similarly, a calculation which treats capital as an input yields the effective protective rates for labor (plus any other factors). This calculation has been made by Basevi (1966) for the U.S. tariff.[8] But there are some conceptual problems here which must be explored. In particular, how do tariffs on capital goods enter the calculation?

First of all, at this stage fixed physical capital-output ratios must be assumed just as fixed labor-output ratios were needed before. Now let b_k be the cost of a unit of physical capital per annum to the users, just as the wage rate is the cost of a unit of labor; it is the equivalent of the price of a tradable input. It is b_k which has to be constant, except when it is increased by tariffs or their equivalents. Since

$$b_k = (r + q)p_k,\tag{5}$$

where p_k is the price of capital goods, r is the rate of interest, and q is the annual rate of depreciation on capital, it follows that p_k, r, and q must all be constant in response to changes in demand for capital from protected industries. Now q can be regarded as a fixed coefficient (dependent on the method of depreciation chosen), and r is constant if we assume (as Basevi does) that the interest rate is a given world market rate. But what about p_k? Extending our earlier analysis, this is given when the capital goods are tradables and is not given when they are non-tradables. Traded capital goods with annual cost per unit of b_{kt} must really be distinguished from non-traded capital goods with annual cost per unit of b_{kn} where

$$b_{kt} = (r + q_t)p_{kt},\tag{5.1}$$

$$b_{kn} = (r + q_n)p_{kn}.\tag{5.2}$$

Only the annual service of tradable capital goods can be treated as an input, like tradable goods themselves, and only when it is legitimate to assume in addition a perfectly elastic supply of capital funds. The resulting effective rate will then be the protective rate for labor, for producers of non-tradables, whether capital goods or consumer goods, and for land. In our formula (4.2) there is needed for the capital cost (referring only to tradable capital goods) an equivalent of the tariff on an input. This must incorporate the tariff on capital goods, any other taxes or subsidies affecting the total investment cost, such as investment allowances, and any taxes or other measures which alter the rate of interest. This equivalent is db_{kt}/b_{kt}. From (5.1), taking differentials

$$db_{kt} = rdp_{kt} + p_{kt}dr + q_t dp_{kt}. \tag{6}$$

From (6)

$$\frac{db_{kt}}{b_{kt}} = \frac{rp_{kt}}{b_{kt}} \left[\frac{dr}{r} + t_k \left(1 + \frac{q_t}{r} \right) \right], \tag{6.1}$$

where

$$t_k = \frac{dp_{kt}}{p_{kt}}.$$

In (6.1) the percentage increase in the rate of interest resulting from the tax structure is dr/r, the tariff on capital goods minus any investment subsidies as a percentage of the capital cost is t_k, and rp_{kt}/b_{kt} is the share of interest charges in the capital cost.

h. Substitution

So far, fixed physical input ratios of material inputs to outputs have been assumed. Let us now allow for the possibility that changes in price relationships bring about substitution between material inputs and inputs of primary factors and that this substitution in turn causes changes in the input coefficients. So the tariff structure itself, through its effects on internal price relationships, may induce changes in input coefficients. Two questions then arise. The first concerns the nature of the thing which ideally we are trying to measure when we calculate an effective protective rate. The second question is to define the direction of the error, if any, which results on account of induced changes in input coefficients when certain practicable methods of calculation are used. Thus, first, we define the ideal measure and then we relate the results of measures which are practicable to the ideal.

The exposition will be in terms of a very simple model, though probably most of the conclusions would apply even when some of the constraints of the model are removed. We assume for each tradable product j a twice-differentiable linear homogenous production function $j = f_j(i, y)$, where input i is a tradable material and input y a primary factor, with positive marginal products and a diminishing marginal rate of substitution. We assume competitive pricing. Both the material input i and the primary factor y can be regarded as bundles of inputs, but we must then assume fixed ratios between inputs within each bundle. We focus, in fact, on one particular substitution relationship, that between the material inputs and the primary factors. Prices are p_j, p_i, and p_y, where p_j is a product price, p_y a factor price, and p_i is both. The only changes in prices we consider are due to tariffs or similar taxes or subsidies. When p_j, p_i, and p_y are defined as representing prices in the free-trade situation, then the tariff on the final product t_j is dp_j/p_j, and the tariff on the material t_i is dp_i/p_i. Since prices of inputs must be equal to the value of their marginal products, it follows that the marginal physical products of i and y, respectively, are p_i/p_j and p_y/p_j. We denote the physical ratio of material input i to output j in the free-trade situation as b (the input coefficient) and the physical ratio of material input i to primary factor input y in the free-trade situation as c (the factor ratio). Therefore

$$a_{ij} = b\frac{p_i}{p_j}. \tag{7}$$

We must note here the well-known relationship between input substitution and input coefficients which holds when one assumes a given linear homogenous production function with two inputs only and with continuous substitution between these inputs. The input coefficients (that is, the ratios of each input to output) depend only on the ratio between the inputs and must change when there is substitution between the inputs. In our model, the input coefficient is b, namely, the ratio of material input to output. This must rise whenever there is substitution away from y toward i, so that c rises. If c falls, b falls; and if c does not change, b does not change.

It was explained earlier that the calculation of effective rates is designed to indicate the direction in which resources will be pulled by the tariff structure. It should not incorporate the effects of these resource shifts. Therefore, the effective rate can no longer be the actual percentage rise in returns per unit to the primary factors (and non-traded inputs) resulting from the tariffs, since that depends partly on the substitution effects which have actually taken place. Thus, g_j cannot be defined as dp_y/p_y in the present model. Rather, we want to know what the rise in the rate of return to a factor is before any resources move in response to this rise. Hence, the effective rate should be the percentage rise in the return to the primary factor which would result if there were no substitution between inputs and, hence, if there were no change in the input coefficient. It follows that the ideal calculation should use the input coefficient of the free-trade situation; the formula which we have been using remains the correct one and, with or without actual substitution, the coefficient to use is b and, in value terms, a_{ij}. The difficulty is that, while previously the physical input coefficients were the same in the protection as in the free-trade situation, when there is a possibility of substitution between inputs they may be different. So starting with the protection situation, we no longer know the input coefficient required for the formula. If, nevertheless, we use the coefficient of the protection situation, we need at least to know whether we will be understating or overstating the effective rate.

In the protection situation the information available consists of the two tariff rates t_j and t_i and the share of material input in total cost a'_{ij}:

$$a'_{ij} = b' \frac{(p_i + dp_i)}{(p_j + dp_j)}, \tag{8}$$

where b' is the physical ratio of material input i to output j (the input coefficient) in the protection situation. Primes refer to the protection situation. Since $t_j = dp_j/p_j$ and $t_i = dp_i/p_i$, we have from (7) and (8)

$$a'_{ij} = \frac{1 + t_i}{1 + t_j} \frac{a_{ij}}{w}, \tag{9}$$

where $w \equiv b/b'$ (that is, w is the ratio of the free trade to the protection physical input coefficients). We have

$$g_j = \frac{t_j - a_{ij}t_i}{1 - a_{ij}}. \tag{4}$$

Substituting (9) in (4), we have

$$g_j = \frac{t_j - a'_{ij}wt_i(1 + t_j)/(1 + t_i)}{1 - a'_{ij}w(1 + t_j)/(1 + t_i)}, \tag{10}$$

which may be rewritten as follows:

$$g_j = \frac{1 - a'_{ij}w}{1/(t_j + 1) - a'_{ij}w/(t_i + 1)} - 1.[9] \tag{10.1}$$

The author's calculations (Corden, 1963, pp. 208–13), those of the Australian committee (Committee of Economic Enquiry, 1965, app. L 4), and the calculations by Basevi (1966) of the U.S. effective rates represent an application of this formula on the assumption that $w = 1$, that is, that the input coefficients in the free-trade and the protection situation are the same. They would be the same if there were a fixed ratio between inputs. Even when there are substitution possibilities, they will be the same if $t_j = t_i$, so that p_i/p_j does not change. For p_i/p_j is equal to the marginal physical product of i, which can stay constant in this model only if the input ratio also stays constant. If $t_j > t_i$, so that p_i/p_j falls, there will be substitution toward $i(c' > c)$ so that the input coefficient rises ($b' > b$) and thus $w < 1$. If $t_j < t_i$, the substitution will be away from i, so that $w > 1$.

Now consider the effect of a change in w on g_j. From (10.1)

$$\frac{\partial g_j}{\partial w} = (t_j - t_i)\frac{a'_{ij}}{(t_j + 1)(t_i + 1)[1/(t_j + 1) - a'_{ij}w/(t_i + 1)]^2}. \tag{11}$$

It follows that $\partial g_j/\partial w > 0$ if $t_j > t_i$ and $\partial g_j/\partial w < 0$ if $t_j < t_i$.

Bringing all this together, we arrive at a rather surprising conclusion. Suppose that $t_j > t_i$, so that there is substitution toward i. A correct calculation of the effective rate requires then a value of $w < 1$. But the actual calculation which is made assumes that $w = 1$. Therefore, w has been overstated, and we must ask whether this leads to an understatement or overstatement of g_j. It can be seen from (11) that when $t_j > t_i, \partial g_j/\partial w > 0$, so that if w is too high g_j must also be too high. Therefore, by assuming $w = 1$ (no substitution), the effective rate has been *overstated*. Next we do the same exercise for the case where $t_j < t_i$, so that there is substitution against i and $w > 1$. This time, by assuming that $w = 1$, we have understated it. But it has also been seen from (11) that when $t_j < t_i, \partial g_j/\partial w < 0$, so that if w is too low g_j is too high. In other words, by assuming that $w = 1$, the effective rate has again been *overstated*. We may conclude that calculations of effective rates which use the data of the protection situation will always tend to overstate the effective rates if there is any substitution from primary inputs toward material inputs or vice versa and, of course, unless other errors are offsetting.

i. Use of Foreign Input Coefficients
Instead of using the input coefficients in the protection situation of the country for which the effective rates are to be calculated, an alternative is to use the input coefficients of another country, the prices of which are not distorted to the same extent by tariffs. This method is used by Balassa. [10] Can one then generalize about the direction of the error?

If the production functions are the same in the country which supplies the coefficients (say, the Netherlands) as in the country for which the effective rates are required (say, Australia) and if price ratios in the Netherlands are the same as free-trade price ratios in Australia, then there will be no error. In fact, production functions do not even have to be the same; they may differ neutrally (in the Harrod, not Hicks, sense), so that the input coefficient b stays constant even though the factor ratio c varies. The assumption of similar production functions (or ones that differ only neutrally) is perhaps not unreasonable. But the existence of transport costs may cause the Netherlands price ratio to diverge from the free-trade Australian ratio. Suppose that the Netherlands is the exporting country and that her exports are not differentially priced; so her internal prices are identical with Australian f.o.b. import prices, excluding duty. The Australian internal free-trade price ratio, that is, the ratio of c.i.f. prices, will then differ from the Netherlands ratio if the percentages of transport costs differ between the material and the finished good. Let us work through the implications in a special, and not implausible, case. Suppose that the transport-cost percentage is higher for materials than for finished goods, so that p_i/p_j is lower in the Netherlands than it would be in free-trade Australia; that the elasticity of substitution in the production function is less than unity, so that a_{ij} is less in the Netherlands than in free-trade Australia; and that $t_j > t_i$, so that an understatement of a_{ij} understates the effective rate g_j. It follows that the use of Netherlands coefficients understates effective rates in Australia, the answer depending in fact on a combination of three assumptions. Though each of these assumptions seems rather more reasonable than its alternative, it is clear that, in contrast to the previous case, there is no general presumption about the direction of error resulting from the method used.

j. Other Assumptions
In conclusion, attention should be drawn to assumptions (ii) and (iii), maintained throughout this paper. Removing assumption (iii), namely, that all tradable goods continue to be traded even after tariffs and other taxes have been imposed, presents few difficulties in principle. Part of a tariff can now be redundant. As is well known, many tariff structures have redundant elements in them ("water in the tariff"), and it is these elements which trade negotiators are usually most ready to sacrifice. Since a redundant tariff has no effect of any kind other than as an insurance to protected industries against falls in import prices, all calculations should ideally be based only on the *utilized* parts of tariffs—an ideal which requires detailed price data and which may not always be practical. It should also be noted that, once imports of an input cease, further protection of the input requires the tariff on the final good to be increased (up to the point where imports of the final good cease). Thus, not only does the protection for the final product depend on both its own tariff and the tariffs on its inputs, but the protection of the inputs depends on their own tariffs and the tariff on the final good. Finally, removing as-

sumption (ii), namely, that the export-demand and import-supply elasticities are all infinite, presents considerable difficulties; and, when the elasticities for inputs are less than infinite, the effective-protective-rate concept strictly interpreted appears to break down. But perhaps if the elasticities are generally close to infinite, the calculation of effective rates and the derivation of various conclusions from the calculations are justified as reasonable approximations. The present author applied the concept in Australia, a country which, like most countries of the "periphery", faces import-supply curves which are commonly accepted to be infinitely elastic. Some export-demand curves are no doubt less than infinitely elastic, but the exportable content in protected import-competing production is fairly unimportant. So, for Australia and similar countries, no difficulty arises.

This paper has benefited greatly from comments by H. W. Arndt and H. G. Johnson. I am indebted also to members of seminars at the L.S.E., Oxford, M.I.T., Yale, Brookings, Chicago, Berkeley, and Stanford, who commented on an earlier presentation of some of the main ideas.

References

Balassa, B. (1965), "Tariff protection in industrial countries: an evaluation", *Journal of Political Economy*, vol. 73, pp. 573–94.

Barber, C. L. (1955), "Canadian tariff policy", *Canadian Journal of Economics and Political Science*, vol. 21, pp. 513–30.

Basevi, G. (1966), "The U.S. tariff structure: estimate of effective rates of protection of U.S. industries and industrial labor", *Review of Economics and Statistics*, vol. 48.

Committee of Economic Enquiry (1965), *Report of the Committee of Economic Enquiry*, Canberra.

Corden, W. M. (1963), "The tariff", in A. Hunter, ed., *The Economics of Australian Industry*, Melbourne University Press.

Humphrey, D. D. (1962), *The United States and the Common Market*, Praeger.

Johnson, H. G. (1965), "The theory of tariff structure with special reference to world trade and development", *Trade and Development*, Institut Universitaire des Hautes Etudes Internationales.

Meade, J. E. (1955), *Trade and Welfare*, Oxford University Press.

Travis, W. P. (1964), *The Theory of Trade and Protection*, Harvard University Press.

Young, J. H. (1957), *Canadian Commerical Policy*, Royal Commission on Canada's Economic Prospects.

IV
**Gains from Trade,
Distortions, and Recent
Extensions**

10

The Gains from International Trade Once Again

Paul A. Samuelson

Introduction

In 1939 I wrote a paper that showed how some international trade makes a society potentially better off than it would be if restricted to autarky (Samuelson, 1939). Although this paper has received a flattering amount of notice, I had always regarded it as somewhat incomplete and had long planned to follow it with a more definite companion piece. For it was written with two purposes in mind other than to say all that can be said about the gains from international trade.

First, it was an attempt to show how the new theories of revealed preference could be used to demonstrate important theorems in welfare economics. And second, it was intended to mediate the dispute between two of many famous teachers, Jacob Viner (then of Chicago) and Gottfried Haberler (Harvard), over the doctrine of opportunity cost in international trade and value theory: my 1939 article was shaped to show how the eclectic doctrine of general equilibrium could take changes in factor supplies in its stride and by the index-number methods of revealed preference illustrate how the Haberlerian transformation curve could be generalized.

Even after the passage of twenty years, the final chapter seemed still to be lacking in the literature. And an interesting Danish criticism of my earlier paper's treatment of income distribution by Mr. Erling Olsen (1958) led me to defend the argument and at long last take up the thorough completion. This time there was no need to worry about the obsolete doctrine of opportunity cost; nor to use index numbers of revealed preference, since for better or worse this approach had already won its

This paper was originally published in *The Economic Journal* 72 (1962): 820–829. Also published in Jagdish Bhagwati, editor, *International Trade: Selected Readings*, Penguin Books, 1969.

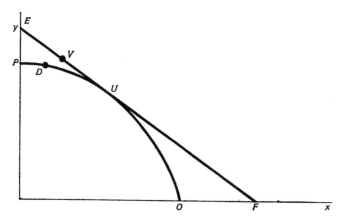

Figure 1. With no trade, we end up at D. With free trade, production ends up at U, consumption at V, with UV the vector of algebric imports.

place in the literature of economic theory. Good fortune, however, brought Dr. Murray Kemp to MIT as a visiting professor in 1959–61 on his way from Canada to a chair at the University of New South Wales. For, in discussing the present paper, Professor Kemp showed that my alternative approach of 1939 could indeed be carried through all the way to achieve the same final goals (Kemp, 1962). In a real sense, therefore, our two papers are complementary and benefit from simultaneous publication.

The Small Country Case

On the special assumption that our country under consideration is too small to affect its terms of trade, and on the assumption that the price ratios abroad differ from those that would prevail at home under autarky, figure 1's heavy line EUF represents our "consumption possibility frontier" with some trade. With autarky the consumption possibility frontier is given by the production locus $PDUQ$. Since the trade frontier lies everywhere[1] north-east of the autarky frontier, our society can have more of all goods (and less of all irksome inputs) with some trade. It is in this sense that trade makes us potentially better off.

An Important Envelope

I wish to increase the generality of my 1939 argument by now dropping the assumption that our country is small. Let us be large enough to affect

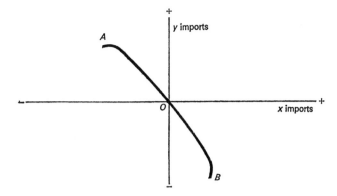

Figure 2. *AOB* is the familiar Marshallian offer curve of the rest of the world, but plotted in terms of our algebraic imports.

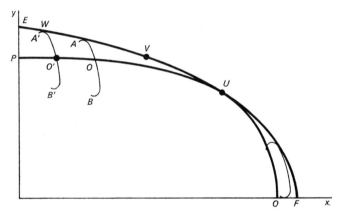

Figure 3. The important Baldwin envelope *EF* is generated by sliding *AOB* along *PO* in such a way as to trace out the frontier of consumable product. The slopes at *W* are necessarily equal to the slope at *O'*.

our terms of trade as we move along figure 2's Marshallian offer curve of the rest of the world for our two-goods.

Now draw up the envelope frontier[2] of figure 3 by sliding the origin of the AOB offer curve along the domestic production possibility locus PQ in such a way as to trace out the maximal amount of each good that is available for given amounts consumed of the other good.[3] The resulting envelope may be called society's *cum*-trade consumption possibility frontier. Like figure 1's EUF, of which it is a generalization, the new consumption frontier lies uniformly (save for one point like U) outside the autarky consumption frontier.[4] *Hence our society is potentially better off in the sense that there is a way of reallocating the enlarged totals of goods so as to make every person better off.*

It may be noted that the envelope frontier could be attained by an optimal Mill-Bickerdike tariff or by more direct means. The Kahn-Graaff paradox (Graaff, 1957, ch. 9) that the size of the optimal tariff depends only on foreigners' demand elasticity and not on home consumers' demand, is easily resolved as follows: the envelope's slope at any point like W is related to the slope of $O'W$ as determined by the AOB curve alone; but never forget that home demand must tell us *which* W will be the equilibrium one.

The Utility Possibility Frontier

Practical men and economic theorists have always known that trade may help some people and hurt others. Our problem is to show that trade lovers are theoretically able to compensate trade haters for the harm done them, thereby making everyone better off. The ordinal utility diagram of figure 4 is the natural tool to use for this purpose.[5]

The horizontal axis represents ordinal utility of one of our citizens. The vertical axis represents ordinal utility of a second citizen. And for simplicity I suppose there are only two citizens, or two classes of identical citizens in our country. A point represents the simultaneous position of both men: because utility need not be numerically measurable, only north and south and east and west relationships count.

The point d corresponds to point D of figure 1. The broken locus $d'dd''$ represents the utility possibility frontier if the fixed goods totals of D are allocated in favour of man 1 or man 2 by ideal-sum transfers so that there is no "inefficiency" or deadweight loss involved in the transfers. On the other hand, the envelope pq is generated by treating every point on PQ the way we have treated D and then drawing in the north-east frontier.

What is the envelope ef? It is the frontier traced out by *all* the points

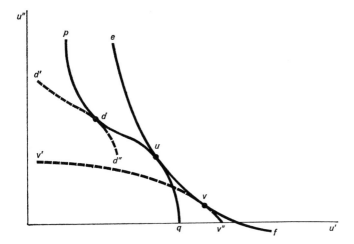

Figure 4. The *ef* social utility frontier lies outside the autarky frontier *pq*. But the *vv'* frontier corresponding to reallocation of the actual post-trade totals may well loop inside the autarky point. (Utilities being ordinal not cardinal, the curvatures of the loci are of no definite signs.)

on *EF*. Thus, it is tangential at *v* to the broken locus *v'vv''* representing the ideal reallocation of the goods at the post-trade point *V*. Since *EF* lies north-east of *PQ*, *ef* must obviously lie north-east of *pq*.[6]

Now let us carefully compare the pre-trade point *d* with a post-trade point *v*. Since *v* is south-east of *d*, it would be dangerous to say that trade has made the world better off: man 1 is better off, man 2 is worse off. But let us ideally reallocate the goods of *v*, moving north-west on *vv'* to compensate man 2. Can we in this way make both men better off? Mr. Olsen's reply would be—not necessarily. If I may translate his analysis into my terminology, he argues: The *v'v* locus of reallocation may pass north-east of the autarky point *d*, or it may pass south-west of that point.

I have no dispute with this last possibility. In fact, figure 4 is drawn with *vv'* passing below *d* so that the gainers from trade cannot (by reallocating the given totals) bribe the losers into acquiescing to trade.

But nothing in my 1939[7] or present arguments required that the compensation or bribing be possible out of *fixed totals*. What I was concerned to argue was that the *cum*-trade utility envelope frontier *ef*— not *vv'*—lay outside the autarky frontier *pq*. And this is true despite the Olsen contention.

As a matter of fact, imagine compensation beginning to take place at *v* and *V*. *This will automatically change the pattern of imports*, moving *v* north-westward on *ef* and moving *V* north-westward on *EF*. Where will the process end? If the losers are fully compensated—and my argument proves conclusively that they *can* be—the points v and V will be moved so far north-westward as to cause the Olsen effect to disappear necessarily. Thus, we end up north-east of d.

I hope no one will think that I advocate: (1) compensation, or (2) non-compensation. We need a Bergson social-welfare function to answer these questions, and I have always pointed out the illogic of those new welfare economists who used to try to reach normative conclusions on the basis of insufficient norms.

Scitovsky Collective Indifference Curves

In 1939, two years before Professor Tibor Scitovsky[8] introduced his collective indifference curves, I, of course, did not use them in my exposition. Nor have I yet used them here. But in that Olsen has used them, I ought to mention them briefly.

Through D in figure 1 (or as well in figure 3), Olsen would draw a Scitovsky indifference curve: this gives the minimum required totals of the goods needed to keep all men as well off as they actually were under autarky. Olsen then argues that the after-trade point V could conceivably lie *under* this Scitovsky curve, not above it. This I freely admit (as in my figure 4's passing of vv' below d).

But what do I need for my argument that some trade makes a society potentially better off in the sense of making it possible for all men to be made better off, the gainers being able to more than compensate the losers? Not that V lie above the D Scitovsky indifference curve, but rather the weaker, and inevitable, condition that the EF envelope frontier *somewhere* pass above the Scitovsky indifference curve. Figure 5 shows how inevitable this is, and how irrelevant the crossing of the V and D Scitovsky curves is.

Index Number Comparisons

Finally, let me review and extend the index-number type of argument used in my 1939 paper. For simplicity, I shall revert back to figure 1's case where the country is too small to affect its terms of trade.[9] In figures 1 and 5 the tangent line of the equilibrium point V contains U inside of it, and *a fortiori* because of the strong curvature of PQ it must contain D inside of it: in terms of index number comparisons,[10] this means

$$\sum P_V Q_V \geqslant \sum P_V Q_D.$$

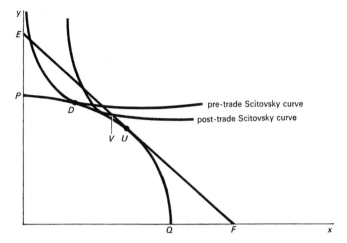

Figure 5. The Scitovsky community indifference curve of the actual post-trade configuration V may well pass above the community indifference curve of the actual autarky configuration D. But for the winners to be able ideally to compensate the losers requires only that UE cut somewhere above the autarky community indifference curve—as is always the case. The fact that the post-trade community indifference curve always passes above the autarky point means that trade satisfies the 1941 Scitovsky test for an improvement—namely, the losers from trade can never afford to bribe the trade gainers into unanimously repealing all trade.

If only a single individual or a "representative man" standing for identical citizens were involved we could, from the familiar economic theory of index numbers (see Samuelson, 1947, ch. 6), deduce that the post-trade point was "better than" the autarky point. Most of my 1939 paper dealt with this one-person case; and the remainder, to which Mr. Olsen's remarks all apply, was well advised not to use the index-number method.

What does the above index-number comparison mean when there are different men in our economy so that it must be written

$$\sum P_V(q_V' + q_V'' + \ldots) \geqslant \sum P_V(q_D' + q_D'' + \ldots),$$

and when we observe only the totals in parentheses?

Professor Hicks stated in 1940 a beautiful theorem (Hicks, 1940; Samuelson, 1950, pp. 7–10) that gives a partial answer. By it, the index-number comparison alone will tell us that the post-trade point v in figure 4 necessarily lies outside the autarky loci pq or dd''. Thus, Mr. Olsen's conclusion—which he derived in his last paragraph by perceiving that the Scitovsky collective indifference curve through V would have to lie outside the point D (and indeed outside all autarky points of PQ)—

follows: those hurt by trade are never able to bribe the trade winners into going back to autarky.

In terms of welfare economics, Mr. Olsen has proved that the post-trade situation satisfied the 1941 test (Scitovsky, 1941) added by Scitovsky to supplement the Kaldor-Hicks 1939 test that the gainers from trade— or any improvement—be capable of bribing the losers. Though Mr. Olsen has proved that the Scitovsky test holds, I believe he has not thereby shown that my proof of the Kaldor-Hicks tests' holding is faulty. Actually, my proof I deem satisfactory, and by it I establish something stronger— that an *infinity* of tests or comparisons between the pre-trade and post-trade utility frontiers show the latter to be the frontier farther out. (All this is specified at a glance in figure 4.)

In this sense trade makes a country potentially better off.

A Warning About Feasibility

What in the way of policy can we conclude from the fact that trade is a *potential* boon? As I pointed out in my 1950 paper, we can actually conclude very little.

To see this turn to figure 6, which is much like figure 4. Suppose the social-welfare function, if we knew it, "favoured" the man hurt by trade, man 2—as shown by the Bergson contours of welfare indifference. And suppose, as is the simple truth, that ideal lump-sum redistributions are never really available to us. Instead the only feasible redistributions must cause harmful substitution and other effects. Then the feasibility focus upon which we are free to move looks like the dotted curve in figure 6, *vg*, looping inside the *ef* frontier. Now it is quite possible that this feasibility locus might even loop inside the autarky point *d*. It evidently follows that, with the given Bergson contours, autarky is preferable to the post-trade situation—showing how difficult must be any rigorous interpretation of "potential" improvement.[11]

Conclusions

Rather than summarize what has been a lengthy argument, I shall simply stand by my earlier position and jot down some truths that are perhaps better understood today than twenty years ago.[12]

1. If the laws of returns were appropriate for perfect competition (no external effects, indivisibilities, monopolies, dynamic uncertainties, learning processes, etc.), free trade[13] and ideal transfers could be used to give

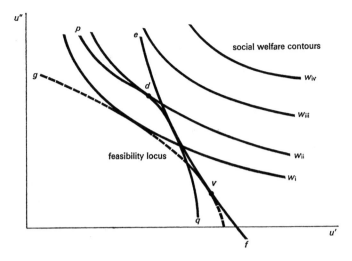

Figure 6. If lump-sum transfers are not feasible, so that vg rather than ef is the feasibility frontier, the highest social-welfare contour obtainable from free trade might be lower than that obtainable under autarky.

maximal *world* production in the sense of a farthest out world production possibility frontier.

2. Free trade and ideal transfers could give a similar maximal world utility frontier for all individuals.

3. Free trade will *not* necessarily maximize the real income or consumption and utility possibilities of *any one country*—even though by ideal bribes the international winning countries could bribe the losers into a unanimous vote for free trade.

4. Free trade will not necessarily maximize the income, consumption and utility possibilities of a *subset* of persons or factors within a country.

5. If all but one country will always trade freely it (almost) always pays that one country to behave monopolistically, imposing optimum Mill-Bickerdike tariffs or other interferences to take advantage of less-than-infinitely-elastic international demand.

6. Whatever the fixed pattern of tariffs abroad, it usually pays one country to introduce an optimum duty unilaterally. Some countries may then end up better off than under free trade; or perhaps none will end up better off. But never can *all* countries end up better off; and indeed, the losers from the tariff pattern can always theoretically offer the winners large enough ideal bribes to get rid of all tariffs and interferences with free trade.

7. Only at a point reachable by free trade would an international individualistic social welfare function be at its *maximum maximorum*.

8. For a given country, autarky cannot be optimal if ideal transfers are possible. Some trade is better than no trade in the sense of making the nation better off, with a farther out consumption-possibility frontier and farther out utility-possibility frontier.

If ideal lump-sum reallocations of income are not feasible the above conclusions need serious modification and qualification. The same is true when we introduce imperfections of competition, uncertainties, induced changes of an irreversible type and game-theoretic struggles for power and welfare.

Grateful acknowledgment is made to the Ford Foundation for research assistance.

References

Baldwin, R. E. (1948), "Equilibrium in international trade: a diagrammatic analysis", *Quarterly Journal of Economics*, vol. 62, pp. 748–62.

Baldwin, R. E. (1952), "The new welfare economics and gains in international trade", *Quarterly Journal of Economics*, vol. 65, pp. 91–101.

Baldwin, R. E. (1953–54), "A comparison of welfare criteria", *Review of Economic Studies*, vol. 21.

Boiteux, M. (1956), "Sur la question des Monopoles Publics astreints à l'équilibre budgétaire', *Econometrica*, vol. 24, pp. 22–40.

Graaff, J. de V. (1957), *Theoretical Welfare Economics*, Cambridge.

Hicks, J. R. (1940). "The valuation of social income", *Economica*, new series, vol. 7, pp. 105–24.

Kemp, M. C. (1962), "The gain from international trade", *Economic Journal*, vol. 72, pp. 803–19.

Kenen, P. B. (1957), "On the geometry of welfare economics", *Quarterly Journal of Economics*, vol. 71, pp. 426–7.

Lipsey, R. G. and Lancaster, R. K. (1956–7), "The general theory of the second best", *Review of Economic Studies*, vol. 24, pp. 11–32.

Little, I. M. D. (1957), *A Critique of Welfare Economics*, Oxford, 2nd edition.

Olsen, E. (1958), "Undenrigschandelens Gevinst", *Nationalokonomisk Tidskrift*, haefte 1–2, pp. 76–9.

Samuelson, P. A. (1938), "Welfare economics and international trade", *American Economic Review*, vol. 28, pp. 261–8.

Samuelson, P. A. (1939), "The gains from international trade", *Canadian Journal of Economic and Political Science*, vol. 5, pp. 195–205. (Reprinted in H. S. Ellis and L. A. Metzler, eds., *Readings on the Theory of International Trade*, Blakiston, 1949.)

Samuelson, P. A. (1947), *Foundations of Economic Analysis*, Harvard University Press.

Samuelson, P. A. (1950), "Evaluation of real national income", *Oxford Economic Papers*, new series, vol. 2, pp. 1–29.

Samuelson, P. A. (1956), "Social indifference curves", *Quarterly Journal of Economics*, vol. 70, pp. 1–22.

Scitovsky, T. (1941), "A note on welfare propositions in economics", *Review of Economic Studies*, vol. 8, pp. 77–88.

Scitovsky, T. (1941–42), "A reconstruction of the theory of tariffs", *Review of Economic Studies*, vol. 9, pp. 89–110. (Reprinted in H. S. Ellis and L. A. Metzler, eds., *Readings in the Theory of International Trade*, Blakiston, 1949.)

11

Optimal Trade Intervention in the Presence of Domestic Distortions

Harry G. Johnson

I. Introduction

In the period since the war, the concern of economists with the problems of the underdeveloped countries and the formulation of policies to stimulate economic development has led to renewed interest in the economic arguments for protection. I use the description 'economic arguments' to distinguish arguments that recommend protection as a means of increasing real income or economic welfare from arguments that recommend protection as a means of achieving such essentially non-economic objectives as increasing self-sufficiency for political and military reasons, diversifying the economy to provide a richer way of life for the citizenry and so strengthening national identity, or preserving a valued traditional way of life. In the first place, writers on economic development have taken over and made considerable use of the theory of the optimum tariff, originated by Bickerdike and revived in the 1940s and early 1950s as a by-product of the contemporary debate over the legitimacy of welfare propositions in economics. Secondly, writers in the economic development area have laid considerable stress on the traditional 'external economies' and 'infant industry' arguments for protection; in recent years they have also developed new, or at least heretofore not much emphasized, arguments for protection based on the alleged fact that in underdeveloped countries wages in manufacturing exceed the opportunity cost of labor in the economy—the marginal productivity of labor in the agricultural sector. Two distinct reasons for the alleged discrepancy between industrial wage rates and the opportunity costs of labor are

This paper was originally published in R. Caves, H. G. Johnson, P. B. Kenen, editors, *Trade, Growth and the Balance of Payment*, Rand McNally, 1965. Also published in Jagdish Bhagwati, editor, *International Trade: Selected Readings*, Penguin Books, 1969.

advanced, it not always being recognized that they are distinct. One, which can be associated with the name of Arthur Lewis (1954; 1958), is that industrial wages are related to earnings in the agricultural sector, and that these earnings are determined by the average product of labor, which exceeds the marginal product of labor because agricultural labor has familial or traditional claims on the rent of land. The other reason, associated with the name of Everett Hagen (1958) but equally attributable to Lewis (1954, pp. 150–51), is that the industrial wage rate exceeds the agricultural wage rate by a margin larger than can be explained by the economic costs of urban life;[1] this difference Hagen associates with the dynamic need for a growing economy to transfer labor from agriculture to industry, although it can also be explained by social influences on industrial wage determination.

The theory of the optimum tariff rests on the proposition that if a country possesses monopolistic or monopsonistic power in world markets, world market prices for its exports and imports will not correspond to the marginal national revenue from exports or marginal national cost of its imports, and asserts that by appropriately chosen export and import duties—taxes on trade—the country can equate the relative prices of goods to domestic producers and consumers with their relative opportunity costs in international trade. In other words, the theory of the optimum tariff rests on the existence of a distortion in international markets, viewed from the national standpoint, such that market prices diverge from opportunity costs; and the optimum tariff is recommended as a means of off-setting this distortion. The other economic arguments for protection, with which this paper is concerned, rest on the presence of distortions in the domestic economy, which create a divergence between domestic prices and domestic opportunity costs; in these arguments, protection is recommended as a means of offsetting the distortions that prevent domestic prices from reflecting domestic opportunity costs.

The purpose of this paper is to explain and elaborate on two propositions concerning arguments for protection derived from the existence or alleged existence of domestic distortions. The first proposition is that such distortions do not logically lead to the recommendation of protection, in the sense of taxes on international trade; instead, they lead to the recommendation of other forms of government intervention which do not discriminate between domestic and international trade and which differ according to the nature of the distortion they are intended to correct. The second proposition is that if protection is adopted as a means of correcting domestic distortions, not only will the result be that economic welfare will fall short of the maximum obtainable, but economic welfare may even be reduced below what it would be under a policy of free trade. These two propositions can be combined in the proposition that the only valid argument for protection as a means of maximizing economic welfare is the optimum tariff argument; all other arguments for protection of this kind are in principle arguments for some form of government intervention in the domestic economy, and lead to the recommendation of protection only when supported both by practical considerations that render the appropriate form of intervention unfeasible, and empirical evidence that protection will in fact increase economic welfare.

II. Definitions and Assumptions

As a preliminary to the development of the main theme, it is necessary to comment briefly on certain aspects of the setting of the problem and the definition of terms.

In the first place, it is necessary to define the word 'protection.' Economists generally use this word in a very loose sense, which carries the connotation of a tariff on imports but also lends itself to extension to any policy that raises the price received by domestic producers of an importable commodity above the world market price. Not only can the effect of a tariff be achieved in the modern world by other devices, such as import restrictions, exchange controls, and multiple exchange rates— devices which may achieve the effect of raising the domestic relative price of importable goods above their relative price in the world market by operating to restrict exports as well as to restrict imports—but the domestic relative price received by producers of importable goods can be raised above the world price by two quite different means—by raising the domestic price to both producers and consumers above the world price, through tariffs or equivalent devices, and by raising the domestic price to producers only above the world price, while leaving consumers free to buy at world prices, through subsidies on production or equivalent taxation of production of alternative products. These two means of raising prices to domestic producers above world prices differ sharply in their economic implications, as will appear from what follows, and the confusion of them in the loose usage of the term 'protection' has been responsible for serious analytical errors in the literature. In this paper, I confine the term 'protection' to policies that create a divergence between the relative prices of commodities to domestic consumers and producers, and their relative prices in world markets. This usage does not preclude anyone who wishes to describe policies of subsidizing domestic production by one means or another as protection from doing so, and interpreting my analysis as showing that production by subsidies is economically desirable in certain cases of domestic distortion, provided that he clearly distinguishes protection by subsidy from protection by tariff. It is perhaps worth noting in passing—though this is not part of the subject of this paper—that the identification of protection with the tariff is a potent source of confusion in other contexts than the relation of protection to economic welfare; for example, the degree of protection afforded to a particular industry by a tariff structure depends not only on the tariff rate on its product but on the tariffs and other taxes levied or subsidies paid both on its inputs and on the other goods that could be produced by the resources it uses;[2] and these complications include the effects of overvaluation or undervaluation of the exchange rate.

Second, it is necessary to be precise about the meaning attached to an improvement or deterioration in economic welfare. Disagreement on this question was the foundation of the classic debate between Gottfried Haberler and Thomas Balogh that followed on Haberler's attempt to analyse the issues discussed in this paper with the assistance of a criterion of improvement in welfare that has subsequently been shown to be objectionable (Haberler, 1950, 1951; Balogh, 1951). This paper employs the concept of welfare in the modern sense of potential welfare, and regards a change in the economic environment as producing a potential improvement in economic welfare if, in the new environment, everyone could be made better off—in the usual sense of enjoying a higher consumption of goods and services—than in the old environment, if income were distributed in accordance with any social welfare function applied consistently in the new and the old environment. This approach permits the use of community indifference curves to represent the potential welfare of the community. One might indeed go further and maintain that the assumption that some social welfare function exists and is implemented is essential to any rational discussion of national economic policy.

Third, it is assumed in this paper, in accordance with the conventions of theoretical analysis of these problems, that government intervention is a costless operation: in other words, there is no cost attached to the choice between a tax and a subsidy. This assumption ignores the empirical consideration, frequently introduced into arguments about protection, that poor countries have considerably greater difficulty in levying taxes to finance subsidies than they have in levying tariffs on imports. This consideration is of practical rather than theoretical consequence, and to constitute a case for tariffs requires supplementation by empirical measurement of both the relative administrative costs and the economic effects of the alternative methods of promoting favored industries—as has already been mentioned. Its relevance to practical policy-making is probably less than is frequently assumed, since on the one hand the intent of a protective tariff is not to yield revenue, and on the other hand the effect of a subsidy on one type of production can be achieved by taxes levied on alternative lines of production. The assumption also ignores the possibility that the income or other taxes levied to finance subsidies to production may have a distorting effect on the supply or allocation of resources. Abandonment of this assumption would also lead to the necessity of empirical assessment of the relative economic costs of alternative methods of promoting favored industries.

Finally, something should be said about the bearing of theoretical analysis of the arguments for protection on practical policy-making and the assessment of actual tariff systems. The demonstration that in certain carefully defined circumstances a tariff levied at a theoretically specified rate would make a country better off than it would be under free trade is not—contrary to the implication of many economic writings on protection—equivalent to a demonstration that past or present tariffs have in fact made the nations imposing them better off than they would have been under free trade, or a justification of whatever tariffs legislators might choose to adopt. Modern economic analysis of the cases in which a tariff or other governmental intervention in the price system would improve economic welfare, in other words, does not constitute a defense of indiscriminate protectionism and a rejection of the market mechanism; rather, it points to a number of respects in which the market mechanism fails to work as it should, and indicates remedies designed to make the market function properly. The usefulness of the exercise depends precisely on the assumption that legislators do not normally know what makes for improvement of economic welfare, and would be prepared to act on better information if it could be provided. If economists did not customarily accept this assumption, their work on economic policy would have to be oriented entirely differently; in particular, research on commercial policy would—depending on the theory of government adopted—be concerned with inferring from actual tariff structures either the divergences between social and private costs and benefits discovered by the collective wisdom of the legislators to exist in the economy, or the political power of various economic groups in the community, as measured by their capacity to extort transfers of income from their fellow-citizens.

III. The Two Propositions

With the preliminary definitions, assumptions, and observations established, I turn to the main theme of the paper, the two propositions concerning optimal government intervention in the presence of domestic distortions. The first proposition, that the correction of such distortions does not require intervention in the form of taxes on international trade (taxes here include negative taxes or subsidies), follows directly from the well-known first-order marginal conditions of Pareto optimality. These conditions specify that the marginal rate of substitution between goods in consumption should be equal to the marginal rate of transformation between goods in production, and in an open economy include transformation through international exchange as well as transformation through domestic production. It follows that any distortion that prevents market prices from corresponding to marginal social rates of substitution or transformation should be corrected by a tax, a subsidy, or a combination of taxes and subsidies that restores the necessary marginal equalities; for simplicity, it is convenient to consider the simplest remedy, a tax or subsidy imposed at the point where the distortion occurs. Where there is a distortion in foreign markets, owing to imperfectly elastic foreign demand or supply, Pareto optimality requires the imposition of taxes on trade designed to equate the domestic price ratios facing producers and consumers with the marginal rates of transformation between commodities in international trade—that is, the imposition of the optimum tariff structure.[3] In the case of domestic distortions, Pareto optimality requires the imposition of taxes or subsidies on consumption, production, or factor supply, as the situation requires.

Where externalities in consumption make social marginal rates of substitution diverge from private, taxes or subsidies on consumption are required; where external economies in production exist, or where monopolistic influences raise prices above marginal costs, marginal subsidies on production are required, and where external diseconomies are present, marginal taxes on production are required; and where the price of a factor in a particular occupation exceeds its price in other occupations by more than can be accounted for by the nonpecuniary disadvantages of that occupation, a subsidy on the use of that factor in that occupation is required. The point of central importance is that the correction of domestic distortions requires a tax or subsidy on either domestic consumption or domestic production or domestic factor use, not on international trade.

The imposition of any tax or subsidy on international trade, other than what is indicated by the optimum tariff analysis, for the purpose of correcting a domestic distortion, itself introduces an inequality between either the marginal rate of substitution in domestic consumption or the marginal rate of transformation in domestic production and the marginal rate of transformation in foreign trade, and so constitutes a violation of Pareto optimality. A tax on luxury imports, for example, designed to discourage an undesirable demonstration effect and therefore to correct an external diseconomy of consumption, permits the marginal rate of transformation of domestic resources into the importable good in question to exceed the marginal rate of transformation through foreign trade. A tax on imports or subsidy to exports of goods subject to external economies or monopolistic pricing in domestic production, designed to offset these distortions, makes the relative marginal cost of these goods to consumers higher than their marginal cost to the economy. Since the offsetting of domestic distortions by taxes or subsidies on trade necessarily removes one distortion at the expense of introducing another, interventions in international trade introduced for this purpose cannot lead to a situation of Pareto optimality. Consequently, tariffs and other trade interventions justified on grounds of the existence of domestic distortions cannot lead to the maximization of real income. The only forms of intervention that can do so are interventions that offset the existing distortions without introducing new distortions; such interventions are confined to taxes and subsidies on domestic consumption, production, or factor use.

The second proposition, that taxes or subsidies on international trade designed to offset domestic distortions will not necessarily increase economic welfare by comparison with the free trade situation, is a direct application of the theory of second best developed by Meade, Lipsey and Lancaster, and others (Meade, 1955; Lipsey and Lancaster, 1956–57). One implication of that theory is that it is impossible to predict on *a priori* grounds—that is, without comprehensive empirical information on the tastes and technology of the economy—whether the substitution of one violation of the Pareto optimality conditions for another will worsen or improve economic welfare. Since the use of intervention in trade to offset domestic distortions necessarily involves precisely this kind of substitution, it is impossible to say whether the result will be an improvement in welfare or not. For example, in the consumption externality case mentioned above, free trade produces the result $MRT_d = MRT_f > MRS$; and an import tariff produces the result $MRT_d > MRT_f = MRS$. In the case of external economies in production or monopolistic pricing, free trade produces the result $MRT_d < MRT_f = MRS$, and an import tariff produces the result $MRT_d = MRT_f < MRS$. In the case of a distortion in the market for factors, there are additional violations of the Pareto optimality conditions in the factor markets under both free trade and protection.[4]

The remainder of the paper is concerned with illustrating these propositions by reference to various arguments for protection. For this purpose, it is convenient to follow the general outline of Haberler's classic article (1950), modified to include fuller treatment of the arguments emphasized in the recent literature on underdeveloped countries, and to divide the arguments for protection into four groups. These are: arguments derived from immobility of factors and downward rigidity of factor prices; arguments derived from distortions in commodity markets; arguments derived from distortions in factor markets; and the infant industry argument. The first class of argument, to which Haberler devoted considerable space, grew out of the unemployment problem of the 1930s and the associated revival of protectionism. The second includes both the classical problems of external economies and diseconomies, and the problem of monopolistic distortions to which considerable attention was devoted in the 1930s following the development of the theory of monopolistic (imperfect) competition. The third involves the essential elements of the new case for protection developed on the basis of the disequilibrium in the labor market alleged to be characteristic of underdeveloped countries. The fourth is, of course, the orthodox accepted exception to the case for free trade.

IV. The Standard Trade Model

To provide a frame of reference for the analysis of these arguments, it is convenient to use the standard model of international trade. This model simplifies the problem by assuming that the economy produces two commodities only, by employing only two factors of production, the available quantities of which are assumed to be given; the production functions for the two commodities are assumed to be subject to constant returns to scale, an assumption which eliminates externalities in production; and perfect competition is assumed in the commodity and factor markets, which assumption includes perfect flexibility of prices and mobility of factors between industries. These assumptions permit the production conditions of the economy to be summarized in a community transformation curve between the two commodities, such that at any exchange ratio between the commodities production will be represented by the point on the transformation curve at which the slope of that curve is equal to the exchange ratio. On the demand side, factor owners are assumed to be indifferent between occupations—utility depends only on the quantities of goods consumed—and consumers' welfare is assumed to depend only on personal consumption, which assumption eliminates externalities in consumption. (Such consumption externalities are ignored in the remainder of this paper, since they have not been advanced as an important argument for protection, and the relevant analysis follows directly from the proposition already presented, and from analogy with the cases of production distortion dealt with below.) The individual tastes and distribution of income that determine the demand for the two commodities are assumed to be summarizable in a set of community indifference curves, such that for any given income and exchange ratio the consumption of the two commodities will be that which places the community on the highest attainable indifference curve. Since in a competitive economy the distribution of income depends on the distribution of factor ownership and varies with factor prices, the set of community indifference curves has to be interpreted as embodying either the concept of potential welfare employed in modern welfare economics, or the expression of a particular social welfare function in a particular invariant distribution of income among the members of the community. The conclusions concerning the effects of alternative types of government intervention on economic welfare derived below are to be interpreted as referring to welfare in either of these two senses. Since the concern of the paper is with government intervention in the presence of domestic distortions, it is convenient to exclude distortions in foreign markets by assuming that the opportunity to trade internationally consists in the opportunity to exchange goods in the world market at an exchange ratio different from that which would rule in the economy in the absence of the opportunity to trade, which international exchange ratio is assumed to be independent of the direction or magnitude of the trade of the country under analysis. The two commodities will be referred to as X and Y, and it is assumed throughout that the country's true comparative advantage lies in Y, in the sense that the comparative cost of Y in the absence of the opportunity to trade is lower than the comparative cost of Y embodied in the international exchange ratio.

This standard model of international trade is represented in the accompanying figure 1, where TT is the transformation curve and U_0, U_1, U_2 are the community indifference curves. In the absence of the opportunity to trade, the community would produce and consume at P, C, the closed-economy exchange ratio between the goods being represented by

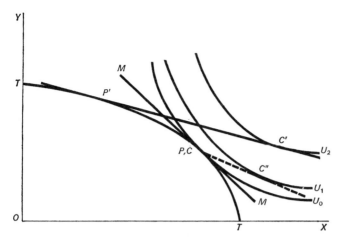

Figure 1

the slope of the common tangent MM to the transformation and indifference curves at that point. The opportunity to trade (represented by the slope P' C') allows the economy to increase its welfare from U_0 to U_2, by shifting from production and consumption at P, C to production at P' and consumption at C'. The gain in welfare resulting from trade can be divided into two components: the increase in welfare from U_0 to U_1 resulting from the opportunity to exchange the goods produced in the absence of trade for the more attractive consumption combination C''—the consumption or exchange gain; and the increase in welfare from U_1 to U_2 resulting from the opportunity to produce a combination of goods more valuable at the international price ratio than the closed-economy output—the production or specialization gain. The adjustment to the higher international price of Y necessarily involves an increase in the relative price of the factor used relatively intensively in producing that commodity, and a reduction in the relative price of the factor used relatively intensively in producing the importable commodity X.

V. Factor Immobility and Price Rigidity

For the analysis of arguments for protection derived from immobility of factors and downward rigidity of factor prices, it is convenient to pose the problem in terms of whether the opening of the opportunity to trade makes a country worse off when these conditions exist, so that a prohibitive tariff would secure a higher level of welfare than could be attained under free trade, even though in reality the argument for protection on these grounds usually arises when trade is already established and the international price of imports suddenly falls. The difference of assumptions merely simplifies the problem without altering the conclusions.

As Haberler has shown, there is a fundamental difference between the effects of immobility of factors, combined with flexibility of factor prices, and of downward rigidity of factor prices, whether combined with immobility or not. As the analysis of the standard model of trade shows, the country would enjoy a consumption or exchange gain from trade even if production remained at the closed-economy equilibrium point. Production would remain at that point if factors were completely immobile but their prices were perfectly flexible; if factors were partially mobile, production would shift to some point within the transformation curve but necessarily entailing a higher value of production at world market prices, that is, yielding some production or specialization gain. It follows that so long as factor prices are flexible, immobility of factors cannot prevent the country from being better off under free trade than with protection. The fundamental reason for this is that immobility does not by itself entail a distortion of the first-order conditions of Pareto optimality. So long as factor prices are flexible, and immobility is taken as an immutable fact of life (more is said on this point below), factor prices will reflect the alternative opportunity costs of factors to the economy; hence there is no domestic distortion to be offset by protection, and protection will simply introduce a distortion of the marginal conditions for optimality in foreign trade.

Downward rigidity of factor prices does introduce a distortion, if (as Haberler has carefully pointed out) such rigidity does not reflect a perfectly elastic supply of the factor in question (derived, for example, from an infinite elasticity of substitution between leisure and consumption) but instead reflects institutional limitations on voluntary choice (imposed, for example, by conventional pricing of labor services or collective bargaining).[5] Analysis of the effects of downward rigidity of factor prices requires definition of the terms in which factor prices are rigid downwards, since factor prices may be rigid in terms of one commodity or the other or of the utility level enjoyed, and consideration of various possible combinations of downward price rigidity and immobility.

If factor prices are rigid in terms of X and both factors are immobile, production will remain where it was in the absence of trade (at point P in figure 2). The result will be the same as with factor price flexibility, since the marginal productivities of the factors in the X industry in terms of X are unchanged, while the marginal productivities of the factors in the Y industry are unchanged in terms of Y but greater in terms of X, because

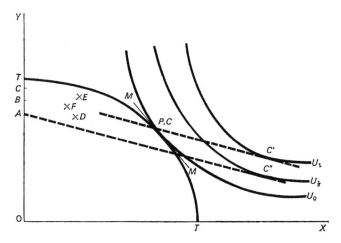

Figure 2

the price of X in terms of Y has fallen as a result of trade. If both factor prices are rigid in terms of Y or of constant-utility combinations of X and Y, and both factors are immobile, production of X will cease, and both factors used in producing X will become wholly unemployed (the economy will produce at point A in figure 2, level with P, C). This result follows from the fact that the marginal productivities of the factors in the X industry will be unchanged in terms of X but lower in terms of Y or any combination of X and Y, because the price of X in terms of Y has decreased as a result of trade. Since the value of each factor's marginal product is now below its price when the factors are combined in the ratio optimal at these factor prices, and since neither factor price can change to induce factor substitution and raise the marginal productivity of the other factor, the cost of production of X must exceed its price at any positive level of output.

  If both factor prices are rigid (in terms of X or of Y or of a constant-utility combination of X and Y), and both factors are perfectly mobile, production of X will cease and factors will be transferred into production of Y. Some of the factor used intensively in producing X must, however, become unemployed, so that production of Y will be less than the maximum possible production shown by the transformation curve, since full employment of both factors necessitates a reduction of the price of that factor in terms of both commodities, according to the well-known Stolper-Samuelson analysis (1941). The amount of unemployment of the factor in question will be greater, and the increase in production of Y less, if factor prices are rigid in terms of Y than if they are rigid in terms of X, since a given factor price expressed in Y now buys more X, and the marginal productivity of the surplus factor in the Y industry can fall if factor prices are rigid in terms of X but not if they are rigid in terms of Y. (The extremes are represented for illustrative purposes by points B and C in figure 2: if factor prices are rigid in terms of utility, production of Y will fall somewhere between these points.)

If both factors are immobile but the price of one of them is flexible, whereas the price of the other is rigid in terms of Y or of a constant-utility combination of X and Y, production of X will not cease altogether; instead, enough of the rigid-priced factor in that industry will become unemployed to lower its ratio to the other factor to what is consistent with its rigid price. Obviously, the unemployment of that factor and the decrease in production of X will be greater if that factor's price is rigid in terms of Y than if it is rigid in terms of a constant-utility combination of X and Y, and in the latter case will be less the less important is Y in the factor's consumption. (This case is represented in figure 2 by the single point D, in the same horizontal line as A and P, C.) If one of the factors is mobile, and its price is rigid in terms of X or of a constant-utility combination of X and Y, whereas the other factor is immobile and flexible-priced, some of the rigid-priced factor will transfer to the Y industry, increasing output there. The transfer will proceed to the point where its effect in raising the ratio of the mobile factor to the other in the Y industry lowers the marginal productivity of the mobile factor in the Y industry to the level set by its price rigidity. (This case is represented by point E in figure 2; E may be vertically above D as in the diagram or to the left of it, and must correspond to a higher value of output at world prices than D.) If one of the factors is mobile and flexible-priced, whereas the other factor is immobile and its price is rigid in terms of X or of Y or of a constant-utility combination of X and Y, production of Y will increase and of X decrease as compared with the case of immobility of both factors; production of X may or may not cease entirely depending on the elasticities of substitution between the factors in the two industries and on the terms in which the immobile factor's price is rigid. (This case is represented by point F in the diagram, and may or may not correspond to a higher value of output than at D.)

Whatever the combination of factor immobility and factor price rigidity assumed, production will be altered to some point in the interior of the transformation curve corresponding to production of less X and possibly no more Y than in the closed-economy equilibrium (except for the extreme case of complete immobility and factor price rigidity in terms of X already noted). This does not, however, necessarily imply that free trade makes the country worse off than it would be under the self-sufficiency obtainable by a prohibitive tariff. It may, or it may not. Figure 2 illustrates the possibility of the country's being better off with free trade than with a prohibitive tariff even in the extreme case in which production of X ceases altogether, with no consequent increase in the production of Y, owing to a combination of complete factor immobility with factor price rigidity. In this case, as the diagram shows, the country could be made still better off than under free trade by subsidizing production of the initial output of X sufficiently to permit the factors being paid the minimum prices they demand, but trading at the international exchange ratio. In the less extreme cases, more complex forms of subsidy may be necessary to achieve the output combination that has the highest value at the international exchange ratio attainable under the relevant restrictions on factor mobility.

VI. Distortions in the Commodity Market

The second group of arguments for protection to be discussed comprises arguments derived from the existence of distortions in the markets for commodities that have the effect of raising the market price of the commodity in which the country has a comparative advantage above its alternative opportunity cost. One possibility is the presence of monopoly or oligopoly conditions in the production of the good, which have the effect of raising the price to consumers above the marginal cost of production. Another is the presence of external economies or diseconomies, which make marginal cost as it appears to producers higher than marginal social cost. The marginal social cost of increased output of a particular commodity may be lower than the marginal private cost because expansion of the industry producing it yields economies of scale external to the individual firm, or because contraction of the industry from which this industry draws its factors of production lowers costs of production in the former because that industry is subject to diseconomies of scale, or because expansion of the one industry lowers the cost of production of the other through any one of a variety of effects.

The result of either type of distortion, in terms of the simple model of international trade, is that the market price ratio at which a particular combination of X and Y will be produced will be less steep than the slope of the transformation curve, reflecting the assumption that the relative price of Y (the good in which the country is assumed to have a comparative advantage) exceeds its social opportunity cost. In the absence of the opportunity to trade, the country will therefore in equilibrium produce

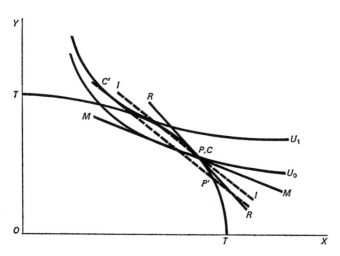

Figure 3

more X and less Y than would be socially optimal; the closed-economy
equilibrium is represented in figure 3 by the point P, C, the slope of MM
corresponding to the market price ratio and that of RR to the true comparative cost ratio. The opening of the opportunity to trade at an international price ratio at which the country's true comparative advantage lies
in Y has two alternative possible results, according to the relation between
the international price ratio and the closed-economy market price ratio:
this relation may indicate either an apparent comparative advantage in
X, in which case the country specializes in the wrong direction, or an
apparent comparative advantage in Y corresponding to the country's
true comparative advantage, in which case the country specializes in the
right direction but to a suboptimal extent.

The first case is represented in figure 3 by the international price ratio
II, which leads the country to the production equilibrium P' and the
consumption equilibrium C', involving the export of X, in which the
country is at a true comparative disadvantage. The point P' necessarily
represents a lower value of output at the international price ratio than
the closed-economy production point P; but C' may lie on either a lower
indifference curve than the closed-economy consumption point C, or a
higher one, the latter possibility being illustrated in the diagram. In other
words, trade leads to a production loss and a consumption gain, and the
latter may or may not offset the former.

The argument for protection in this case is that the country will gain
by imposing a tariff on imports to raise their price to consumers above

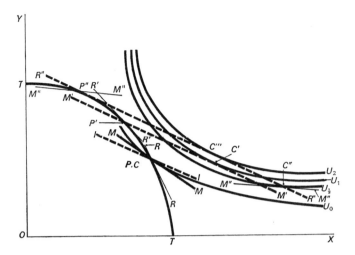

Figure 4

the world price, compensating for the distortion that makes the apparent cost of domestically produced importables exceed their true social cost. (Alternatively, the country could levy a tax on exports to compensate for the distortion that makes their true social cost exceed their apparent cost.) Since the country's true comparative advantage lies in the good it imports, the imposition of an import tariff (or an export duty) at a rate just sufficient to compensate for the distortion would effect a return to self-sufficiency at the production and consumption equilibrium P, C, since a tax on trade cannot reverse the direction of trade. The effect of the tariff would be to increase the value of the country's output at the international price ratio; but, as the diagram exemplifies, the resulting pattern of consumption might yield a lower level of economic welfare than would be attained in the absence of protection. In short, the imposition of the tariff to correct the distortion of domestic prices from opportunity costs achieves a production gain at the expense of a consumption loss, and the net-effect may be a gain or a loss, by comparison with free trade. Thus free trade in the wrong direction may be superior to protection designed to correct a distortion of domestic market prices; which policy is actually superior depends on the magnitudes of the distortion of domestic prices from opportunity costs and the difference between the closed-economy exchange ratio and the international exchange ratio, and the shape of the community's preference system.[6]

The second case is illustrated in figure 4, where at the international price ratio II the country's apparent comparative advantage lies in the commodity in which it has a true comparative advantage, and the opportunity to trade leads to the production equilibrium P' and consumption equilibrium C', involving the export of commodity Y. P' necessarily represents a higher value of national output at the international exchange ratio than the closed-economy production point P, so that the country enjoys both a consumption gain and a production gain from trade; but the volume of international trade falls short of the optimum level, owing to the excess of the price of Y over its comparative cost.

In this case, the arguments for intervention in international trade to correct the distortion of domestic prices would indicate an export subsidy on Y (or import subsidy on X). The same policy might be recommended to overcome the inability of the tariff to promote exports in the circumstances of the case previously considered. (In either case, to be effectively a subsidy on trade rather than on production, the export subsidy would have to be accompanied by measures preventing reimportation.) The introduction of such a subsidy at a rate just sufficient to offset the distortion would lead to the production equilibrium P'' and consumption equilibrium C'' shown in figure 4, the new domestic price ratio being represented by $M''\,M''$. The subsidy would necessarily raise the value of output at the international exchange ratio above what it would be under free trade, but, as the diagram illustrates, it might nevertheless lead to a consumption pattern yielding a lower level of welfare than that enjoyed under free trade, owing to the consumption loss induced by the effect of the subsidy in raising the domestic relative price of the exported good Y above the world market price. In order to achieve the maximum attainable economic welfare (C''' in figure 4), the country should subsidize production of Y (or tax production of X) at a rate sufficient to compensate for the domestic distortion, without discriminating between domestic and foreign consumers by a tax (in the first case) or subsidy (in the second case) on international trade.[7]

One further comment on arguments for governmental intervention derived from distortions in domestic commodity markets is worth making. The foregoing analysis lumps together distortions originating in external economies and diseconomies, and distortions originating in imperfectly competitive market organization; and it assumes that the distortions are independent of the governmental intervention, so that intervention can be designed to offset them. This assumption is legitimate for the first type of distortion, but of doubtful validity for the second. Monopolistic practices are generally intimately interrelated with commercial policy, and there is reason to believe that producers often collude to exploit the profit opportunities created by protection. Where this is so, the attempt to offset monopolistic distortions by protective interventions in trade (taxes or subsidies on trade) may well be offset by increased distortions, so that intervention generates a consumption loss without a countervailing production gain; the same reaction could render nugatory the attempt to employ optimal intervention in the form of production taxes or subsidies. In these circumstances, the only effective means of achieving maximum economic welfare would be a direct attack on the source of the distortion, through trust-busting policies, although it is worth noting that genuine free trade may be the most effective policy for controlling monopoly.

VII. Distortions in the Factor Market

The third group of arguments for protection comprises arguments derived from the existence of distortions in the markets for factors that, by raising the price of a factor used in producing the commodity in which the country has a comparative advantage above the factor's marginal productivity in the rest of the economy, raises the private cost of production of the commodity above its alternative opportunity cost. As mentioned, two reasons for such a distortion are commonly advanced in the literature on economic development, both of which pertain to a distortion in the labor market and are used to favor protection of industry—that earnings of labor in agriculture exceed the marginal productivity of labor there, so that the industrial wage must exceed the alternative opportunity cost of labor, and that industrial wages exceed wages in agriculture by a margin greater than can be accounted for by the disutility or higher cost of urban life.

The effect of such distortions in factor markets is twofold: first, they make the allocation of factors between industries inefficient, so that production is below the maximum attainable–in terms of the model of international trade, the transformation curve is pulled in toward the origin, except at the extreme points of specialization on one or the other commodity. Second, they will normally cause the market exchange ratio between the commodities to differ from the social opportunity cost ratio, the only exception occurring when a distortion in the market for one factor is exactly offset by an opposite distortion in the market for the others. In particular, if the marginal productivity of one particular factor in one industry must exceed its marginal productivity in the other, the price of the commodity produced by the former industry must exceed its opportunity cost. Consequently, in this case the country's economic welfare will be below the maximum attainable, both in the absence of the opportunity to trade and under free trade, for two reasons: first, the country will be on a transformation curve inferior to the transformation curve that would be available to it in the absence of the distortion in the factor market; and second, owing to the discrepancy between private costs of production and social costs in the commodity market resulting from the distortion in the factor market, the country will choose a suboptimal position on the restricted transformation curve available to it.

Given the existence of a distortion in the market for a factor requiring its marginal productivity to be higher in the industry in which the country has a comparative advantage, the opportunity to trade may have either of the two consequences analysed in connection with distortions in the commodity markets; and, as demonstrated in that analysis, the protectionist policy of remedying the effects of the distortion by an export or import duty (if the country specializes on the commodity in which it has a comparative disadvantage) or an export or import subsidy (if the country specializes on the commodity in which it has a comparative advantage) may make the country either worse off or better off than it would be under free trade. A policy of subsidization of production of the commodity overpriced by the distortion, or of taxation of production of the other commodity, would maximize the economic welfare attainable from the restricted transformation curve. The important point, however, is that all of these policies aimed at offsetting the distortion by operating on the prices received by producers of commodities would leave the country on a transformation curve restricted by the inefficiency of factor use induced by the factor market distortion. This particular cause of suboptimal economic welfare could be eliminated in four different ways —by a tax on the use in one industry or subsidy on the use in the other of either factor, the rate of tax or subsidy being chosen to exactly offset the distortion. But only two of these—a subsidy on the use of the factor subject to distortion in the industry in which its marginal productivity is required to be higher, or a tax on its use in the other industry—would simultaneously eliminate the associated distortion of commodity prices from opportunity costs, the other two accentuating the distortion in the commodity market. Thus the attainment of maximum economic welfare in this case requires subsidization or taxation of the use of the factor subject to distortion; taxation or subsidization of commodity production can maximize welfare subject to the inefficiency of factor use but cannot correct that inefficiency; taxation or subsidization of commodity trade not only fails to eliminate inefficiency in factor allocation but may even reduce welfare, given the inefficiency of factor allocation, below what it would be under free trade.

The foregoing argument has accepted the validity of the contention that in underdeveloped countries there is a distortion in the labor market such that the marginal productivity of labor in industry must be higher than the marginal productivity of labor in agriculture (the alternative opportunity cost of labor). Before leaving this group of arguments for protection, it is appropriate to express some doubts about the validity of this contention and its implications for economic policy. As already mentioned, there are two separate arguments supporting this contention —that industrial wages exceed agricultural wages, and that industrial wages are comparable to agricultural earnings but that the latter exceed the marginal productivity of labor in agriculture because agricultural workers claim a share of agricultural rent.

So far as the first argument is concerned, the mere fact that industrial wages exceed agricultural wages is not sufficient to prove a distortion, since the difference may be accounted for by the higher cost of disutility of urban living, the greater skill or stamina required of urban industrial labor, or the economic cost of migration, factors which necessitate compensation in the form of a higher industrial than agricultural wage if allocation of the labor force is to be efficient. An attempt to iron out wage differences due to these factors would involve misallocation of labor. There are, however, two plausible reasons for believing that observed industrial-agricultural wage differences may entail a genuine distortion.[8] The first is that frequently in underdeveloped countries either trade union organization or social legislation and popular sentiment impose industrial wage levels well above the alternative opportunity cost of labor; this possibility is substantiated by the evidence of persistent large-scale urban unemployment, and by the fact that wage levels tend to increase with size of establishment. In so far as trade union organization or political pressure forces industry to pay wages above the alternative opportunity cost of labor, however, any attempt to remedy the distortion by subsidization of the use of labor or by protection might be frustrated by the exaction of still higher wages. The second reason is suggested by an interpretation of migration from rural to urban employment as an investment in the formation of human capital, the investment involving both a transportation and an education cost; insofar as the market for capital to finance investment in human beings is imperfect, the marginal rate of return on such investment may be far higher than the social opportunity cost of capital to the economy.

So far as the second reason for distortion is concerned—the excess of agricultural earnings over the marginal productivity of agricultural labor —since this implies that the private return on capital invested in agriculture is less than the social return, the distortion in the labor market may be more than offset by an opposite distortion in the capital market, so that rather than indicating the desirability of subsidization of the use of labor in industry, this argument may in fact indicate the desirability of subsidization of the use of capital in agriculture.

VIII. The Infant Industry Argument

The fourth type of argument for protection to be considered is the infant industry argument. Although this argument is frequently confused, at least in description, with the 'external economies' argument, the two are logically distinct. The external economies argument is static, in the sense that the assumed distortion due to external economies or diseconomies is by implication a permanent characteristic of the technology of production that would require correction by government intervention of a permanent kind. The infant industry argument, by contrast, is explicitly dynamic or more accurately an argument for temporary intervention to correct a transient distortion, the justification for protection being assumed to disappear with the passage of time.

The infant industry argument bases the case for temporary protection on the assertion that the industry in question (or, more commonly in the literature on economic development, manufacturing in general) would eventually be able to compete on equal terms with foreign producers in the domestic or world market if it were given temporary tariff protection to enable it to establish itself, but would be unable to establish itself against free competition from established foreign producers owing to the temporary excessive costs it would have to incur in the initial stages. Since the incurring of costs for a limited period in return for future benefits is a type of investment, the infant industry argument is essentially an assertion that free competition would produce a socially inefficient allocation of investment resources. For the argument to be valid, it is not sufficient to demonstrate that present costs, in the form of losses on production in the infancy of the industry, must be incurred for the sake of future benefits in the form of higher income than would otherwise be earned. For if the higher income accrues to those who incur the costs, and the capital market functions efficiently, the investment will be privately undertaken unless the rate of return on it is below the rate of return available on alternative investments, in which case the investment would be socially as well as privately unprofitable. To provide an argument for government intervention, it must be demonstrated either that the social rate of return exceeds the private rate of return on the investment, or that the private rate of return necessary to induce the investment exceeds the private and social rates of return available on alternative investment, by a wide enough margin to make a socially profitable investment privately unprofitable.

The social rate of return on investment in an infant industry may exceed the private rate of return for a variety of reasons, of which two may be of particular relevance to the problems of underdeveloped countries (Kemp, 1960). One relates to the fact that, once created, the product of investment in the acquisition of knowledge, unlike the product of material investments, can be enjoyed by additional users without additional cost of production. In other words, once knowledge of production technique is acquired, it can be applied by others than those who have assumed the cost of acquiring it; the social benefit at least potentially exceeds the private benefit of investment in learning industrial production techniques, and the social use of the results of such learning may even reduce the private reward for undertaking the investment. Where the social benefits of the learning process exceed the private benefits, the most appropriate governmental policy would be to subsidize the learning process itself, through such techniques as financing or sponsoring pilot enterprises on condition that the experience acquired and techniques developed be made available to all would-be producers. The other reason why the social benefit may exceed the private hinges on the facts that much of the technique of production is embodied in the skill of the labor force, and that the institutions of the labor market give the worker the property rights in any skills he acquires at the employer's expense. Consequently, the private rate of return to the employer on the investment in on-the-job training may be lower than the social rate of return, because the trained worker may be hired away by a competitor. The appropriate policy in this case would entail the government either financing on-the-job training or establishing institutions enabling labor to finance its own training out of the higher future income resulting from training.[9] In either of the two cases just described a subsidy on production or on investment in the infant industry would in principle be economically inefficient, since neither type of subsidy would necessarily stimulate the type of investment in knowledge subject to an excess of social over private return.

The private rate of return necessary to induce investment in infant industries may also exceed the private and social rates of return on alternatively investments for a variety of reasons. Entrepreneurs may be excessively pessimistic about the prospects of success, or unwilling to take chances; in this case the most appropriate policy would involve publication of expert estimates of the prospects for the industries in question. Alternatively, imperfections in the capital market may make the cost of finance for investment in new industries excessively high, especially if these industries require an initially large scale for economical production by the firm; in this case, subsidization of provision of capital would be the appropriate policy.

Whatever the distortion in the allocation of investment capital used to support the infant industry argument for protection, it is apparent from the general principles governing optimal governmental intervention in the presence of domestic distortions that the optimal policy entails some sort of subsidy to the infant industries, rather than protection. Where infant industry distortions exist, protection justified by their presence may have the effect of reducing economic welfare rather than raising it. The reason is that protection increases the social cost of the investment in the learning process of the infant industry, by adding to the cost of a transitional subsidy the consumption cost of protection; the additional cost may be sufficient to reduce the social rate of return on the investment below the social rate of return on alternative investments.

It has been mentioned above that, for the infant industry argument to justify government intervention, investment in the learning process of the infant industry must be socially profitable. This requirement implies that the customary formulations of both the infant industry argument and the most potent argument used against it are seriously defective. The customary formulation argues that there is a case for protection on infant industry grounds if the industry could eventually compete in the domestic or world market without protection. This argument is invalid because protection involves a present cost which can only be justified economically by an increase in future income above what it would otherwise be; and a necessary condition for this is that the infant industries should eventually be able to compete while paying higher returns to the factors they employ than those factors would have enjoyed if the infant industries had not been assisted to maturity by protection. The most potent argument against infant industry protection is that the infant industries in fact never grow up but instead continue to require protection. The argument overlooks the possibility that, although the continuance of protection is a political fact, it is not always an economic necessity: protection may be continued even though intramarginal firms or units of production do not require it, and the country may gain from infant industry protection even though such protection continues indefinitely. The possibility of such a gain is illustrated in figure 5, where as a result of infant industry protection the transformation curve shifts outwards from TT to TT', and the community as a consequence enjoys the welfare

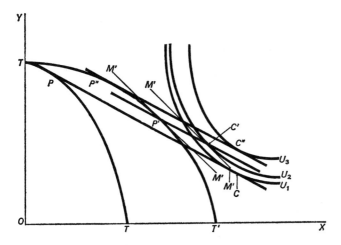

Figure 5

level U_2 in place of the welfare level U_1 in the long run. If the cost of protection, in terms of a lower welfare level in the period of transition from TT to TT', is low enough, the increase in welfare from U_1 to U_2 great enough, and the social rate of return required to justify the investment low enough, the eventual welfare level U_2 may be superior to the eventual welfare level U_1, even though U_2 is inferior to the welfare level U_3 that could be enjoyed if the infant industry tariff were removed once it had served it purpose.

IX. Conclusion: Noneconomic Arguments for Protection

This paper has been concerned with elaborating on two propositions concerning arguments for protection based on the alleged existence of domestic distortions creating a divergence between marginal private and marginal social benefits or costs. These are that welfare maximization requires a correction of the relevant domestic distortion by an appropriate tax or subsidy on production, consumption, or factor use, and not a tax or subsidy on international trade; and that, given the presence of a domestic distortion, protection designed to offset it may decrease welfare rather than increase it. In conclusion, it is appropriate to comment on two further matters, the reasons why economists who admit the need for correction of domestic distortions are so prone to concede the argument for tariffs in these cases, and the bearing of the analysis on noneconomic arguments for protection.

The explanation for the propensity of economists to concede the argument for protection rather than present the case for more appropriate and theoretically reliable remedies seems to lie in two factors—the tendency of economists when confronted with policy problems to ignore the rather elusive principle of consumers' sovereignty and to adopt the apparently but illusively firmer welfare criterion of an increase in the value of production, and the historical emphasis of the theory of international trade on the real cost approach to economic welfare as contrasted with the opportunity cost approach, an emphasis ultimately derived from the labor theory of value. The latter emphasis has been a major source of weakness in the theoretical analysis of contemporary international trade problems, both in connection with the theory of tariffs and in connection with the more recently evolved theory of customs unions and discriminatory tariff reduction.

While this paper has concentrated on the economic arguments for protection—specifically, on arguments for protection as a means of correcting domestic distortions leading to inequalities between marginal social and marginal private costs or benefits—the analysis does have some important implications for what have been described in the introduction as noneconomic arguments for protection.[10] Such arguments stress the non-economic value of changes in production and consumption or resource allocation patterns achieved by protection. Conceptually, they can be divided into arguments that stress the noneconomic value of increased *domestic production* of, and arguments that stress the noneconomic value of increased *self-sufficiency* in (a reduced volume of imports of) certain types of commodities that under free trade would be imported. The argument of this paper has shown that where domestic distortions make the production of a commodity lower than it should be, optimal government intervention entails subsidization of production rather than interferences with international trade. The same conclusion can be shown to hold for noneconomic arguments based on the desirability of larger domestic production, such as the national identity and way-of-life arguments mentioned above. On the other hand, it can be shown that for noneconomic arguments based on the desirability of a smaller volume of imports, the method of tariff protection is superior to the method of subsidization. The reason is that in the first case an increase of domestic production achieved by protection, as contrasted with an increase achieved by subsidization, involves an additional cost in the form of a consumption loss. In the second case, however, the reduction in consumption achieved by the tariff is to be regarded as a gain, since it also contributes to the reduction of imports; and since at the margin the production loss from subsidizing production is proportional to the rate

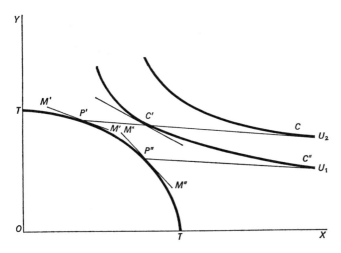

Figure 6

of subsidy, and the consumption loss from taxing consumption is proportional to the rate of tax, it follows that a given reduction in imports can
be achieved more efficiently by means of the tariff, which subsidizes
production and taxes consumption at the same rate, than by means of a
production subsidy alone, which subsidy would necessarily be at a higher
rate than the required tariff rate.

These propositions are illustrated in figure 6, where P' represents the
production point and C' the consumption point achieved by the imposition of a tariff that distorts the domestic exchange ratio and transformation ratio from the international exchange ratio $P'C'$ to $M'M'$. It is
obvious that the country could reach the consumption point C and the
associated higher welfare level U_2, while keeping domestic production
at the same level P', by replacing the tariff by a subsidy on production of
X (or a tax on production of Y). If, however, the object of policy is not
the domestic production pattern shown by P' but the restriction of international trade to the level represented by the distance $P'C'$, achievement of this object by means of subsidization of domestic production
necessarily involves a greater loss of welfare than achievement of it by
means of tariff protection. To appreciate this, consider the production
subsidy represented by the domestic price ratio $M''M''$, which combined
with free trade places the country on the indifference curve U_1 reached
with the tariff. It follows from the tangencies of the transformation curve
and the indifference curve U_1 to the tariff-distorted domestic exchange
ratio at P' and C' that the distance between the production point P'' and

consumption point C'' achieved with a subsidy welfare-indifferent to the tariff is greater than that between the production point P' and consumption point C' achieved with the tariff. In short, for a given welfare loss, trade is restricted less by a production subsidy than by a tariff; therefore, the achievement of a given restriction of trade requires a smaller welfare loss if trade is restricted by a tariff than if trade is restricted by a production subsidy.

This paper originated as a guest lecture at the Claremont Colleges, California, delivered in March 1963. It was originally scheduled for publication in the *Indian Economic Review*, but the editors of that journal have graciously released it for inclusion in this volume (*Trade, Growth and the Balance of Payments*) on the grounds that its contents bear witness to the depth and durability of Gottfried Haberler's contribution to the pure theory of international trade and economic welfare.

The paper represents a condensation of analysis developed in lectures and writings over a period of years. The organization of the argument around the two central propositions of the paper, however, is derived from discussion with Jagdish Bhagwati, and particularly from an early reading of his brilliant joint article with V. K. Ramaswami, "Domestic distortions tariffs and the theory of optimum subsidy", *Journal of Political Economy*, vol. 71 (1963), pp. 44–50. To these two authors belongs the credit for reducing a mass of *ad hoc* arguments concerning tariffs to a simple application of second-best welfare theory. The present paper extends their analysis to some arguments for protection not considered by them, elaborates more fully on the infant industry argument, and adds to their results two propositions about non-economic arguments for protection. I should like also to acknowledge a debt to Erling Olsen, whose comments on an earlier draft prompted improvements in the presentation of the factor-price rigidity case.

References

Balogh, T. (1951), "Welfare and freer trade–a reply", *Economic Journal*, vol. 61, March, pp. 72–83.

Becker, G. S. (1962), "Investment in human capital: a theoretical analysis", *Journal of Political Economy*, vol. 70, pp. 9–49.

Bhagwati, J. N., and Ramaswami, V. K. (1963), "Domestic distortions, tariffs and the theory of optimum subsidy", *Journal of Political Economy*, vol. 71, pp. 44–50.

Corden, W. M. (1957), "Tariffs, subsidies and the terms of trade", *Economica*, vol. 24, pp. 235–42.

Fishlow, A., and David, p. (1961), "Optimal resource allocation in an imperfect market setting", *Journal of Political Economy*, vol. 69, pp. 529–46.

Haberler, G. (1950), "Some problems in the pure theory of international trade", *Economic Journal*, vol. 60, June, pp. 223–40.

Haberler, G. (1951), "Welfare and freer trade–a rejoinder", *Economic Journal*, vol. 61, December, pp. 777–84.

Hagen, E. E. (1958), "An economic justification of protectionism", *Quarterly Journal of Economics*, vol. 72, pp. 496–514.

Johnson, H. G. (1953–4), "Optimum tariffs and retaliation", *Review of Economic Studies*, vol. 22, pp. 142–53. (Reprinted as chapter 2 in H. G. Johnson, *International Trade and Economic Growth*, Allen and Unwin, 1958.)

Johnson, H. G. (1963), "The Bladen plan for increased protection of the Canadian automotive industry", *Canadian Journal of Economics and Political Science*, vol. 29, pp. 212–38.

Kemp, M. C. (1960), "The Mill-Bastable infant industry dogma", *Journal of Political Economy*, vol. 68, pp. 65–7.

Kenen, P. B. (1963), "Development, mobility and the case for tariffs", *Kyklos*, vol. 16, pp. 321–4.

Lewis, W. A. (1954), "Economic development with unlimited supplies of labour", *Manchester School of Economic and Social Studies*, vol. 22, pp. 139–91.

Lewis, W. A. (1958), "Unlimited labour: further notes", *Manchester School of Economic and Political Studies*, vol. 26, pp. 1–32.

Lipsey, R. G., and Lancaster, K. (1956–7), "The general theory of the second best", *Review of Economic Studies*, vol. 24, pp. 11–32.

Manoilesco, M. (1931), *The Theory of Protection and International Trade*, P. S. King.

Meade, J. E. (1955), *Trade and Welfare*, Oxford University Press.

Stopler, W. F., and Samuelson, P. A. (1941). "Protection and real wages", *Review of Economic Studies*, vol. 9, pp. 58–73. (Reprinted as chapter 15 in H. S. Ellis and L. A. Metzler, eds., *Readings in the Theory of International Trade*, Blakiston, 1949.)

Viner, J. (1932), "Review of M. Manoilesco's *The Theory of Protection and International Trade*", *Journal of Political Economy*, vol. 40, pp. 121–5.

Young, J. H. (1957), *Canadian Commercial Policy*, Royal Commission on Canada's Economic Prospects.

Editor's Note

Johnson essentially argues that (1) tariffs are the first-best policy instrument whenever there is a foreign distortion (in the terminology developed in Bhagwati, chapter 12, in this volume) and that (2) if there is a domestic distortion, offsetting it fully by a tariff (or trade subsidy) will not necessarily improve welfare. These two propositions of Bhagwati and Ramaswami (*Journal of Political Economy*, February 1963) are quite correct.

However, it is incorrect to infer, as Bhagwati and Ramaswami did (and the tenor of Johnson's argumentation and explicit indebtedness to their paper for his own without rejection of their further inference definitely imply that Johnson did as well), that a tariff may not exist which *improves* welfare vis-à-vis free trade when there is a domestic distortion. This error was spotted by Kemp and Negishi and the analysis developed yet further by Bhagwati, Ramaswami, and Srinivasan in their response to Kemp and Negishi (*Journal of Political Economy*, November/ December 1969), and the correct analysis can be found in Bhagwati, chapter 12. All this should be carefully noted by the readers of Johnson's excellent paper, lest they infer, as they are bound to unless warned, that trade policy instruments may not at times be capable of improving welfare over free trade in the presence of domestic distortions.

12

The Generalized Theory of Distortions and Welfare

Jagdish N. Bhagwati

The theory of trade and welfare has recently developed independently in seven areas that have apparently little analytical relationship among themselves:

1. The Suboptimality of Laissez-Faire Under Market Imperfections It has been shown that, when market imperfections exist, laissez-faire (otherwise described as "a policy of unified exchange rates" [5]) will not be the optimal policy. Among the market imperfections for which the suboptimality of laissez-faire has been demonstrated are four key types: (i) factor market imperfection, a wage differential between sectors;[1] (ii) product market imperfection, a production externality;[2] (iii) consumption imperfection, a consumption externality;[3] and (iv) trade imperfection, monopoly power in trade.[4]

2. Immiserizing Growth   Examples have been produced where a country, after growth (in factor supplies and/or technological know-how), becomes worse off, phenomena described as *immiserizing growth*. I produced an example of such a phenomenon in 1958 [1] (as also did Harry Johnson independently at the time) where growth led to such a deterioration in the country's terms of trade that the loss from the worsened terms of trade outweighted the primary gain from growth. Subsequently, Johnson [19] produced another example of immiserization, in which the country had no ability to influence her terms of trade but there was a tariff (which is necessarily welfare reducing in view of the assumed absence of monopoly power in trade) in both the pregrowth and the postgrowth situations, and growth impoverished the country in certain cases. I later produced yet other examples of immiserizing growth [6], one in which there was a wage

This paper was originally published in Jagdish N. Bhagwati, Ronald W. Jones, Robert A. Mundell, Jaroslav Vanek, editors, *Trade, Balance of Payments, and Growth: Papers in International Economics in Honor of Charles P. Kindleberger*, North-Holland Publishing Company, 1971.

differential in the factor market, and another in which the country had monopoly power in trade (as in my original 1958 example), but the country had an optimum tariff (before growth) which became suboptimal after growth.

3. Ranking of Alternative Policies under Market Imperfections   For the four major imperfections described earlier, the optimal policy intervention has been analyzed by several economists. Hagen [16] has argued that the optimal policy for the case of the wage differential would be a factor tax-cum-subsidy. For the production externality, Bhagwati and Ramaswami [2] have shown that the optimal policy intervention is a production tax-cum-subsidy. For the consumption externality case, it follows from the general arguments in Bhagwati and Ramaswami [2] that a consumption tax-cum-subsidy ought to be used. Finally, for the case of monopoly power in trade, it has been known since the time of Mill and has been demonstrated rigorously by (among others) Graaff [14] and Johnson [17] that a tariff is the optimal policy. Recent work of Bhagwati, Ramaswami, and Srinivasan [8] has then extended the analysis, for each market imperfection, to the ranking of *all* alternative policies: the tariff (trade subsidy) policy, the production tax-cum-subsidy policy, the consumption tax-cum-subsidy policy, and the factor tax-cum-subsidy policy.[5]

4. Ranking of Tariffs   Yet another area of research in trade and welfare has raised the question of ranking policies that constitute impediments themselves to the attainment of optimality. Thus, for example, Kemp [22] has analyzed, for a country without monopoly power in trade (and no other imperfections), the question as to whether a higher tariff is worse than a lower tariff. Similarly, Bhagwati and Kemp [10] have analysed the problem for tariffs around the optimal tariff for a country *with* monopoly power in trade.

5. Ranking of Free Trade and Autarky   A number of trade theorists have compared free trade with autarky, when there were market imperfections such as wage differentials (Hagen [16]) and production externality (Haberler [15]), to deduce that free trade was no longer necessarily superior to self-sufficiency. Melvin [26] and Kemp [23] have recently considered the comparison between free trade and autarky when there are commodity taxes.

6. Ranking of Restricted Trade and Autarky   Aside from the case in which trade is tariff restricted (wherein the comparison between restricted trade and autarky becomes the comparison of tariffs discussed in item 4) Bhagwati [4] has considered the ranking of other policies (e.g., production tax-cum-subsidies) that restrict trade and autarky.

7. Noneconomic Objectives and Ranking of Policies   Finally, a number

of economists have addressed themselves to the question of optimal policy intervention when the values of different variables are constrained, as noneconomic objectives, so that full optimality is unattainable. Four key types of noneconomic objectives have been analyzed. Corden [12] has shown that a production tax-cum-subsidy is optimal where the constrained variable is production (for reasons such as defense production). Johnson [18] has shown a tariff to be optimal when imports are constrained instead (in the interest of "self-sufficiency"). Bhagwati and Srinivasan [7] have demonstrated that a factor tax-cum-subsidy is optimal when the constrained variable is employment of a factor in an activity (i.e., in the interest of "national character") and a consumption tax-cum-subsidy when the constrained variable is domestic availability of consumption (i.e., to restrict "luxury consumption"). Bhagwati and Srinivasan have also extended the analysis to the ranking of *all* policy instruments for a number of these noneconomic objectives.

This paper is aimed at putting these diverse analyses into a common analytical framework. This results in the logical unification of a number of interesting and important results, leading in turn to fresh insights while also enabling us to derive remarkable "duality" relationships between the analysis of policy rankings under market imperfections and policy rankings to achieve noneconomic objectives.

Alternative Types of Distortions

It can be readily shown, in fact, that the diverse results reviewed so far belong to what might aptly be described as the theory of distortions and welfare.

The theory of distortions is built around the central theorem of trade and welfare: that laissez-faire is Pareto optimal for a perfectly competitive system with no monopoly power in trade.[6] Ruling out the phenomenon of diminishing cost of transformation between any pair of commodities (i.e., the concavity of the production possibility set in the familiar, two-commodity system),[7] the Pareto optimality of the laissez-faire policy follows quite simply from the fact that the economic system will operate with technical efficiency (i.e., on the "best" production possibility curve, if we think again of two commodities for simplicity). The economic system will also satisfy further the (first-order) conditions for an economic maximum: $DRT = FRT = DRS$ (where DRT represents the marginal rate of transformation in domestic production, FRT represents marginal foreign rate of transformation, and DRS represents the marginal rate of substitution in consumption).[8]

The theory of distortions is then concerned with the following four pathologies which may characterize, singly or in combination, the economic system:

Distortion 1: FRT $\neq$ DRT $=$ DRS
Distortion 2: DRT $\neq$ DRS $=$ FRT
Distortion 3: DRS $\neq$ DRT $=$ FRT
Distortion 4: Nonoperation on the efficient production possibility curve.

"Endogenous" Distortions

These distortions (implying departures from full optimality) may arise when the economy is characterised by *market imperfections* under a policy of laissez-faire. Thus, the presence of national monopoly power in trade will lead to Distortion 1, because foreign prices will not equal FRT. The case of the Meade type of production externality[9] leads to Distortion 2. Distortion 3 will follow when sellers of the importable commodity, for example, charge a uniform premium on imported as well as home-produced supplies. Distortion 4 follows when there is a factor market imperfection resulting from a wage differential, for a factor, between the different activities.[10] In these cases, therefore, the resulting distortions (arising from the market imperfections) are appropriately described as "endogenous" distortions.

"Policy-Imposed" Distortions

On the other hand, the four varieties of distortions listed earlier may be the result of economic policies, as distinct from endogenous phenomena such as market imperfections. Thus, Distortion 1 will arise for a country with no monopoly power in trade if the country has a tariff; it will also arise for a country with monopoly power in trade if the tariff is less or greater than the optimal tariff. Distortion 2 will follow if the government imposes a production tax-cum-subsidy. Distortion 3 will be the consequence similarly of a consumption tax-cum-subsidy policy. Finally, the adoption of a factor tax-cum-subsidy policy will result in Distortion 4.[11] These are instances therefore of "policy-imposed" distortions.

But as soon as we probe the reasons for the existence of such policy-imposed distortions, two alternative interpretations are possible. Either we can consider these policies as *autonomous* (i.e., a tariff, which leads to Distortion 1, may for example be a historic accident), or we may consider these policies as *instrumental* (a tariff, leading to Distortion 1, may be the policy instrument used in order to reduce imports)—as in the case of the theory of noneconomic objectives when Distortion 1 is created through the deployment of a tariff when the objective is to reduce imports in the interest of "self-sufficiency."

We thus have altogether three sets of "causes" for the four varieties of distortions that can be distinguished: *endogenous*; *autonomous, policy-imposed*; and *instrumental, policy-imposed*. The entire literature that I reviewed earlier can then be given its logical coherence and unity around these alternative classes and causes of distortions.

Before formulating the general theory of distortions and generalizing the theorems discussed in the introduction into other areas, it would be useful to underline the precise manner in which these theorems relate to the different varieties of distortions that we have distinguished so far.

1. The theorems on the suboptimality of different market imperfections clearly relate to the theory of endogenous distortions. Within a static welfare context, they demonstrate that these market imperfections result in the different types of Distortions 1–4, thus resulting in the breakdown of the Pareto optimality of laissez-faire in these cases.

2. The theorems on immiserizing growth, on the other hand, relate to the comparative statics of welfare when distortions are present. The theorems developed in this literature involve cases in which growth takes place under given distortions, either endogenous or policy imposed, and the primary improvement in welfare (which would have accrued if fully optimal policies were followed both before and after growth) is outweighed by the accentuation of the loss from the distortion in the postgrowth situation [6].

Thus, in the original Bhagwati example of immiserizing growth, the assumed free trade and hence failure to impose an optimum tariff (to exploit the monopoly power in trade) in both the pregrowth and the postgrowth situations involves welfare-reducing "distortionary" policies in both situations. Immiserization occurs therefore because the gain, which would necessarily accrue from growth if the optimal tariff were imposed in both situations, is smaller than the incremental loss arising from the accentuation (if any) in the postgrowth situation of the welfare loss resulting from the "distortionary" free-trade policy (implying an endogenous Distortion 1 in this instance) in both situations.

Harry Johnson's example of immiserization where the country has no monopoly power in trade but a tariff (which thus constitutes an autonomous policy-imposed Distortion 1) in both the pregrowth and the postgrowth situations, is to be explained in terms of the same logic. In the absence of monopoly power in trade, the tariff is necessarily "distortionary" and, compared with the fully optimal free-trade policy, causes a loss of welfare in each situation. If the growth were to occur with free trade, there would necessarily be an increment in welfare. However, since growth occurs under a tariff, there arises the possibility that the loss from the tariff may be accentuated after growth, and that this incremental loss may outweigh the gain (that would occur under the optimal, free-trade policy), thus resulting in immiserization. Thus, the policy-imposed distortion (i.e., the tariff) generates the possibility of immiserizing growth.

3. The theorems that rank alternative policies under market imperfections are addressed to a different range of questions. They relate to endogenous distortions, of each of the four varieties we have distinguished, and then seek to rank the different, available policy instruments (extending to the full complement: production, consumption, trade, and factor tax-cum-subsidies) in relation to one another and vis-à-vis laissez-faire itself. The problem has been posed in this fashion by Bhagwati, Ramaswami, and Srinivasan [8] in their recent work.

4. The theorems of Kemp [22] and Bhagwati and Kemp [10], which rank tariffs in relation to one another, however, belong to a yet different genre. They relate to policy-imposed distortions, autonomous in the sense defined in this paper, and aim at ranking different levels at which policy may impose the specified distortion (e.g., Distortion 1 in the cases in which tariffs are ranked).

5. The ranking of free trade and autarky under situations involving market imperfections or taxes involves, on the other hand, a comparison of essentially two levels (the zero tariff level and the prohibitive tariff level) at which a policy-imposed distortion (the tariff) is used, in a situation which is itself characterized by another distortion (either endogenous, such as the wage differential in Hagen [16], or policy-imposed, such as a tax on consumption of a commodity).

6. The ranking of a situation with trade restricted by a nontariff policy with a situation of autarky (with therefore an implicit, prohibitive tariff) involves an altogether different type of comparison: of one distortion with another, both autonomous policy-imposed in Bhagwati's analysis [4].

7. The theory of noneconomic objectives [7], on the other hand, relates to the optimal nature of intervention and the ranking of alternative policies, when certain variables are precluded from specified ranges of values in the interest of "noneconomic" objectives. It is therefore, from an analytical point of view, a theory of how optimally (i.e., at minimum cost) to *introduce* distortions in the economic system, when the attainment of the full optimum is precluded by the noneconomic-objective constraints and also of what the relative costs of alternative policies or methods of introducing such distortions, in pursuit of the noneconomic objectives, are. It is thus a theory pertaining to the ranking of instrumental, policy-

imposed distortions, with each distortion being defined under a common set of economic and noneconomic constraints.

It is clear, therefore, that these diverse theorems relate to different types of distortions and raise a number of diverse questions relating thereto. But as soon as we grasp this central fact, it is possible to unify and extend the entire body of this literature and thus to develop a general theory of distortions and welfare.

Distortions and Welfare: General Theory

This generalized theory of distortions and welfare can be developed in terms of seven central propositions.

PROPOSITION 1 There are four principal types of distortions:
1. $\text{FRT} \neq \text{DRT} = \text{DRS}$;
2. $\text{DRT} \neq \text{DRS} = \text{FRT}$;
3. $\text{DRS} \neq \text{DRT} = \text{FRT}$; and
4. Nonoperation on the efficient production possibility curve.

These, in turn, can be caused by factors that are
1. Endogenous;
2. Autonomous, policy-imposed; and
3. Instrumental, policy-imposed.

This proposition is merely a recapitulation of the concepts and analysis developed in the preceding section and requires no further comment. Note merely, by way of reemphasis, that in each of the $(4 \times 3 = 12)$ distortionary situations, the economic system departs from full Pareto optimality.

PROPOSITION 2
i. Optimal policy intervention, in the presence of distortions, involves a tax-cum-subsidy policy addressed directly to offsetting the source of the distortions, when the causes are endogenous or autonomous, policy-imposed. Dual to (i) is the theorem that:
ii. When distortions have to be introduced into the economy, because the values of certain variables (e.g., production or employment of a factor in an activity) have to be constrained, the optimal (or least-cost) method of doing this is to choose that policy intervention that creates the distortion affecting directly the constrained variable.

These two propositions, which constitute a remarkable duality of theorems, extend between themselves to all the classes of Distortions 1 to 4 and their three possible causes, endogenous, autonomous policy-imposed, and instrumental policy-imposed. Furthermore, each proposition is readily derived from the theorems on market imperfections and on noneconomic objectives.

Proposition 2(i) was formulated, in essentially similar form, by Bhagwati and Ramaswami [2] and later by Johnson [18], for the case of endogenous distortions. For Distortion 1, resulting from monopoly power in trade under laissez-faire, it is well known that the optimal policy intervention is a tariff. For Distortion 2, Bhagwati and Ramaswami showed that the optimal policy was a production tax-cum-subsidy. For Distortion 3, correspondingly, the optimal policy is a consumption tax-cum-subsidy. Finally, when a wage differential causes Distortion 4, Hagen [16] showed that the optimal intervention was through a factor tax-cum-subsidy. In each instance, therefore, the policy required is one that directly attacks the source of the distortion.

It follows equally, and trivially, that if these distortions are autonomous policy-imposed, the optimal intervention is to eliminate the policy itself: hence, again the optimal policy intervention is addressed to the source of the distortion itself. Thus, with a suboptimal tariff leading to Distortion 1, the optimal policy is to change the tariff to an optimal level (equal to zero, if there is no monopoly power in trade). Similarly, if a consumption tax-cum-subsidy causes Distortion 3, the optimal policy is to offset it with an equivalent consumption tax-cum-subsidy (which leaves zero net consumption tax-cum-subsidy and thus restores full optimality).

But the extension of these results, via the "dual" Proposition 2(ii), to the class of instrumental, policy-imposed distortions, is far from trivial. And the duality is remarkable. Corden [12] has shown that the optimal policy, if the binding noneconomic constraint relates to production, is a *production* tax-cum-subsidy. Johnson [18] has demonstrated that the optimal policy, if the binding noneconomic constraint relates to import (export) level, is a *tariff or trade subsidy*. Bhagwati and Srinivasan [7] have extended the analysis to show that, if the binding noneconomic constraint relates to the level of employment of a factor of production in a sector, the optimal policy is to use a *factor* tax-cum-subsidy that directly taxes (subsidises) the employment of the factor in the sector where its employment level must be lowered (raised) to the constrained level.[12] They have also demonstrated that the optimal policy for raising (lowering) consumption to a constrained level is a *consumption* tax-cum-subsidy policy.

To put it somewhat differently, a trade-level noneconomic objective is achieved at least cost by introducing a policy-imposed Distortion 1 via a trade tariff or subsidy; a production noneconomic objective by introducing a policy-imposed Distortion 2 via a production tax-cum-subsidy; a consumption noneconomic objective by introducing a policy-imposed Distortion 3 via a consumption tax-cum-subsidy; and a factor-employment (in a sector) non-economic objective by introducing a policy-imposed Distortion 4 via a factor tax-cum-subsidy.

PROPOSITION 3

i. For each distortion, whether endogenous or autonomous, policy-imposed, in origin, it is possible to analyse the welfare ranking of all alternative policies, from the (first best) optimal to the second best and so on.

ii. a. When distortions have to be introduced into the economy, because the values of certain variables have to be constrained (e.g., production or employment of a factor in an activity), the policy interventions that do this may similarly be welfare ranked. b. The ranking of these policies is further completely symmetrical with that under the "corresponding" class of endogenous or autonomous policy-imposed distortions (e.g., the ranking of policies for production externality, an endogenous Distortion 2, is identical with the ranking of policies when production is constrained as a noneconomic objective).

Since there are four different types of policies (factor, production, consumption, and trade tax-cum-subsidies), the propositions listed here are aimed at ranking *all* of them for each of the (twelve) varieties of distortions and establishing "duality" relations of the kind we discovered for optimal policies alone in Proposition 2(ii).

Bhagwati, Ramaswami, and Srinivasan [8] have recently analyzed the welfare ranking of all policies for endogenous distortions and established the following rankings:[13]

Distortion 1: FRT $\neq$ DRT = DRS

This is the case of monopoly power in trade. The ranking of policies then is

i. First best: tariff;

ii. Second best: either production or consumption or factor tax-cum-subsidy (all policies are superior to laissez-faire but cannot be ranked uniquely vis-à-vis one another).[14]

Distortion 2: DRT $\neq$ DRS = FRT

This is the case of a pure production externality. The ranking of policies then is

i. First best: production tax-cum-subsidy;

ii. Second best: either tariff (trade subsidy) or factor tax-cum-subsidy (both policies are superior to laissez-faire but cannot be ranked uniquely vis-à-vis each other);

iii. Consumption tax-cum-subsidy will not help.[15]

Distortion 3: DRS ≠ DRT = FRT

This is the case in which, for example, the sellers of a commodity uniform premium to buyers over the cost of supplies, whether imported or domestically produced. The ranking of policies then is

i. First best: consumption tax-cum-subsidy;

ii. Second best: tariff;

iii. Production or factor tax-cum-subsidy will not help.[16]

Distortion 4: Nonoperation on the efficient production possibility curve

This is the case in which there is a wage differential, a factor market imperfection. In this case, the ranking of policies is

i. First best: factor tax-cum-subsidy;

ii. Second best: production tax-cum-subsidy;

iii. Third best: tariff (trade subsidy);

iv. Consumption tax-cum-subsidy will not help.[17]

It is clear that the extension of these rankings to the corresponding cases where the distortions are autonomous policy-imposed (e.g., Distortion 2 resulting from the autonomous levy of a governmental tax, or Distortion 4 resulting from the grant of a governmental subsidy on employment of a factor in one activity) is total and trivial. It is interesting and remarkable, however, that these rankings carry over also to the class of instrumental, policy-imposed distortions.

Thus, for the case of noneconomic objectives, Bhagwati and Srinivasan [7] have provided the basis for analyzing the rankings of different policies, which I now proceed to develop fully:

Trade-level as a Constraint: The ranking of policies in this case is

i. First best: tariff;

ii. Second best: either production tax-cum-subsidy or factor tax-cum-subsidy or consumption tax-cum-subsidy (these policies cannot be ranked vis-à-vis one another).[18]

Note the complete symmetry with the rankings under Distortion 1 earlier.

Production level as a Constraint: The ranking of policies in this case is

i. First best: production tax-cum-subsidy;

ii. Second best: either tariff (trade subsidy) or factor tax-cum-subsidy (these policies cannot be ranked vis-à-vis each other);

iii. Consumption tax-cum-subsidy will not help.[19]
Note again the complete symmetry with the rankings under Distortion 2.

Consumption level as a Constraint: The ranking of policies in this case is
i. First best: consumption tax-cum-subsidy;
ii. Second best: tariff;
iii. Production or factor tax-cum-subsidy, when it helps meet the consumption constraint, will be third-best.[20]
Again, the symmetry with the ranking under Distortion 3 is total.

Factor Employment (in a Sector) as a Constraint: The ranking of policies in this case is
i. First best: factor tax-cum-subsidy;
ii. Second best: production tax-cum-subsidy;
iii. Third best: tariff (trade subsidy);
iv. Consumption tax-cum-subsidy will not help.[21]
In this final case as well, the symmetry with the corresponding Distortion 4 is complete.

Thus, the duality of the policy rankings, for endogenous and autonomous policy-imposed distortions on the one hand and instrumental policy-imposed distortions on the other hand, is altogether complete and remarkable.

PROPOSITION 4 For each kind of distortion, growth may be immiserizing.

For endogenous and autonomous policy-imposed distortions, belonging to each of the varieties 1 to 4 that we have distinguished, this proposition has already been demonstrated by Bhagwati [6].

Thus, for example, where Distortion 1 obtains endogenously under laissez-faire because of monopoly power in trade, Bhagwati's 1958 analysis [1] demonstrates the possibility of immiserization. Where Distortions 2 and 4 obtain simultaneously as a result of an endogenous wage differential, the same possibility has again been demonstrated by Bhagwati [6]. Johnson's demonstration [19] of immiserization when a country has no monopoly power in trade but a tariff, illustrates Proposition 2 for the case of an autonomous policy-imposed Distortion 1.

Note again that the underlying reason for immiserizing growth is that the growth takes place in the presence of a distortion. This distortion produces a loss of welfare from the fully optimal welfare level. Thus, if there is an accentuation in this loss of welfare, when growth has occurred and the distortion has continued, this incremental loss could outweigh the gain that would have accrued if fully optimal policies had been followed in the pregrowth and postgrowth situations [6]. It also follows

that such immiserizing growth would be impossible if fully optimal policies were followed in each situation, i.e., if the distortions resulting from
the endogenous and policy-imposed cause were offset by optimal policy
intervention, as discussed under Proposition 2(i) earlier.[22]

But so far we have discussed only distortions resulting from endogenous
and policy-imposed, autonomous factors. However, Proposition 4 applies
equally, and can be generalized, to *instrumental* policy-imposed distortions as well.

In complete symmetry with the endogenous and autonomous policy-
imposed distortions, the phenomenon of immiserizing growth will be
precluded when the constrained variable (e.g., production in the case of a
production objective) is attained (in the pregrowth and the postgrowth
situations) by optimal policy. On the other hand, immiserization becomes
possible as soon as any of the second-best (or third best) policies is adopted
to constrain the variable (to a preassigned value in both the pregrowth
and postgrowth situations).

This generalization of the theory of immiserizing growth is readily
illustrated with reference to production as the constrained variable.
Remember that a production tax-cum-subsidy is the optimal policy in
this case and a tariff a second best policy. Figure 1a then illustrates how
it is impossible, after growth, to become "worse off" if the production
level of a commodity is constrained to the required level by a suitable
production tax-cum-subsidy policy. The y production is constrained to
level $\bar{y}$; the production possibility curve shifts out from AP to $A'B'$. With
a suitable production tax-cum-subsidy used in both the pregrowth and
the postgrowth situations, to constrain y production to $\bar{y}$, it is clear that
it is impossible to worsen welfare after growth. Figure 1b illustrates,
however, the possibility of immiserizing growth when the suboptimal
tariff policy is followed instead in each case to constrain y output to
level $\bar{y}$. Note that this demonstration, where the welfare level reduces
after growth to U' from U, does not require the assumption of inferior
goods.

Similar illustrations could be provided for the other three cases, where
consumption, factor employment in a sector, and trade-level are constrained. In each case, only the pursuit of a suboptimal policy to achieve
the specified noneconomic objective could lead to immiserization.

PROPOSITION 5 Reductions in the "degree" of an only distortion are
successively welfare increasing until the distortion is fully eliminated.

This theorem holds whether we take endogenous or policy-imposed
distortions. However, it needs to be qualified, so as to exclude inferior

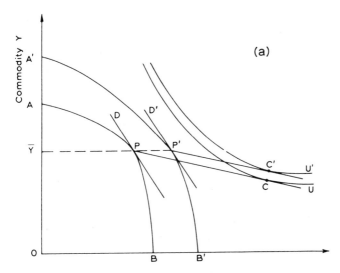

Figure 1a. AB is the pregrowth production possibility curve; $A'B'$ the postgrowth production possibility curve. The international price ratio is given at $PC = P'C'$. Production of y is constrained to level $\bar{y}$. A suitable production tax-cum-subsidy takes production, before growth, to P at domestic, producer price ratio DP. After growth, a suitable production tax-cum-subsidy takes producer price ratio to $D'P'$ and production to P'. Welfare level has increased, after growth, to U' ($> U$).

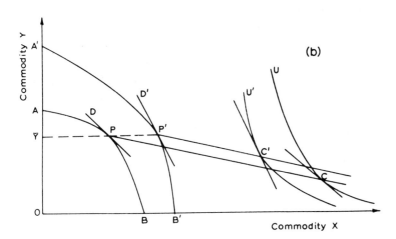

Figure 1b. The production possibility curve shifts, after growth, from AB to $A'B'$. In each case, the production of y is constrained to $\bar{y}$ by a tariff. In the pregrowth case, this tariff leads to production at P (with domestic price ratio DP), consumption at C, and welfare at U. After growth, production is at P', consumption at C', and welfare has reduced to U' ($< U$), implying immiserizing growth.

goods for all cases except where a *consumption* tax-cum-subsidy is relevant.

For autonomous, policy-imposed Distortion 1, the Kemp [22] and Bhagwati-Kemp [10] theorems are special cases of Proposition 5: Each further requires the exclusion of inferior goods and attendant multiple equilibria if the possibility of the competitive system "choosing" an inferior-welfare equilibrium under the lower degree of distortion is to be ruled out.[23] In point of fact, identical propositions could be derived for alternative forms of autonomus policy-imposed distortions, factor tax-cum-subsidy, production tax-cum-subsidy, and consumption tax-cum-subsidy.[24]

Similarly, we can argue that reduction in the degree of each market imperfection, insofar as it reduces the degree of its consequent distortion, will raise welfare. Thus, for example, a reduction in the degree of production externality will reduce the degree of Distortion 2 and increase the level of welfare.[25]

Finally, identical conclusions apply if we reduce the degree of "required" distortion, of the instrumental policy-imposed type, by relaxing the binding constraint on the "noneconomic"-objective variable. Thus, marginally relaxing the constraint on production will suffice to improve welfare. As is clear from figure 2a, the relaxation of the constraint on y production, from $\bar{y}$ to $\bar{y}_n$, will necessarily improve welfare by shifting the "availability line" outwards—if, in each case, the policy. adopted is a production tax-cum-subsidy policy.

If, however, as figure 2b illustrates, a (suboptimal) tariff policy is followed instead, to constrain y-production to the required level, the result of a relaxation in the constraint is identical; the only qualification is relating to that arising from inferior goods. Further, an identical conclusion holds, as in the case of a production tax-cum-subsidy, for the case of a factor tax-cum-subsidy instead.

Thus, Proposition 5 applies in the case of instrumental policy-imposed distortions, no matter *which* policy is considered (in other words, no matter which distortion is introduced in pursuit of the specific noneconomic objective).

PROPOSITION 6 Reductions in the "degree" of a distortion will not necessarily be welfare increasing if there is another distortion in the system.

This proposition is readily established for endogenous or autonomous policy-imposed distortions.

Let us first consider a case in which reductions in one distortion *do* lead to improvement in welfare despite the presence of another distortion in the system. Thus, consider the case in which a production externality,

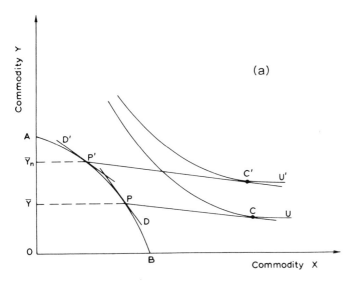

Figure 2a. With AB as the production possibility curve, $\bar{y}$ and $\bar{y}_n$ are the successive noneconomic constraints on y production, which are met by use of a suitable production subsidy policy in each case. For $\bar{y}$, production then is at P, consumption at C, and welfare level at U. For $\bar{y}_n$, a relaxation in the constraint, production shifts to P' (with producer price ratio at $D'P'$ now), consumption to C', and welfare has increased to U' ($> U$).

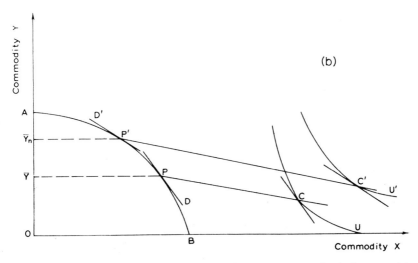

Figure 2b. With production of y-commodity constrained successively at $\bar{y}$ and $\bar{y}_n$, a tariff used for that purpose, and production possibility curve AB, the production for $\bar{y}$ constraint is at P, consumption at C, and welfare at U. Relaxation in the constraint to $\bar{y}_n$ leads to production at P' and consumption at C' (at price $D'P'$) and welfare increases to U' ($> U$).

an endogenous Distortion 2 where DRT $\neq$ DRS = FRT, is combined with a consumption tax-cum-subsidy, an autonomous policy-imposed Distortion 3 where DRS $\neq$ FRT = DRT, but there is no monopoly power in trade. Assume further that the two distortions combine so as to yield altogether the initial situation where DRT $\neq$ DRS $\neq$ FRT (so that they are not mutually offsetting as far as one inequality is concerned). In this case, successive reductions in the consumption tax-cum-subsidy will necessarily be welfare increasing, given the production externality; and successive reductions in the production externality will improve welfare (except for the complication introduced by inferior goods).[26]

Next, however, consider the case where there is a production externality (endogenous, DRT $\neq$ DRS = FRT) combined with a tariff without monopoly power in trade (autonomous policy-imposed FRT $\neq$ DRS = DRT) and assume that the resulting initial situation is characterized by FRT $\neq$ DRT $\neq$ DRS. In this case, successive reductions in the tariff will not necessarily improve welfare steadily, if at all, and the gains may turn into losses.[27] The theorems on the possible inferiority of free trade (i.e., zero tariff) to no trade (i.e., prohibitive tariff) when there is a production externality [15] or a wage differential [2] [16] are only special cases of this general theorem that illustrates Proposition 6.

It is interesting to note further that this theorem can with equal insight be analyzed in terms of Proposition 4 if we recognize that, if optimal policies are followed in *both* the autarkic and the trading "situations", the trade situation must necessarily enable the economy to be "better off"—as is obvious to trade theorists familiar with the Baldwin-envelope technique. If then there is a distortion common to both situations, as with an endogenous wage differential or production externality or with an autonomous policy-imposed production tax-cum-subsidy, the transition to the (free) trading situation may well be immiserizing (i.e., therefore, free trade inferior to autarky) if the loss from this distortion is accentuated and outweighs the primary gain from the shift to (free) trade itself.

PROPOSITION 7 Distortions cannot be ranked (uniquely) vis-à-vis one another.

This is a readily apparent proposition and applies clearly to all the classes of distortions we have discussed.

Bhagwati's demonstration [4] that Kemp's theorem [22] of the superiority of tariff-restricted trade over no trade will not extend to cases where the trade is restricted instead by policies such as consumption and production tax-cum-subsidies becomes intuitively obvious as soon as it is seen that it falls into the class of theorems belonging to Proposition 7. For, in this instance, two distortions are being compared: (i) a consumption tax-cum-subsidy leading to Distortion 3, DRS ≠ DRT = FRT, with a situation of autarky and hence implicit prohibitive tariff, thus involving Distortion 1, FRT ≠ DRT = DRS; and (ii) a production tax-cum-subsidy leading to Distortion 2, DRT = DRS = FRT, with autarky involving Distortion 1, FRT ≠ DRT = DRS. In principle, of course, the demonstration of impossibility of unique ranking between autarky and restricted trade could be carried equally into the case where trade-restriction occurs via use of a factor tax-cum-subsidy involving Distortion 4 along with 2.

Concluding Remarks

We have thus succeeded in unifying a considerable body of literature on the welfare economics of trade into a series of major propositions that consitute a generalized theory of distortions and welfare. Aside from the intrinsic elegance of such unification, this has resulted in a number of insights into, and extensions of, the theorems to date in this significant area of economic policy.

This paper is the result of thinking and research over a period of many years, originating in my 1958 paper on immiserizing growth [1] and developing considerably since my joint paper with the late V. K. Ramaswami in 1963 [2] on domestic distortions. Since 1965, T. N. Srinivasan and I have collaborated on research in related matters, pertaining to the theory of optimal policy intervention when noneconomic objectives are present [7], a subject pioneered by Max Corden's brilliant work [12]. In many ways, therefore, this paper has grown out of the ferment of ideas in Delhi during 1963–1968, when Srinivasan, Ramaswami, and I happened to work together and independently on the diverse subjects which are brought together in this paper. The work of others, particularly Murray Kemp [23], [24] and Harry Johnson [18], has also contributed to the development of my thinking.

References

[1] Bhagwati, J. "Immiserizing Growth: A Geometrical Note." *Review of Economic Studies*, 25 (June 1958).

[2] Bhagwati, J., and Ramaswami, V. K. "Domestic Distortions, Tariffs and the Theory of Optimum Subsidy." *Journal of Political Economy*, 71 (February 1963).

[3] Bhagwati, J. "Non-Economic Objectives and the Efficiency Properties of Trade." *Journal of Political Economy*, 76 (October 1968).

[4] Bhagwati, J. "Gains from Trade Once Again." *Oxford Economic Papers*, 20 (July 1968).

[5] Bhagwati, J. *The Theory and Practice of Commercial Policy*. Frank Graham Memorial Lecture (1967), Special Papers in International Economics No. 8, Princeton University, 1968

[6] Bhagwati, J. "Distortions and Immiserizing Growth: A Generalization," *Review of Economic Studies*, 35 (November 1968).

[7] Bhagwati, J. and Srinivasan, T. N. "Optimal Intervention to Achieve Non-Economic Objectives. "*Review of Economic Studies*, 36 (January 1969).

[8] Bhagwati, J., Ramaswami, V. K. and Srinivasan, T. N. "Domestic Distortions, Tariffs and the Theory of Optimum Subsidy: Some Further Results." *Journal of Political Economy*, 77 (November/December 1969).

[9] Bhagwati, J., "Optimal Policies and Immiserizing Growth." *American Economic Review*, 59 (December 1969).

[10] Bhagwati, J. and Kemp, M. C. "Ranking of Tariffs under Monopoly Power in Trade." *Quarterly Journal of Economics*, 83 (May 1969).

[11] Bhagwati, J. and Srinivasan, T. N. "The Theory of Wage Differentials: Production Response and Factor Price Equalisation", *Journal of International Economics*, 1 (February 1971).

[12] Corden, W. M. "Tariffs, Subsidies and the Terms of Trade." *Economica*, 24 (August 1957).

[13] Fishlow, A. and David, P. "Optimal Resource Allocation in an Imperfect Market Setting." *Journal of Political Economy*, 69 (December 1961).

[14] Graaff, J. "On Optimum Tariff Structures." *Review of Economic Studies*, 17 (1949–1950).

[15] Haberler, G. "Some Problems in the Pure Theory of International Trade," *Economic Journal*, 30 (June 1950).

[16] Hagen, E. "An Economic Justification of Protectionism," *Quarterly Journal of Economics*, 72 (November 1958).

[17] Johnson, H. G. *International Trade and Economic Growth*, London: George Allen and Unwin Ltd, 1958.

[18] Johnson, H. G. "Optimal Trade Intervention in the Presence of Domestic Distortions." in R. E. Caves, H. G. Johnson and P. B. Kenen (eds.), *Trade, Growth and the Balance of Payments*, Amsterdam: North-Holland Publishing Company, 1965.

[19] Johnson, H. G. "The Possibility of Income Losses from Increased Efficiency or Factor Accumulation in the Presence of Tariffs." *Economic Journal*, 77 (March 1967).

[20] Johnson, H. G. "Factor Market Distortions and the Shape of the Transformation Curve." *Econometrica*, 34 (July 1966).

[21] Kemp, M. C. *The Pure Theory of International Trade*. Englewood Cliffs, N. J.: Prentice-Hall, 1964

[22] Kemp, M. C. "The Gain from International Trade." *Economic Journal*, 72 (December 1962).

[23] Kemp, M. C. "Some Issues in the Analysis of Trade Gains." *Oxford Economic Papers*, 20 (July 1968).

[24] Kemp, M. C. and Negishi, T. "Domestic Distortions, Tariffs and the Theory of Optimum Subsidy," *Journal of Political Economy*, 77 (November/December 1969).

[25] Melvin, J. "Demand Conditions and Immiserizing Growth." *American Economic Review*, 59 (September 1969).

[26] Melvin, J. "Commodity Taxation as a Determinant of Trade." University of Western Ontario, *mimeographed*, 1968.

[27] Matthews R. C. O. "Reciprocal Demand and Increasing Returns." *Review of Economic Studies*, 17 (1949–1950).

[28] Samuelson, P. A. "The Gains from International Trade." *Canadian Journal of Economics and Political Science*, 5 (May 1939).

[29] Samuelson, P. A. "The Gains from International Trade Once Again." *Economic Journal*, 72 (December 1962).

[30] Tinbergen, J. *International Economic Cooperation, Amsterdam:* North-Holland Publishing Company, 1946.

13

Optimal Commercial Policy for a Minimum-Wage Economy

Richard A. Brecher

1. Introduction

The standard Heckscher-Ohlin analysis of an open economy has been extended to consider the welfare implications of various factor-market imperfections. Two such imperfections may be seen as polar types.[1] In one of these cases, there is a distortive wage differential between sectors, with perfect flexibility of the real wage ensuring full employment of labor. In the other case, there is wage equality between sectors, with downward inflexibility of the (uniform) real wage leading to unemployment of labor. For the first case, Bhagwati and Ramaswami (1963) and Bhagwati, Ramaswami and Srinivasan (1969) have established a welfare ranking of alternative commercial policies. The present paper performs a similar type of exercise for the second case, which has been discussed by Haberler (1950), Johnson (1965), Bhagwati (1968) and Brecher (1974).[2]

Section 2 briefly reviews the model in which the entire labor market is subject to an exogenously specified floor, or minimum, that constrains the real wage to exceed the maximum level consistent with full employment. Within this constrained-wage context, section 3 considers various commercial policies of the home country (i.e., the minimum-wage country), assuming that this economy has monopoly power in trade and remains incompletely specialized. Three policy combinations are ranked in increasing order of social-welfare optimality, as follows: (1) a trade tax (subsidy) in the absence of complementary commercial intervention; (2) a trade tax (subsidy) together with a consumption tax-cum-subsidy favoring one commodity; and (3) a trade tax together with a factor tax-cum-subsidy favoring the use of labor uniformly in all sectors, which is a first-best policy package. In case some of these taxes and subsidies are

This paper was originally published in *Journal of International Economics* 4 (1974): 139–149.

unavailable (see below), the discussion has been designed to show how to make the most of whichever ones actually can be used. In proceeding upwards through the policy ranking, there is an increase not only in the maximum achievable level of social welfare, but also in this level's corresponding quantity of overall labor employment.

2. The Model

Section 2.1 considers the production side of a minimum-wage economy. Then, home and foreign demand are introduced in section 2.2, so that the full international equilibrium can be determined in section 2.3. Finally, section 2.4 derives the consumption-possibility frontier to be used in section 3.

2.1. Production

Before introducing the wage constraint, recall the standard two-factor, two-good model of trade theory. Two commodities (one and two) are produced in amounts X_1 and X_2, using L_1 and L_2 units of labor plus K_1 and K_2 units of capital, with strictly concave production functions exhibiting homogeneity of degree one:

$$X_i = F_i(K_i, L_i) = L_i f_i(k_i), \qquad i \equiv 1, 2, \tag{1}$$

where $k_i \equiv K_i/L_i$ and $f_i \equiv F_i/L_i$. The economy is endowed with fixed, overall factor supplies ($\bar{L}$ and $\bar{K}$) which constrain the total employment levels (L and K):

$$L \equiv L_1 + L_2 \leqq \bar{L}, \tag{2}$$

$$K \equiv K_1 + K_2 \leqq \bar{K}. \tag{3}$$

Both factors are perfectly mobile domestically. Entrepreneurs maximize profits under perfect competition. In addition, it will be assumed throughout this paper that home production remains incompletely specialized at all times.

Now subject the entire labor market to a wage floor, which is exogenously given in real[3] terms. Let this minimum real wage be set by some institutional arrangement (such as custom, unions or law), and be specified in terms of the second[4] good at some fixed[5] level denoted by $\bar{w}_2$. This minimum-wage constraint can be written as

$$w_2 \geqq \bar{w}_2, \tag{4}$$

where w_2 is the economy's (uniform) wage in terms of good two, and (by profit maximization) equals MPL_2 which is the economy's (uniform)

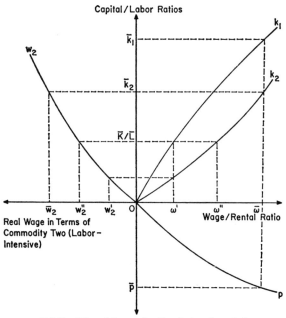

Figure 1

marginal product of labor in terms of good two. Because of this wage floor, labor may be unemployed. However, since the reward of capital is perfectly flexible, capital must be fully utilized. Thus,

$$\bar{K} = K \equiv L_1 k_1 + L_2 k_2. \tag{5}$$

Figure 1 illustrates the familiar relationships between w_2 and k_2 (in the second quadrant) and between $k_i (i = 1, 2)$ and ω (in the first quadrant), where ω denotes the economy's (uniform) wage/rental ratio.[6] It is well known that, given endowment ratio $\bar{K}/\bar{L}$, full employment of both factors is consistent only with $\omega' \leq \omega \leq \omega''$,[7] and hence only with $w_2' \leq w_2 \leq w_2''$. However, constraint (4) implies $w_2 > w_2''$, since $\bar{w}_2 > w_2''$ by assumption. In this case, unemployment of labor is necessary, since $\bar{w}_2$ has been specified to exceed the maximum w_2 (and MPL_2) consistent with full employment. This unemployment of labor implies that constraint (4) is binding, with $w_2 = \bar{w}_2$ and hence with $\omega = \omega$. This binding case is the interesting one, and the only case considered in this paper.

Figure 1 also shows the well-known Samuelson (1949) relationship between ω and p (in the fourth quadrant), where p is the relative price of the second good in terms of the first. The equilibrium wage/rental

Commodity Two
(Labor-Intensive)

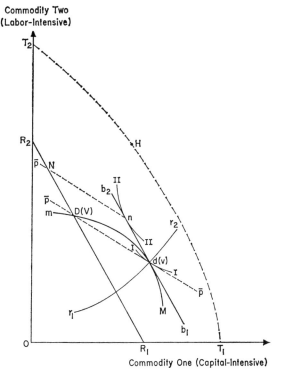

Figure 2

ratio ($\bar{\omega}$) corresponds to the equilibrium values $\bar{p}$, $\bar{k}_1$ and $\bar{k}_2$. Since $\bar{k}_1 > \bar{k}_2$, good one (two) is relatively capital-intensive (labor-intensive) in the relevant range.[8] Substituting $\bar{k}_1$ and $\bar{k}_2$ into equations (1) and (5), it follows after simple manipulation that

$$X_1 = \alpha - \beta X_2, \tag{6}$$

where α and β are constants defined as $\alpha \equiv \bar{K} f_1(\bar{k}_1)/\bar{k}_1$ and $\beta \equiv \bar{k}_2 f_1(\bar{k}_1)/\bar{k}_1 f_2(\bar{k}_2)$. Equation (6) describes the minimum-wage transformation curve, illustrated by the straight line $R_2 R_1$ in figure 2. The equilibrium price line (for $\bar{p}$) is flatter than $R_2 R_1$, since $\bar{k}_1 > \bar{k}_2$ implies $\bar{p} > \beta$. [The first-order conditions for profit maximization can be manipulated to yield $\beta = \bar{p}(\bar{\omega} \bar{k}_2 + \bar{k}_1 \bar{k}_2)/(\bar{\omega} \bar{k}_1 + \bar{k}_1 \bar{k}_2) < \bar{p}$, where β was defined as the ratio of capital's average products, and $\bar{p}$ equals the ratio of capital's (and labor's) marginal products.] As output of the (labor-intensive) second good increases with upward movements along $R_2 R_1$, total employment of labor increases. [That is, $dL/dX_2 = (\bar{k}_1 - \bar{k}_2)/\bar{k}_1 f_2(\bar{k}_2) > 0$;

where equation (5) has been differentiated after substituting from equation (1), using the fact that $L_1 \equiv L - L_2$, and setting $k_i = \bar{k}_i$.] Line $R_2 R_1$ lies completely below the conventional (flexible-wage, full-employment) production-possibility frontier, $T_2 T_1$, to reflect the existence of unemployed labor. The minimum-wage transformation curve,[9] $R_2 R_1$, is a well-known Rybczynski line described by Mundell (1968).

2.2. Demand

Foreign demand is given by the function $g(E)$; where $g(0) = 0$, $g'(E) \equiv dg/dE > 0$ and $dg'(E)/dE < 0$;[10] and where E denotes foreign net imports (and home net exports) of good two, exchanging for $g(E)$ of foreign net exports (and home net imports) of good one. If $E > (<) 0$, in which case $g > (<)0$, the home country exports (imports) the second good and imports (exports) the first good. The function g may be represented in figure 2 by a conventional foreign offer curve like mDM, whose origin (D) has been placed on the transformation curve $(R_2 R_1)$ in the Baldwin (1948) manner.

Home consumption of good i, $C_i (i = 1, 2)$, can now be written as

$$C_2 = X_2 - E, \tag{7}$$

$$C_1 = \alpha - \beta X_2 + g(E), \tag{8}$$

where use has been made of equation (6). The levels of C_1 and C_2 completely determine social welfare in the traditional way, according to the conventional utility function $U(C_1, C_2)$; where U is a concave function; and the partial derivatives of U, $U_i \equiv \partial U(C_1, C_2)/\partial C_i (i = 1,2)$, are assumed to be positive if C_1 and C_2 are both finite.[11] The function U may be represented by a conventional set of community indifference curves,[12] like I-I and II-II in figure 2. It is assumed throughout this paper that neither good is inferior in home consumption.

2.3. Free-Trade Equilibrium

As usual, free-trade equilibrium requires equality among the domestic price ratio $(\bar{p})$, the world price ratio (g/E), and the marginal rate of substitution in home consumption (U_2/U_1):

$$g(E)/E = \bar{p}, \tag{9}$$

$$U_2(C_1, C_2)/U_1(C_1, C_2) = \bar{p}. \tag{10}$$

Equations (7), (8), (9) and (10) together are sufficient to determine all equilibrium values. Free-trade equilibrium may be illustrated in figure 2 as follows. Home production is at D. The domestic and world price ratio is $\bar{p}$. Home consumption is at d, where indifference curve I-I touches the social budget line (for $\bar{p}$) drawn through D. The home country trades (at price ratio $\bar{p}$) to point d on foreign offer curve mDM, in this case importing the first good and exporting the second. Throughout this paper, equilibrium in world markets is assumed to be unique and stable.

2.4. The Consumption-Possibility Frontier

An important construction for section 3 is the consumption-possibility frontier, or Baldwin (1948) envelope, which shows the maximum possible consumption level of one good for a given consumption level of the other good. This frontier is found by maximizing C_2, subject to a given level of C_1, and subject to equations (7) and (8). The first-order conditions of this maximization can be manipulated to yield

$$g'(E) = \beta, \tag{11}$$

whose unique solution is denoted $\tilde{E}$. Substituting $\tilde{E}$ into equations (7) and (8),

$$C_1 = \gamma - \beta C_2, \tag{12}$$

where γ is a constant defined as $\gamma \equiv \alpha + g(\tilde{E}) - \beta\tilde{E}$. Equation (12) describes the consumption-possibility frontier, partially illustrated in figure 2 by the straight line $b_2 b_1$, which (given its slope of $-1/\beta$) is parallel to $R_2 R_1$. Line $b_2 b_1$ is part of the outer envelope traced by mDM, as the origin of mDM is allowed to slide along $R_2 R_1$ with the axes of mDM kept parallel to those of $R_2 R_1$.[13]

3. Policy Ranking

This section shows how taxes and subsidies may be used to maximize welfare when different policy combinations are available. A welfare ranking is established for three such combinations, assuming that the home country has monopoly power in trade and remains incompletely specialized. Sections. 3.1, 3.2 and 3.3 consider respectively the third-best, second-best and first-best of the three policy packages analyzed. As the discussion progresses from the third-best optimum to the second-best and then to the first-best, the optimal level of employment increases with the optimal level of social welfare.

3.1. Taxes (Subsidies) on Trade

Suppose that trade taxes and trade subsidies are the only forms of commercial intervention available. These policies create a wedge between the domestic (producer and consumer) price ratio ($\bar{p}$) and the world price ratio (g/E). The ad valorem trade tax (subsidy), t, is then given by

$$t = \frac{[g(E)/E] - \bar{p}}{\bar{p}}, \tag{13}$$

when the home country imports the first good (with $E, g > 0$), and by

$$t = \frac{\bar{p} - [g(E)/E]}{g(E)/E}, \tag{14}$$

when the home country imports the second good (with $E, g < 0$). As $t \gtreqless 0$, trade is taxed, free or subsidized, respectively. Made here is a conventional assumption that the government redistributes (finances) all trade taxes (subsidies) in lump-sum fashion.

The formal problem for optimal trade policy is to maximize $U(C_1, C_2)$, subject to constraints (7), (8) and (10). The first order conditions of this maximization can be manipulated to yield

$$g'(E) = \beta. \tag{11}$$

The unique solution of equation (11), $\tilde{E}$ as before, can be substituted into equation (13) (if $\tilde{E} > 0$) or into equation (14) (if $\tilde{E} < 0$) to calculate the optimal value of t, denoted $\tilde{t}$.

The optimal trade strategy is now illustrated in figure 2 for the case of $E > 0$. Welfare maximization is achieved by moving up the income-consumption curve ($r_2 r_1$) corresponding to constraint (10), until such movement is halted (at v) by the consumption-possibility frontier ($b_2 b_1$) characterized by equation (11). The value of $\tilde{t}$ can be determined by comparing the slope of the domestic price line (Dd) with the slope of the (optimal) world price line (Vv). (V is the optimal production point where the origin of mDM lies when this curve touches $b_2 b_1$ at v.) Figure 2 (in which v coincides with d and V coincides with D) shows the special case in which free trade is the optimal strategy. This prescription arises because the free-trade slope of mDM (at d) equals the slope of $R_2 R_1$, thereby indicating that the second good's marginal cost (in terms of the first good) is the same through free trade as through domestic production. If mDM were redrawn slightly so that its free-trade slope at d were steeper (flatter) than $R_2 R_1$ in figure 2, the optimal policy would be a trade tax (subsidy) instead of free trade.

Whatever the value of $\tilde{t}$, the following two results always hold. First, the optimal trade strategy does not achieve full employment[14] (on $T_2 T_1$ in figure 2), and therefore is clearly not a first-best policy. Second, the optimal trade policy is not even second-best, since it leaves $U_2/U_1 =$

$\bar{p} \neq \beta$, as at point v in figure 2 where indifference curve I-I is not tangent to $b_2 b_1$.

3.2. Taxes (Subsidies) on Both Trade and Consumption

Now suppose that it is possible to use consumption[15] tax-cum-subsidies, in addition to trade taxes (subsidies). The added policy gives an additional degree of freedom, by allowing a wedge between the domestic producer price ratio ($\bar{p}$) and the domestic consumer price ratio (equal to U_2/U_1). An ad valorem trade tax (subsidy) of t is still given by equation (13) or (14). An ad valorem consumption tax (subsidy) of τ, imposed on the first good, is given by

$$\tau = \frac{\bar{p} - [U_2(C_1, C_2)/U_1(C_1, C_2)]}{U_2(C_1, C_2)/U_1(C_1, C_2)}. \tag{15}$$

As $\tau \gtreqless 0$, consumption of the first good is taxed, unaffected or subsidized, respectively. It is assumed that all such consumption taxes (subsidies) are redistributed (financed) by the government in lump-sum fashion.[16]

The formal problem for optimal trade policy is now to maximize $U(C_1, C_2)$, subject to constraints (7) and (8) as before—but no longer subject to constraint (10) of the previous section, since τ is now available. The first-order conditions of this maximization can be manipulated to yield

$$g'(E) = \beta, \tag{11}$$

as before, and

$$U_2(C_1, C_2)/U_1(C_1, C_2) = \beta, \tag{16}$$

which differs from equation (10) since $\bar{p} \neq \beta$. The unique solution of equation (11), $\tilde{E}$ as before, can be substituted into equation (13) or into equation (14) to yield the optimal t, which is clearly $\tilde{t}$ as before. That is, the optimal trade tax (subsidy) is the same whether or not it can be combined with the optimal consumption policy. By equations (15) and (16), the optimal value of τ (denoted $\tilde{\tau}$) is $\tilde{\tau} = (\bar{p} - \beta)/\beta$—which is positive (recalling $\bar{p} > \beta$), independent of $\tilde{E}$, and hence independent of $\tilde{t}$. Thus, consumption of the capital-intensive good should always be taxed at the same rate, no matter what the optimal trade tax (subsidy).

The optimal strategy is now illustrated in figure 2. Welfare maximization is achieved by consuming on the consumption-possibility frontier ($b_2 b_1$) characterized by equation (11), at the point (n) where an indifference curve (II-II) is tangent to $b_2 b_1$ in accordance with equation (16). As before, $\tilde{t}$ is obtained by comparing the slope of the domestic producer price line (Dd) with the slope of the (optimal) world price line (Nn parallel to Vv). (N is the optimal production point where the origin of mDM lies when this curve touches $b_2 b_1$ at n). The value of $\tilde{t}$ is given by comparing the slope of the domestic producer price line (dD) with the slope of the (optimal) domestic consumer price line ($b_2 b_1$).

Whatever the value of $\tilde{t}$ combined with (the positive) $\tilde{\tau}$, the following results always hold. First, optimal welfare and its corresponding level of optimal employment[17] always increase when $\tilde{\tau}$ is added to $\tilde{t}$—as in figure 2, where welfare is greater at n than at v, and employment is greater at N than at V (recalling $dL/dX_2 > 0$). Second, combining $\tilde{t}$ with $\tilde{\tau}$ achieves the highest level of welfare consistent with production constraint (6), as in figure 2 where n lies on the highest indifference curve consistent with production on $R_2 R_1$. Third, the combination of $\tilde{t}$ and $\tilde{\tau}$ does not achieve full employment, and is therefore not a first-best policy package.

3.3. Taxes and Subsidies on Both Trade and Factors

Now suppose that it is possible to impose tax-cum-subsidies on factor use, in addition to trade taxes and trade subsidies. With an ad valorem labor subsidy of s, applied uniformly in both sectors, the producer's net cost of a unit of labor is $\bar{w}_2(1 - s)$ in terms of good two. Under profit maximization, $\bar{w}_2(1 - s) = MPL_2$, which implies

$$s = (\bar{w}_2 - MPL_2)/\bar{w}_2. \tag{17}$$

In other words, a labor subsidy can be used to drive a wedge between the marginal product of labor and the minimum wage. This subsidy may be financed either in lump-sum fashion, or by taxing capital uniformly in both sectors (since the supply of capital is perfectly inelastic). By combining a labor subsidy with a trade tax, it is possible to reach the first-best solution, as will now be shown.

If the wage were unconstrained, welfare could be maximized simply by application of the conventional (positive) optimal tariff, denoted t^*. Imposing t^* in the absence of wage rigidity would bring production to the first-best point on $T_2 T_1$ in figure 2, say point H, where labor's marginal product would be MPL_2^*. However, there actually is a binding minimum-wage constaint, which implies that $\bar{w}_2 > MPL_2^*$. (Recall that $\bar{w}_2$ has been specified to exceed the maximum MPL_2 consistent with full employment.) This optimal wedge between wage and marginal product at H can be created with an optimal labor subsidy (denoted s^*), given by $s^* = (\bar{w}_2 - MPL_2^*)/\bar{w}_2$ according to equation (17). This s^* must be applied (in both sectors) along with t^* to achieve the first-best solution.

The unemployment effect of the minimum wage is cancelled by s^*, while t^* restricts trade to the conventional optimal level.[18] This first-best policy combination goes directly to the sources of distortion, in keeping with the general prescription of Bhagwati and Ramaswami (1963). The labor subsidy is used to correct a domestic distortion due to wage rigidity in the home labor market. The trade tax is used to correct a foreign distortion arising from monopoly power in international trade.

This paper draws upon parts of my Ph.D. thesis (1971). For their guidance and encouragement of this work, I am deeply indebted to Richard E. Caves, chairman of my dissertation committee, and to Jagdish N. Bhagwati and Thomas O. Horst, members of this committee. I also wish to thank Lucy A. Cardwell, Vahid F. Nowshirvani and Ian C. Parker for discussing the material with me extensively, T. N. Srinivasan for suggesting major improvements in the paper, and anonymous referees for providing helpful comments and suggestions. Of course, I alone am responsible for any remaining errors or shortcomings.

References

Baldwin, R. E., 1948, Equilibrium in international trade: A diagrammatic analysis, *Quarterly Journal of Economics* 62, Nov., 748–762.

Bhagwati, J. N., 1968, *The theory and practice of commercial policy: Departures from Unified Exchange Rates*, Frank D. Graham Memorial Lecture, Princeton, 1967, Special Papers in International Economics, no. 8 (Princeton University, Princeton).

Bhagwati, J. N. and V. K. Ramaswami, 1963, Domestic distortions, tariffs and the theory of optimum subsidy, *Journal of Political Economy* 71, no. 1, 44–50.

Bhagwati, J. N. and T. N. Srinivasan, 1969, Optimal intervention to achieve non-economic objectives, *Review of Economic Studies* 36, no. 105, 27–38.

Bhagwati, J. N., V. K. Ramaswami and T. N. Srinivasan, 1969, Domestic distortions, tariffs, and the theory of optimum subsidy: Some further results, *Journal of Political Economy* 77, no. 6, 1005–1010.

Brecher, R. A., 1971, Minimum wage rates and the pure theory of international trade, unpublished Ph.D. dissertation (Harvard University, Cambridge).

Brecher, R. A., 1974, Minimum wage rates and the pure theory of international trade, *Quarterly Journal of Economics* 88, no. 1, 98–116.

Haberler, G., 1950, Some problems in the pure theory of international trade, *Economic Journal* 60, no. 238, 223–240.

Johnson, H. G., 1965, Optimal trade intervention in the presence of domestic distortions, in R. E. Baldwin et al., eds., *Trade growth and the Balance of Payments: Essays in Honor of Gottfried Haberler* (Rand McNally, Chicago) 3–34.

Lefeber, L., 1971, Trade and minimum wage rates, in J. N. Bhagwati et al., eds., *Trade, Balance of Payments, and Growth: Papers in International Economics in Honor of Charles P. Kindleberger* (North-Holland, Amsterdam) 91–114.

Mundell, R. A., 1968, International trade and factor mobility, in *International Economics* (The Macmillan Company, New York) 85–99.

Samuelson, P. A., 1949, International factor-price equalisation once again, *Economic Journal* 59, no. 234, 181–197.

Srinivasan, T. N. and J. N. Bhagwati, 1973, *Alternative Policy Rankings in a Large, Open Economy with Sector-Specific, Minimum Wages*, mimeo., Working Paper no. 109 (Massachusetts Institute of Technology, Cambridge).

14

Dynamic Stability and the Theory of Factor-Market Distortions

J. Peter Neary

Although international monetary economists have devoted much attention to the process of adjustment from one equilibrium to another, the pure theory of international trade has traditionally confined its attention to comparisons between long-run equilibria.[1] The same point applies to those branches of theory, such as the neoclassical theory of tax incidence, which make use of models identical in structure to the Heckscher-Ohlin-Samuelson model of international trade. The aim of this paper is to suggest that this neglect has overlooked many interesting problems, and to argue that the study of adjustment mechanisms in two-sector neoclassical models is both of interest in itself, and of value in providing information on the comparative static properties of these models. In particular, it is shown that the use of explicit adjustment mechanisms permits some considerable simplifications of the theory of factor-market distortions.

Many of the recent writings on factor-market distortions by international trade theorists have been concerned with the elucidation of a number of paradoxes (paradoxes at least in the light of accepted trade theory) which can arise in the presence of such distortions. (See especially Jagdish N. Bhagwati and T. N. Srinivasan; Ronald W. Jones, 1971a; Stephen P. Magee, 1971, 1976.) One writer has gone as far as to say that the introduction of factor-market distortions into international trade models opens a "Pandora's Box of paradoxes" (see Raveendra N. Batra, p. 279). A necessary and sufficient condition for the occurrence of many of these paradoxes is that the economy exhibit a particular condition (which cannot arise if factor markets are undistorted): namely, the level of initial distortions must be such that the ranking of the two sectors in terms of *physical* factor intensities is the opposite of their ranking in

This paper was originally published in *American Economic Review* 68, no. 4 (September 1978): 671–682.

terms of *value* factor intensities; in other words, in the sector which uses a higher physical ratio of capital to labor, the share of payments to capital in the total value of output is lower than in the other sector. The implications of this condition may be seen by noting the principal paradoxes to which it gives rise:

1. Perverse Price–Output Response   An increase in the relative price of one good leads to a fall in its output, assuming the levels of factor-market distortions are unchanged.

2. Perverse Distortion–Output Response   An increase in the rate of subsidy to one sector (whether an output or an input subsidy) leads to a fall in the output of that sector, assuming relative output prices are unchanged.

3. Lack of Correspondence between Rybczynski and Stolper-Samuelson Theorems   Each of these theorems continues to hold in isolation, but the former must be expressed in terms of physical factor intensities, and the latter in terms of value factor intensities. Hence, if labor force growth at constant commodity prices increases the output of good X, an increase in the relative price of X assuming a constant labor force will *reduce* rather than increase the real wage. More surprisingly still, a country may be capital abundant relative to the rest of the world, and exporting its physically capital-intensive commodity, with all the other conditions for the Heckscher-Ohlin theorem holding, and yet a protection-induced increase in the domestic price of the import-competing good will *reduce* the real return of the scarce factor (labor).

These examples are sufficient to demonstrate that international trade theory becomes apparently much more complicated when allowance is made for factor-market distortions. However, a major object of this paper is to show that *all these paradoxes are theoretical curiosa which will "almost never" be observed in real world economies.* More formally, sections I and II below demonstrate that in a small open economy, equilibria where the value and physical factor-intensity rankings of the two sectors differ are necessarily *unstable* under a variety of plausible adjustment mechanisms.

Section I concentrates on the "short-run capital specificity" adjustment process, which is one exception to the general neglect of adjustment processes by international trade theorists, having been studied by Mayer (1974b), Michael Mussa and Neary (1978a), drawing on earlier work by Jones (1971b). A more general class of adjustment mechanisms, permitting both labor and capital to be sector specific in the short run, is examined in section II. Section III extends the analysis to the case where relative commodity prices are endogenous and derives a general stability condition for this case also. The implications of these findings are examined in section IV: it is shown that they permit a considerable simplification of both international trade theory and the general equilibrium theory of tax incidence, and also that they may be interpreted in terms of the relationship between Walrasian and Marshallian stability conditions. Finally the principal conclusions of the paper are summarized in section V.

I. Short-Run Capital Specificity in a Small Open Economy

In this section, I examine the process of adjustment to an exogenous change in the level of factor-market distortion in a small open economy which obeys all the assumptions of the Heckscher-Ohlin-Samuelson model of international trade (including perfect competition, constant returns to scale and fixed aggregate factor supplies) with two exceptions: firstly, long-run equilibrium is characterized by constant proportional differentials between the value marginal products of capital and labor in the two sectors:[2]

$$w_Y = \alpha w_X \tag{1a}$$

$$r_Y = \beta r_X \tag{1b}$$

and secondly, while the labor force is instantaneously reallocated to ensure that (1a) is satisfied at all times, capital goods are sector specific in the short run, and move between sectors in the medium run in response to deviations from (1b).[3]

To investigate the short-run effect on the intersectoral differential in capital rentals of a once and for all increase in the labor-market distortion parameter α (attributable, for example, to an increase in the rate of labor subsidy to sector X), I invoke the well-known conditions, implied by profit maximization and constant returns to scale, that the proportional change in the price of each good must equal a weighted average of the changes in factor prices in each sector, the weights being the share of each factor in the value of output of that sector (a circumflex indicates a proportional rate of change: $\hat{w} = d \log w$):

$$\hat{p}_X = \theta_{LX}\hat{w}_X + \theta_{KX}\hat{r}_X, \tag{2}$$

$$\hat{p}_Y = \theta_{LY}\hat{w}_Y + \theta_{KY}\hat{r}_Y. \tag{3}$$

With both commodity prices held constant because of the "small country" assumption, equations (1a), (2), and (3) may be manipulated to express the change in the intersectoral rental differential as a function of changes in the labor-market distortion parameter and the wage in the X sector:

$$\theta_{KX}\theta_{KY}(\hat{r}_X - \hat{r}_Y) = -|\theta|\hat{w}_X + \theta_{LY}\theta_{KX}\hat{\alpha}, \tag{4}$$

where $|\theta|$ is the determinant of the matrix of sectoral factor shares, and is positive if and only if the X sector is relatively labor intensive in the *value* sense. To eliminate the change in w_X from (4), use the full-employment condition, which is expressed by equating the sum of the labor demand schedules of each sector to the fixed labor endowment:

$$L_X\left(\frac{w_X}{p_X}, K_X\right) + L_Y\left(\frac{w_Y}{p_Y}, K_Y\right) = \bar{L}. \tag{5}$$

Differentiating (5), holding commodity prices and capital allocations constant, and using equation (1a), one may express the short-run proportional change in the wage rate in sector X as a function of the change in the labor market distortion parameter:[4]

$$\hat{w}_X = -\frac{1}{\Delta}\lambda_{LY}\frac{\sigma_Y}{\theta_{KY}}\hat{\alpha}, \tag{6}$$

where

$$\Delta = \lambda_{LX}\frac{\sigma_X}{\theta_{KX}} + \lambda_{LY}\frac{\sigma_Y}{\theta_{KY}} > 0. \tag{7}$$

Finally, substituting from (6) into (4):

$$\theta_{KX}\theta_{KY}(\hat{r}_X - \hat{r}_Y) = \frac{1}{\Delta}(\sigma_X\lambda_{LX}\theta_{LY} + \sigma_Y\lambda_{LY}\theta_{LX})\hat{\alpha}. \tag{8}$$

Assuming that the capital market is in long-run equilibrium before the change, this shows that an increase in the wage differential in favor of sector Y will increase the relative rental on capital in the other sector in the short run. Hence, in the medium run, capital will begin to reallocate from sector Y to sector X, *irrespective of the relative factor intensities* (in either the physical or value sense) of the two sectors.

But this capital reallocation will itself affect the intersectoral rental differential. To see this, again differentiate equation (5), this time holding commodity prices and factor-market distortions constant:

$$\hat{w}_X = \frac{1}{\Delta}(\lambda_{LX}\hat{K}_X + \lambda_{LY}\hat{K}_Y). \tag{9}$$

This gives the effect on the X sector wage rate of any arbitrary changes in the capital stocks in each sector. However, when a reallocation of the given stock of capital is considered, the changes in each sector are not arbitrary, but must continue to satisfy the capital endowment constraint:

$$K_X + K_Y = \bar{K},$$

or in differential form:

$$\lambda_{KX}\hat{K}_X + \lambda_{KY}\hat{K}_Y = 0. \tag{10}$$

Substituting from (10) into (9) gives

$$\hat{w}_X = \frac{|\lambda|}{\Delta} \frac{\hat{K}_X}{\lambda_{KY}}, \tag{11}$$

where $|\lambda|$ is the determinant of the matrix of factor-to-sector allocations, and is positive if and only if sector X is relatively labor intensive in the *physical* sense. Finally, substituting from (11) into (4), holding constant the level of the labor-market distortion parameter α, one derives

$$\hat{r}_X - \hat{r}_Y = -\frac{1}{\Delta} \frac{|\lambda| |\theta|}{\theta_{KX}\theta_{KY}} \frac{\hat{K}_X}{\lambda_{KY}}. \tag{12}$$

This shows that a reallocation of capital into sector X will reduce the proportional gap between the rentals in the two sectors, if and only if the product of the two determinants, $|\lambda|$ and $|\theta|$, is positive; in other words, if and only if the rankings of the two sectors by physical and value factor intensities are the same.[5] Hence, if these rankings differ, the initial reallocation of capital in response to an increase in the wage differential will widen the intersectoral rental differential, leading to an increased flow of capital from Y to X, moving progressively further away from the new long-run equilibrium predicted by the comparative static analysis. One may conclude, therefore, that under the short-run capital specificity adjustment process, an equilibrium where the physical and value factor intensity rankings differ in a small open economy must be locally unstable.

II. Stability in a Small Open Economy when Both Capital and Labor Adjust Sluggishly

In the last section I examined the stability of equilibrium following a particular exogenous change (a change in the level of distortion in the labor market), and assuming a particular adjustment mechanism (the short-run capital-specificity process). In this section I generalize this to the case where both capital and labor adjust sluggishly, and show that the same stability criterion applies. I continue to adopt the small open economy assumption of fixed relative commodity prices.

The dynamic assumptions of this section are that both capital and labor follow adjustment processes of the same form (though not necessarily of the same speed). Both factors are now sector specific in the short run, but complete flexibility of the wage and rental rate within each sector ensures that both factors are fully employed throughout the adjustment period.[6] As before, a long-run equilibrium is defined as a state where each factor earns the same return in both sectors, taking into account the distortion parameters α and β as in equations (1a) and (1b). Starting from such an equilibrium, any exogenous shock will bring about a short-run intersectoral divergence of the distortion-inclusive returns of each factor. These divergences in turn will lead in the medium run to a gradual reallocation (or "migration") of each factor out of the sector where it earns a lower return into the sector where it earns a higher return. The rate at which this reallocation takes place will depend in general on a variety of considerations, including migration costs, rates of time preference and expectations of future price changes on the part of factor owners. However, since our primary interest lies not in these influences themselves, but rather in their implications for stability, we may subsume them into general migration functions of the following form (where D is the time derivative operator):

$$DK_X = \phi \left\{ \beta \frac{r_X}{r_Y} - 1 \right\}, \qquad \phi' > 0,\ \phi(0) = 0, \tag{13}$$

$$DL_X = \psi \left\{ \alpha \frac{w_X}{w_Y} - 1 \right\}, \qquad \psi' > 0,\ \psi(0) = 0. \tag{14}$$

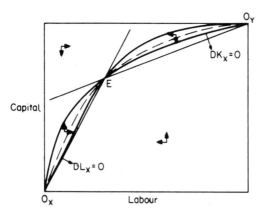

Figure 1

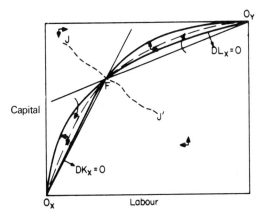

Figure 2

It turns out that these dynamic assumptions may be conveniently analyzed by locating directly in the Edgeworth-Bowley box the stationary loci of (13) and (14)[7] (i.e., equations (1a) and (1b)) as well as the distorted efficiency locus (*DEL*) or contract curve of the Edgeworth-Bowley box, whose equation is

$$\frac{\alpha}{\beta} \frac{w_X}{r_X} = \frac{w_Y}{r_Y}. \tag{15}$$

The details of this construction are outlined in Appendix A. Figure 1 presents the case where sector X is capital intensive in the physical sense ($|\lambda| < 0$), and where the rankings of the two sectors by physical and value factor intensities correspond ($|\lambda| |\theta| > 0$). For all points other than the long-run equilibrium point E, the directions of movement are shown by the arrows. These may be verified by reference to equations (A3) and (A5) in the Appendix, and are in any case intuitively plausible. For example, an upward movement away from any point on the capital-market equilibrium locus (*KMEL*) implies an increase in the capital-labor ratio in X and a decrease in that in Y; at constant commodity prices this implies a fall in the rental in X and an increase in that in Y; hence capital is encouraged to move out of the X sector into Y. The direction of labor migration at all points off the labor-market equilibrium locus (*LMEL*) may be established in a similar manner. The conclusion to be drawn from the figure is that the equilibrium at E is globally as well as locally stable.

A very different conclusion is drawn from figure 2, however, where the physical and value factor-intensity rankings of the two sectors differ. At the equilibrium point F, the *KMEL* cuts the *DEL* from below, while the *LMEL* cuts it from above. As a result, the point *F* is a saddle point: there is one knife-edge path, indicated by the dotted line *JJ'*, along which factor allocations will converge towards *F*. But this path is itself unstable: the slightest divergence from it will lead to a cumulative movement away from *F*. Hence, while the condition $|\lambda| \, |\theta| < 0$ does not precisely imply global instability, equilibria where this condition is met are likely in practice to be highly unstable.

Two special cases of the general adjustment mechanism may be mentioned in passing. The first, where the labor force is assumed to be reallocated instantaneously, is simply the short-run capital specificity adjustment process of section I. Only points along the *LMEL* in figures 1 and 2 are now admissible, and it is clear that point *E* in figure 1 is still globally stable while point *F* in figure 2 is now globally unstable, thus reinforcing the conclusions of section I. A second special case is where capital goods are sector specific in the long run (or, more plausibly, "capital" in each sector is a different fixed factor, for example, plant and machinery in the manufacturing sector *X*, and land in agriculture *Y*, as in Jones, 1971b). In this case, it may be seen that no instability problem arises, even in figure 2. We may conclude therefore that the comparative static paradoxes and the associated problem of instability arise only when *both* capital and labor are assumed to be intersectorally mobile in the long run.

Finally, having shown that, when the rankings of sectors by physical and value factor intensities differ, the economy will not move towards the new equilibrium predicted by the comparative static analysis, one must establish where it will tend towards. In brief, the answer is either towards a *specialized* equilibrium, or towards a new nonspecialized equilibrium where the initial ranking of the sectors by *value* factor intensity has been reversed, so that the physical and value rankings now coincide. To illustrate this, refer again to figure 2. As the diagram is drawn, all paths other than those starting along the line *JJ'* converge towards either O_X or O_Y, implying that the economy specializes in good *Y* or good *X*, respectively. Nevertheless, it is possible that the process of factor reallocation may reverse the value factor-intensity ranking of the sectors, in which case a new stable long-run equilibrium may be attained at some point other than *F* on the *DEL*. At such a point, both the *KMEL* and the *LMEL* would again intersect the *DEL*, and a local stability analysis similar to that of figure 1 would be appropriate. However, if this reversal does not occur (for example, it cannot occur if both production functions are Cobb-Douglas), then the factor reallocation will continue until the economy specializes in the production of one or other good.

III. Preexisting Distortions and Stability of Equilibrium when Commodity Prices are Variable

So far I have been exclusively concerned with a small open economy, where prices are parametrically given. However, the adjustment processes just considered may be extended to examine the stability of equilibrium when commodity prices are variable. To investigate this, follow Jones (1965, 1971a) and assume that the aggregate demand function, in differential form, is given by

$$\hat{X} - \hat{Y} = -\sigma_D(\hat{p}_X - \hat{p}_Y). \tag{16}$$

This may be interpreted as referring to a closed economy where aggregate preferences are homothetic, in which case the parameter σ_D is the elasticity of substitution in demand. Equation (16) could alternatively be interpreted as a composite demand function, representing the combined effects of home and foreign demand in an open economy which possesses some monopoly power in international trade. In both cases, assume that σ_D is positive.

In addition to specifying the demand function (16), assume that relative commodity prices move instantaneously to clear the commodity market at all times. When this assumption is made, it is shown in Appendix B that a necessary and sufficient condition for local stability is

$$\frac{1}{\sigma_D}(\sigma_D|\lambda|\,|\theta| + \sigma_X Q_X + \sigma_Y Q_Y) > 0, \tag{17}$$

where

$$Q_X = \lambda_{LX}\theta_{KX} + \lambda_{KX}\theta_{LX}$$

and

$$Q_Y = \lambda_{LY}\theta_{KY} + \lambda_{KY}\theta_{LY}.$$

Hence, the stability condition (assuming that σ_D is positive) is that the expression in parentheses in (17) be positive. This expression, denoted by σ, has been termed by Jones (1965) the economy's "aggregate elasticity of substitution." Its importance for the comparative static results of the two-sector model is well known, but its crucial role in affecting stability does not appear to have been noted by previous writers. Note that the stability criterion for the fixed-prices model of sections I and II is a special case of (17), corresponding to the limiting value as σ_D tends to infinity.

While the local stability criterion $\sigma > 0$ is just 'as convenient as that for the small open economy model $|\lambda|\,|\theta| > 0$, the analysis of global stability is more complicated when prices are variable, since there is no guarantee that either factor-market equilibrium locus will slope upwards. There are now three configurations which the phase diagram may exhibit in the neighborhood of a long-run equilibrium point: (i) both loci may slope upwards; in this case the analysis of figures 1 and 2 is directly applicable: the equilibrium will be locally stable if and only if the *KMEL* cuts the *DEL* from above and the *LMEL* cuts it from below; (ii) one locus may be upward sloping and the other downward sloping; in this case condition (17) is necessarily fulfilled and the equilibrium is locally stable; or (iii) both loci may be downward sloping; here (17) requires that the slope of the *KMEL* be greater (i.e., less negative) than that of the *LMEL* for local stability. Finally, as in section II, it is quite possible for multiple equilibria to exist, with the two equilibrium loci crossing and recrossing the *DEL*, implying a succession of alternately stable and unstable equilibria.

IV. Implications of the Stability Criteria

Evidently, the importance of obtaining stability conditions derives from the fact that they may be combined with Samuelson's Correspondence Principle, to assert that, since all empirically interesting equilibria must be stable, long-run equilibria where the stability conditions do not hold will "almost never" be observed.

The implications of the stability condition $|\lambda|\,|\theta| > 0$ for the theory of factor-market distortions in an open economy are immediately obvious: all of the comparative static paradoxes mentioned in the introduction become inconsistent with stable unspecialized equilibrium. However, it is important not to claim too much for this stability condition. For example, as Bhagwati and Srinivasan and others have shown, there is no necessary relationship between the reversal of physical and value factor intensities and the curvature of the distortion-constrained transformation curve. Hence, the stability condition $|\lambda|\,|\theta| > 0$ does not imply that the transformation curve must be concave to the origin in the neighborhood of an equilibrium point. Nor does it rule out the possibility that international factor price equalization may be prevented by the existence of factor-market distortions. Furthermore, there are a number of "paradoxes" which are attributable to factor-market distortions but which can occur even when the physical and value factor-intensity rankings are the same.[8] Clearly, nothing in the present paper rules out the possibility of any of these paradoxes.

Turning to the stability criterion for a closed economy $\sigma > 0$, it is of considerable importance, for the aggregate elasticity of substitution is the key parameter in most of the comparative static derivations for the two-sector model. For example, as shown by Jones (1965, equation (15)), an increase in the aggregate capital-labor ratio will raise the wage rental ratio if and only if σ is positive: our stability condition therefore rules out "capital-intensity perversities" in the two-sector model with homogeneous capital. It can also be shown (see the author, 1976) that provided σ is positive the conclusions of Harberger concerning factor-tax incidence in a closed economy and those of Harry G. Johnson and Peter Mieszkowski concerning the income distribution effect of unionization continue to hold in a wide variety of circumstances.[9] Finally, this condition may be related to the two-sector neoclassical growth model of Hirofumi Uzawa: a necessary and sufficient condition for uniquencess of momentary equilibrium in this model is that σ be positive, as Avinash K. Dixit and others, following Frank H. Hahn, have shown. The approach adopted here therefore draws attention to the unity of the two-sector framework, whether applied to the theories of public finance, international trade, or economic growth.[10]

A rather different application of this stability condition is the light

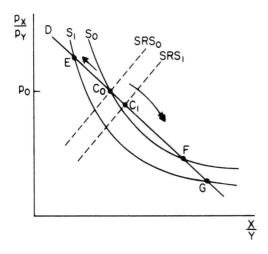

Figure 3

it throws on the relationship between the so-called Marshallian and Walrasian stability criteria. For example, in examining closed-economy equilibria where the aggregate supply schedule slopes downwards, Jones (1971a) assumed that its intersection with the aggregate demand schedule should exhibit Walrasian stability. Such an intersection is shown at C_o in figure 3: the downward-sloping long-run supply schedule S_o cuts the demand schedule D from above, implying that excess demand is positive for prices just below and negative for prices just above the equilibrium price p_o.

Is the stability criterion $\sigma > 0$ satisfied at C_o in figure 3? It is easily seen that it is not. For at that point, the algebraic value of the elasticity of the aggregate demand schedule is less than that of the long-run aggregate supply schedule, or in symbols: $-\sigma_D < \sigma_{LRS}$. Invoking the expression for the long-run supply elasticity derived by Jones (1965), this may be rewritten as

$$\sigma_D + \frac{\sigma_X Q_X + \sigma_Y Q_Y}{|\lambda|\,|\theta|} > 0. \tag{18}$$

But, since the aggregate supply curve is downward sloping, the term $|\lambda|\,|\theta|$ is negative. Hence, multiplying (18) by $|\lambda||\theta|$ reverses the sign of the inequality:

$$\sigma_D|\lambda|\,|\theta| + \sigma_X Q_X + \sigma_Y Q_Y < 0.$$

This shows that the equilibrium at C_o is indeed unstable in the long-run sense. For example, the granting of a subsidy to sector X shifts the long-run supply curve from S_o to S_1, implying that the new long-run equilibrium should be at E (note that the variability of commodity prices does not affect the comparative static prediction of a perverse distortion-output response in the long run). But the adjustment path which the economy actually follows involves a sequence of short-run equilibria, moving down the demand curve in the direction of the double-headed arrow, and converging towards a new stable long-run equilibrium at G. At this point the long-run supply curve cuts the demand curve from below, implying that the stability condition $\sigma > 0$ is indeed fulfilled there. Hence, contrary to Jones, the correct ciriterion for the stability of long-run equilibrium in this model is that the aggregate supply and demand schedules exhibit Marshallian, not Walrasian, stability.[11]

Does this mean that there is no role for the Walrasian stability criterion? The answer to this is no, for the model must also exhibit Walrasian stability, but this refers to the intersection of the demand curve with the *short-run* supply curve. A different short-run supply curve is implied by each of the adjustment mechanisms considered. For example, if, as in sections II and III, both capital and labor are sector specific in the short run but remain fully employed, the short-run supply curve is vertical. Alternatively, under the adjustment mechanism assumed in section I, the short-run supply curve is upward sloping, as shown in figure 3. In the latter case, the effect of increasing the rate of subsidy in the X sector is to shift the short-run supply curve to the right, leading to a new equilibrium at C_1. But irrespective of the adjustment mechanism assumed, as factor markets move towards long-run equilibrium, the short-run supply curve shifts progressively to the right, tracing out a sequence of short-run equilibria where each short-run supply curve intersects the demand curve. At each of these intersections Walrasian stability must prevail. It should be noted that this analysis is perfectly consistent with the usual explanation for the difference between Marshallian and Walrasian stability (see Mark Blaug, pp. 411–14); that the former assumes it is quantities which adjust out of equilibrium whereas the latter assigns that role to prices. The present paper confirms this analysis, and supplements it by showing that under the adjustment mechanisms considered above, the two stability criteria are complementary; since in full long-run equilibrium both must hold, though the Marshallian criterion must be interpreted with respect to the long-run supply curve, whereas the Walrasian criterion is applicable to the short-run supply curve.

V. Summary and Conclusion

This paper has examined the implications for the theory of factor-market distortions of a class of dynamic adjustment mechanisms, of which the short-run capital specificity assumption is an interesting special case. It was shown that the existing literature requires modification in a number of respects:

1. A small open economy (i.e., an economy facing fixed commodity prices) can *never* be in a stable unspecialized equilibrium where one sector is relatively labor intensive in physical terms, but relatively capital intensive in value terms. This conclusion rules out a number of paradoxical outcomes (such as a "perverse" price-output response) which have received a great deal of attention in the literature on factor-market distortions.

2. A closed economy, or an open economy which has some influence over its terms of trade, *can* be in a stable unspecialized equilibrium where the rankings of the two sectors by physical and value factor intensities

do not correspond. The condition for such an equilibrium to be stable is that Jones' "aggregate elasticity of substitution" be positive. This stability condition is important since it permits us to sign unambiguously a great many comparative static results of the two-sector model; and in this case too, many paradoxical outcomes may be ruled out.

3. Finally, contrary to Jones (1971a), when the rankings of the two sectors by physical and value factor intensities differ, the condition for the economy to be in stable equilibrium implies that the intersection of the demand schedule and the long-run supply schedule must exhibit Walrasian instability.

One final qualification to the conclusions of this paper must be noted. It involves what might be called the Ambiguity of the Correspondence Principle: while the assumption of stability is a powerful tool in deducing comparative static results, it may yield different results depending on which particular disequilibrium adjustment mechanism is assumed. Thus all of the conclusions given above are conditional on the particular class of adjustment mechanisms which has been examined. However, while it is not difficult to devise alternative mechanisms, there is no reason to believe that they would imply different stability conditions.[12]

Clearly, it would be desirable to develop still more complicated adjustment mechanisms, insofar as the objective is to model the actual process of adjustment towards long-run equilibrium in real world economies.[13] Bur for the present it seems reasonable to accept the conclusions derived from the adjustment mechanisms studied in this paper, with their attractive implication that the long-run predictions of the theory of factor-market distortions are much more consistent with simple economic intuition than has been thought.

Appendix A

This section derives the properties which must be satisfied in figures 1 and 2 by the three loci, the labor-market equilibrium locus ($LMEL$) equation (la), the capital-market equilibrium locus ($KMEL$) equation (lb), and the distorted efficiency locus (DEL) equation (15). The procedure adopted is to totally differentiate each locus, and then to convert each to a differential function of changes in relative commodity prices and factor allocations to sector X only. The latter is accomplished by invoking: (a) the price-equal-to-unit-cost equations, (2) and (3); (b) the relationship between the capital-labor ratio and the marginal product of capital in sector X, in differential form,

$$\hat{K}_X - \hat{L}_X = -\frac{\sigma_X}{\theta_{LX}}(\hat{r}_X - \hat{p}_X) \tag{A1}$$

as well as the corresponding equation for sector Y; and (c) the full-employment constraints: equation (10) for capital, and for labor:

$$\lambda_{LX}\hat{L}_X + \lambda_{LY}\hat{L}_Y = 0. \tag{A2}$$

This procedure yields the following expressions for the three loci:

$$KMEL: \hat{p}_X - \hat{p}_Y - A_1\hat{K}_X + B_1\hat{L}_X = 0, \tag{A3}$$

$$A_1 = \frac{\theta_{LX}}{\sigma_X} + \frac{\theta_{LY}}{\sigma_Y}\frac{\lambda_{KX}}{\lambda_{KY}} \quad \text{and} \quad B_1 = \frac{\theta_{LX}}{\sigma_X} + \frac{\theta_{LY}}{\sigma_Y}\frac{\lambda_{LX}}{\lambda_{LY}}; \tag{A4}$$

$$LMEL: \hat{p}_X - \hat{p}_Y + A_2\hat{K}_X - B_2\hat{L}_X = 0, \tag{A5}$$

$$A_2 = \frac{\theta_{KX}}{\sigma_X} + \frac{\theta_{KY}}{\sigma_Y}\frac{\lambda_{KX}}{\lambda_{KY}} \quad \text{and} \quad B_2 = \frac{\theta_{KX}}{\sigma_X} + \frac{\theta_{KY}}{\sigma_Y}\frac{\lambda_{LX}}{\lambda_{LY}}; \tag{A6}$$

$$DEL: A_3\hat{K}_X - B_3\hat{L}_X = 0, \tag{A7}$$

$$A_3 = \frac{1}{\sigma_X} + \frac{1}{\sigma_Y}\frac{\lambda_{KX}}{\lambda_{KY}} \quad \text{and} \quad B_3 = \frac{1}{\sigma_X} + \frac{1}{\sigma_Y}\frac{\lambda_{LX}}{\lambda_{LY}}. \tag{A8}$$

Assuming commodity prices and the distortion parameters to be fixed, we now have three loci to locate in the Edgeworth-Bowley box, with the elasticity of each given by $B_i/A_i(i = 1, 3)$. We may note first that at any point of long-run equilibrium all three must intersect; moreover, at such a point the difference between their slopes will have the same sign as the difference between their elasticities. Hence, by comparing the elasticities of $KMEL$, $LMEL$, and DEL, the following relationships between the slopes of the three loci, at any point of long-run equilibrium, may be established:

$$|\lambda| |\theta| > 0: 0 < \left.\frac{dK_X}{dL_X}\right|_{KMEL} < \left.\frac{dK_X}{dL_X}\right|_{DEL} < \left.\frac{dK_X}{dL_X}\right|_{LMEL}, \tag{A9}$$

$$|\lambda| |\theta| < 0: \left.\frac{dK_X}{dL_X}\right|_{KMEL} > \left.\frac{dK_X}{dL_X}\right|_{DEL} > \left.\frac{dK_X}{dL_X}\right|_{LMEL} > 0. \tag{A10}$$

Finally, by comparing the elasticities of $KMEL$ and $LMEL$ with the elasticities of rays from the two origins of the Edgeworth-Bowley box (the elasticity of a ray from O_X, expressed in terms of K_X and L_X is one, while the corresponding elasticity of a ray from O_Y is $\lambda_{LX}\lambda_{KY}/\lambda_{LY}\lambda_{KX}$), the following additional relationships may be derived for *any* point G along

KMEL and *any* point *H* along *LMEL* (not just long-run equilibrium points):

$$|\lambda| \gtrless 0: \frac{dK_X}{dL_X}\bigg|_{O_XG} \lesseqgtr \frac{dK_X}{dL_X}\bigg|_{KMEL} \lesseqgtr \frac{dK_X}{dL_X}\bigg|_{O_YG}$$

and

$$\frac{dK_X}{dL_X}\bigg|_{O_XH} \lesseqgtr \frac{dK_X}{dL_X}\bigg|_{LMEL} \lesseqgtr \frac{dK_X}{dL_X}\bigg|_{O_YH}. \tag{A11}$$

Appendix B

To examine local stability when commodity prices are variable, equation (16) is equated with the economy's aggregate supply function, written (in differential form) as a function not of relative commodity prices, but of the allocations of factors to each sector:

$$\hat{X} - \hat{Y} = \theta_{LX}\hat{L}_X + \theta_{KX}\hat{K}_X - \theta_{LY}\hat{L}_Y - \theta_{KY}\hat{K}_Y. \tag{A12}$$

Using (A2) and (10) to eliminate $\hat{L}_Y$ and $\hat{K}_Y$, this becomes

$$\hat{X} - \hat{Y} = B_L\hat{L}_X + B_K\hat{K}_X, \tag{A13}$$

where

$$B_L = \theta_{LX} + \theta_{LY}\frac{\lambda_{LX}}{\lambda_{LY}}$$

and

$$B_K = \theta_{KX} + \theta_{KY}\frac{\lambda_{KX}}{\lambda_{KY}}.$$

Combining (16) and (A13) with (A3) and (A5) yields differential expressions for the two factor-market equilibrium loci which take into account the endogenous changes in relative commodity prices:

$$KMEL: -A_4\hat{K}_X + B_4\hat{L}_X = 0 \tag{A14}$$

where

$$A_4 = \frac{B_K}{\sigma_D} + \frac{\theta_{LX}}{\sigma_X} + \frac{\theta_{LY}}{\sigma_Y}\frac{\lambda_{KX}}{\lambda_{KY}}$$

and

$$B_4 = -\frac{B_L}{\sigma_D} + \frac{\theta_{LX}}{\sigma_X} + \frac{\theta_{LY}}{\sigma_Y}\frac{\lambda_{LX}}{\lambda_{LY}};$$

$$LMEL: A_5\hat{K}_X - B_5\hat{L}_X = 0, \tag{A15}$$

where

$$A_5 = -\frac{B_K}{\sigma_D} + \frac{\theta_{KX}}{\sigma_X} + \frac{\theta_{KY}}{\sigma_Y}\frac{\lambda_{KX}}{\lambda_{KY}}$$

and

$$B_5 = \frac{B_L}{\sigma_D} + \frac{\theta_{KX}}{\sigma_X} + \frac{\theta_{KY}}{\sigma_Y}\frac{\lambda_{LX}}{\lambda_{LY}}.$$

Taking a Taylor series approximation to the adjustment functions (13) and (14) (setting their elasticities equal to unity without loss of generality), and substituting from (A14) and (A15) gives the following matrix equation:

$$\begin{bmatrix} DK_X \\ DL_X \end{bmatrix} = \begin{bmatrix} -A_4 & B_4 \\ A_5 & -B_5 \end{bmatrix} \begin{bmatrix} K_X - K_X^0 \\ L_X - L_X^0 \end{bmatrix} \tag{A16}$$

Since the diagonal terms are negative, a necessary and sufficient condition for local stability is that the determinant of the coefficient matrix in (A16) be positive. This yields condition (17) in the text.

The author, Heyworth research fellow at Nuffield College, Oxford, is indebted to Nick Stern for detailed comments on earlier drafts, and to George Borts, Dermot McAleese, and an anonymous referee for helpful suggestions.

References

Raveendra N. Batra, *Studies in the Pure Theory of International Trade*, London 1973.

J. N. Bhagwati, "The Theory of Immiserizing Growth: Further Applications," in Michael B. Connolly and Alexander K. Swoboda, eds., *International Trade and Money*, London 1973.

———— and T. N. Srinivasan, "The Theory of Wage Differentials: Production Response and Factor Price Equalization," *J. Int. Econ.*, Feb. 1971, *1*, 19–35.

Mark Blaug, *Economic Theory in Retrospect*, 2d ed., London 1968.

A. Bosch, A. Mas-Colell, and A. Razin, "Instantaneous and Non-Instantaneous Adjustment to Equilibrium in Two-Sector Growth Models," *Metroecon.*, May/Aug. 1973, *25*, 105–18.

Avinash K. Dixit, *The Theory of Equilibrium Growth*, London 1976.

F. H. Hahn, "On Two-Sector Growth Models," *Rev. Econ. Stud.*, Oct. 1965, *32*, 339–46.

A. C. Harberger, "The Incidence of the Corporation Income Tax," *J. Polit. Econ.*, June 1962, *70*, 215–40.

K. -I. Inada, "Investment in Fixed Capital and the Stability of Growth Equilibrium," *Rev. Econ. Stud.*, Jan. 1966, *33*, 19–30.

H. G. Johnson and P. Mieszkowski, "The Effects of Unionization on the Distribution of Income: a General Equilibrium Approach," *Quart, J. Econ.*, Nov. 1970, *84*, 539–61.

R. W. Jones, "The Structure of Simple General Equilibrium Models," *J. Polit. Econ.*, Dec. 1965, *73*, 557–72.

———, (1971a) "Distortions in Factor Markets and the General Equilibrium Model of Production," *J. Polit. Econ.*, June 1971, *79*, 437–59.

———, (1971b) "A Three-Factor Model in Theory, Trade and History," in Jagdish N. Bhagwati et al., eds., *Trade, Balance of Payments and Growth: Essays in Honor of C. P. Kindleberger*, Amsterdam 1971.

———, "Income Distribution and Effective Protection in a Multicommodity Trade Model," *J. Econ. Theory*, Feb. 1975, *11*, 1–15.

M. C. Kemp, Y. Kimura and K. Okuguchi, "Monotonicity Properties of a Dynamical Version of the Heckscher-Ohlin Model of Production," *Econ. Stud. Quart.*, Dec. 1977, *28*, 249–53.

C. E. McLure, Jr., "A Diagrammatic Exposition of the Harberger Model with One Immobile Factor," *J. Polit. Econ.*, Jan./Feb. 1974, *82*, 56–82.

Stephen P. Magee, "Factor Market Distortions, Production, Distribution, and the Pure Theory of International Trade," *Quart. J. Econ.*, Nov. 1971, *85*, 623–43.

———, *International Trade and Distortions in Factor Markets*, New York 1976.

W. Mayer, (1974a) "Variable Returns to Scale in General Equilibrium Theory: a Comment," *Int. Econ. Rev.*, Feb. 1974, *15*, 225–35.

———, (1974b) "Short-run and Long-run Equilibrium for a Small Open Economy," *J. Polit. Econ.*, Sept./Oct. 1974, *82*, 955–67.

M. Mussa, "Tariffs and the Distribution of Income: the Importance of Factor Specificity, Substitutability, and Intensity in the Short and Long Run," *J. Polit. Econ.*, Nov./Dec. 1974, *82*, 1191–204.

J. P. Neary, "Factor Tax Incidence in a Stationary Two-Sector Economy: Simplification and Extensions," mimeo, Nuffield College, Oxford 1976.

———, (1978a) "Short-Run Capital Specificity and the Pure Theory of International Trade," *Econ. J.*, Sept. 1978, *88*, 488–510.

———, (1978b) "Capital Subsidies and Employment in an Open Economy," *Oxford Econ. Pap.*, Nov. 1978, *30*, 336–56.

Paul A. Samuelson, *Foundations of Economic Analysis*, Cambridge, Mass. 1947.

H. Uzawa, "On a Two-Sector Model of Economic Growth," *Rev. Econ. Stud.*, Oct. 1961, *29*, 40–47.

A. L. Vandendorpe and A. F. Friedlaender, "Differential Incidence in the Presence of Initial Distorting Taxes," *J. Publ. Econ.*, Oct. 1976, *6*, 205–29.

15

Optimal Trade Policy and Compensation under Endogenous Uncertainty: The Phenomenon of Market Disruption

Jagdish N. Bhagwati
and T. N. Srinivasan

1. Introduction

The fact that 'market disruption' permits or prompts importing countries to invoke quantitative import restrictions (or, what is more fashionable in recent times, voluntary export restrictions by the exporting countries, at the urging of the importing countries) immediately implies that the exporting country faces a situation of endogenous uncertainty: its own export level can affect the probability of such quantitative restrictions (QR's) being imposed. It simultaneously raises the following analytical questions which have obvious policy implications:

1. What is the optimal trade policy for an exporting country which is faced by such potential QR-intervention?

2. Since the possibility of such QR-intervention must restrict the trade opportunity set relative to that which would obtain in the absence of the QR-possibility, can one meaningfully define the loss that such a QR-possibility imposes on the exporting country and therefore the compensation that could be required to be paid to the exporting country under, say, a modified set of GATT rules?

2. Optimal Trade Policy: Two-Period Model with Zero Adjustment Costs

To analyze the problem of optimal trade policy for the exporting country in the presence of a market-disruption-induced possibility of QR-intervention, we will deploy the usual trade-theoretic model of general equilibrium, but will extend it to a two-period framework in sections 2–5.

This paper was originally published in *Journal of International Economics* 6 (1976): 317–336. The version published here omits a long section where the analysis was extended to a steady state with an infinite time horizon so that we could analyze effects of continuous uncertainty.

In section 4, we will also introduce adjustment costs, beginning with a simple formulation which has putty in period 1 and clay in period 2, and then extending the analysis in section 5 to lesser rigidity of redeployment of resources in period 2.

Thus, consider a two-commodity model of international trade. We then assume a two-period time horizon such that the level of exports E in the first period affects the probability $P(E)$ of a quota $\bar{E}$ being imposed at the beginning of the next period.[1]

Let $U[C_1, C_2]$ be the standard social utility function defined in terms of the consumption C_i of commodity $i(i = 1, 2)$. By assumption, it is known at the beginning of the next period whether the quota $\bar{E}$ has been imposed or not. Thus, the policy in the next period will be to maximize U subject to the transformation function $F[X_1, X_2] = 0$ and the terms of trade function π if no quota is imposed, and with an additional constraint $E \leq \bar{E}$ if the quota is imposed.

Let now the maximal welfare with and without the quota be $\underline{U}$ and $\bar{U}$ respectively. Clearly then, we have $\bar{U} > \underline{U}$ when the quota is binding. The expected welfare in the second period is then clearly

$$\underline{U}P(E) + \bar{U}[1 - P(E)].$$

The objective function for the first period is therefore:

$$\phi = U[X_1 - E, X_2 + \pi E] + \rho[\underline{U}P(E) + \bar{U}\{1 - P(E)\}],$$

where ρ is the discount factor. This is then to be maximized subject to the domestic transformation constraint, $F[X_1, X_2] = 0$. In doing this, assume that $P(E)$ is a convex function of E, i.e. the probability of a quota being imposed increases, at an increasing rate as E is increased, and that, in the case where π depends on E, πE is concave in E. Then, the first-order conditions for an interior maximum are:

$$\frac{\partial \phi}{\partial X_1} = U_1 - \lambda F_1 = 0, \tag{1}$$

$$\frac{\partial \phi}{\partial X_2} = U_2 - \lambda F_2 = 0, \tag{2}$$

$$\frac{\partial \phi}{\partial E} = -U_1 + U_2\{\pi + E\pi'\} - \rho(\bar{U} - \underline{U})P'(E) = 0. \tag{3}$$

Now equations (1) and (2) yield the familiar result that the marginal rate of substitution in consumption equals the marginal rate of transformation. Equation (3) moreover can be written as

$$\frac{U_1}{U_2} = (\pi + \pi'E) - \frac{\rho\{\bar{U} - \underline{U}\}}{U_2} P'(E). \tag{3'}$$

If (*i*) monopoly power is absent ($\pi' = 0$) and if (*ii*) the first period's exports do not affect the probability of a quota being imposed in the second period, then (3') clearly reduces to the standard condition that the marginal rate of substitution in consumption equals the (average = marginal) terms of trade. If (*i*) does not hold but (*ii*) holds, then U_1/U_2 equals the marginal terms of trade ($\pi + \pi'E$), leading to the familiar optimum tariff. If both (*i*) and (*ii*) are present, there is an *additional* tariff element: $(p[\bar{U} - \underline{U}]/U_2)P'(E)$. This term can be explained as follows: if an additional unit of exports takes place in period 1, the probability of a quota being imposed and hence a discounted loss in welfare of $\rho(\bar{U} - \underline{U})$ occurring, increases by $P'(E)$. Thus, at the margin, the expected loss in welfare is $\rho(\bar{U} - \underline{U})P'(E)$ since there is no loss in welfare if the quota is not imposed. Converted to numeraire terms, this equals $[\rho(\bar{U} - \underline{U})P'(E)]/U_2$, and must be subtracted from the marginal terms of trade ($\pi + \pi'E$), the effect of an additional unit of exports on the quantum of imports.[2]

It is then clear that the market-disruption-induced QR-possibility requires optimal intervention in the form of a tariff (in period 1). It is also clear that, compared to the optimal situation *without* such a QR-possibility, the resource allocation in the QR-possibility case will shift against exportable production, i.e. comparative advantage, in the welfare sense, shifts away, at the margin, from exportable production. Moreover, denoting the utility level under the optimal policy intervention with quota possibility as ϕ_Q^{OPT}, that under laissez faire with the quota possibility as ϕ_Q^{L}, and that under laissez faire without this quota possibility as $\phi_{\text{NQ}}^{\text{L}}$, we can argue that

$$\phi_Q^{\text{OPT}} > \phi_Q^{\text{L}}, \qquad \phi_{\text{NQ}}^{\text{L}} > \phi_Q^{\text{L}}.$$

This result is set out, with the attendant periodwise utility levels achieved under each option, in table 1 (which is self-explanatory).[3]

For the case of a small country, with no monopoly power in trade (except for the quota possibility), the equilibria under alternative policies are illustrated in figure 1.[4] Thus, $\bar{U}$ represents the utility level in the absence of a quota, $\underline{U}$ the utility level when the quota is imposed, and U^* the first-period utility level reached under the optimal policy intervention option. Note that equilibrium with U^* naturally requires that the export level is being restricted below the level that would be reached with nonintervention (at $\bar{U}$), while exceeding the level reached in equilibrium

Table 1
Alternative Outcomes under Different Policies.

	Alternative outcomes		
	Optimal policy intervention with possible quota	Laissez faire with possible quota	Laissez faire with no quota possibility
Period 1	U^*	$\bar{U}$	$\bar{U}$
Period 2	$\rho[\underline{U}P^* + \bar{U}(1 - P^*)]$	$\rho[\underline{U}\bar{P} + \bar{U}(1 - \bar{P})]$	$\rho\bar{U}$
ϕ (social utility level)	ϕ_Q^{OPT}	ϕ_Q^{L}	$\phi_{\text{NQ}}^{\text{L}}$

$$\phi_Q^{\text{OPT}} > \phi_Q^{\text{L}}, \quad \phi_{\text{NQ}}^{\text{L}} > \phi_Q^{\text{L}}$$

$\underline{U}$ is utility level if quota is imposed.
$\bar{U}$ is utility level if quota is not imposed.
U^* is utility level with optimal policy intervention when quota can be imposed in second period.
$P(E)$ is the probability of second-period quota of $\bar{E}$ being imposed, as a function of the first-period exports E. With optimal policy intervention in the situation with possible quota, the exports of the first period result in a value of P^* for $P(E)$. With laissez faire, the exports in the first period will be different and the corresponding value for $P(E)$ is $\bar{P}$.
ρ is the discount factor.
$\phi_{\text{NQ}}^{\text{L}} > \phi_Q^{\text{OPT}}$ necessarily only for small countries with no influence on terms of trade.
$\phi_{\text{NQ}}^{\text{OPT}}$, when the country is optimally exercising its monopoly power in trade and there is no QR possibility, is not listed above.

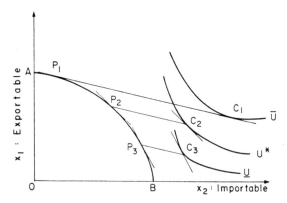

Figure 1

when the quota is invoked (at $\underline{U}$). Also, note that the optimal policy for restricting the first-period level of exports is a tariff: a conclusion that is, of course, familiar from the theory of optimal intervention under non-economic objectives as considered in Johnson (1965) and Bhagwati and Srinivasan (1969).

3. Defining the Loss from Market-Disruption-Induced QR-Possibility

Consider now the measure of the loss to the exporting country from this possibility of a market-disruption-induced QR. One can think of alternative ways in which this loss could be defined:

MEASURE I Taking expected utilities, one can define the loss of welfare to exporting country as the difference between ϕ_{NQ}^{L} and ϕ_{Q}^{L}: i.e. the loss in expected welfare that follows, in the absence of optimal intervention by the exporting country, from the QR-possibility.

This measure clearly is $\rho\bar{P}\{\bar{U} - \underline{U}\}$ and is, of course, nothing but the expected loss in period 2 from the possible imposition of the quota, duly discounted.

Now, it is also clear that this measure will lie between the ex post period-2 loss if the quota *is* invoked (which loss, duly discounted, is $\rho(\bar{U} - \underline{U})$) and the ex post period-2 loss if the quota is not invoked (which loss is, of course, zero). Thus, one must regard the actual period-2 loss when the quota *is* invoked as an upper bound on the loss in this model.

It also follows that there is a welfare loss, measured as $\rho\bar{P}\{\bar{U} - \underline{U}\}$ *even if the quota is not actually invoked in period 2* and, (in our two-period model), the actual equilibrium allocations in each period are identical between the QR-possibility and the no-QR-possibility situations. This follows clearly from the fact that, in period 1, consumers face the prospect of uncertain prices in period 2 as the QR may or may not be invoked.

MEASURE II Alternatively one may measure the loss to the exporting country as the difference between ϕ_{NQ}^{OPT} and ϕ_{Q}^{OPT}: the difference between expected welfare when there is no QR possibility, but the optimal tariff to exploit monopoly power *is* being exercised, and that when the government of the exporting country intervenes with optimal policy to maximize expected welfare when there *is* a QR-possibility. This alternative measure would be more meaningful for exporting countries with governmental trade agencies or exporters' associations with the ability to regulate their overall export levels, whereas Measure I would be more meaningful for exporting countries with (only) atomistic exporters.

4. Adjusting for Adjustment Costs: A Putty-Clay Model

So far, our analysis was based on the assumption that the choice of optimal production in period 2 was not constrained by the choice of production in period 1. Thus, in figure 1, the economy could move from P_1 or P_2 in period 1 to P_3 in period 2, along the (long-run) transformation curve AB. However, this procedure fails to take into consideration possible adjustment costs: i.e. we were essentially dealing with a putty model.

However, this procedure eliminates an important aspect of the problem raised by market disruption. So, in this section, we modify our model and analysis to allow for adjustment costs. However, to simplify the analysis, we take initially the extreme polar case of a putty-clay model, where the production choice made in period 1 cannot be modified *in any way* in period 2.

With this modification, the choice variables now are: X_i, the production of commodity i in periods 1 and 2 ($i = 1, 2$); E_1, the net exports of commodity 1 in period 1; and E_2, the net exports of commodity 1 in period 2 when *no* quota is imposed. As before, $\bar{E}$ is the net export of commodity 1 when the quota *is* imposed. Superscripts refer to periods 1 and 2.

Clearly then, the expected welfare ϕ is now as follows:

$$\phi = U^1[X_1 - E_1, X_2 + \pi E_1] + \rho P(E_1)U^2[X_1 - \bar{E}, X_2 + \pi\bar{E}]$$

$$+ p\{1 - P(E_1)\}\bar{U}^2[X_1 - E_2, X_2 + \pi E_2].$$

This is then maximized subject to the implicit transformation function, $F(X_1, X_2) = 0$, as before. The first-order conditions for an interior maximum then are:

$$\frac{\partial\phi}{\partial X_1} = U_1^1 + \rho P(E_1)\underline{U}_1^2 + \rho\{1 - P(E_1)\}\bar{U}_1^2 - \lambda F_1 = 0, \tag{4}$$

$$\frac{\partial\phi}{\partial X_2} = U_2^1 + \rho P(E_1)\underline{U}_2^2 + \rho\{1 - P(E_1)\}\bar{U}_2^2 - \lambda F_2 = 0, \tag{5}$$

$$\frac{\partial\phi}{\partial E_1} = -U_1^1 + \{\pi(E_1) + E_1\pi'(E_1)\}U_2^1 - \rho P'(E_1)\{\bar{U}^2 - \underline{U}^2\} = 0, \tag{6}$$

$$\frac{\partial\phi}{\partial E_2} = \rho[-\bar{U}_1^2 + \{\pi(E_2) + E_2\pi'(E_2)\}\bar{U}_2^2]\{1 - P(E_1)\} = 0, \tag{7}$$

where

$$U_j^1 = \frac{\partial U[X_1 - E_1, X_2 + \pi E_1]}{\partial X_j},$$

$$\bar{U}_j^2 = \frac{\partial U[X_1 - E_2, X_2 + \pi E_2]}{X_j},$$

$$\underline{U}_j^2 = \frac{\partial U[X_1 - \bar{E}_2, X_2 + \pi \bar{E}_2}{\partial X_j},$$

and $\lambda =$ the Lagrangean multiplier associated with the constraint, $F(X_1, X_2) = 0$.

The interpretation of these first-order conditions is straightforward. Condition (7) states that, *given the optimal production levels*, the level of exports in period 2 *when no quota is imposed* must be such as to equate the marginal rate of substitution in consumption to the marginal terms of trade. Condition (6) is identical in form to the one obtained earlier: the optimal exports in period 1 must *not* equate the marginal rate of substitution in consumption in *that* period to the marginal terms of trade, but must instead also allow for the marginal change in expected welfare arising out of the change in probability of a quota being imposed—the latter equals $P'(E_1)(\bar{U}^2 - \underline{U}^2)$, where $\bar{U}^2 = U[X_1 - E_2, X_2 + \pi E_2]$ and $\underline{U}^2 = U[X_1 - \bar{E}, X_2 + \pi \bar{E}]$. Thus, condition (6) ensures the optimal choice of exports in period 1, *given the production levels*. Conditions (4) and (5) then relate to the optimal choice of production levels and, as we would expect, the introduction of adjustment costs does make a difference. Writing (4) and (5) in the familiar ratio form, we get

$$\frac{F_1}{F_2} = \frac{U_1^1 + \rho P(E_1)\underline{U}_1^2 + \rho\{1 - P(E_1)\}\bar{U}_1^2}{U_2^1 + \rho P(E_1)\underline{U}_2^2 + \rho\{1 - P(E_1)\}\bar{U}_2^2}. \tag{8}$$

Clearly therefore the marginal rate of transformation in production (in periods 1 and 2, identically, as production in period 1 will carry over into period 2 by assumption), i.e. F_1/F_2, must *not* equal the marginal rate of substitution in consumption in period 1, i.e. U_1^1/U_2^1 (unlike our earlier analysis without adjustment costs in sections 2 and 3). Rather, F_1/F_2 should equal a term which properly takes into account the fact that production choices once made in period 1 cannot be changed in period 2 to suit the state (i.e. the imposition or absence of a quota) obtaining in period 2. Equation (8) can be readily interpreted as follows.

The LHS is, of course, the marginal rate of transformation in production. The RHS represents the marginal rate of substitution in consumption, if *reinterpreted* in the following sense. Suppose that the output of commodity 1, the exportable, is increased by one unit in period 1 (and hence in period 2 as well, by assumption). Given an optimal trade policy, then, the impact of this on welfare can be examined by adding it to consumption in each period. Thus social utility is increased in period 1 by U_1^1 while in period 2 it will increase by $\bar{U}_1^2$ if no quota is imposed and by $\underline{U}_1^2$ if the quota is imposed. Thus, the discounted increase in period-2 expected welfare is given as $\rho[\underline{U}_1^2 P(E_1) + \bar{U}_1^2(1 - P(E_1))]$. Thus, the total expected welfare impact of a unit increase in the production of commodity 1 is

$$U_1^1 + \rho[\underline{U}_1^2 P(E_1) + \bar{U}_1^2(1 - P(E_1))].$$

Similarly, a decrease in the production of commodity 2 by a unit in period 1 (and hence in period 2 as well) reduces expected welfare by

$$U_2^1 + \rho[\underline{U}_2^2 P(E_1) + \bar{U}_2^2(1 - P(E_1))].$$

Hence, the ratio of these two expressions, just derived, represents the 'true' marginal rate of substitution, and this indeed is the RHS in equation (8) to which the marginal rate of transformation in production—F_1/F_2, the LHS in equation (8)—is to be equated for optimality.

The optimal policy interventions in this modified model with adjustment costs are immediately evident from equations (6)–(8) and the preceding analysis. Thus, in period 1, the ratio U_1^1/U_2^1 is clearly the relative price of commodity 1 (in terms of commodity 2) facing consumers, while $\pi(E_1)$ is the average terms of trade. Thus U_1^1/U_2^1 differs from $\pi(E_1)$ by $[\pi'E_1 - (\rho P'(E_1)\{\bar{U}^2 - \underline{U}^2\}/U_2^1)]$ and this difference constitutes a consumption tax on the importable, commodity 2. An identical difference between F_1/F_2, the relative price facing producers, and $\pi(E_1)$ would define a production tax on commodity 2 at the same rate, so that a tariff at this rate would constitute the appropriate intervention in the model with no adjustment costs. However, *with adjustment costs*, equation (8) defines, for period 1, the appropriate production tax-cum-subsidy which, in general, will diverge from the appropriate consumption tax: so that the optimal mix of policies in the model with adjustment costs will involve a tariff (reflecting both the monopoly power in trade and the QR possibility) *plus* a production tax-cum-subsidy in period 1.[5] In period 2, in both the models (with and without adjustment costs), an appropriate intervention in the form of a tariff (to exploit monopoly power) would be called for; however, with production fixed at period 1 levels in the adjustment-cost model, a consumption tax-cum-subsidy would equally suffice. Specifically, note that in period 2, with adjustment costs, the price ratio facing consumers would be $\bar{U}_1^2/\bar{U}_2^2$ if no quota is imposed, with the average terms of trade at $\pi(E_2)$ and the producer's price ratio (as defined along the putty-transformation frontier) would be F_1/F_2; on the other hand, if the quota is imposed, these values change to $\underline{U}_1^2/\underline{U}_2^2$, $\pi(\bar{E})$ and F_1/F_2 respectively. The consumption tax-cum-subsidy and the equivalent tariff (with no impact on production decision already frozen at period-1 levels) are then defined by these divergences, depending on whether the quota obtains or not.

A tabular comparison of the characteristics of the optimal solution, with and without adjustment costs, is presented in table 2 and should assist the reader.

Note that the above results are quite consistent with the basic propositions of the theory of distortions, as developed in Bhagwati-Ramaswami (1963), Johnson (1965) and Bhagwati (1971): the first-best, optimal policy intervention for the case with adjustment costs requires a trade policy to adjust for the foreign distortion (represented by the effect of current exports on the period-2 probability of a quota being invoked)[6] and a production tax-cum-subsidy to adjust for the existence of adjustment costs in production. It also follows, from the equivalence propositions, that the combination of the optimal tariff and the optimal production tax-cum-subsidy can be reproduced identically by a tariff set at the 'net' production tax-cum-subsidy required by the optimal solution plus a consumption tax-cum-subsidy. Similarly, while our analysis has been focussed on first-best policy intervention, the fundamental results of the theory of distortions and welfare on second-best policies also can be immediately applied to our problem. Thus, if there are zero adjustment costs so that there is only the foreign distortion in period 1, then clearly

Table 2
Characteristics of Optimal Solutions in Models with and without Adjustment Costs

	No adjustment costs	Adjustment costs
Period 1	$DRS_1 \neq FRT_1$ $DRS_1 = DRT_1$	$DRS_1 \neq FRT_1$ $DRS_1 \neq DRT_1$
Period 2	$DRS_2 = DRT_2$ $= FRT_2$	$DRS_2 = FRT_2$ (DRT_2 not relevant as production is frozen at period-1 levels)

Note: *DRS*, *DRT* and *FRT* represent the marginal rates of substitution in consumption, domestic transformation, and foreign transformation respectively. For an earlier use of these abbreviations see Bhagwati, Ramaswami and Srinivasan (1969). Since we are considering an interior maximum, the inequalities do *not* include corner equilibria, of course. The subscripts refer to the periods, 1 and 2.

a production tax-subsidy will *improve* (but not maximize) welfare. Similarly, if there are adjustment costs as well, then there will be *two* distortions, and then applicable here would be the Bhagwati-Ramaswami-Srinivasan (1969) proposition that no feasible, welfare-improving form of intervention may exist if both of the policy measures that will secure optimal intervention cannot be used simultaneously.

5. Adjustment Costs: A General Formulation

So far, we have considered only the extreme version of an adjustment-costs model, where the period-1 production levels are frozen in period 2. We may now briefly consider however a more general formulation, (with basically the same results, of course, for optimal policy intervention), where the clay nature of period 1 allocation is partially relaxed: some reallocation is now permitted in period 2.

The simplest way to do this is to write out the period-2 implicit transformation function as $\underline{G}[\underline{X}_1^2, \underline{X}_2^2, X_1^1, X_2^1] = 0$ for the quota case and as $\bar{G}[\bar{X}_1^2, \bar{X}_2^2, X_1^1, X_2^1] = 0$ for the no-quota case, such that the feasible output levels in period 2 are explicitly made a function of the (allocation-cum-) output levels of period 1, X_1^1 and X_2^1. Our welfare problem then becomes one of maximizing,

$$\phi = U[X_1^1 - E_1, X_2^1 + \pi E_1] + \rho P(E_1)\underline{U}[\underline{X}_1^2 - \underline{E}_2, \underline{X}_2^2 + \underline{E}_2\pi]$$
$$+ \rho\{1 - P(E_1)\}\bar{U}[\bar{X}_1^2 - \bar{E}_2, \bar{X}_2^2 + \bar{E}_2\pi],$$

subject to:

$$F(X_1^1, X_2^1) = 0, \tag{9}$$

for period 1;

$$\underline{G}[\underline{X}_1^2, \underline{X}_2^2, X_1^1, X_2^1] = 0, \tag{10}$$

for period 2, with quota imposed;

$$\bar{G}[\bar{X}_1^2, \bar{X}_2^2, X_1^1, X_2^1] = 0, \tag{11}$$

for period 2, with no quota imposed; and

$$\underline{E}_2 \leq \bar{\bar{E}}, \tag{12}$$

where $\bar{\bar{E}}$ is the quota level.[7]

The first-order conditions for an interior maximum then are

$$\frac{\partial \phi}{\partial X_1^1} = U_1^1 - \lambda_1 F_1 - \lambda_2 \underline{G}_3 - \lambda_3 \bar{G}_3 = 0, \tag{13}$$

$$\frac{\partial \phi}{\partial X_2^1} = U_2^1 - \lambda_1 F_2 - \lambda_2 G_4 - \lambda_3 \bar{G}_4 = 0, \tag{14}$$

$$\frac{\partial \phi}{\partial \underline{X}_1^2} = \rho P(E_1) \underline{U}_1^2 - \lambda_2 \underline{G}_1 = 0, \tag{15}$$

$$\frac{\partial \phi}{\partial \underline{X}_2^2} = \rho P(E_1) \underline{U}_2^2 - \lambda_2 \underline{G}_2 = 0, \tag{16}$$

$$\frac{\partial \phi}{\partial \bar{X}_1^2} = \rho \{1 - P(E_1)\} \bar{U}_1^2 - \lambda_3 \bar{G}_1 = 0, \tag{17}$$

$$\frac{\partial \phi}{\partial \bar{X}_2^2} = \rho \{1 - P(E_1)\} \bar{U}_2^2 - \lambda_3 \bar{G}_3 = 0, \tag{18}$$

$$\frac{\partial \phi}{\partial E_1} = - U_1^1 + (\pi + \pi' E_1) U_2^1 - \rho [\bar{U}^2 - \underline{U}^2] P'(E_1) = 0, \tag{19}$$

$$\frac{\partial \phi}{\partial \underline{E}_2} = \rho P(E_1) [- \underline{U}_1^2 + (\pi + \pi' \underline{E}_2) \underline{U}_2^2] - \gamma = 0, \tag{20}$$

$$\frac{\partial \phi}{\partial \bar{E}_2} = \rho \{1 - P(E_1)\} [- \bar{U}_1^2 + (\pi + \pi' \bar{E}_2) \bar{U}_2^2] = 0, \tag{21}$$

where λ_1, λ_2, λ_3 and γ are the Lagrangean multipliers associated with constraints (9)–(12) respectively, and G_i is the partial derivative with respect to the ith argument.

It is then easy to see that, while $\underline{DRS}^2 = \underline{DRT}^2$ (because equations (15) and (16) imply that $\underline{U}_1^2/\underline{U}_2^2 = \underline{G}_1/\underline{G}_2$) and $\overline{DRS}_2 = \overline{DRT}_2$ (because equations (17) and (18) imply that $\bar{U}_1^2/\bar{U}_2^2 = \bar{G}_1/\bar{G}_2$), as before, one can see the effect of adjustment costs more readily, from equations (13) and (14), i.e. $DRT_1 \neq DRS_1$, as follows:

$$\frac{F_1}{F_2} = \frac{U_1^1 - \lambda_2 \underline{G}_3 - \lambda_3 \bar{G}_3}{U_1^2 - \lambda_2 \underline{G}_4 - \lambda_3 \bar{G}_4}, \tag{22}$$

or, alternatively,

$$\frac{F_1}{F_2} = \frac{U_1^1 - \rho P(E_1) \underline{U}_1^2 \left(\dfrac{\underline{G}_3}{\underline{G}_1}\right) - \rho \{1 - P(E_1)\} \bar{U}_1^2 \left(\dfrac{\bar{G}_3}{\bar{G}_1}\right)}{U_1^2 - \rho P(E_1) \underline{U}_2^2 \left(\dfrac{\underline{G}_4}{\underline{G}_2}\right) - \rho \{1 - P(E_1)\} \bar{U}_2^2 \left(\dfrac{\bar{G}_4}{\bar{G}_2}\right)}. \tag{22'}$$

Now, it is easy to see that, if we have the polar case with no reallocation possible in period 2 (the putty-clay model of section 4), the transformation curve in period 2 reduces to the single point (X_1^1, X_2^1). As such, the partial derviatives $\underline{G}_i$, $\bar{G}_i$ $(i = 1, 2, 3, 4)$ are not defined. However, one could define G in such a way that putty-clay is a limiting case and, in the limit, $\bar{G}_3 = \underline{G}_3 = -G_1$ and $\bar{G}_4 = \underline{G}_4 = -G_2$. This is analogous to obtaining the Leontief fixed coefficient production function as a limiting case of the CES production function. Therefore, equation $(22')$ reduces to equation (8), as it should. If, however, we have no adjustment costs (as in section 2), then $\bar{G}_3 = \underline{G}_3 = \bar{G}_4 = \underline{G}_4 = 0$ and equation $(22')$ will reduce to $U_1^1/U_2^1 = F_1/F_2$ (which is what equations (1) and (2) imply in section 2). For any situation with *some*, but not total, inflexibility of resource allocation in period 2, the ratios $-\underline{G}_3/\underline{G}_1$, $-\bar{G}_3/\bar{G}_1$, $-\underline{G}_4/\underline{G}_2$ and $-\bar{G}_4/\bar{G}_2$ will lie between 0 and 1.

The parametric values of these ratios will clearly reflect the 'pattern of inflexibility' that one contends with. Thus, if one assumes total factor price flexibility but no resource mobility, as in Haberler (1950), then the putty–clay model is relevant. On the other hand, one might assume just the opposite, where factor prices are inflexible but resources are fully mobile—this being the case systematically analyzed by Brecher (1974). Variations on these two polar possibilities include analyses such as that of Mayer (1974) which assumes an activity-specific factor with no mobility in the short run (interpret 'short run' as period 2 for our purposes) but with factor price flexibility.

Whatever the source of adjustment costs in period 2, what they do imply is that the transformation curve of period 1 is not feasible in period 2. Hence the illustration of optimal-policy equilibrium in period 2 would be as in figure 2, where AB is the (putty) period-1 transformation curve, P^1 the production point on it in period 1 representing therefore (X_1^1, X_2^1), CP^1D the clay transformation curve for period 2 and QP^1R

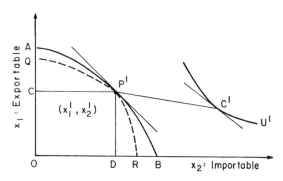

Figure 2

the (partial-clay) transformation curve when resources in period 2 are partially mobile. With equilibrium production at P^1 (with tangency in period 1 to AB) and consumption at C^1, and assuming for simplicity that the international terms of trade are fixed at P^1C^1, we can then illustrate that $F_1/F_2 \neq U_1^1/U_2^1$ (i.e. that the tangents to AB and to the social utility curve U^1 are not equal), as required by equation (22') for the case of adjustment costs.

6. Concluding Remarks

The preceding analysis of the phenomenon of market-disruption-induced QR-imposition can be shown both to have other applications and to be generalizable in many directions.

Thus, it is readily seen that the phenomenon of a trade *embargo* on a country's *imports* can be analyzed in the same way as the market-disruption phenomenon. The analysis, and results, would in fact be identical if we were to assume that the probability of the imposition of an export embargo (e.g. by OPEC) by the exporting country was an increasing function of the import level by the importing country (e.g. import of oil by the U.S.).[8] In this case, the optimal policy intervention by the importing country, faced by such an (import-level-related) embargo-prospect of reduced (or eliminated) feasible import level, would be a trade tariff if there were no adjustment costs, and a trade tariff plus production tax-cum-subsidy if there were adjustment costs as well. The analysis would however have to be slightly modified if the embargo problem were modeled rather as one where the probability of the exporting country allowing reduced, permissible exports were made a function instead of the ratio of imports to domestic production (as this may be a better index of import dependence). In this case, since the probability of the quota being invoked is now a function of a ratio involving *both* trade and production levels, one should expect that the optimum tariff would now be replaced by a *combination* of a tariff *and* a production tax-cum-subsidy, on this account (even in the absence of adjustment costs). Finally, if one models the probability of an embargo imposition as independent of a country's trade level or import-to-production ratio, so that the uncertainty is *exogenous*, then clearly the optimal policy for a small country (with no monopoly power in trade) is free trade with zero adjustment costs and, if there are adjustment costs, it will consist of a production tax-cum-subsidy related to these adjustment costs.

As for the generalizations of our analysis in other directions, we may indicate some. Thus, for example, an important extension would be to incorporate technical change as a source of export expansion and hence accentuated probability of a triggering of market-disruption-induced QR's: this would provide yet another instance of immiserizing growth, while also carrying implications for optimal imports of technology in developing countries, to mention only two possible analytically-interesting consequences. Again, our analysis has explicitly modeled only the exporting country as far as welfare implications of the market-disruption phenomenon are concerned. However, one could take a 'world-welfare' approach and model the importing country also more explicitly. If this was done, then one could no longer meaningfully take the importing country's QR-imposition policy as 'given,' and the basic model of this paper would have to be modified in an essential manner.

The research underlying this paper was financed partly by UNCTAD, through its Manufactures Division; needless to say, the paper does not necessarily represent the views of the UNCTAD Secretariat. Our thanks are due to Peter Diamond, Murrary Kemp, Paul Krugman, Clive Bell, Charles Blitzer, Graham Pyatt, and Wolfgang Mayer for helpful comments on an earlier draft.

References

Bhagwati, J. and V. K. Ramaswami, 1963, Domestic distortions, tariffs and the theory of optimum subsidy, *Journal of Political Economy* 71, 44–50.

Bhagwati, J. and T. N. Srinivasan, 1969, Optimal intervention to achieve non-economic objectives, *Review of Economic Studies* 36, 27–38.

Bhagwati, J., V. K. Ramaswami and T. N. Srinivasan, 1969, Domestic distortions, tariffs, and the theory of optimum subsidy: Some further results, *Journal of Political Economy* 77, 1005–1010.

Bhagwati, J. 1971, The generalized theory of distortions and welfare, in: J. Bhagwati, et al., eds., *Trade, Balance of Payments and Growth* (North-Holland, Amsterdam) 69–90.

Brecher, R., 1974, Optimal commercial policy for a minimum-wage economy, *Journal of International Economics* 4, 139–150.

Haberler, G., 1950, Some problems in the pure theory of international trade, *Economic Journal* 60, 223–240.

Johnson, H. G., 1965, Optimal trade intervention in the presence of domestic distortions, in: R. E. Caves et al., eds., *Trade, Growth and the Balance of Payments* (North-Holland, Amsterdam) 3–34.

Mayer, W., 1974, Short-run and long-run equilibrium for a small open economy, *Jorunal of Political Economy* 82, 955–967.

16
Smuggling, Production and Welfare
Munir A. Sheikh

1. Introduction

In many less developed countries, smuggling (i.e., illegal trade) is a significant economic phenomenon. Until recently, smuggling was completely ignored in the analysis of the theory of international trade. Now, in a path-breaking article, Bhagwati and Hansen (1973) have successfully incorporated the smuggling phenomenon into the standard international trade model. Their analysis has recently been further extended by Bhagwati and Srinivasan (1973) and Johnson (1974).

In the model used by Bhagwati and Hansen, however, it is assumed—in the tradition of trade theory as also of Samuelson's (1954) well-known method of treating transport costs—that the real costs of smuggling are incurred in the form of the (two) tradeable goods which comprise the standard two-good trade-theoretic model.[1] In this paper, on the other hand, it is postulated that the activity of smuggling requires the use of a non-traded good which directly uses domestic, primary factors. This model is spelled out in section 2.[2] Next, we derive the production, consumption and welfare effects of smuggling in section 3 and section 4. Finally, section 5 focuses on the main differences in the results of our model and the Bhagwati-Hansen Model.

2. The Model with Smuggling

Our model assumes the production of only two consumption goods, X the exportable commodity and M the importable commodity, plus the smuggling activity. Only two factors, capital denoted by K and labour denoted by L, are available, and are assumed to be fully employed. All

This paper was originally published in *Journal of International Economics* 4 (1974): 355–364.

production functions are assumed to be subject to constant returns to scale. Furthermore, perfect competition is assumed in both the product and factor markets. On the demand side, we use the simplifying device of a social utility function, defined on the total availability of the two goods, whether smuggled or not.

To introduce smuggling we must specify some additional assumptions. We assume smuggling not to be associated with capital flows and hence we retain the usual balance-of-trade equilibrium in our model. Furthermore, government spends resources on various law enforcement activities, and smuggling being one of the illegal activities is also affected by government law enforcement policy. We shall assume that the government is spending a fixed amount of resources on law enforcement irrespective of whether there is any smuggling or not. This is done to separate the implications of trade restrictions on smuggling as changes in government policy towards law enforcement could also affect smuggling. The transformation curve is thus a net transformation curve derived after a fixed amount of resources have been taken away by the government by means of direct taxation so as not to affect any prices.[3]

We assume two countries in the world, the home country and the rest of the world. The rest of the world supplies importables of the home country and demands its exportables at unique terms of trade, making no distinction whether it is dealing with the smugglers or non-smugglers. Smugglers thus receive the goods at the international terms of trade and pay no import tariff. Any costs which are undertaken in smuggling are thus entirely inside the home country.

Smugglers face two kinds of costs, the risk costs and the real resource costs.[4] In the presence of law enforcement by the government, smuggling entails certain risks. Risk cost includes the possibility of confiscation of smuggled goods, and punishment and fines for the illegal activity. Smugglers face such risks and are assumed to include them in their cost calculations. We further assume that real resources are required within the home country for smuggling (additional to those in legal trade) in the form of a transportation commodity, denoted by T.[5] T is assumed to be produced under conditions of constant returns to scale. We thus have a three-good two-factor model.

2.1. Production Possibility Curve in the Presence of Smuggling
In figure 1, $Q\bar{Q}$ is the production possibility curve for the two commodities X and M, which is the usual concave-to-the-origin production possibility curve in a two-commodity two-factor case. As T is required by assumption only to undertake smuggling, $Q\bar{Q}$ may be regarded as the non-smuggling

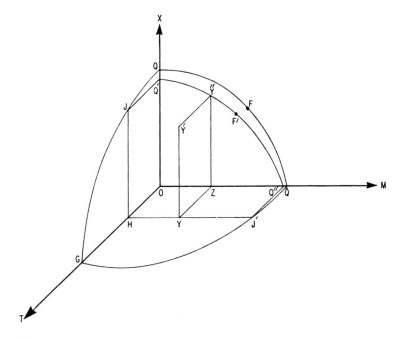

Figure 1

production possibility curve for the economy. The introduction of smuggling and the production of T gives a smooth concave-to-the-origin "ruled" production possibility surface $Q\bar{Q}G$ in this three-commodity two-factor case. In each coordinate plane, the set of possible production points constitutes a gross transformation curve for the two relevant commodities.[6]

We now wish to derive the production possibility curve for X and M, our two consumption goods, if T is also produced when smuggling exists. Let OH be an arbitrarily determined output level of T. With no output of M, the maximum possible output of X is $HJ = OQ'$. Similarly with no output of X, the maximum possible output level of M is $HJ' = OQ''$.

We thus have two extreme points for the production possibility curve in X, M space for a given level of output of T. Assume now that for the same level (OH) of T, the output of M is OZ. By drawing $Y'Y''$ parallel to YZ we then obtain point Y'' in the XM space, which shows that with full employment of factors and an output level of T equal to YZ and of M equal to OZ, the maximum output of X is ZY''. By repeating this procedure, we can derive the production possibility curve $Q'Y''Q''$ for X and M, which would correspond to the *given level of output of T* (equal to OH). This production surface $Q'Y''Q''$ will be concave to the origin.[7]

To determine the effect of smuggling on the production of X and M, our next task therefore is to determine the output level of T.

2.2. Determination of Quantity of Illegal Imports and Production of T

In our three-good two-factor model, with international prices of the two tradeable goods fixed, it is easy to establish the level of smuggling corresponding to any given tariff rate. Let P_T be the price of T in terms of X, P the relative price of M in terms of X, W the wage-rental ratio, and k_X, k_M, k_T the capital-labour ratios in X, M and T, respectively. Taking a unit of X to be the numeraire, let C_M and C_T be the minimized unit costs of production of M and T. With P^* as the international price of M in terms of X, and t as the ad valorem tariff rate, $P^*(1 + t)$ is the domestic price of M in terms of X, given a non-redundant tariff throughout the analysis (an assumption which is relaxed for the smuggling situation in section 4).

The model works very simply. In figure 2, the basic relationships are set out on the assumption that $k_M > k_T > k_X$, so that C_M, C_T and C_T/C_M

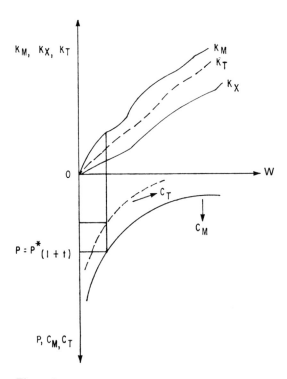

Figure 2

decline as W increases. With the tariff rate given, the domestic price (P) of M is determined; this, in turn, equalizes with M's unit cost of production C_M, thus determining W, k_i ($i = M, X, T$) and the equilibrium unit cost C_T of T. It is now easy to determine the quantity of smuggling (and the associated quantity of T) in this model, by deriving the supply curve of total imports.

Thus, assume that the amount of T required to smuggle a unit of M is a unit of T and let this ratio remain constant irrespective of the level of smuggling. Then the real cost per unit of smuggled imports is ($P^* + C_T$). If $S(q)$[8] denotes the unit risk costs when q units are smuggled in, then we can derive the supply curve of *smuggled* imports as $S^{-1}[P - P^* - C_T]$[9] where $S^{-1}[\ \ ]$ is the inverse function of $S(q)$. Obviously $P \geqq P^* + C_T$ for smuggling to be feasible. We shall need a strict inequality if risk costs in smuggling are positive. This supply curve will be positively sloped if there are increasing risk costs in smuggling.[10]

The supply curve of *legal* imports, on the other hand, is infinitely elastic with our small-country assumption and is given by $P = P^*(1 + t)$. Putting legal and smuggled imports together, the effective *aggregate* supply curve ABC for import is then derived in figure 3.

Equilibrium in the smuggling market then exists when OD quantity of M is illegally imported.[11] As the units of T produced must equal the units of M smuggled in, the required production of T is OD for this given rate of tariffs.[12]

3. Production, Consumption and Welfare Effects of Smuggling

We have so far shown how the quantity of smuggling, and hence the output level of T, are determined once the tariff rate is specified in our model. Returning to figure 1, we can find now the production surface in the XM plane for a given commodity price ratio as output of T is now determined. Suppose this output level of T is given by $OH(= OD$ in figure 3). The tangency of the tariff-inclusive commodity price ratio between X and M to the production possibility curve $Q'Q''$ will determine the production level; of X and M, at F' in figure 1. In the absence of smuggling, the tangency point of QQ' with the same tariff-inclusive commodity price ratio will give the non-smuggling production levels of X and M, at F.

It is then clear that there is a perfect analogy between the theory of immiserising growth and the theory of smuggling, at this point of analysis. If one compares the smuggling with the non-smuggling situation, it is identical to comparing a pre-growth with a post-growth situation—in the

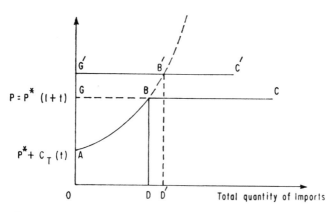

Figure 3

(X, M) space—subject to the distortion defined by the tariff in this small
country. Johnson (1967) has already shown that growth subject to such a
tariff may be immiserising; and it follows equally that the non-smuggling
situation may be welfarewise inferior to the smuggling situation.[13]

It is also clear that such improvement in welfare due to smuggling can
occur only if $X_s^* > X^*$ and $M_s^* < M^*$ (where X^*, M^* are the non-
smuggling and X_s^*, M_s^* the smuggling situation output levels of X and
M, respectively). In all other cases, smuggling must reduce welfare.

Hence, it is necessary to examine how smuggling will affect the outputs
of X and M. This is readily done in the framework of the Findlay-Grubert
(1959) type of analysis, as below, and the outcome depends on the relative
factor-intensities of the commodities in the system.

Let the aggregate capital-labour ratio of the economy be $\bar{k}$. Let l_X, l_M
$(= 1 - l_X)$ denote the proportion of labour force denoted to the production respectively of X and M when there is no smuggling, given the tariff
t. Let l_X^s, l_M^s and $l_T^s(= 1 - l_X^s - l_M^s)$ denote the proportion of labour
force denoted to the production respectively of X, M and T in the presence
of smuggling with the same tariff rate t. Given t, k_X, k_M and k_T are
uniquely determined. Hence:[14]

$$l_X k_X + l_M k_M = \bar{k}, \tag{1}$$

$$l_X^s k_X + l_M^s k_M + l_T^s k_T = \bar{k}. \tag{2}$$

Now, subtracting (1) from (2) we get:

$$(l_X^s - l_X)(k_X - k_T) + (l_M^s - l_M)(k_M - k_T) = 0, \tag{3}$$

which can also be written as:

$$(l_X^s - l_X)(k_X - k_M) + l_T^s(k_T - k_M) = 0, \tag{4}$$

$$(l_M^s - l_M)(k_M - k_X) + l_T^s(k_T - k_X) = 0. \tag{5}$$

Next, using equations (3)–(5), we can derive various production and welfare effects of smuggling. We illustrate only for the case where $k_M > k_X$. The following five cases are then possible.

A. If $k_M > k_T > k_X$, then from (5) $l_M^s < l_M$ and from (4) $l_M^s < l_X$. This means that $X_s^* < X^*$ and $M_s^* < M^*$.[15] Smuggling decreases the production of both X and M. [In figure 1, it can be shown that the welfare level in the presence of smuggling (U_s^*) will be lower than the non-smuggling welfare level (U^*).][16]

B. If $k_M > k_X = k_T$, then from (5) $l_M^s = l_M$, and from (4) $l_X^s < l_X$, so that $X_s^* < X^*$ and $M_s^* = M^*$. (Again, $U_s^* < U^*$.)

C. If $k_T = k_M > k_X$, then from (4) $l_X^s = l_X$ and from (5) $l_M^s < l_M$, so that $M_s^* < M^*$ and $X_s^* = X^*$. (Again, $U_s^* < U^*$.)

D. If $k_M > k_X > k_T$, then from (5) $l_M^s > l_M$ and from (4) $l_X^s < l_X$, so that $M_s^* > M^*$ and $X_s^* < X^*$. (Smuggling reduces welfare as $U_s^* < U^*$.)

E. If $k_T > k_M > k_X$, then from (5) $l_M^s < l_M$ and from (4) $l_X^s > l_X$. Hence $X_s^* > X^*$ and $M_s^* < M^*$. (In this case it is possible that $U_s^* \gtreqless U^*$.)[17]

4. Redundant Tariff under Smuggling

So far, we have assumed that the tariff is not redundant under either the non-smuggling or the smuggling situation. Thus, in figure 3, the tariff defines the height of the line GC, the supply curve of legal imports, and the quantity of imports in smuggling equilibrium is greater than or equal to OD.

We now propose to re-examine the smuggling equilibrium under the assumption that the supply curve of imports would yield a quantity of smuggled imports in excess of total imports demanded: thus leading to a redundancy of the tariff, and hence zero legal imports, in smuggling equilibrium. This analysis is best done by assuming an initial tariff leads to a smuggling equilibrium such that legal imports are *just* eliminated, and then increasing the tariff.

Returning to figure 3, we then start with an initial tariff t, equilibrium imports are OD, and legal imports are zero. Assume that the tariff is increased so that GC shifts up to $G'C'$, leading to illegal imports, in equilibrium, being $OD'(>OD)$ *provided* that the ABB' curve also does not shift. To ensure the latter, we merely need to make C_T invariant to the tariff increase: the assumption that $k_M > k_X = k_T$ will do this.[18] But the higher domestic price of the importable ensures that the consumption of total imports will fall, so that the tariff change must lead to excess supply of importables in the domestic market. Hence the domestic price of importables must fall back to G, defined by the *initial* tariff rate, to restore equilibrium. Thus the incremental tariff is redundant, in the smuggling situation, although it is not in the non-smuggling situation.

Thus, at this higher tariff, it is clear that the analysis of section 3 must be modified. Whereas, in section 3, the comparison of the smuggling and non-smuggling situations was identical to the comparison of pre-growth and post-growth situations for a small country with a *constant* tariff in the theory of immiserising growth, now the comparison involves adding one more loss-causing element to the non-smuggling situation: i.e., the non-smuggling situation has an additional tariff which imposes an additional loss, since a higher tariff is inferior to a lower tariff in a small country.[19] Hence it follows that, given a tariff which leads to the elimination of legal imports under smuggling and also to redundancy in the tariff in that situation such that the domestic price of the importable is below that given by the tariff inclusive price thereof, the conditions under which smuggling will improve welfare over the non-smuggling situation are even less stringent than those spelled out for the cases of co-existence of legal and illegal trade considered in section 3.[20]

5. Concluding Remarks

We have presented above a model of smuggling, different from the Bhagwati-Hansen Model in its assumption of how the real costs of smuggling are incurred. This difference in assumptions leads to specific and important differences in some of the conclusions reached regarding the effects of smuggling.

In particular, the Bhagwati-Hansen Model, in assuming that the real costs of smuggling are incurred in the form of the (two) tradeables which enter the utility function, enables the analysis to be conducted by assuming that these real costs lead to an inferior foreign transformation curve for illegal trade than for legal trade, while assuming the domestic transformation curve among the two goods to be invariant to the mix of legal and illegal trade. Our model, on the other hand, implies that the presence of illegal trade, in requiring the use of a non-tradeable good using domestic primary resources, leads to a direct impact on the domestic transformation curve among the two tradeable goods entering the utility function.

This central difference implies that smuggling can affect the domestic production of the two tradeables even if the domestic, tariff-inclusive price of the importables is unaffected by smuggling: whereas, in the Bhagwati-Hansen Model the production of the tradeables cannot change unless the effect of the smuggling is to eliminate legal trade and simultaneously to lead to a redundancy in the tariff.

More important, in follows that legal and illegal trade can co-exist in our model and yet illegal trade may have *improved* welfare, whereas in the Bhagwati-Hansen Model the co-existence of legal and illegal trade implics an excess (terms of trade) cost on illegal trade whereas the consumption and production costs are identical under the legal and illegal trade situations so that the illegal trade situation must have *lower* welfare than the legal trade situation.

Economic Council of Canada: This paper is a revised version of a chapter of Sheikh's Ph.D. dissertation (1973). The author gratefully acknowledges the assistance provided to him by Professors J. C. Leith, J. R. Melvin and K. L. Avio at every stage in the writing of this thesis. Melvin's ideas were particularly useful in the development of this paper. Thanks are also due to J. Bhagwati and an anonymous referee whose suggestions have considerably improved the contents of this paper. Any remaining errors are, however, the sole responsibility of the author. Research on this project was partially supported by a grant from the Ghana Development workshop at the University of Western Ontario which is also gratefully acknowledged.

References

Batra, R. N. and F. Casas, 1973, Intermediate products and the pure theory of international trade: A neo-Heckscher-Ohlin framework, *American Economic Review* 63, 297–311.

Bhagwati, J., 1968, Distortions and immiserising growth: A generalisation, *The Review of Economic Studies* 35, 481–485.

Bhagwati, J., 1968, The gains from trade once again, Oxford Economic Papers 20, 137–148.

Bhagwati, J., ed., 1974, *Illegal transactions and international trade: Theory and measurement* (North-Holland, Amsterdam).

Bhagwati, J. and B. Hansen, 1973, A theoretical analysis of smuggling, *Quarterly Journal of Economics* 87, 172–187.

Bhagwati, J. and B. Hansen, 1974, A theoretical analysis of smuggling: A reply, *Quarterly Journal of Economics*, forthcoming.

Bhagwati, J. and T. N. Srinivasan, 1973, Smuggling and trade policy, *Journal of Public Economics* 2, 377–389.

Findlay, R. and H. Grubert, 1959, *Factor intensities, technological progress, and the terms of trade*, Oxford Economic Papers, 11, 111–121.

Johnson, H. G., 1965, Optimal intervention in the presence of domestic distortions, in: R. E. Caves, P. B. Kenen and H. G. Johnson, eds., *Trade, growth and the balance of payments* (Rand McNally, Chicago) ch. 1.

Johnson, H. G., 1967, The possibility of income losses from increased efficiency or factor accumulation in the presence of tariffs, *Economic Journal* 77, 151–154.

Johnson, H. G., 1974, Notes on the economic theory of smuggling, in: J. Bhagwati, ed., *Illegal transactions and international trade: Theory and measurement* (North-Holland, Amsterdam).

Melvin, J. R., 1968, Production and trade with two factors and three goods, *American Economic Review* 58, 1249–1268.

Melvin, J. R., 1970, Commodity taxation as a determinant of trade, *Canadian Journal of Economics* 36, 62–78.

Musgrave, R. A., 1959, *The theory of public finance, A study in public economy* (McGraw Hill, Toronto).

Samuelson, P. A., 1954, The transfer problem and transportation costs, II: Analysis of effects of trade impediments, *Economic Journal* 64, 264–289.

Sheikh, M. A., 1973, Economics of smuggling: Theory and application, unpublished Ph.D. dissertation (The University of Western Ontario, London).

Vanek, J., 1965, *The general equilibrium of international discrimination* (Harvard University Press, Cambridge, Mass.).

17

Shadow Prices for Project Selection in the Presence of Distortions: Effective Rates of Protection and Domestic Resource Costs

T. N. Srinivasan and Jagdish N. Bhagwati

Until recently, theorists of trade and welfare have, by and large, ignored the ever-increasing literature on project evaluation. This is puzzling since the bulk of the project evaluation literature attempts to derive shadow prices to replace the market prices that, in distorted situations, clearly will not reflect true opportunity costs whereas the major advances in the welfare theory of international trade have consisted precisely in the analysis of issues in trade and welfare when the market is characterized by a number of alternative endogenous or policy-imposed distortions.[1]

Trade theorists have generally considered second-best problems characterizing the nature of optimal policy intervention when the given distortions cannot be (directly) removed. Project analysis, on the other hand, poses a related, but different, question: if the given distortions defining current resource (and expenditure) allocations cannot be removed, would the introduction of a project which withdraws resources from this existing allocation for project use be welfare-improving? The solution to this latter problem naturally follows from the derivation of the shadow prices of factors and outputs for use in project evaluation.

As it happens, this problem has been posed by Findlay and Wellisz (1976) in a most elegant, recent contribution, illuminating how trade-theoretic tools can be deployed to advantage in analyzing it.[2] We follow them in section I, essentially taking over their simple model of trade theory, with primary factors producing traded goods (including the project output), with no intermediates and with fixed international prices for the traded goods, and considering with Findlay and Wellisz the case of a trade distortion (i.e., a tariff or trade subsidy). We parallel the Findlay-Wellisz analysis, using somewhat different analytical techniques, managing therefore to both complement and correct it in critical ways.

This paper was originally published in *Journal of Political Economy* 86, no. 1 (1978).

Next, in section II, we relate these results on the appropriate shadow prices in project evaluation to the two measures which have been proposed as project-evaluation criteria in the developmental and trade literature: the effective rate of protection (ERP) and the domestic resource cost (DRC). It is shown that the ERP is an inappropriate measure for this purpose: and that DRCs, if they must yield the correct social evaluation of a project, must use the second-best shadow prices that are derived in section I, that is, they must be appropriately defined DRCs. Thus we succeed in casting light on the inconclusive debate among the ERP and DRC proponents—as typified, for example, by the controversy in this *Journal* among Balassa and Schydlowsky (1968, 1972), Bruno (1972), and Krueger (1972)—as to their relative merits as techniques of project appraisal.[3]

Finally, in section III, we analyze the derivation of shadow factor prices when the given distortions arise from three alternative, polar types of factor market imperfections familiar to trade theorists, rather than from the presence of a trade tariff or subsidy.

I. The Model and Derivation of Shadow Prices

As stated above, we consider the usual trade-theoretic model with two primary factors, k and l, producing two traded outputs, X_1 and X_2, that enjoy fixed international prices p_1^* and p_2^*. The "small" project being considered will produce commodity X_3, at fixed international price p_3^*. It is assumed that the planner is working with a well-behaved social utility function. The problem of project analysis then is to evolve suitable prices, for the primary factors and output (X_3) in the project, which would enable the analyst to decide whether the project should be accepted or rejected.

The problem would be straightforward indeed if there were no distortions in the system: the correct valuations of the primary factors would clearly be those in the market, as reflected by the international price-ratio p_1^*/p_2^*, and the correct valuation for X_3 would be the international price p_3^*. But the situation we must now introduce is one where the domestic price-ratio between commodities X_1 and X_2 is *distorted* by a tariff and/or trade subsidy and it is further assumed that this distortion must be taken as *given*. The problem then, as noted by Findlay and Wellisz (1976, p. 545) is "an inherently second best one" in which "the criterion for acceptance of the project is whether or not it will increase the value of total production at world prices as compared with the existing situation, assuming that the distortional policy on the existing goods continues unchanged":[4] this

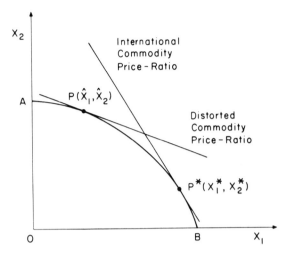

Figure 1

being, of course, the procedure suggested by Little and Mirrlees (1969) in their celebrated *Manual* and also by Bruno (1962, 1967b) in his important analytical work on project evaluation.

In applying this criterion for a "small" project, we note first that the introduction of the project will use labor and/or capital that are withdrawn from their present use. As such, the answer to the question whether or not the project (producing X_3) will increase the value of production at world prices is the *same* as to the question whether the world price of a unit of output of the project exceeds or falls short of its cost of production as obtained by evaluating the labor and capital used in producing X_3 at their *shadow* prices, that is, at prices that equal their marginal contribution in their existing use to the value of total production at world prices.

Turn now to figure 1. Here AB is the production possibility curve, defined on commodities X_1 and X_2. At free trade, production would be at $P^*(X_1^*, X_2^*)$ reflecting the international commodity prices. However, with trade distortion, the commodity price-ratio is more favorable to commodity X_2 and production is at $P(\hat{X}_1, \hat{X}_2)$. Now, the planner is assumed unable to correct the situation directly, so that the commodity price-ratio, the factor price-ratio, and factor proportions for X_1 and X_2 are to be held fixed at their respective values at $P(\hat{X}_1, \hat{X}_2)$. Denote then the corresponding input coefficients as $(\hat{k}_1, \hat{l}_1)$ and $(\hat{k}_2, \hat{l}_2)$ and factor rentals as $\hat{w}$ and $\hat{\gamma}$.

Now, as noted above, the *second-best* shadow prices of labor ($\hat{w}^*$) and capital ($\hat{\gamma}^*$) in this situation must equal the change in the quantities of X_1 and X_2 output, evaluated at *international* prices p_1^* and p_2^*, resulting from a marginal change in labor and capital, respectively, starting at $P(\hat{X}_1, \hat{X}_2)$ and maintaining the distored commodity price-ratio for production decisions.[5] Thus, defining $W = p_1^* X_1 + p_2^* X_2$ and the total availability of capital and labor as $\bar{K}$ and $\bar{L}$, respectively, it is clear that the shadow price of labor will be $dW/d\bar{L}$ and that of capital will be $dW/d\bar{K}$, where the derivatives must be evaluated for the distored situation. This is readily done as follows. First, since capital supply is fixed $(\bar{K})$, we have: $\hat{k}_1(dX_1/d\bar{L}) + \hat{k}_2(dX_2/d\bar{L}) = 0$, and, for labor, the corresponding equation is: $\hat{l}_1(dX_1/d\bar{L}) + \hat{l}_2(dX_2/d\bar{L}) = 1$. Therefore, $dX_1/d\bar{L} = -\hat{k}_2/(\hat{k}_1\hat{l}_2 - \hat{k}_2\hat{l}_1)$ and $dX_2/d\bar{L} = \hat{k}_1/(\hat{k}_1\hat{l}_2 - \hat{k}_2\hat{l}_1)$. Hence, the shadow price of labor, defined as: $\hat{w}^* = p_1^*(dX_1/d\bar{L}) + p_2^*(dX_2/d\bar{L})$ is seen to be equal to

$$\hat{w}^* = \frac{p_2^* \hat{k}_1 - p_1^* \hat{k}_2}{\hat{k}_1\hat{l}_2 - \hat{k}_2\hat{l}_1}. \tag{1}$$

Similarly, we can see that the shadow price of capital is

$$\hat{\gamma}^* = \frac{p_1^* \hat{l}_2 - p_2^* \hat{l}_1}{\hat{k}_1\hat{l}_2 - \hat{k}_2\hat{l}_1}. \tag{2}$$

It is readily seen that these are also the values of $\hat{w}^*$ and $\hat{\gamma}^*$ that satisfy the equations

$$p_1^* = \hat{w}^* \hat{l}_1 + \hat{\gamma}^* \hat{k}_1, \tag{3}$$

$$p_2^* = \hat{w}^* \hat{l}_2 + \hat{\gamma}^* \hat{k}_2.^{6} \tag{4}$$

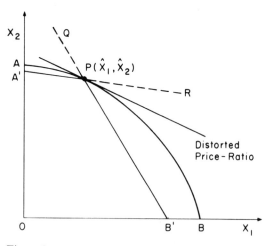

Figure 2

Now, it is easy to see that the shift in outputs, as labor (capital) is withdrawn from P, maintaining the distortion and hence the distorted commodity price-ratio, is yielded by the corresponding Rybczynski line. So, assuming that X_1 is K-intensive at P (i.e., $\hat{k}_1/\hat{l}_1 > \hat{k}_2/\hat{l}_2$), one can see, in figure 2, that the economy will move from P down line PB' as labor is reduced, up line PQ as labor is increased, up PA' as capital is reduced, and down PR as capital is increased. It equally follows, from the evaluation of these shifts at the *international* (rather than the distorted) commodity price-ratio, that $\hat{w}^*$ will be negative if the international price line is steeper that PB' (i.e., $p_1^*/p_2^* > \hat{k}_1/\hat{k}_2$) and $\hat{\gamma}^*$ will be negative if the international price line is flatter than PA' (i.e., $p_1^*/p_2^* < \hat{l}_1/\hat{l}_2$); and that nonnegative values for $\hat{w}^*$ and $\hat{\gamma}^*$ will obtain only when the international price-ratio is in the range spanned by PB' and PA'.

That it is possible for $\hat{w}^*$ *or* $\hat{\gamma}^*$ to be negative would appear to be a paradox. For, it of course implies, for instance, that when (say) $\hat{w}^* < 0$, it would pay society to implement a project with zero output (X_3) and positive labor input: in other words, that if labor were withdrawn from existing production, thanks to the project, this will increase the value of such production at international prices. But then this paradox is only yet another instance of "immiserizing growth"; the presence of the marginal labor is immiserizing, given the distortion;[7] and thus the paradox is readily resolved.

In their derivation of shadow factor prices for the above problem, however, Findlay and Wellisz (1976) bypass this possibility of negative factor prices by deriving these prices instead via the solution to a programming problem which is tantamount to (see figure 2) deriving the shadow factor prices corresponding to the international prices *but* subject to a "feasible" production possibility curve defined by $A'PB'$. These Findlay-Wellisz shadow prices ($\hat{w}^*, \hat{\gamma}^*$) are clearly yielded by putting the international price-ratio tangent to $A'PB'$, in the usual way, and are illustrated to advantage in figure 3.

Figure 3 is the all-too-familiar Samuelson diagram and needs no explanation. Now, movement along the *unrestricted* production possibility curve APB in figure 2 corresponds to movement along the curve QPR in figure 3, relating the commodity price-ratio to the corresponding factor price-ratio. Similarly, movement along the *restricted* production possibility curve $A'PB'$ in figure 2 corresponds in figure 3 to following the y-axis in the fourth quadrant from ∞ up to the point S where $OS = \hat{k}_1/\hat{k}_2$, then along the curve $SPNZ$ up to Z (where N is at a distance $\hat{l}_1/\hat{l}_2$ from the x-axis) and then following a straight line parallel to the x-axis. The (restricted) curve $SPNZ$, depicting w/γ as a function of p_1/p_2, can

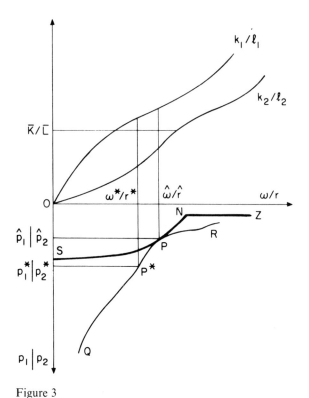

Figure 3

be shown to be increasing and concave, with a common tangent with the (unrestricted) curve QPR at P. Thus, the Findlay-Wellisz shadow price-ratio $\hat{w}^*/\hat{\gamma}^*$ will be infinite for $p_1^*/p_2^* \geqslant \hat{k}_1/\hat{k}_2$ and zero for $p_1^*/p_2^* \leqslant \hat{l}_1/\hat{l}_2$, while taking positive values in the range spanned by $\hat{k}_1/\hat{k}_2$ and $\hat{l}_1/\hat{l}_2$. This procedure therefore clearly will yield shadow prices that coincide with the correct ones yielded by our procedure only when $\hat{w}^*/\hat{\gamma}^* \geqslant 0$, that is, in figures 1 and 2, only for the parametric case where the international price-ratio lies in the range spanned by PA' and PB'. For the parametric cases where the international price-ratio lies outside of this range, the Findlay-Wellisz procedure will incorrectly yield, not negative shadow factor prices, but a shadow factor price-ratio, $\hat{w}^*/\hat{\gamma}^* = 0$ or ∞, according to whether the production specialization, corresponding to the international price-ratio, occurred in figure 2 at B' (on X_1) or A' (on X_2).[8]

II. ERPs, DRCs, et al.

We have thus deduced, in the preceding section, the precise shadow prices that must be used, in a distorted situation, for project appraisal. We are therefore now in a position to decide on the competing claims of the ERP and DRC proponents as to their relative merits as techniques of project appraisal. As careful reading of this debate in this *Journal* (1972), already cited, will unmistakably reveal, the first priority in this area is to define one's concepts unambiguously.

Since these and other economists distinguish between direct and indirect use of factors, thus including intermediates which were not included in the analysis in Section I above, we should first state that our project-acceptance criterion, suitably amended, is the following:

$$p_3^* \geqslant k_3 \hat{\gamma}^* + l_3 \hat{w}^* + f_1 p_1^*, \tag{5}$$

where it is now assumed that X_1 is used in project (X_3) with coefficient f_1 per unit output of X_3 and where k_3, l_3, and f_1 are assumed fixed so that one is essentially treating each process as a project. What the criterion says, of course, is that the project, to be accepted, must produce output which, when evaluated at international prices, exceeds or equals the cost of production evaluated at the (second-best) shadow factor prices. Now, note that the right-hand side of (5) is written in a form that includes the primary and intermediate inputs. But, it can *equivalently* be written in the form including direct *plus* indirect primary factors, that is, by decomposing intermediates into primary factors:

$$p_3^* \geqslant (k_3 + f_1 \hat{k}_1) \hat{\gamma}^* + (l_3 + f_1 \hat{l}_1) \hat{w}^*. \tag{6}$$

Now, noting that the DRC concept implies that one is measuring the domestic resources used in an activity to produce a unit of foreign exchange, we can distinguish sharply among the following, alternative concepts that correspond, in one way or another, to the concepts that are often apparently used indistinguishably in the literature.

Note, initially, that by first best we will refer to factor valuations (w^*, γ^*) corresponding to the *first-best* optimal situation at $P^*(X_1^*, X_2^*)$ in figure 1. By second best, we will denote instead the factor valuations $(\hat{w}^*, \hat{\gamma}^*)$ that reflect the second-best optimal situation, given the distortion. Finally, by "private" we will denote the factor valuations $(\hat{w}, \hat{\gamma})$ that actually obtain in the distorted situation at P.

Next, we should also note that the debate includes additionally a distinction among measures working with intermediates or alternatively with the intermediates decomposed into the primary factors producing them. Hence, we will distinguish also between decomposed-intermediates and direct-intermediates measure.[9] We will thus have altogether six measures of DRCs and one for ERP. We may therefore now state these alternative concepts/measures in regard to the project producing X_3, with brevity, noting that, in the denominator of all the measures set out below, commodities $(X_1, X_2,$ and $X_3)$ are always valued at their international prices.[10]

DRC_I: First-Best, Direct-Intermediates Measure

Here, we have the evaluation of the primary factors at first-best shadow wage and rental (w^*, γ^*), corresponding to the situation where the international commodity prices obtain domestically and therefore the distortions have been eliminated. These are also the shadow prices suggested by Bacha and Taylor (1971). In this case, we define

$$DRC_I = \frac{k_3\gamma^* + l_3 w^*}{p_3^* - f_1 p_1^*} \tag{7}$$

for the project, using the "direct" formulation: $f_1 p_1^*$ in the denominator, rather than decomposing that into $[(f_1 k_1^*)\gamma^* + (f_1 l_1^*)w^*]$ as in the next measure DRC_{II} (where k_1^* and l_1^* are the coefficients corresponding to first-best shadow prices).

DRC_{II}: First-Best, Decomposed-Intermediates Measure

Here, DRC_I modifies equivalently therefore to

$$DRC_{II} = \frac{k_3\gamma^* + l_3 w^*}{p_3^* - [(f_1 k_1^*)\gamma^* + (f_1 l_1^*)w^*]}. \tag{8}$$

(Now, note that we have been referring *only* to formulations that deal with *value added* in the denominator. These DRC measures are therefore "net" measures. Alternatively, we could have also chosen "gross" measures, rewriting DRC_I, for example, as $[k_3\gamma^* + l_3 w^* + f_1 p_1^*]/p_3^*$, and DRC_{II}, for example, as $[(k_3 + f_1 k_1^*)\gamma^* + (l_3 + f_1 l_1^*)w^*]/p_3^*$. But, as already remarked earlier, none of the DRC practitioners have used gross measures; hence they are not added here.)

DRC_{III}: Second-Best, Direct-Intermediates Measure

Here, we replace the first-best shadow factor prices with the second-best shadow prices, to alter DRC_I to

$$DRC_{III} = \frac{k_3\hat{\gamma}^* + l_3 \hat{w}^*}{p_3^* - f_1 p_1^*}. \tag{9}$$

DRC_{IV}: Second-Best, Decomposed-Intermediates Measure

Similarly, we alter DRC_{II} here to

$$DRC_{IV} = \frac{k_3\hat{\gamma}^* + l_3 \hat{w}^*}{p_3^* - [(f_1\hat{k}_1)\hat{\gamma}^* + (f_1\hat{l}_1)\hat{w}^*]}, \tag{10}$$

which is equivalent to DRC_{III}.

DRC_V: *Private, Direct-Intermediates Measure*
Here, we use the market prices and hence get a "private" DRC measure:

$$\text{DRC}_V = \frac{k_3\hat{\gamma} + l_3\hat{w}}{p_3^* - f_1 p_1^*}. \tag{11}$$

DRC_{VI}: *Private, Decomposed-Intermediates Measure*
Here, we get:

$$\text{DRC}_{VI} = \frac{k_3\hat{\gamma} + l_3\hat{w}}{p_3^* - [(f_1\hat{k}_1)\hat{\gamma} + (f_1\hat{l}_1)\hat{w}]}, \tag{12}$$

which is clearly *not* equivalent to DRC_V since the factor quantities yielded by the decomposition are being evaluated at the distorted, actual factor prices whereas the intermediates in DRC_V are directly being evaluated at the undistorted, international prices.

ERP
Then, finally, we have the well-known ERP measure:

$$\text{ERP} = \left[\frac{\hat{p}_3 - f_1\hat{p}_1}{p_3^* - f_1 p_1^*}\right] - 1, \tag{13}$$

where $\hat{p}_3$ is chosen such that $(\hat{p}_3 - f_1\hat{p}_1) = (\hat{k}_3\hat{\gamma} + \hat{l}_3\hat{w})$. Note that, in consequence, the numerator in the bracketed part of the ERP measure refers to the evaluation of domestic primary factors via the valuation of output and intermediates at actual (rather than shadow) prices; the numerators of (the bracketed term in) ERP and DRC_V *as also* DRC_{VI} are therefore identical. However, the denominator in the ERP measure represents value added at international prices and is identical with the denominator of DRC_V *but not* DRC_{VI}.

Now, the relevant question before us is whether, if a project is accepted by our (correctly derived) criterion, it will also be accepted if we were instead to compute the ERP or DRC for it and for the existing activities and then rank it correspondingly vis-à-vis these other activities. In short, would the ERP, and the DRC, be less for an acceptable project (X_3) than for the existing activities $(X_1$ and $X_2)$?

To answer this question, note first the fact that, for the existing activities $(X_1$ and $X_2)$ at first-best *or* second-best *shadow* factor prices, the DRCs must necessarily be unity.[11] It is equally evident that the DRCs at the *private* factor prices will differ from unity. Thus we have DRC_I to $\text{DRC}_{IV} = 1$, but DRC_V and DRC_{VI} are not necessarily unity.

By comparing the above with our project acceptance criterion, we then see right away that, if we do have to take the distorted situation as given, the measures DRC_{III} and DRC_{IV} will be unity for the existing activities and less than unity for the project if the project is acceptable. Hence, the DRCs using appropriately derived second-best shadow factor prices (and international-price valuation of the traded commodities) will lead to a correct acceptance/rejection of a project.

However, it is equally evident that neither the DRCs using the first-best shadow factor prices (i.e., DRC_I and DRC_{II}) nor those using private, market prices of factors (i.e., DRC_V and DRC_{VI}) can, as a general rule, lead to the correct acceptance/rejection of the project.[12] In particular, it is clear that the ERP measure, which corresponds to DRC_V, will identically therefore be quite inappropriate to the task.[13]

While therefore ERP is an inappropriate measure to use for project analysis, it may be suggested that it be replaced by a so-called social ERP measure. The only operational implication of such a suggestion would be to convert ERP into (the *correct* criterion) DRC_{III}, that is, to replace the incorrect numerator $(\hat{p}_3 - f_1\hat{p}_1)$ in the bracketed term in ERP by the correct numerator $(k_3\hat{r}^* + l_3\hat{w}^*)$. But this implies revaluing domestic factors *directly* at the second-best prices, in the manner set out in section I, whereas the essence of the ERP approach (which was developed in the context of the quite different, "positive," problem of predicting resource-allocational effects of a tariff structure) has always been to arrive at the numerator *indirectly* as the difference between the domestic values of inputs and outputs (yielding equivalently value added at domestic, "private," prices, of course). To derive DRCs, by estimating (as must be done) the correct shadow factor prices $(\hat{w}^*$ and $\hat{r}^*)$, and then to rechristen them as "social ERPs" is therefore likely to lead to confusion; and, in our judgment, it is best therefore to drop the terminology and concept of ERPs altogether from cost-benefit analysis.

Next, it is also evident that it makes absolutely no difference whether one uses the direct-intermediates measure DRC_{III} or the measure DRC_{IV} where the intermediates are decomposed into the primary factors used up in them; *as long as* second-best shadow factor prices are used for project appraisal, as indeed they should be, the two methods are identical and equally correct. Thus demonstration, therefore, also seems to bear out Bruno's (1972) rejection of the Balassa-Schydlowsky (1968) contention that this distinction matters: Bruno (1966, 1967a) was clearly working within an institutionally (quantity-) constrained framework which therefore yielded second-best shadow prices.

Furthermore, note that if the project analyst were to use the following "hybrid" DRC measure,

$$\text{DRC}_{\text{VII}} = \frac{k_3 \hat{\gamma}^* + l_3 \hat{w}^*}{p_3^* - f_1 \hat{p}_1} \tag{14a}$$

$$= \frac{k_3 \hat{\gamma}^* + l_3 \hat{w}^*}{p_3^* - (f_1 \hat{k}_1 \hat{\gamma} + f_1 \hat{l}_1 \hat{w})}, \tag{14b}$$

then clearly the numerator is correct but the denominator is erroneous; but this clearly is *not* what Bruno (1972) proposes. In fact, this would be precisely the opposite kind of error to that which ERP would imply as a project criterion: for, with ERP, the denominator is correct but the numerator is not.

Finally, the question has been raised in this ERP versus DRC debate: what if the introduction of the garment project *leads* (via a rule for example which requires that domestic fabrics *must* be used) to the licensing and creation of a tariff-protected fabric industry?[14] If such is indeed the case, we should naturally wish to redefine and consider, as a project, the *vertically integrated* project involving *both* the garments and the fabrics that are produced for the garments. And then, the correct project appraisal would be along exactly the same lines as before, with DRC_{III} and DRC_{IV}, all using second-best shadow factor prices, providing the correct method for doing project appraisal for this redefined project.

III. Alternative Factor Market Distortions and Second-Best Shadow Factor Prices

It this section, we briefly extend our analysis to three standard factor market distortions which trade theorists have analyzed in great depth, deriving second-best shadow prices in each case in the manner set out in section I. The three distortions are: (*a*) a sector-specific sticky wages;[15] (*b*) a generalized sticky wage;[16] and (*c*) a wage differential between sectors.[17]

Sector-Specific Sticky Wage

Consider a typical two-sector model of the Harris-Todaro variety.[18] Here, the minimum wage is set in the manufacturing sector, producing X_2, in terms of X_2 at $\bar{w}$. The workers from the agricultural sector, producing X_1, migrate to the manufacturing sector until the agricultural wage equals the *expected* manufacturing wage. The expected wage is defined as the sticky manufacturing wage, $\bar{w}$, multiplied by the probability of a worker in the manufacturing sector obtaining employment therein. This probability, in turn, is assumed equal to the ratio of actual employment (L_2) in manufacturing to the total labor force there, (i.e., $\bar{L} - L_1$).

Assuming perfect competition and the production functions in the two sectors to be strictly concave functions of employment, and denoting the latter by F_1 and F_2 and the international price-ratio as p_1^*/p_2^* as before, we can now write the Harris-Todaro equilibrium as

$$F_2'(L_2) = \bar{w} \tag{15}$$

$$\frac{p_1^*}{p_2^*} \cdot F_1'(L_1) = \bar{w} \cdot \frac{L_2}{\bar{L} - L_1}. \tag{16}$$

Since the availability of foreign exchange in this model is given by $Z = F_2 + (p_1^*/p_2^*) \cdot F_1$, the second-best shadow price of labor is clearly

$$\hat{w}^* = \frac{dZ}{d\bar{L}} = \frac{p_1^*}{p_2^*} \cdot F_1' \left[\frac{F_1'}{F_1' - (\bar{L} - L_1)F_1''} \right]. \tag{17}$$

With $F_1'' < 0$ by strict concavity of F_1, and $\bar{L} > L_1$, we then see that the second-best shadow wage for labor is less than the agricultural wage which, in turn, is less than the manufacturing wage. Note also that the shadow wage is positive, instead of zero, despite the unemployed labor; this is because any withdrawal of labor from the labor force ($\bar{L}$), while initially reducing unemployment, will simultaneously raise the expected wage in manufacturing and hence result in reduction of agricultural employment and output.

The foregoing analysis assumes that the employment (at whatever wage rate) in the project has no impact on the expected wage in the manufacturing sector except insofar as it affects the manufacturing labor force. Thus writing ε as the employment in the project and η as the resulting migration from agriculture, the expected wage in the manufacturing sector after migration is $\bar{w}L_2/(\bar{L} - \varepsilon) - (L_1 - \eta)$ which is equated in turn to the agricultural wage $p_1^* F_1'(L_1 - \eta)$. However, if we were to assume that the project laborers are employed at some wage, w^p, and that project employment at this wage affects the expected wage in the manufacturing sector, the latter would be $wL_2 + w^p \varepsilon / \bar{L} - (L_1 - \eta)$ which again is equated to $p_1^* F_1'(L_1 - \eta)$. Solving the latter for η and noting that the shadow wage is the loss in agricultural output per unit of project employment, that is, $p_1^* F_1'(\eta/\varepsilon)$, we get shadow wage $= (w^p \cdot F_1')/ [F_1' - F_1''(\bar{L} - L_1)]$. In the case where $F_1'' = 0$, this reduces to w^p, the wage paid to the project laborer. If we make the further assumption that $w^p = \bar{w}$, that is, the project employs labor at the manufacturing wage, the shadow wage equals the manufacturing wage: a highly special case, as we have just shown, but one which has been focused upon in the standard cost-benefit analysis of the Harris-Todaro model.

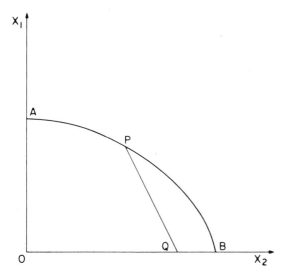

Figure 4

Generalized Sticky Wage

Shift now to the model where the wage is sticky across the two sectors at the level $\bar{w}$. Assuming then that commodity X_2 is capital-intensive, that is, $(K_2/L_2 > K_1/L_1)$, we now get:

$$\frac{F_2}{L_2} - \frac{K_2}{L_2} \cdot F_2^K \geqslant \bar{w} \tag{18}$$

$$\frac{F_2}{L_2 F_2^K} - \frac{K_2}{L_2} = \frac{F_1}{L_1 F_1^K} - \frac{K_1}{L_1} \tag{19}$$

where F_1^K, F_2^K, F_1^L, and F_2^L are the partial derivatives with respect to K and L, respectively; that is, they are marginal products of capital and labor; and F_2/L_2 and F_1/L_1 are the average products of labor in production of X_2 and X_1, respectively.

We can then see that, in terms of figure 4, the production possibility curve is APB, P representing the point at which $(F_2/L_2 - K_2/L_2 \cdot F_2^K) = \bar{w}$. At points to the left [right] of P, $(F_2/L_2 - K_2/L_2 \cdot F_2^K) > [<] \bar{w}$. It is evident then that, with the minimum wage constraint, the feasible production possibility curve will be APQ where PQ is the Rybczynski line (for variations in labor) and, at points on PQ other than P, there is unemployed labor. Let the capital-labor ratios at P then be $\bar{K}_2/\bar{L}_2$ and $\bar{K}_1/\bar{L}_1$.

Now, when the international price-ratio p_1^*/p_2^* yields tangency along AP, the market and shadow wages will be naturally identical, and will exceed $\bar{w}$ if the tangency is off P. For the price-ratio tangent to APB at P, the production equilibrium however may be anywhere between P and Q, the different production equilibria implying different labor availabilities. Therefore, for this tangential price-ratio, the shadow and actual wages will be $\bar{w}$ for production at P, whereas the actual wage will be $\bar{w}$ but the shadow wage will be zero for points other than P on PQ.[19] Finally, for all commodity price-ratios steeper than the price-ratio tangent at P, there will be complete specialization on X_2 at Q and the corresponding actual wage will be $\bar{w}$ while the shadow wage will be zero.[20]

Hence, unlike in the sector-specific wage stickiness case, the unemployment of labor can indeed be taken to imply a zero shadow wage for labor. However, associated with this, the shadow rental of capital will exceed its market rental, so that the standard prescription of putting the wage of unemployed labor equal to zero but using the market rental of capital is wrong.

The Wage-Differential Case

Take, finally, the distorion where the wage in X_2 is a multiple λ of that in X_1. In this case, it is well known that the production possibility curve will shrink to AQB, in figure 5. Furthermore, AQB need not be concave to the origin, the market equilibrium need not be unique for any commodity price-ratio, and the commodity price-ratio will not equal the marginal rate of transformation along AQB.[21]

Let the market equilibrium in the initial, distorted situation be at Q.

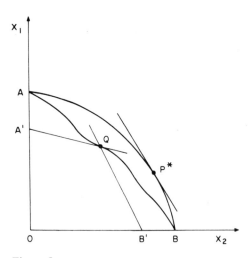

Figure 5

Then, we can derive the two Rybczynski lines, QB' (for variations in labor availability) and QA' (for variations in capital availability), assuming as earlier that X_2 is capital intensive.

Now, the international price-ratio equals the ratio of *marginal* products of capital in producting X_2 and X_1 with the techniques corresponding to Q (i.e., $p_1^*/p_2^* = F_K^2/F_K^1$, the latter derivatives as at Q). On the other hand, the slope of QB' (measured against the vertical axis) will equal the ratio of the corresponding *average* products.

If follows then that the international price-line would be flatter than QB' and steeper than QA', given the capital intensity of X_2 relative of X_1, provided there were no wage differential λ. However, in the presence of the wage differential, the international price-line may well be steeper (flatter) than $QB'(QA')$, with the wage in X_2 exceeding that in X_1 by factor $\lambda(>1)$, the condition for this "reversal" of relative slopes of the price-ratio and the Rybczynski line being that X_2 ceases to be capital intensive relative to X_1 if the factor intensities are compared on a *differential-weighted* basis.[22]

It is then easy to see that, as in section I, the second-best shadow wage of labor, that is, $[p_1^*(\bar{K}_2/F_2) - p_2^*(\bar{K}_1/F_1)]/[(\bar{K}_2/F_2)(\bar{L}_1/F_1) - (\bar{K}_1/F_1)(\bar{L}_2/F_2)]$, or the shadow rental on capital, that is, $[p_2^*(\bar{L}_1/F_1) - p_1^*(\bar{L}_2/F_2)]/[(\bar{K}_2/F_2)(\bar{L}_1/F_1) - (\bar{K}_1/F_1)(\bar{L}_2/F_2)]$, will be negative when such reversal of relative slopes exists; and, once again, the Findlay-Wellisz procedure of deriving shadow prices would yield an incorrect zero wage (rental).

IV. Concluding Remarks

A few concluding observations are in order. First, while our results on project appraisal have been shown to be successfully convertible into appropriately defined DRCs, this is not the same thing of course as having shown that these were precisely the DRC definitions (as against the many others that we have distinguished) that one or more of the DRC proponents, in the project-appraisal debate among the DRC and ERP proponents, had in mind.

Second, while we have confined our analysis to "small" projects, drawing infinitesimal resources away from the existing distorted situation, it is equally clear from our analysis that the results can hold also for "large" projects. Given the Rybczynski-line properties of the different models, the shadow prices of factors will be identical for small and large shifts of factors into the project.[23]

Third, we might as well note explicitly that our analysis could be extended to models involving nontraded goods; this would permit the introduction of the real exchange rate in a meaninglful manner into the analysis. The extension to models with sector-specfic factors is not merely readily done;[24] it will however introduce no special insights that qualify what has been learned from the present paper.

Fourth, note that we are implicitly assuming that, in respect of projects which will be chosen under shadow prices but *not* under actual market prices, the resulting losses are covered in some nondistortionary way. However, if the losses can be covered only by some form of distortionary taxation, then the shadow prices (for both inputs and outputs) have to be calculated reflecting this fact. *Alternatively*, our analysis can be held to apply without modification to the case where the planning authorities are investigating the social profitability of a private project which is com-mercially viable at market prices. In this instance, if social profitability is absent, the planning authorities can decide to eliminate the activity by prohibiting it, and the revenue problem does not arise.

Fifth, note also that we evaluated the project at a given technique. Thus, if a projects can exploit alternative techniques, from which entre-preneurs would choose the cost-minimizing one, then the revenue problem will arise *also* because a suitable factor-use tax-cum-subsidy will have to be provided so that the "correct" technique (i.e., that using coefficients k_3, l_3, and f_1 if the project X_3 has been shown to be socially profitable) is chosen.

Finally, it is also clear that implicit in our analysis is the assumption that problems of income distribution and saving can be tackled through deployment of appropriate nondistortionary instruments. Obviously, if this is not possible, the shadow prices will have to be calculated afresh by introducing additional constraints which reflect the feasible set of public policy instruments.

The research underlying this paper was supported by NSF grant SOC74-13210. Thanks are due to Peter Diamond for helpful conversations and to Michael Bruno, Henry Wan, Ian Little, Christopher Heady, Richard Brecher, Takashi Negishi, Koichi Hamada, Hiroshi Atsumi, Bela Balassa, and Jacob Frenkel for valuable comments on an earlier draft of this paper. The views expressed are those of the authors and should not be ascribed to the World Bank or to its affiliated institutions.

References

Bacha, Edmar, and Taylor, Lance. "Foreign Exchange Shadow Prices: A Critical Review of Current Theories." *Q.J.E.* 85 (May 1971): 197–224.

Balassa, Bela, and Schydlowsky, Daniel M. "Effective Tariffs, Domestic Cost of Foreign Exchange, and the Equilibrium Exchange Rate." *J.P.E.* 76 (May/June 1968): 348–60.

———. "Domestic Resource Costs and Effective Protection Once Again." *J.P.E.* 80 (January/Feburary 1972): 63–69.

Bhagwati, Jagdish N. "Immiserizing Growth: A Geometrical Note." *Rev. Econ. Studies* 25 (June 1958): 201–5.

———. "Distortions and Immiserizing Growth: A Generalization." *Rev. Econ. Studies* 35 (October 1968): 481–85.

———. "The Generalized Theory of Distortions and Welfare." In *Trade, Balance of Payments, and Growth*, edited by J. N. Bhagwati et al. Amsterdam: North-Holland, 1971.

———. *Anatomy and Consequences of Exchange Control Regimes.* Cambridge, Mass.: Ballinger & Co., 1979.

Bhagwati, J. N., and Desai, Padma, *India: Planning for Industrialization: Industrialization and Trade Policies since 1951.* London: Oxford Univ. Press, for OECD Development Centre, 1970.

Bhagwati, J. N., and Ramaswami, V. K. "Domestic Distortions, Tariffs and the Theory of Optimum Subsidy." *J.P.E.* 71, no. 1 (February 1963): 44–50.

Bhagwati, J. N.; Ramaswami, V. K.; and Srinivasan, T. N. "Domestic Distortions, Tariffs, and the Theory of Optimum Subsidy: Some Further Results." *J.P.E.* 77, no. 6 (November/December 1969): 1005–10.

Bhagwati, J. N., and Srinivasan, T. N. "Thy Theory of Wage Differentials: Production Response and Factor Price Equalisation," *J. Internat. Econ.* 1 (February 1971): 19–35.

———. "On Reanalyzing the Harris-Todaro Model: Policy Rankings in the Case of Sector-Specific Sticky Wages." *A.E.R.* 64 (June 1974): 502–8.

———. *Foreign Trade Regimes and Economic Development: India.* New York: Columbia University Press, 1978.

Bhagwati, J. N.; Srinivasan, T. N.; and Wan, Henry, Jr. "Value Subtracted, Negative Shadow Prices of Factors in Project Evaluations, and Immiserizing Growth: Three Paradoxes in the Presence of Trade Distortions." *Econ. J.*, 1977 (forthcoming).

Bhagwati, J. N., and Wan, Henry, Jr. "Shadow Prices in Project Evaluation, with and without Distortions, and with Many Goods and Factors." *American Economic Review* 69 (June 1979): 261–73.

Brecher, Richard A. "Minimum Wage Rates and the Pure Theory of International Trade," *Q.J.E.* 88 (February 1974): 98–116 (*a*)

———. "Optimum Commercial Policy for a Minimum Wage Economy." *J. Internat. Econ.* 4 (May 1974): 139–50. (*b*)

Bruno, Michael. *Interdependence, Resource Use and Structural Change in Israel.* Jerusalem: Bank of Israel, 1962.

————. "A Programming Model for Israel." In *The Theory and Design of Economic Development*, edited by I. Adelman and E. Thorbecke. Baltimore: Johns Hopkins Univ. Press, 1966.

————. "Optimal Patterns of Trade and Development." *Rev. Econ. and Statis.* 49 (November 1967): 545–54. (*a*)

————. "The Optimal Selection of Import-substituting and Export-promoting Projects." In *Planning the External Sector: Techniques, Problems and Policies*. New York: United Nations (ST/TAO/SER. C/91), 1967. (*b*)

————. "Domestic Resource Costs and Effective Protection: Clarification and Synthesis." *J.P.E.* 80, no. 1 (January/February 1972): 16–33.

Corden, W. M. *Trade Policy and Economic Welfare*. London: Oxford Univ. Press, 1974.

Diamond, Peter A., and Mirrlees, James A. "Private Constant Returns and Public Shadow Prices." *Rev. Econ. Studies* 43 (February 1976): 41–48.

Findlay, Ronald, and Wellisz, Stanislaw. "Project Evaluation, Shadow Prices, and Trade Policy." *J.P.E.* 84, no. 3 (June 1976): 543–52.

Haberler, Gottfried. "Some Problems in the Pure Theory of International Trade." *Econ. J.* 60 (June 1950): 223–40.

Hagen, Everett E. "An Economic Justification of Protectionism." *Q.J.E.* 72 (November 1958): 496–514.

Harris, John R., and Todaro, Michael. "Migration, Unemployment and Development: A Two-Sector Analysis." *A.E.R.* 60 (March 1970): 126–42.

Herberg, Horst, and Kemp, Murray C. "Factor Market Distortions, the Shape of the Locus of Competitive Outputs, and the Relation between Product Prices and Equilibrium Outputs." In *Trade, Balance of Payments, and Growth*, edited by J. N. Bhagwati et al. Amsterdam: North-Holland, 1971.

Johnson, Harry G. "Optimal Trade Intervention in the Presence of Domestic Distortions." In *Trade, Growth, and the Balance of Payments*, edited by R. E. Caves et al. Amsterdam: North-Holland, 1965.

————. "Factor Market Distortions and the Shape of the Transformation Curve." *Econometrica* 34 (July 1966): 686–98.

————. "The Possibility of Income Losses from Increased Efficiency or Factor Accumulation in the Presence of Tariffs." *Econ. J.* 77 (March 1967): 151–54.

Jones, Ronald W. "Distortions in Factor Markets and the General Equilibrium Model of Production." *J.P.E.* 79, no. 3 (May/June 1971): 437–59. (*a*)

————. "A Three-Factor Model in Theory, Trade, and History." In *Trade, Balance of Payments, and Growth*, edited by J. N. Bhagwati et al. Amsterdam: North-Holland, 1971. (*b*)

Joshi, V. "The Rationale and Relevance of the Little-Mirrlees Criterion." *Bull. Oxford Inst. Econ. and Statis.* 34 (February 1972): 3–33.

Krueger, Anne O. "Evaluating Restrictionist Trade Regimes: Theory and Measurement." *J.P.E.* 80, no. 1 (January/February 1972): 48–62.

Lal, Deepak. "Methods of Project Analysis: A Review." World Bank Occasional Paper no. 16, Washington, D.C., 1974, Distributed by Johns Hopkins Press, Baltimore.

Lefeber, Louis. "Trade and Minimum Wage Rates." In *Trade, Balance of Payments, and Growth*, edited by J. N. Bhagwati et al. Amsterdam: North-Holland, 1971.

Little, I. M. D., and Mirrlees, James A. *Manual of Industrial Project Analysis in Developing Countries*. Vol. 2. Paris: Org. Econ. Cooperation and Development, 1969.

Magee, Stephen. *International Trade and Distortions in Factor Markets*. New York: Marcel Dekker, 1976.

Srinivasan, T. N., and Bhagwati, Jagdish N. "Alternative Policy Rankings in a Large Open Economy with Sector-Specific Minimum Wages." *J. Econ. Theory* 1, no. 3 (December 1975): 256–71.

V
Tariff Discrimination: Customs Unions et al.

18

The Theory of
Customs Unions:
A General Survey

Richard Lipsey

This paper is devoted mainly to a survey of the development of customs-union theory from Viner to date; since, however, the theory must be meant at least as an aid in interpreting real-world data, some space is devoted to a summary of empirical evidence relating to the gains from European Economic Union. It is necessary first to define customs-union theory. In general, the tariff system of any country may discriminate between commodities and/or between countries. Commodity discrimination occurs when different rates of duty are levied on different commodities, while country discrimination occurs when the same commodity is subject to different rates of duty, the rate varying according to the country of origin. The theory of customs unions may be defined as that branch of tariff theory which deals with the effects of geographically discriminatory changes in trade barriers.

Next we must turn our attention to the scope of the existing theory. The theory has been confined mainly to a study of the effects of customs unions on welfare rather than, for example, on the level of economic activity, the balance of payments or the rate of inflation. These welfare gains and losses, which are the subject of the theory, may arise from a number of different sources: (1) the specialization of production according to comparative advantage which is the basis of the classical case for the gains from trade; (2) economies of scale; (3) changes in the terms of trade; (4) forced changes in efficiency due to increased foreign competition; and (5) a change in the rate of economic growth.[1] The theory of customs unions has been almost completely confined to an investigation of (1) above, with some slight attention to (2) and (3), (5) not being dealt with at all, while (4) is ruled out of traditional theory by the assumption (often

This paper was originally published in *The Economic Journal* 70 (1960): 496–513. Also published in Jagdish Bhagwati, editor, *International Trade: Selected Readings*, Penguin Books, 1969.

contradicted by the facts) that production is carried out by processes which are technically efficient.

Throughout the development of the theory of customs unions we will find an oscillation between the belief that it is possible to produce a general conclusion of the sort: "Customs unions will always, or nearly always, raise welfare", and the belief that, depending on the particular circumstances present, a customs union may have any imaginable effect on welfare. The earliest customs-union theory was largely embodied in the oral tradition, for it hardly seemed worthwhile to state it explicitly, and was an example of an attempt to produce the former sort of conclusion. It may be summarized quite briefly. Free trade maximizes world welfare; a customs union reduces tariffs and is therefore a movement towards free trade; a customs union will, therefore, *increase* world welfare even if it does not lead to a world-welfare *maximum*.

Viner showed this argument to be incorrect. He introduced the now familiar concepts of trade creation and trade diversion (Viner, 1950, ch, 4) which are probably best recalled in terms of an example. Consider the figures in the following table:

Table 1
Money Prices (at Existing Exchange Rates) of a Single Commodity (*X*) in Three Countries

Country	A	B	C
Price	35s.	26s.	20s.

A tariff of 100 per cent levied by country A will be sufficient to protect A's domestic industry producing commodity X.[2] If A forms a customs union with either country B or country C she will be better off; if the union is with B she will get a unit of commodity X at an opportunity cost of 26 shillings-worth of exports instead of at the cost of 35 shillings-worth of other goods entailed by domestic production.[3] This is an example of trade creation. If A had been levying a somewhat lower tariff, a 50 per cent tariff, for example, she would already have been buying X from abroad before the formation of any customs union. If A is buying a commodity from abroad, and if her tariff is non-discriminatory, then she will be buying it from the lowest-cost source—in this case country C. Now consider a customs union with country B. B's X, now exempt from the tariff, sells for 26s., while C's X, which must still pay the 50 per cent tariff, must be sold for 30s. A will now buy X from B at a price, in terms of the value of exports, of 26s., whereas she was formerly buying it from C at a price of only 20s. This is a case of Viner's trade diversion, and since it entails a movement from lower to higher real cost sources of supply, it represents a movement from a more to a less efficient allocation of resources.

This analysis is an example of what Mr. Lancaster and I have called *the general theory of second best* (Lipsey and Lancaster, 1956–57): "if it is impossible to satisfy *all* the optimum conditions (in this case to make all relative prices equal to all rates of transformation in production), then a change which brings about the satisfaction of *some* of the optimum conditions (in this case making some relative prices equal to some rates of transformation in production) may make things better or worse.[4]

Viner's analysis leads to the following classification of the possibilities that arise from a customs union between two countries, A and B:

1. Neither A nor B may be producing a given commodity. In this case they will both be importing this commodity from some third country, and the removal of tariffs on trade between A and B can cause no change in the pattern of trade in this commodity; both countries will continue to import it from the cheapest possible source outside of the union.

2. One of the two countries may be producing the commodity inefficiently under tariff protection while the second country is a non-producer. If country A is producing commodity X under tariff protection this means that her tariff is sufficient to eliminate competition from the cheapest possible source. Thus if A's tariff on X is adopted by the union the tariff will be high enough to secure B's market for A's inefficient industry.

3. Both countries may be producing the commodity inefficiently under tariff protection. In this case the customs union removes tariffs between country A and B and ensures that the least inefficient of the two will capture the union market.[5]

In case 2 above any change must be a trade-diverting one, while in case 3 any change must be a trade-creating one. If one wishes to predict the welfare effects of a customs union it is necessary to predict the relative strengths of the forces causing trade creation and trade diversion.

This analysis leads to the conclusion that customs unions are likely to cause losses when the countries involved are complementary *in the range of commodities that are protected by tariffs.* Consider the class of commodities produced under tariff protection in each of the two countries. If these classes overlap to a large extent, then the most efficient of the two countries will capture the union market and there will be a reallocation of resources in a more efficient direction. If these two classes do not overlap to any great extent, then the protected industry in one country is likely to capture the whole of the union market when the union is formed, and there is likely to be a reallocation of resources in a less efficient direction. This point of Viner's has often been misunderstood and read to say that, in some general sense, the economies of the two countries should be competitive and not complementary. A precise way of making the point is to say that the customs union is more likely to bring gain, the greater is the degree of overlapping between the class of commodities produced under tariff protection in the two countries.

A subsequent analysis of the conditions affecting the gains from union through trade creation and trade diversion was made by Drs. Makower and Morton (1953). They pointed out that, *given that trade creation was going to occur*, the gains would be larger the more dissimilar were the cost ratios in the two countries. (Clearly if two countries have almost identical cost ratios the gains from trade will be small.) They then defined competitive economies to be ones with similar cost ratios and complementary economies to be ones with dissimilar ratios, and were able to conclude that unions between complementary economies would, if they brought gain at all, bring large gains. The conclusions of Viner and Makower and Morton are in no sense contradictory. Stated in the simplest possible language, Viner showed that gains will arise from unions if both countries are producing the same commodity; Makower and Morton showed that these gains will be larger the larger is the difference between the costs at which the same commodity is produced in the two countries.[6]

We now come to the second major development in customs-union theory—the analysis of the welfare effects of *the substitution between commodities* resulting from the changes in relative prices which necessarily accompany a custom union. Viner's analysis implicitly assumed that commodities are consumed in some fixed proportion which is independent of the structure of relative prices. Having ruled out substitution between commodities, he was left to analyse only bodily shifts of trade from one country to another. The way in which Viner's conclusion that trade diversion necessarily lowers welfare depends on his implicit demand assumption is illustrated in figure 1. Consider the case of a small country, A, specialized in the production of a single commodity, Y, and importing one commodity, X, at terms of trade independent of any taxes or tariffs levied in A. The fixed proportion in which commodities are consumed is shown by the slope of the line OZ, which is the income- and price-consumption line for all (finite) prices and incomes, OA indicates country A's total production of commodity Y, and the slope of the line AC shows the terms of trade offered by country C, the lowest cost producer of X. Under conditions of free trade, country A's equilibrium will be at e, the point of intersection between OZ and AC. A will consume Og of Y,

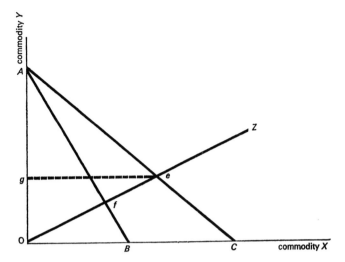

Figure 1

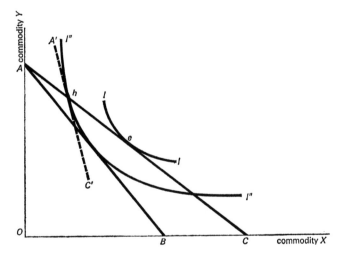

Figure 2

exporting Ag in return for ge of X. Now a tariff which does not affect A's terms of trade and is not high enough to protect a domestic industry producing Y will leave her equilibrium position unchanged at e.[7] The tariff changes relative prices, but consumers' purchases are completely insensitive to this change and, if foreign trade continues at terms indicated by the slope of the line AC, the community must remain in equilibrium at e. Now consider a case where country A forms a trade-diverting customs union with country B. This means that A must buy her imports of X at a price in terms of Y higher than she was paying before the union was formed. An example of this is shown in figure 1 by the line AB. A's equilibrium is now at f, the point of intersection between AB and OZ; less of both commodities are consumed, and A's welfare has unambiguously diminished. We conclude therefore that, under the assumed demand conditions, trade diversion (which necessarily entails a deterioration in A's terms of trade) *necessarily* lowers A's welfare.

Viner's implicit assumption that commodities are consumed in fixed proportions independent of the structure of relative prices is indeed a very special one. A customs union necessarily changes relative prices and, in general, we should expect this to lead to some substitution between commodities, there being a tendency to change the volume of already existing trade with more of the now cheaper goods being bought and less of the now more expensive. This would tend to increase the volume of imports from a country's union partner and to diminish both the volume of imports obtained from the outside world and the consumption of home-produced commodities. The importance of this substitution effect in consumption seems to have been discovered independently by at least three people, Professor Meade (1956), Professor Gehrels (1956–57) and myself (1957).

In order to show the importance of the effects of substitutions in consumption we merely drop the assumption that commodities are consumed in fixed proportions. I shall take Mr. Gehrels's presentation of this analysis because it illustrates a number of important factors. In figure 2 OA is again country A's total production of Y, and the slope of the line AC indicates the terms of trade between X and Y when A is trading with country C. The free-trade equilibrium position is again at e, where an indifference curve is tangent to AC. In this case, however, the imposition of a tariff on imports of X, even if it does not shift the source of country A's imports, will cause a reduction in the quantity of these imports and an increase in the consumption of the domestic commodity Y. A tariff which changes the relative price in A's domestic market to, say, that indicated by the slope of the line $A'C'$ will move A's equilibrium position to point h. At this point an indifference curve cuts AC with a slope equal to the line $A'C'$; consumers are thus adjusting their purchases to the market rate of transformation and the tariff has had the effect of reducing imports of X and increasing consumption of the home good Y. In these circumstances it is clearly possible for country A to form a trade-diverting customs union and yet gain an increase in its welfare. To show this, construct a line through A tangent to the indifference curve I'' to cut the X axis at some point B. If A forms a trade-diverting customs union with country B and buys her imports of X from B at terms of trade indicated by the slope of the line AB, her welfare will be unchanged. If, therefore, the terms of trade with B are worse than those given by C but better than those indicated by the slope of the line AB, A's welfare will be increased by the trade-diverting customs union. A's welfare will be diminished by this trade-diverting union with B only if B's terms of trade are worse than those indicated by the slope of AB.

The common-sense reason for this conclusion may be stated as follows:

The possibility stems from the fact that whenever imports are subject to a tariff, the position of equilibrium must be one where an indifference curve [surface or hyper-surface as the case may be] cuts (*not* is tangent to) the international price line. From this it follows that there will exist an area where indifference curves higher than the one achieved at equilibrium lie below the international price line. In Figure 2 this is the area above I'' but below AC. As long as the final equilibrium position lies within this area, trade carried on in the absence of tariffs at terms of trade worse than those indicated by AC, will increase welfare. In a verbal statement this possibility may be explained by referring to the two opposing effects of a trade-diverting customs union. First, A shifts her purchases from a lower to a higher cost source of supply. It now becomes necessary to export a larger quantity of goods in order to obtain any given quantity of imports. Secondly, the divergence between domestic and international prices is eliminated when the union is formed. The removal of the tariff has the effect of allowing ... consumer[s] in A to adjust ... purchases to a domestic price ratio which now is equal to the rate at which [Y] can be transformed into ... [X] by means of international trade. The final welfare effect of the trade-diverting customs union must be the net effect of these two opposing tendencies; the first working to lower welfare and the second to raise it.[8]

On this much there is general agreement. Professor Gehrels, however, concluded that his analysis established a general presumption in favour of gains from union rather than losses. He argued that 'to examine customs unions in the light only of *production* effects, as Viner does, will give a biased judgement of their effect on countries joining them' (Gehrels, 1956–57, p. 61), and he went on to say that the analysis given above established a general presumption in favour of gains from union. Now we seemed to be back in the pre-Viner world, where economic analysis

Table 2

Free trade (col. 1)	Uniform ad valorem tariff on all imports (col. 2)	Customs union with country B (col. 3)
$\dfrac{P_{Ad}}{P_{Bd}} = \dfrac{P_{Ai}}{P_{Bi}}$	$\dfrac{P_{Ad}}{P_{Bd}} < \dfrac{P_{Ai}}{P_{Bi}}$	$\dfrac{P_{Ad}}{P_{Bd}} = \dfrac{P_{Ai}}{P_{Bi}}$
$\dfrac{P_{Ad}}{P_{Cd}} = \dfrac{P_{Ai}}{P_{Ci}}$	$\dfrac{P_{Ad}}{P_{Cd}} < \dfrac{P_{Ai}}{P_{Ci}}$	$\dfrac{P_{Ad}}{P_{Cd}} < \dfrac{P_{Ai}}{P_{Ci}}$
$\dfrac{P_{Bd}}{P_{Cd}} = \dfrac{P_{Bi}}{P_{Ci}}$	$\dfrac{P_{Bd}}{P_{Cd}} = \dfrac{P_{Bi}}{P_{Ci}}$	$\dfrac{P_{Bd}}{P_{Cd}} < \dfrac{P_{Bi}}{P_{Ci}}$

Note: Subscripts A, B and C refer to countries of origin, d to prices in A's domestic market, and i to prices in the international market.

established a general case in favour of customs unions. In Lipsey (1956–57) I attempted to point out the mistake involved. The key is that Gehrels' model contains only two commodities: one domestic good and one import. There is thus only one optimum condition for consumption: that the relative price between X and Y equals the real rate of transformation (in domestic production or international trade, whichever is relevant) between these two commodities. The general problems raised by customs unions must, however, be analysed in a model containing a minimum of three types of commodities: domestic commodities (A), imports from the union partner (B) and imports from the outside world (C). When this change is made Gehrels's general presumption for gain from union disappears. Table 2 shows the three optimum conditions that domestic prices and international prices should bear the same relationship to each other for the three groups of commodities, A, B and C.[9] In free trade all three optimum conditions will be fulfilled. If a uniform tariff is placed on both imports, then the relations shown in column 2 will obtain, for the price of goods from both B and C will be higher in A's domestic market than in the international market. When a customs union is formed, however, the prices of imports from the union partner, B, are reduced so that the first optimum condition is fulfilled, but the tariff remains on imports from abroad (C) so that the third optimum cindition is no longer satisfied. The customs union thus moves country A from one non-optimal position to another, and in general it is impossible to say whether welfare will increase or diminish as a result. We are thus back to a position where the theory tells us that welfare may rise or fall, and a much more detailed study is necessary in order to establish the conditions under which one or the other result might obtain.

The above analysis has led both Mr. Gehrels and myself to distinguish between *production effects* and *consumption effects* of customs unions (Gehrels, 1956–57, p. 61; Lipsey, 1957, pp. 40–41). The reason for attempting this is not hard to find. Viner's analysis rules out substitution in consumption and looks to shifts in the location of production as the cause of welfare changes in customs unions. The analysis just completed emphasizes the effects of substitution in consumption. The distinction on this basis, however, is not fully satisfactory, for consumption effects will themselves cause changes in production. A more satisfactory distinction would seem to be one between *inter-country substitution* and *inter-commodity substitution*. Inter-country substitution would be Viner's trade creation and trade diversion, when one country is substituted for another as the source of supply for some commodity. Inter-commodity substitution occurs when one commodity is substituted, at least at the margin, for some other commodity as a result of a relative price shift. This is the type of substitution we have just been analysing. In general, either of these changes will cause shifts in both consumption and production.

Now we come to Professor Meade's analysis. His approach is taxonomic in that he attempts to classify a large number of possible cases, showing the factors which would tend to cause welfare to increase when a union is formed and to isolate these from the factors which would tend to cause welfare to diminish.[10] Figure 3a shows a demand and a supply curve for any imported commodity. Meade observes that a tariff, like any tax, shifts the supply curve to the left (to $S'S'$ in figure 3a) and raises

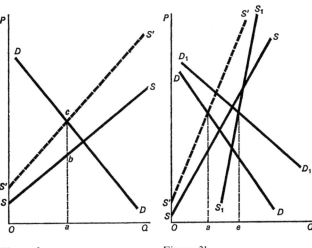

Figure 3a   Figure 3b

the price of the imported commodity. At the new equilibrium the demand price differs from the supply price by the amount of the tariff. If the supply price indicates the utility of the commodity to the suppliers and the demand price its utility to the purchasers, it follows that the utility of the taxed import is higher to purchasers than to suppliers, and the money value of this difference in utility is the value of the tariff. Now assume that the marginal utility of money is the same for buyers and for sellers. It follows that, if one more *unit of expenditure* were devoted to the purchase of this commodity, there would be a net gain to society equal to the proportion of the selling price of the commodity composed of the tariff. In figure 3a the rate of tariff is *cb/ab* per cent, the supply price is *ab* and the demand price is *ac*, so that the money value of the 'gain' ('loss') to society resulting from a marginal increase (decrease) in expenditure on this commodity is *bc*.

Now assume that the same *ad valorem* rate of tariff is imposed on all imports so that the tariff will be the same proportion of the market price of each import. Then the gain to society from a marginal increase in expenditure (say one more 'dollar' is spent) on any import is the same for all imports, and this gain is equal to the loss resulting from a marginal reduction in expenditure (one less 'dollar' spent) on any import. Now consider *a marginal reduction* in the tariff on one commodity. This will cause a readjustment of expenditure, in the various possible ways analysed by Meade, so that in general more of some imports and less of others will be purchased. Since, *at the margin*, the gain from devoting one more unit of expenditure to the purchase of any import is equal to the loss from devoting one less unit of expenditure to the purchase of any import, the welfare consequences of this discriminatory tariff reduction may be calculated by comparing the increase in the volume of imports (trade expansion) with the decrease in the volume of other imports (trade contraction). If there is a net increase in the volume of trade the customs union will have raised economic welfare. A study of the welfare consequences of customs unions can, therefore, be devoted to the factors which will increase or decrease the volume of international trade. If the influences which tend to cause trade expansion are found to predominate it may be predicted that a customs union will raise welfare. The main body of Meade's analysis is in fact devoted to a study of those factors which would tend to increase, and to those which would tend to decrease, the volume of trade. Complications can, of course, be introduced, but they do not affect the main drift of the argument.[11]

Meade's analysis, which makes use of demand and supply curves, suffers from one very serious, possibly crippling, limitation. It will be noted that we were careful to consider only *marginal reductions* in tariffs. For such changes Meade's analysis is undoubtedly correct. When, however, there are *large* changes in many tariffs, as there will be with most of the customs unions in which we are likely to be interested, it can no longer be assumed that the demand and supply curves will remain fixed; the *ceteris paribus* assumptions on which they are based will no longer hold, so that both demand and supply curves are likely to shift. When this happens it is no longer obvious how much welfare weight should be given to any particular change in the volume of trade (even if we are prepared to make all of the other assumptions necessary for the use of this type of classical welfare analysis). In figure 3b for example, if the demand curve shifts to $D_1 D_1$ and the supply curve to $S_1 S_1$, what are we to say about the welfare gains or losses when trade changes from Oa to Oe?

There is not time to go through a great deal of Professor Meade's or my own analysis which attempts to discover the particular circumstances in which it is likely that a geographically discriminatory reduction in tariffs will raise welfare. I shall, therefore, take two of the general conclusions that emerge from various analyses and present these in order to illustrate the type of generalization that it is possible to make in customs-union theory.

The first generalization is one that emerges from Professor Meade's analysis and from my own. I choose it, first, because there seems to be general agreement on it and, second, although Professor Meade does not make this point, because it is an absolutely general proposition in the theory of second best; it applies to all sub-optimal positions, and customs-union theory only provides a particular example of its application. Stated in terms of customs unions, this generalization runs as follows: when only some tariffs are to be changed, welfare is more likely to be raised if these tariffs are merely *reduced* than if they are completely *removed*. Proofs of this theorem can be found in both Meade (1956, pp. 50–51) and Lipsey and Lancaster (1956–57, section 5), and we shall content ourselves here with an intuitive argument for the theorem in its most general context. Assume that there exist many taxes, subsidies, monopolies, etc., which prevent the satisfaction of optimum conditions. Further assume that all but one of these, say one tax, are fixed, and inquire into the second-best level for the tax that is allowed to vary. Finally, assume that there exists a unique second-best level for this tax.[12] Now a change in this one tax will either move the economy towards or away from a second-best optimum position. If it moves the economy away from a second-best position, then, no matter how large is the change in the tax, welfare will be lowered. If it moves the economy in the direction of the second-best optimum it may move it part of the way, all of the way or past it. If the economy is moved sufficiently far past the second-best optimum welfare will be lowered by the change. From this it follows that, if there is a unique second-best level for the tax being varied, a small variation is more likely to raise welfare than is a large variation.[13]

The next generalization concerns the size of expenditure on the three classes of goods—those purchased domestically, from the union partner, and from the outside world—and is related to the gains from inter-commodity substitution. This generalization follows from the analysis in my own thesis (Lipsey, 1958, pp. 97–99 and appendix to ch. 6) and does not seem to have been stated in any of the existing customs-union literature. Consider what happens to the optimum conditions, which we discussed earlier, when the customs union is formed (see table 2). On the one hand, the tariff is taken off imports from the country's union partner, and the relative price between these imports and domestic goods is brought into conformity with the real rates of transformation. This, by itself, tends to increase welfare. On the other hand, the relative price between imports from the union partner and imports from the outside world are moved away from equality with real rates of transformation. This by itself tends to reduce welfare. Now consider both of these changes. As far as the prices of the goods from a country's union partner are concerned, they are brought into equality with rates of transformation *vis-à-vis* domestic goods, but they are moved away from equality with rates of transformation *vis-à-vis* imports from the outside world. These imports from the union partner are thus involved in both a gain and a loss and their size is *per se* unimportant; what matters is the relation between imports from the outside world and expenditure on domestic commodities: the larger are purchases of domestic commodities and the smaller are purchases from the outside world, the more likely is it that the union will bring gain. Consider a simple example in which a country purchases from its union partner only eggs while it purchases from the outside world only shoes, all other commodities being produced and consumed at home. Now when the union is formed the 'correct' price ratio (i.e. the one which conforms with the real rate of transformation) between eggs and shoes will be disturbed, but, on the other hand, eggs will be brought into the 'correct' price relationship with all other commodities—bacon, butter, cheese, meat, etc., and in these circumstances a customs union is very likely to bring gain, for the loss in distorting the price ratio between eggs and shoes will be small relative to the gain in establishing the correct price ratio between eggs and all other commodities. Now, however, let us reverse the position of domestic trade and imports from the outside world, making shoes the only commodity produced and consumed at home, eggs still being imported from the union partner, while everything else is now bought from the outside world. In these circumstances the customs union is most likely to bring a loss; the gains in establishing the correct price ratio between eggs and shoes are indeed likely to be very small compared with the losses of distorting the price ratio between eggs and all other commodities. If, to take a third example, eggs are produced at home, shoes imported from the outside world, while everything else is obtained from the union partner, the union may bring neither gain nor loss; for the union disturbs the 'correct' ratio between shoes and everything else except eggs, and establishes the 'correct' one between eggs and everything else except shoes. This example serves to show that the size of trade with a union partner is not the important variable; it is the relation between imports from the outside world and purchases of domestic goods that matters.

This argument gives rise to two general conclusions, one of them appealing immediately to common sense, one of them slightly surprising. The first is that, *given a country's volume of international trade*, a customs union is more likely to raise welfare the higher is the proportion of trade with the country's union partner and the lower the proportion with the outside world. The second is that a customs union is more likely to raise welfare the lower is the total volume of foreign trade, for the lower is foreign trade, the lower must be purchases from the outside world relative to purchases of domestic commodities. This means that the sort of countries who ought to form customs unions are those doing a high proportion of their foreign trade with their union partner, and making a high proportion of their total expenditure on domestic trade. Countries which are likely to lose from a customs union, on the other hand, are those countries in which a low proportion of total trade is domestic, especially if the customs union does not include a high proportion of their foreign trade.

We may now pass to a very brief consideration of some of the empirical work. Undoubtedly a serious attempt to predict and measure the possible effects of a customs union is a very difficult task. Making all allowances for this, however, a surprisingly large proportion of the voluminous literature on the subject is devoted to guess and suspicion, and a very small proportion to serious attempts to measure. Let us consider what empirical work has been done on the European Common Market and the Free Trade Area, looking first at attempts to measure possible gains from specialization. The theoretical analysis underlying these measurements is of the sort developed by Professor Meade and outlined previously.

The first study which we will mention is that made by the Dutch economist Verdoorn, subsequently quoted and used by Scitovsky (1958, pp. 64–78). The analysis assumes an elasticity of substitution between domestic goods and imports of minus one half, and an elasticity of substitution between different imports of minus two. These estimates are based on some empirical measurements of an aggregate sort and the extremely radical assumption is made that the same elasticities apply to all commodities. The general assumption, then, is that one import is fairly easily substituted for another, while imports and domestic commodities are not particularly good substitutes for each other.[14]

Using this assumption, an estimate was made of the changes in trade when tariffs are reduced between the six Common Market countries, the United Kingdom and Scandinavia. The estimate is that intra-European trade will increase by approximately 17 per cent, and, when this increase is weighted by the proportion of the purchase price of each commodity that is made up of tariff and estimates for the reduction in trade in other directions are also made, the final figure for the gains from trade to the European countries is equal to about one twentieth of one per cent of their annual incomes. In considering this figure, the crude estimate of elasticities of substitution must cause some concern. The estimate of an increase in European trade of 17 per cent is possibly rather small in the face of the known fact that Benelux trade increased by approximately 50 per cent after the formation of that customs union. A possible check on the accuracy of the Verdoorn method would have been to apply it to the pre-customs union situation in the Benelux countries, to use the method to predict what would happen to Benelux trade and then to compare the prediction with what we actually know to have happened. Whatever allowances are made, however, Scitovsky's conclusion is not likely to be seriously challenged:

The most surprising feature of these estimates is their smallness. . . . As estimates of the total increase in intra-European trade contingent upon economic union, Verdoorn's figures are probably under-estimates; but if, by way of correction, we should raise them five- or even twenty-five-fold, that would still leave unchanged our basic conclusion that the gain from increased intra-European specialization is likely to be insignificant. (Scitovsky, 1958a, p. 67.)

A second empirical investigation into the possible gains from trade, this time relating only to the United Kingdom, has been made by Professor Johnson (1958). Johnson bases his study on the estimates made by *The*

Economist Intelligence Unit of the increases in the value of British trade which would result by 1970, first, if there were only the Common Market and, second, if there were the Common Market and the Free Trade Area. Professor Johnson then asks what will be the size of the possible gains to Britain of participation in the Free Trade Area? His theory is slightly different from that of Professor Meade, but since it arrives at the same answer, namely that the gain is equal to the increased quantity of trade times the proportion of the purchase price made up of tariff, we do not need to consider the details. From these estimates Johnson arrives at the answer that the possible gain to Britain from joining the Free Trade Area would be, *as an absolute maximum*, 1 per cent of the national income of the United Kingdom.

Most people seem to be surprised at the size of these estimates, finding them smaller than expected. This leads us to ask: might there not be some inherent bias in this sort of estimate? and, might not a totally different approach yield quite different answers? One possible approach is to consider the proportion of British factors of production engaged in foreign trade. This can be taken to be roughly the percentage contribution made by trade to the value of the national product, which can be estimated to be roughly the value of total trade as a proportion of G.N.P., first subtracting the import content from the G.N.P. This produces a rough estimate of 18 per cent of Britain's total resources engaged in foreign trade. The next step would be to ask how much increase in efficiency of utilization for these resources could we expect: (1) as a result of their reallocation in the direction of their comparative advantage, and (2) as a result of a reallocation among possible consumers of the commodities produced by these resources. Here is an outline for a possible study, but, in the absence of such a study, what would we guess? Would a 10 per cent increase in efficiency not be a rather conservative estimate? Such a gain in efficiency would give a net increase in the national income of 1.8 per cent. If the resources had a 20 per cent increase in efficiency, then an increase in the national income of 3.6 per cent would be possible. At this stage these figures can give nothing more than a common-sense check on the more detailed estimates of economists such as Verdoorn and Johnson. Until further detailed work has been done, it must be accepted that the best present estimates give figures of the net gain from trade amounting to something less than 1 per cent of the national income (although we may not, of course, have a very high degree of confidence in these estimates).[15]

When we move on from the possible gains from new trade to the question of the economic benefits arising from other causes, such as economies of scale or enforced efficiency, we leave behind even such halting attempts at measurement as we have just considered. Some economists see considerable economies of scale emerging from European union. Others are sceptical. In what follows, I will confine my attention mainly to the arguments advanced by Professor H. G. Johnson.[16] His first argument runs as follows:

It is extremely difficult to believe that British industry offers substantial potential savings in cost which cannot be exploited in a densely-populated market of 51 million people with a G.N.P. of £18 billion, especially when account is taken of the much larger markets abroad in which British industry, in spite of restrictions of various kinds, has been able to sell its products. (Johnson, 1957, p. 35.)[17]

Let us make only two points about Professor Johnson's observation. First, many markets will be very much less than the total population. What, for example, can we say about a product sold mainly to upper middle-class males living more than 20 miles away from an urban centre? Might there not be economies of scale remaining in the production of a commodity for such a market? Secondly, in the absence of some theory that tells us the statement is true for 51 and, say, 31, but not 21, million people, the argument must remain nothing more than an unsupported personal opinion. As another argument, Professor Johnson asks, 'Why are these economies of scale, if they do exist, not already being exploited?' (Johnson, 1958b, p. 10; 1957, p. 35.) It is, of course, well known that unexhausted economies of scale are incompatible with the existence of perfect competition, but it is equally well known that unexhausted economies of scale are compatible with the existence of imperfect competition as long as long-run marginal cost is declining faster than marginal revenue. Here it is worth while making a distinction, mentioned by Scitovsky (1958, pp. 42 ff.), between the long-run marginal cost of producing more goods, to which the economist is usually referring when he speaks of scale effects, and the marginal cost of making and selling more goods (which must include selling costs). This leads to a distinction between increasing sales when the whole market is expanding and increasing sales when the market is static, and thus increasing them at the expense of one's competitors. The former is undoubtedly very much easier than the latter. It is quite possible for the marginal costs of *production* to be declining while the marginal costs of *selling* in a static market are rising steeply. This would mean that production economies would not be exploited by the firms competing in the market, but that if the market were to expand so that *all* firms in a given industry could grow, then these economies would be realized.

Let us also consider an argument put forward in favour of economies of scale. Gehrels and Johnson (1955) argue that very large gains from economies of scale can be expected. In evidence of this they quote the following facts: American productivity (i.e. output per man) is higher than United Kingdom productivity for most commodities; the differential is, however, greatest in those industries which use mass-production methods. From this they conclude that there are unexploited economies of mass production in the United Kingdom. Now this may well be so, but, before accepting the conclusion, we should be careful in interpreting this meagre piece of evidence. What else might it mean? Might it not mean, for example, that the ratios of capital to labour differed in the two countries so that, if we calculate the productivity of a factor by dividing total production by the quantity of one factor employed, we will necessarily find these differences? Secondly, would we not be very surprised if we did not find such differences in comparative costs between the two countries? Are we surprised when we find America's comparative advantage centred in the mass-producing industries, and, if this is the case, must we conclude that vast economies of mass production exist for Europe?

Finally, we come to the possible gains through forced efficency. Business firms may not be adopting methods known to be technically more efficient than those now in use due to inertia, a dislike of risk-taking, a willingness to be content with moderate profits, or a whole host of other reasons. If these firms are thrown into competition with a number of firms in other countries who are not adopting this conservative policy, then the efficiency of the use of resources may increase because technically more efficient production methods are forced on the businessman now facing fierce foreign competition. Here no evidence has as yet been gathered, and, rather than report the opinions of others, I will close by recording the personal guess that this is a very large potential source of gain, that an increase in competition with foreign countries who are prepared to adopt new methods might have a most salutary effect on the efficiency of a very large number of British and European manufacturing concerns.[18]

An earlier version of this paper was read before the Conference of the Association of University Teachers of Economics at Southampton, January 1959.

References

Archibald, G. C. (1959), "The state of economic science", *British Journal of the Philosophy of Science*, June.

Friedman, M. (1953), *Essays in Positive Economics*, University of Chicage Press.

Gehrels, F. (1956–57), "Customs unions from a single country viewpoint", *Review of Economic Studies*, vol. 24.

Gehrels, F., and Johnson, H. G. (1955), "The economic gains from European integration", *Journal of Political Economy*, August.

Johnson, H. G. (1957), "The criteria of economic advantage", *Bulletin of the Oxford University Institute of Statistics*, vol. 19.

Johnson, H. G. (1958a), "The gains from free trade with Europe: an estimate", *Manchester School of Economic and Social Studies*, vol. 26.

Johnson, H. G. (1958b), "The economic gains from free trade with Europe", *Three Banks Review*, September.

Lipsey, R. G. (1958), *The Theory of Customs Unions: A General Equilibrium Analysis*. Unpublished Ph.D. thesis, University of London.

Lipsey, R. G. (1956–57), "Mr. Gehrels on customs unions", *Review of Economic Studies*, vol. 24, pp. 211–14.

Lipsey, R. G. (1957), "The theory of customs unions: trade diversion and welfare", *Economica*, vol. 24.

Lipsey, R. G. (1967), "The balance of payments and the Common Market", *Economics: The Journal of the Economics Association*, Autumn.

Lipsey, R. G., and Stilwell, A. J. (1968), *An Introduction to Positive Economics*, Weidenfeld and Nicolson.

Lipsey, R. G., and Lancaster, K. J. (1956–57), "The general theory of second best", *Review of Economic Studies*, vol. 24.

Makower, H., and Morton, G. (1953), "A contribution towards a theory of customs unions", *Economic Journal*, vol. 62, pp. 33–49.

Meade, J. E. (1956), *The Theory of Customs Unions*, North Holland.

Meyer, F. V. (1956), "Complementarity and the lowering of tariffs", *American Economic Review*, vol. 46.

Scitovsky, T. de (1958), *Economic Theory and Western European Integration*, Allen and Unwin.

Viner, J. (1950), *The Customs Unions Issue*, Carnegie Endowment for International Peace.

19

An Elementary Proposition Concerning the Formation of Customs Unions

Murray Kemp and Henry Wan, Jr.

1. Introduction

In the welter of inconclusive debate concerning the implications of customs unions the following elementary yet basic proposition seems to have been almost lost to sight.[1]

PROPOSITION 1 Consider any competitive world trading equilibrium, with any number of countries and commodities and with no restrictions whatever on the tariffs and other commodity taxes of individual countries and with costs of transport fully recognized. Now let any subset of the countries form a customs union. Then there exists a common tariff vector and a system of lump-sum compensatory payments involving only members of the union, such that each individual, whether a member of the union or not, is not worse off than before the formation of the union.

A detailed list of assumptions, and a relatively formal proof, may be found in section 2. Here we merely note that there exists a common tariff vector which leaves world prices, and therefore the trade and welfare of non-members, at their pre-union levels. If the net trade vector of the union is viewed as a (constant) endowment, it is then plausible that both the union as a whole and (after appropriate internal transfers) each member must be left not worse off by the removal of internal barriers to trade.

The proposition is interesting in that it contains no qualifications whatever concerning the size or number of the countries which are contemplating union, that pre- or post-union trading relationships, their relative states of development or levels of average income, and their propinquities in terms of geography or costs of transportation.

This paper was originally published in Murray Kemp, *Three Topics in the Theory of International Trade: Distribution, Welfare and Uncertainty*, North-Holland Publishing Company, 1976.

The proposition is also interesting because it implies that an incentive to form and enlarge customs unions persists until the world becomes one big customs union, that is, until world free trade prevails. More precisely, given any initial trading equilibrium, there exist finite sequences of steps, at each step new customs unions being created or old unions enlarged, such that at each step no individual is made worse off and such that after the last step the world is free trading. (In general, at each step some individual actually benefits.) Indeed, on the basis of these observations one might attempt to rehabilitate the vague pre-Vinerian view that to form a customs union is to move in the direction of free trade.

Evidently the incentive is insufficiently strong; tariffs and other artificial obstacles to trade persist. That the real world is not free trading must be explained in terms of

(i) the game theoretic problems of choosing partners, dividing the spoils and enforcing agreements, and
(ii) the non-economic objectives of nations.

A role may be found also for
(iii) inertia and ignorance concerning the implications of possible unions (in particular, concerning the long list of lump sum compensatory payments required); and, in the short run, for
(iv) the restraint exercised by international agreements to limit tariffs. However (iv) can form no part of an explanation of the persistence of trading blocks in the long run.

Topics (i)–(iii) form a possible agenda for the further study of customs unions. For a preliminary analysis of (i) the reader may consult Caves (1971); and for suggestive work on (ii) he is referred to Cooper and Massell (1965), Johnson (1965) and Bhagwati (1968).

2. Proof of the Proposition

Suppose that

(ia) the consumption set of each individual is closed, convex and bounded below;
(ib) the preferences of each individual are convex and representable by a continuous ordinal utility function;
(ic) each individual can survive with a consumption bundle each component of which is somewhat less than his pre-union consumption bundle;
(ii) the production set of each economy is closed, convex, contains

the origin and is such that positive output requires at least one positive input (impossibility of free production).

Consider a fictitious economy composed of the member economies but with a net endowment equal to the sum of the member endowments plus the equilibrium pre-union net excess supply of the rest of the world. In view of (i) and (ii), the economy possesses an optimum, and any optimum can be supported by at least one internal price vector (Debreu, 1959. pp. 92–93 and 95–96). Either the pre-union equilibrium of the member countries is a Pareto-optimal equilibrium of the fictitious economy (that is, corresponds to a maximal point of the utility possibility set), or it is not; in the latter case, a preferred Pareto-optimal equilibrium can be attained by means of lump sum transfers among individuals in the fictitious economy. That essentially completes the proof. It only remains to note that the required vector of common tariffs may be computed as the difference between the vector of pre-union world prices and the vector of internal union prices.

Commodities can be indexed by location. Hence the resource-using activity of moving commodities from one country to another is accommodated in the several production sets; no special treatment of cost of transportation is needed.

References

Bhagwati, J. (1968), Trade liberalization among LDCs, trade theory, and Gatt rules, in: J. N. Wolfe (ed.), *Value, Capital, and Growth, Papers in honour of Sir John Hicks*, Edinburgh University Press, Edinburgh, 21–43.

Caves, R. E. (1971), The economics of reciprocity: theory and evidence on bilateral trading arrangements. Harvard Institute of Economic Research, Discussion Paper No. 166.

Cooper, C. A. and B. F. Massell (1965), Towards a general theory of customs unions for developing countries, *Journal of Political Economy*, 73, 461–476.

Debreu, G. (1959), *Theory of Value*, Wiley, New York.

Johnson, H. G. (1965), An economic theory of protectionism, tariff bargaining, and the formation of customs unions, *Journal of Political Economy*, 73, 256–283.

Kemp, M. C. (1964), *The Pure Theory of International Trade*, Prentice-Hall, Englewood Cliffs, N. J.

Vanek, J. (1965), *General Equilibrium of International Discrimination. The Case of Customs Unions*, Harvard University Press, Cambridge, Mass.

Editor's Note

In the Kemp-Wan proposition, the phrase "and other commodity taxes" should be eliminated. Alternatively, as Kemp and Wan have noted in correspondence, a customs union may be *defined* to be free of commodity taxes other than tariffs, in which case the phrase "and other commodity taxes" can be retained.

VI
**Growth, Foreign
Investment, and
Bottlenecks**

20

Factor Intensities,   Ronald Findlay and
Technological Progress   Harry Grubert
and the Terms of Trade

In recent years the problems connected with the secular dollar shortage and the economic development of backward countries have aroused considerable interest in the relationship between economic growth and international trade. Theoretical analysis of the problems involved was pioneered by Professor J. R. Hicks (1953) and further developed by Mr. E. J. Mishan (1955), Professor H. G. Johnson (1955) and Dr. W. M. Corden (1956).

In his contribution Professor Hicks advanced the proposition that in a two-country model with one economy growing and the other static, technological progress in the growing country would turn the terms of trade against it if the progress was concentrated mainly in the export industries or "export-biased," and in favour of it if the progress was mainly in the import-competing industries or "import-biased." Professor Hicks's somewhat loosely formulated model was subjected to stricter analysis by the other authors mentioned. Mr. Mishan pointed out and analysed the importance of income effects on consumption for the direction of change in the terms of trade. Professor Johnson discussed the effects of various types of economic expansion such as population growth, capital accumulation, and technological progress on the terms of trade.

Dr. Corden clarified and refined the results of these authors by an elegant diagrammatic technique derived from Professor J. E. Meade (1952). One conclusion of his analysis is that the terms of trade must turn against the growing country in a two-country, two-commodity model if, at unchanged terms of trade, the economic expansion is "ultra export-biased," and in favour of the growing country if the expansion is "ultra import-biased," provided that there are no inferior goods. By an

This paper was originally published in *Oxford Economic Papers*, 1959, pp. 111–121. Also published in Jagdish Bhagwati, editor, *International Trade: Selected Readings*, Penguin Books, 1969.

"ultra export-biased" expansion is meant one that results in an absolute decline in the domestic production of the imported commodity and by an "ultra import-biased" expansion is meant one that results in an absolute decline in the output of the exported commodity.

This conclusion by itself is obvious since it merely states that if demand exceeds supply the relative price of the commodity must rise and vice versa. The next and more important step in the analysis is to find what types of expansion are "ultra-biased" so that the effect on the terms of trade is certain provided only that one makes the very weak assumption of no inferior goods. It is here that both Johnson and Corden employ a very useful theorem proved by Mr. T. M. Rybcznski (1955). The theorem states that under certain assumptions, an increase in the amount of one factor, with the other factor fixed, must result, at constant relative prices of the two commodities, in an absolute reduction in the output of the commodity that uses the augmented factor relatively less intensively than the other commodity in a two-factor, two-commodity economy.

Professor Johnson also discusses the effect of technological progress but makes the very restrictive assumption that factors are combined in the same proportions before and after the technological change; i.e. innovations are neither "capital-using" nor "labour-using" but "neutral." [1]

Under this assumption he states that if technological progress is confined to the production of one of the goods, then, at constant relative prices for the two goods, the absolute level of the output of the other good must decline. It is thus a further example of "ultra-biased" expansion.

Dr. Corden asserts that by an argument similar to Mr. Rybcznski's it can be shown that if a productivity change is confined to the import-competing good in one country in a two-commodity trade model with the rest of the world static, the terms of trade must turn in the country's favour if the export good is not inferior in domestic consumption. This result follows if, and only if, the productivity change is "ultra-import-biased." Thus Dr. Corden seems to have stated a generalization of Professor Johnson's proporition since he makes no restriction on the factor bias being neutral as Professor Johnson does.

Neither of these authors gives an explicit proof of these propositions. As our analysis indicate, the problem of the effect of factor-biased technological change on the terms of trade, while similar in many ways to the question of the effect of changes in factor endowment, nevertheless presents sufficient additional difficulties to require a considerably more elaborate geometrical argument than that employed by Mr. Rybczynski. We therefore feel that even if it were true Dr. Corden's statement gives a somewhat misleading impression of simplicity to the problem so that a fuller examination would be worth while. However, the statement turns out not to be generally valid, as we shall proceed to show.

Our aim in this paper is to give a systematic analysis, by diagrammatic methods, of the effects of neutral- and factor-biased technological progress on the terms of trade in the framework of the familiar simplified model of only two factor, two commodities, and two countries.

The rest of the paper is divided into three parts. In part I we analyse the shift in relative factor prices necessary to have relative product prices unchanged after technological progress has taken place in one industry and technique in the other is unchanged. In part II we ascertain the direction of the shift in the output of the good produced with unchanged technology, at constant relative product prices, as a result of technological progress in the production of the other good. This will enable us to establish whether technological progress in one good only will always be "ultra-biased" or not. In part III international trade is introduced and the movement of the terms of trade as a consequence of technological progress is deduced from the preceding analysis. Our results are then related to those already in the literature.

Part I

The analytical tool of this section of the paper will be a diagram introduced by Mr. A. P. Lerner in his brilliant paper on factor price equilization in international trade (1952). In figure 1 an isoquant is drawn for each of two goods, which we assume to be the only goods produced in the economy. Let us call them wheat and textiles respectively. The axes represent labour and capital which are assumed to be the only two factors of production. The production functions for both wheat and textiles are assumed to be homogeneous of the first degree. In that case each of the isoquants will represent an infinite family, identical in shape and differing only in scale. The respective output levels for which each of the isoquants is drawn are such that they represent the equilibrium exchange ratio between the two goods prevailing in the economy.

The reader will realize that if we draw a common tangent to the two isoquants it must represent an equilibrium factor price ratio for the economy if it is assumed, as we do, that there is perfect competition with full factor mobility. In figure 1 the isoquants cut each other only once and so it is not possible to draw more than one such common tangent, which we have called *FG*. The capital-labour ratios are *OA* in textiles and *OB* in wheat. Since *OA* is steeper than *OB* we may call textiles the capital-

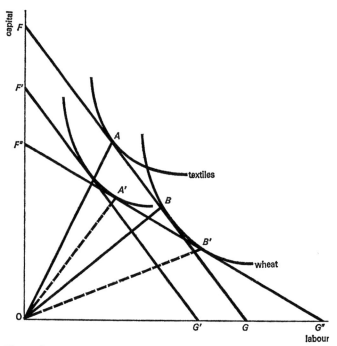

Figure 1

intensive, and wheat the labour-intensive commodity. It is here that the importance of our assumption that the isoquants cut only once lies. If they cut twice then two common tangents could be drawn representing two possible equilibrium factor price ratios. In this case the factor intensities will reverse themselves as we move from one factor price ratio to the other. Our analysis will be confined to the original case, where the isoquants cut only once. We also rule out the case where one isoquant lies entirely within the other except at a single point.[2]

In figure 1 the line FG represents constant total cost along its entire length. The result of technological progress is to reduce the total cost of producing the same amount of a commodity. Let us suppose that there is a technological improvement in textile production. This can be represented in figure 1 by the isoquant for textiles now being tangential to a line $F'G'$, parallel to FG and indicating lower total cost at the original relative factor prices. Suppose that, as in Figure 1, it is tangential to $F'G'$ at the point where OA cuts $F'G'$. This means that, at existing relative factor prices, the new technique has the same capital-labour ratio in equilibrium as the original one. Such technical progress we designate "neutral". The reader should note that this definition of neutrality does

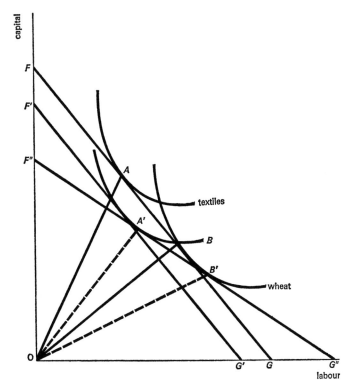

Figure 2

not imply a mere renumbering of the isoquants for the commodity since
the shape of the new isoquant may differ from that of the original family.
For our diagram to remain independent of scale we must also assume
that the new isoquants are also homogeneous of the first degree. This
assumption will be made in all other cases of technological progress also.

It is clear that for the same product price ratio to prevail there must
be a shift in the factor price ratio. The new factor price ratio is obtained
by drawing the common tangent to the wheat isoquant and the new
textile isoquant. As can be seen from Figure 1 the capital-labour ratio
must fall in both industries, to OA' in textile and OB' in wheat. The
factor price ratio, as shown by $F''G''$, shifts in favour of capital.

In figure 2 we depict the case of "labour-using" technical progress in
textiles, since the capital-labour ratio in textiles is lowered at the original
relative factor prices. We have assumed that the "labour-using" bias did
not proceed sufficiently far for the new textile isoquant and the original
wheat isoquant to intersect each other more than once. Therefore, only

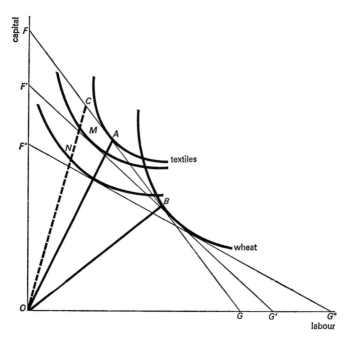

Figure 3

a single common tangent, $F''G''$, can be drawn, which indicates that the capital-labour ratio falls in both industries and the factor price ratio moves in favour of capital. Notice that at the original product price ratio the capital-labour ratio in textiles falls even lower than at the same factor price ratio. The reader can show that "capital-using" technological progress in wheat, provided that textiles remains unambiguously the capital intensive good, will raise the capital-labour ratio in both industries and shift the factor price ratio in favour of labour. The capital-labour ratio in wheat will be higher, at constant relative product prices, than at constant relative factor prices, after the technological change.

In figure 3 we consider the case of capital-using technological progress in textiles. The dotted radial OC represents the new capital intensity of production in textiles at FG, the original factor price ratio. The point M on OC is where a factor price line drawn parallel to FG would be tangential to the higher of the two otherwise identical new isoquants for textiles. $F'G'$ is the common tangent to this isoquant and the wheat isoquant. Relative factor prices have thus shifted against labour but the capital-labour ratio has risen in textiles while it falls in wheat. Had the proportionate reduction in total costs due to technological progress been greater, however, the capital-labour ratio in textiles would also fall, as can be seen by looking at the point where $F''G''$ is tangential to the isoquant which cuts OC at N, which is the point at which a line parallel to FG would be tangential to it. It can be shown that labour-using technical progress in wheat will always cause the capital-labour ratio in textiles to rise, but it may rise or fall in wheat. This completes our analysis of the shift in factor price ratios and factor proportions necessary to have relative product prices unchanged after neutral and biased technical progress in producing either one of the goods.

Part II

In this section of the paper we shall ascertain the shift, at constant relative product prices, in the level of total output of one of the goods as a consequence of technological progress in the production of the other. We assume that the supplies of labour and capital are fixed in amount and that each has a perfectly inelastic supply curve. As a result we can construct an Edgeworth-Bowley box diagram of production for the economy which is shown in figure 4.

Wheat production is measured from the lower left-hand corner of the diagram so that movement to the north-east indicates rising levels of wheat output. The amounts of capital and labour used in wheat production are measured along OY and OX respectively. Textile output is measured from the opposite corner O' and labour used in textile production is therefore measured along $O'Y$ and capital along $O'X$. The solid

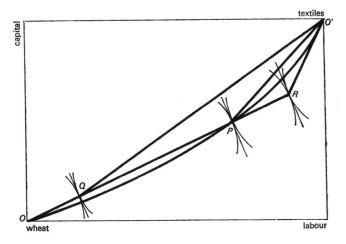

Figure 4

curved line joining O and O' represents the "efficiency locus" which shows the maximum amount that can be produced of one good for any fixed level of the other. At any point on the efficiency locus, such as P, a textile isoquant is tangential to a wheat isoquant. If a line is drawn through P, or any other point on the efficiency locus, such that it is the common tangent to both the isoquants touching at that point, its slope will indicate relative factor prices. The way we have drawn the efficiency locus reflects our assumption that textiles is the capital-intensive and wheat the labour-intensive good. The point on the locus at which production actually takes places will be determined by the tastes of the society. Let us say this point is at P. The difference between P and all other points on the locus is that at this point only is the marginal rate of transformation in production equal to the marginal rate of substitution in consumption.

From figure 4 we see that the equilibrium capital-labour ratios are OP in wheat and $O'P$ in textiles. Suppose now that neutral technological progress takes place in textiles. At the prevailing factor price ratio, indicated by the slope of the straight line through P, there will, by definition, be no change in the equilibrium capital-labour ratio in textile production. The only change is that the point P represents a higher level of textile output than before. The amount of wheat produced at P is of course unchanged. Since the wheat isoquant and the new textile isoquant are tangential at P this point will also lie on the new efficiency-locus. The two loci will not, however, generally coincide at the other points. Only if the technological progress involves a mere renumbering of the textile isoquant will the two loci be identically shaped.

Knowledge of the entire new efficiency locus is conveniently unnecessary for us to determine the shift in wheat output at constant relative product prices. We know from our preceeding analysis that for the product price ratio to remain constant after neutral technological improvement in textile production the capital-labour ratios must fall in both industries. From figure 4 it is at once apparent that wheat output must therefore contract at the same product price ratio. By identical reasoning it can be shown that neutral technological progress in wheat will reduce the level of textile output at constant relative product prices.

Let us now consider labour-using technological progress in textiles. In figure 4 the radial $O'Q$ represents the change in the capital-labour ratio in textiles at unchanged relative factor prices as a result of such a change in technique. The point Q is where the new capital-labour ratio line in textiles intersects OP, the original capital-labour ratio line in wheat. By the first degree homogeneity of the production functions a wheat isoquant and a new textile isoquant must be tangential at Q, so that

Q is therefore a point on the new efficiency locus which has the property that the factor price line passing through it has the same slope as the factor price line through P on the original efficiency locus. It might seem surprising that relative factor prices can remain unchanged after a biased technological change in the production of one of the goods. It is easy to see, however, why this happens. The fixed factor supplies are reallocated between the two goods in such a way that the factor price ratio is left unchanged. As can be seen from figure 4 this entails a reduction in the absolute amount of wheat that is produced. From the analysis of part I we know that for the product price ratio to remain unchanged the capital-labour ratio must fall in wheat and fall even lower than $O'Q$ in textiles. By looking at figure 4 we can see that this must reduce the amount of wheat produced even lower than the output at Q. By similar reasoning the reader can show that capital-using technological progress in wheat will cause textile output to be reduced at constant relative product prices.

The radial $O'R$ in figure 4 represents the rise in the capital intensity of textile production at the original relative factor prices as a result of capital-using technological progress in the production of that good. By the first degree homogeneity property of the production functions R indicates a point at which two isoquants are tangential and it is therefore a point on the new efficiency-locus arising from the capital-using technological change in textiles. It shows that at constant relative facor prices the output of wheat has increased from OP to OR. From the results of part I we know that at the original product price ratio the capital-labour ratio in wheat falls. In order to find out the direction of shift in wheat output it is also necessary to ascertain the change in the capital-labour ratio in textiles.

At this point the reader may find it convenient to refer back to figure 3. By looking at the lower of the two isoquants drawn for textiles it can be seen that the equilibrium capital-labour ratio in textiles after the technical change falls below the original capital-labour ratio in that good. In terms of figure 4 this means that at a constant product price ratio the capital-labour ratio in textiles must be to the left of $O'P$. The output of wheat must therefore contract.

This, however, is by no means a necessary result. From figure 3 again we see that if the proportionate reduction in total cost at the original relative factor prices had been smaller, the capital-labour ratio in textiles would rise above its original slope. The smaller the proportionate reduction in total cost the steeper the capital-labour ratio in textiles becomes. It can never, however, exceed the slope of OC in figure 3 although it can approach arbitrarily close to it. It also follows from figure 3 that the higher the capital-labour ratio in textiles after the technological change in that good, the higher will the capital-labour ratio in wheat be. It is not possible, however, for it to exceed the capital-labour ratio at the original relative factor prices. In terms of figure 4 this means that at the original product-price ratio it is perfectly possible for wheat output to be very close to the level at R and therefore higher than at P. By a similar argument the reader can show that labour-using technological progress in wheat may raise the output of textiles at the former relative product prices.

Part III

We may now proceed directly to the analysis of the impact of technological progress on the international terms of trade. From the box diagram the production-possibilities curve of the economy can be derived. If we are provided with an indifference map revealing the tastes of the society an offer curve can be generated which will indicate the terms on which the country is prepared to trade with the rest of the world. Assuming the offer curve of the rest of the world to be given the equilibrium terms of trade and the optimum production and consumption points for the economy can be established. Let us suppose that the country finds it profitable to import the labour-intensive good, wheat, and export the capital-intensive good, textiles.

Then, using the Hicks-Johnson terminology explained earlier, and assuming that neither good is inferior we have obtained the following results:

1. Neutral technological progress in wheat is "utra import-biased" and in textiles it is "ultra export-biased". Thus the terms of trade shift in favour of the country in the first case and against it in the second.

2. Capital-using technological progress in wheat is "ultra import-biased" and labour-using technological progress in textiles is "ultra export-biased". The movement of the terms of trade will therefore be favourable to the country in the first case and unfavourable in the second.

3. Labour-using technological progress in wheat and capital-using technological progress in textiles have no definite effect, at constant relative product prices, on the direction of shift in the output of whichever of the two goods is produced with unchanged technique. Since such technological changes are not, in general, "ultra-biased" in their effect, the direction of shift in the terms of trade cannot be ascertained merely on the assumption that neither good is inferior. The magnitude of the positive

income elasticities will be important in determining which way the terms of trade move.

We have, however, established that the greater the proportionate reduction in total costs, at the original factor price ratio, the more likely it is that either of these types of technological change will be "ultra-biased."

We may now relate our results to the existing literature on the problem. Our first result was stated by Professor Johnson but we have provided an explicit geometrical proof. Our second result agrees with Dr. Corden's proposition that a change in productivity, if confined to the import-competing good, will turn the terms of trade in the country's favour if the exported good is not inferior. Our third result, however, disproves his proposition and the related one that technological progress confined to the exported good must move the terms of trade against the country.

Dr. Corden employs his proposition to defend Professor Hicks from a criticism made by Mr. Mishan. Professor Hicks stated that import-biased expansion in the U.S.A., in the sense of the output of the import-competing good increasing proportionately more than the output of the exported good, would turn the terms of trade in her favour. Mr. Mishan pointed out that the nature of income effects on consumption could be such as to make it quite possible for the shift to be in the opposite direction. Dr. Corden suggests that what Professor Hicks probably had in mind was the case of practically all of the increase in American productivity being concentrated on the import-competing good and therefore "ultra import-biased," in which case only the assumption of no inferior goods would be necessary to ascertain that the shift in the terms of trade would favour the U.S. Since our analysis has shown that technical progress confined to the import-competing good is not generally "ultra import-biased," Mr. Mishan's criticism still stands even in this case.

In our analysis we have assumed that the rest of the world remains static. The interested reader will be able to work out the consequences of the technological progress being transmitted to the rest of the world, after the first disturbance has resulted in a new equilibrium of the terms of trade. He will find that in some cases the transmission of the technological changes will lead to the initial shift in the terms of trade proceeding further in the same direction and in some cases being reversed. For reasons of space we do not consider it worth while to analyse these cases in detail here.

In conclusion we may point out that our analysis may be used to discuss the problem of the effect of technological progress on the relative shares in the national income of the factors of production.[3]

An earlier version of this paper was presented to a seminar in international economics at M.I.T. The authors are grateful to Professor C. P. Kindleberger and other members of the seminar for helpful criticism. Responsibility for any mistakes is borne by the authors alone. R. Findlay is also indebted to the Ford Foundation for the award of a fellowship enabling him to study at M.I.T.

References

Corden, W. M. (1956), "Economic expansion and international trade: a geometric approach", *Oxford Economic Papers*, vol. 8.

Jones, R. W. (1956–57), "Factor proportions and the Heckscher-Ohlin theorem", *Review of Economic Studies*, vol. 24.

Hicks, J. R. (1935), *The Theory of Wages*, Macmillan.

Hicks, J. R. (1953), "An inaugural lecture", *Oxford Economic Papers*, vol. 5.

Johnson, H. G. (1955), "Economic expansion and international trade", *Manchester School of Economic and Social Studies*, May.

Lerner, A. P. (1952), "Factor prices and international trade", *Economica*, new series, vol. 19.

MacDougall, G. D. A. (1957), *The World Dollar Problem*, Macmillan.

Meade, J. E. (1952), *A Geometry of International Trade*, Allen and Unwin.

Mishan, E. J. (1955), "The dollar shortage: a comment", *Oxford Economic Papers*, vol. 5.

Pearce, I. F., and James, S. F. (1951–52), "The factor-price equalization myth", *Review of Economic Studies*, vol. 19.

Robinson, J. (1937–38), "The classification of inventions", *Review of Economic Studies*, vol. 5. (Reprinted in W. Fellner and B. F. Haley, eds., *Readings in the Theory of Income Distribution*, Blakiston, 1946.)

Rybczynski, T. M. (1955), "Factor endowment and relative commodity prices", *Economica*, new series, vol. 22.

Samuelson, P. A. (1948), "International trade and the equalization of factor prices", *Economic Journal*, June.

Samuelson, P. A. (1949), "International factor-price equalization once again", *Economic Journal*, June.

21

Immiserizing Growth: A Geometrical Note

Jagdish N. Bhagwati

The effect of economic expansion on international trade has been receiving increasing attention from economic theorists since the publication of Professor Hicks' stimulating analysis of the "dollar problem".[1] It has, however, been insufficiently realized that under certain circumstances, economic expansion may harm the growing country itself.[2] Economic expansion increases *output* which, however, might lead to a sufficient deterioration in the terms of trade to offset the beneficial effect of expansion and reduce the *real income* of the growing country. It is the purpose of this note to formulate the conditions under which immiserizing growth will occur. Section 1 sets out the analysis geometrically and arrives at the criterion for immiserizing growth. Section 2 discusses some of the implications of this criterion.

1.

In the ensuing analysis we assume the traditional two-country, two-commodity "real" model where full-employment always obtains. We also assume, to simplify the analysis, that growth is confined to a single country so that the other country (i.e., the rest of the world) is not experiencing any growth in *output*; this assumption enables us to assume the offer curve of the rest of the world as "given" during the course of our analysis. Finally, we simplify the problem by beginning with an investigation of the conditions under which growth would leave the country just as well off as before, and then determining whether the equilibrium actually realized would involve still less favourable terms of trade; this approach has the convenience of avoiding the need for an explicit analysis of the income effect of growth.

This paper was originally published in *Review of Economic Studies*, June 1956.

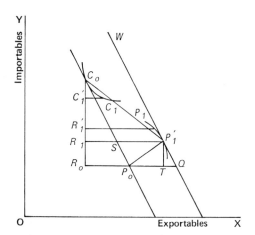

Figure 1

Consider now figure 1 which represents the growing economy. C_0 is the pre-expansion consumption, P_0 the pre-expansion production point, $P_0 C_0$ the pre-expansion terms of trade or price-line, $C_0 R_0$ the imports of Y into the country and $R_0 P_0$ the exports of X from the country. The production possibility curve tangential to $P_0 C_0$ has not been drawn in to avoid cluttering up the diagram; the indifference curve through C_0 is tangential to $P_0 C_0$ at C_0 and has been drawn partially. Consider now growth which pushes the production possibility curve outwards and which, at *constant terms of trade*, would bring production from P_0 to P_1'. Now assume that the terms of trade are changed just enough to offset the gain from growth; the relevant price line being $C_1 P_1$ which is tangential to the old indifference and the *new* production possibility curve. We later assume, legitimately for infinitesimal changes, that $C_1 P_1$ coincides with $C_0 P_1'$.

The combined effect of the expansion and the compensating adjustment of the terms of trade is to reduce the demand for imports from $C_0 R_0$ to $C_1' R_1'$. This reduction can be analysed into the sum of three effects:

1. *The Increase in Production of Importables Due to Economic Expansion* This increase ($R_0 R_1$ in the diagram) may be analysed as follows. Let p_0 and p_1 be the original and the zero-gain prices respectively, measured as the number of units of exportables required to buy a unit of importables. Then the change in total output, valued at *initial* prices, is

$$P_0 T + TQ = P_0 Q = SP_1'$$

and

$$SP_1' = \frac{P_1' R_1 - R_1 S}{C_0 R_1} \cdot C_0 R_1 = (p_1 - p_0) \cdot C_0 R_1.$$

The change in the production of importables is:

$$R_0 R_1 = P_1' T = \frac{\partial Y}{\partial K} \cdot P_0 Q = \frac{\partial Y}{\partial K} \cdot SP_1',$$

where K is defined to be the country's productive capacity which is assumed to be kept fully employed and is measured by the value in terms of exportables of the output the country would produce at the initial terms of trade and Y is the domestic output of importables.
Then,

$$R_0 R_1 = C_0 R_1 \cdot \frac{\partial Y}{\partial K} \cdot (p_1 - p_0).$$

Since we have assumed the changes to be infinitesimal, it follows that we can assume $C_0 R_1 = C_0 R_0$, the initial volume of imports, so that

$$R_0 R_1 = M \cdot \frac{\partial Y}{\partial K} \cdot dp, \tag{1}$$

where M is the quantity of imports.

This shows the change in the production of importables due to the economic expansion itself. The expression is normally positive, indicating that the output of importables increases, consequent on economic expansion, at constant terms of trade. It should be noted here, however, that, as argued in section 2, the output of importables may actually contract due to the expansion.

2. *The Decrease in Consumption of Importables Due to the Price-Change*
The price-change (from p_0 to p_1) shifts consumption *along* the indifference curve to C_1. The consumption of importables is then reduced by

$$C_0 C_1' = -\frac{\partial C}{\partial p} \cdot dp, \tag{2}$$

where C is the total demand for importables.

3. *The Increase in Production of Importables Due to the Price-Change*
The price-change shifts production *along* the production possibility curve to P_1. The production of importables is then increased by

$$R_1 R_1' = \frac{\partial Y}{\partial p} \cdot dp. \tag{3}$$

The total decrease in the domestic demand for *imports*[3] is the sum of the three effects (1), (2) and (3):

$$\left(M \cdot \frac{\partial Y}{\partial K} + \frac{\partial Y}{\partial p} - \frac{\partial C}{\partial p} \right) \cdot dp. \tag{4}$$

This expression measures the decrease in demand for imports when the effect of growth on real income is exactly offset by an adverse movement of the terms of trade. In the abnormal case where output of importables *falls* as a result of growth, the expression may be negative, indicating an *increase* in the demand for imports.

Whether the country will actually be made worse off or not depends on what would happen to the quantity of imports supplied if the terms of trade were adjusted as assumed. The change in imports supplied as a result of such a price change is:

$$\frac{\partial S_m}{\partial p} \cdot dp. \tag{5}$$

The sum of (4) and (5) constitutes the excess supply of imports at the zero-gain terms of trade: if it is positive, the terms of trade will not move against the growing country enough to deprive it of all gain from growth; but if it is negative, the price of imports will have to rise still further to preserve equilibrium, and the growing country will actually be made worse off by growth.

The economic meaning of this criterion for immiserizing growth will be considered in the next section; for this purpose a neater formulation of the criterion is desirable, and this can be derived by subjecting it to some algebraic manipulation.

Multiplying (4) and (5) by $\dfrac{p}{M \cdot dp}$, we get our criterion for immiserizing growth as

$$\left(\frac{C}{M} \cdot \varepsilon + \frac{Y}{M} \cdot \sigma + y + r_m \right) < 0, \tag{6}$$

which may be written as

$$\left(\frac{C}{M} \cdot \varepsilon + \frac{Y}{M} \cdot \sigma + y \right) < -r_m, \tag{7}$$

where

$$\varepsilon = -\frac{p}{C} \cdot \frac{\partial C}{\partial p}, \quad r_m = \frac{p}{M} \cdot \frac{\partial S_m}{\partial p} \qquad (S_m \equiv M),$$

$$\sigma = \frac{p}{Y} \cdot \frac{\partial Y}{\partial p} \quad \text{and} \quad y = p \cdot \frac{\partial Y}{\partial K}.$$

This criterion is also expressible in the alternative equivalent form:

$$\left(\frac{C}{M} \cdot \varepsilon + \frac{Y}{M} \cdot \sigma + y \right) < 1 - n_x, \tag{8}$$

where $n_x = \frac{p}{X^0} \cdot \frac{\partial X^0}{\partial p}$ and X^0 is the quantity of exports. This follows from the fact that n_x and r_m are the *total* elasticities of the rest of the world's offer curve; n_x being the elasticity of the rest of the world's demand for imports (into the rest of the world) in response to an infinitesimal change in the terms of trade and r_m being the elasticity of the rest of the world's supply of (its) exports (to the growing country) in response to an infinitesimal shift in the terms of trade. It is a well-known proposition in theory of international trade that $n_x - r_m = 1$; hence, $1 - n_x = -r_m$.

2.

What are the implications of the criterion that we have derived in section 1? It will be remembered that $\varepsilon = \frac{p}{Y} \cdot \frac{\partial Y}{\partial p}$ and is thus necessarily positive and $\sigma = -\frac{p}{C} \cdot \frac{\partial C}{\partial p}$ which again, being the constant-utility or expenditure-compensated demand-elasticity with respect to a change in the price of importables, is necessarily positive.[4] We can see from (6), (7) or (8) that the *possibility* of immiserizing growth is increased if

(i) $\frac{Y}{M}$, the ratio of domestic production to import of importables is small. Since $\frac{C}{M} = 1 + \frac{Y}{M}$, it follows that $\frac{C}{M}$ will also be small when $\frac{Y}{M}$ is small;

(ii) ε, the constant-utility demand-elasticity for importables with respect to a change in the price of importables, is small; this would depend on the substitution effect against importables being negligible when the price of importables rises; and

(iii) σ, the elasticity in supply of importables when production shifts along the production possibility curve in response to a change in the price of importables, is small.

These are, neither singly nor in combination, sufficient conditions for immiserizing growth. In fact, the *possibility* of immiserizing growth arises only when, with these conditions favourably fulfilled, either or both of the following crucial conditions are fulfilled:

(a) the offer of the rest of the world is inelastic (i.e. r_m is negative, which may be for the *extreme*, and by no means necessary, reason that the growing country's exports are Giffen goods abroad); and

(b) growth actually reduces the domestic production of importables at constant relative commodity prices (i.e. y is negative).

Stringent as the latter condition may appear at first sight, recent analyses have shown that it is feasible under relatively simple assumptions. Thus the Rybczynski proposition states that under a two-commodity, two-factor model where, say, labour and land being the factors, one good is labour-intensive and the other land-intensive, if labour (land) increases in supply, then the output of the land-intensive (labour-intensive) industry must actually contract if the relative commodity prices are maintained constant.[5] Professor Johnson has recently advanced the proposition that under neutral technical progress in one industry, the technology of the other and the total factor endowment remaining unchanged, the output of the other industry must actually fall under constant relative commodity prices.[6] It may be of interest to note that under biased progress as well it is possible to establish conditions under which the output of the non-innovating industry will contract.[7]

References

1. Corden, W. M., "Economic Expansion and International Trade: A Geometric Approach", *Oxford Economic Papers*, June 1956.

2. Findlay, R., and Grubert, H., "Factor Intensity, Technological Progress, and the Terms of Trade", *Oxford Economic Papers*, February 1959.

3. Hicks, J. R., "An Inaugural Lecture", *Oxford Economic Papers*, June 1953.

4. Johnson, H. G., "Equilibrium Growth in an Expanding Economy", *Canadian Journal of Economics and Political Science*, November 1953.

5. Johnson, H. G., "Economic Expansion and International Trade", *Manchester School of Economic and Social Studies*, May 1955.

6. Mishan, E. J., "The Long-Run Dollar Problem: A Comment", *Oxford Economic Papers*, June 1955.

7. Rybczynski, T., "Factor Endowments and Relative Commodity Prices", *Economica*, November 1955.

22

The Possibility of Income Losses from Increased Efficiency or Factor Accumulation in the Presence of Tariffs

Harry G. Johnson

The adoption of more efficient technology and the accumulation of factors of production are generally assumed to increase the real income available to an economy. But when a country is following a protective policy improved efficiency in the protected industry or accumulation of the factor used intensively in that industry will actually reduce the country's real income, over a range of change set by the degree of protection. This possibility of income-reducing growth is relevant to the fact that countries industrialising by means of protectionist and import-substitution policies are frequently dissatisfied with the results. This note presents a formal demonstration of the possibility, in terms of the standard Heckscher-Ohlin model of international trade.

Figure 1 depicts production and consumption equilibrium with the initial technology and factor supplies and the tariff. TT' is the transformation curve, deduced from the standard box-diagram, II is the international price ratio, MM and $M'M'$ are the internal price ratio, which differs from the international price ratio to an extent determined by the rate of protection of Y, and P and C are the production and consumption equilibrium points.

Now suppose that neutral technical progress occurs in the protected Y industry, and in that industry only. As a result, the transformation curve will shift outward except at point T (where no Y is produced) to TT''; and the new equilibrium production point P' must lie to the northwest of P.[1] P' may lie either to the left or to the right of II, depending on the tariff rate, the extent of the technical improvement, and the elasticities of substitution between the factors in the two production functions. The new utility level of the country is given by the community indifference curve that intersects a new II curve through P' with a slope equal to that

This paper was originally published in *The Economic Journal* (March 1967): 151–154.

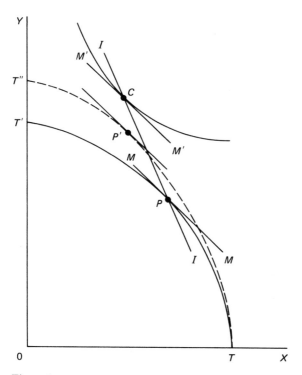

Figure 1

of $M'M'$. It is obvious, on the usual assumption that neither good is
inferior, that the new utility level will be higher if P' lies to the right of
II, and lower if P' lies to the left of II. In the latter case the country is
made worse off by technical progress in its protected industry. Moreover,
it is obvious that for a small enough degree of technical progress in that
industry the country must be made worse off, while with a large enough
degree of progress it must be made better off, by technical improvement.

If, instead of neutral technical progress in the protected industry, there
were an increase in the stock of the factor used intensively in producing
the protected product, the transformation curve would shift outward
throughout its length; but (by the Rybczynski Theorem) the new equilibrium production point P' would in this case also have to be to the northwest of P, again entailing the possibility of loss or gain of real income,
the necessity of loss if the factor increment is small enough, and the
necessity of gain if the factor increment exceeds some initial minimum
quantity.

The analytical results just presented may be understood in the light of the following considerations. Technical progress increases efficiency and therefore potential output per head; but it also shifts resources towards the industry in which progress occurs. If this is the export industry there is an additional gain from the reduction of waste implicit in the excess cost of protected production; but if it is the import-substitute industry there is an offsetting loss from increased waste through the excess cost of additional protected production, which may more than absorb the increase in potential output per head. Similarly, an increase in the supply of a factor increases potential real output, but also reallocates production towards the industry using that factor intensively; and if that industry is protected and so wastes resources through excess production costs, the shift again involves increased waste of resources, which may more than absorb the increase in potential output per head.

It is an interesting reflection on policy that protectionists usually demand increased protection when comparative advantage shifts against the protected industries, in effect claiming that part of the increased productive potential inherent in such a shift should be spent on the increased support of these industries.

In conclusion, it should be noted that the possibility of income-reducing growth demonstrated here is quite different from the possibility of "immiserizing growth" developed by Jagdish Bhagwati.[2] The latter is associated with the adverse effects of growth on the terms of trade; the former is associated with the presence of protection, under conditions in which any terms-of-trade effects of growth are excluded by assumption.

The possibility of income losses from increased efficiency or factor accumulation in the presence of tariffs was first pointed out to the author by J. H. Dales of the University of Toronto, who developed it in connection with his study of the effects of Canadian "National Policy" of industrial protection. The formal demonstration presented here was provoked by the disbelief of H. S. Houthakker.

23

Tariffs, Foreign Capital and Immiserizing Growth

Richard A. Brecher and Carlos F. Díaz Alejandro

Within the standard two-commodity two-factor model of international trade Bhagwati (1973) has demonstrated the possibility of immiserizing growth caused by a tariff-induced inflow of capital from abroad, assuming that the host country is small and continues to import the capital-intensive good while remaining incompletely specialized. The deterioration in welfare may be decomposed (for comparative-static purposes) into the following three contributing effects: (1) the well-known loss due to tariff-created distortions in consumption and production, given only the initial factor endowments; (2) the loss or gain that would result even from accumulation of nationally owned capital in the presence of a tariff, for reasons expounded by Johnson (1967) and further explored by Bertrand and Flatters (1971) and Tan (1969); and (3) the loss arising when foreign profits are subtracted to determine national income.

Assuming that foreign capital receives the full (untaxed) value of its marginal product, the present paper shows that the ambiguous effect (2) plus the negative effect (3) necessarily yield a net loss. Therefore, national reduction in welfare must result on balance, even before the negative effect (1) is added to the "net inflow-impact," which here denotes the combined impact of effects (2) plus (3). In other words, Bhagwati's (1973) possibility (immiseration) is in fact the only outcome that can result from a tariff-induced inflow of untaxed capital from abroad. Of course, if taxation of foreign profits were taken into account as suggested by Bhagwati (1973), host-country deterioration in welfare could be avoided.

Since the inclusion of (negative) effect (1) would serve merely to reinforce the following argument, the analysis will restrict itself only to effects (2) and (3), by starting from the tariff-inclusive but pre-inflow situation. This approach helps not only to simplify the exposition but also to

This paper was originally published in *Journal of International Economics* 7 (1977): 317–322.

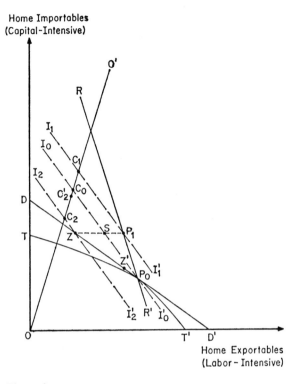

Figure 1

emphasize that, once protection has been granted, further reduction in welfare would result from any exogenous (as well as tariff-induced) inflows of capital from abroad.

In figure 1, the small protectionist country produces (with constant returns to scale) initially at P_0, using only the national endowments of capital and labor which generate the home production-possibility frontier labelled TT'. The domestic (tariff-inclusive) price ratio is given by the slope of line DD', tangent to TT' at P_0; whereas the world price ratio, as fixed by the small-country assumption, is given by the slope of line $I_0 I_0'$. Consumption is at C_0, where $I_0 I_0'$ intersects line OO', which is the income-consumption curve corresponding to domestic prices. Linearity of OO' simplifies the diagram but is not required for the analysis. To avoid cluttering the geometry, the diagram omits the community indifference curves, one of which passes through C_0 with a slope equal to that of DD'.

Effect (2) will first be examined in isolation. The once-for-all increase in the capital stock shifts out the production-possibility frontier (not shown in its new position) and, at constant prices, production moves from P_0 to P_1. Point P_1 lies northwest of P_0, according to the Rybczynski Theorem, and both of these points lie on RR', which is the familiar Rybczynski line corresponding to the (fixed) ratio of domestic prices. Since RR' is steeper than the world-price line in the particular case illustrated, the real value of total output increases at international prices, as the world-price line shifts from $I_0 I_0'$ to $I_1 I_1'$. Therefore, consumption increases from C_0 to C_1 and welfare improves. Alternatively, if the world-price line had been drawn steeper than RR', welfare would have decreased by similar reasoning, and the following analysis clearly would go through *a fortiori* because effect (2) would be negative.

Now effect (3) also will be incorporated, by subtracting foreign profits to leave only national income. Assuming that capital from abroad receives the full (tax-free) value of its marginal product, foreign profits absorb the entire increase in total output valued at domestic prices, by reasoning similar to Mundell's (1957). Expressed in terms of the exportable good, these profits are therefore represented by $P_1 Z$, which is the horizontal distance between point P_1 and line DD'. Supposing that foreign profits are repatriated in terms of home exportables, the home country is left with commodity bundle Z, which can be exchanged internationally along the world-price line $I_2 I_2'$ to achieve consumption at C_2. Since C_2 must lie southwest of C_0, the capital inflow clearly reduces the host country's welfare.

Thus, even though capital accumulation could increase national welfare in the absence of foreign profits, the host country must suffer from foreign investment which receives its market rate of return. By way of extension, the following four observations could be substantiated readily. First, the analysis (qualitatively speaking) depends neither upon the type of goods used to repatriate foreign profits, nor upon the assumption that foreigners consume these profits abroad rather than locally.[1] Second, if host-country taxes were levied to reduce the repatriation of foreign profits from $P_1 Z$ to $P_1 S$ or less, the net inflow-impact [combining effects (2) plus (3)] would be zero or positive, respectively. Third, if home importables were instead labor-intensive—in which case effect (2) is known to be positive—the net inflow-impact necessarily would be positive. Fourth, in the alternative situation of a trade subsidy (i.e. a negative tariff), the net inflow-impact would be positive, assuming that host-country importables are capital-intensive (but negative if these goods were labor-intensive). Of course, if the net inflow-impact were positive for either of these three reasons, effect (1) might be outweighed and tariff-induced inflows of capital from abroad clearly need not be immiserizing.

In figure 1, the inflow of capital reduces home imports of capital-intensive goods, because output of these commodities increases (as production shifts from P_0 to P_1) while consumption of these goods decreases (from the level at C_0 to the level at C_2). Also, the capital inflow shifts the pattern of output in favor of capital-intensive goods at the expense of labor-intensive commodities, as production moves northwestwardly (from P_0 to P_1) along RR'. Until this stage in the discussion, however, the inflow of capital is not large enough to extinguish home-country imports or achieve complete specialization in production. The implications of larger inflows will now be considered briefly.

As Minabe (1974) observes, host-country welfare rises above its tariff-inclusive pre-inflow level if the capital inflow is large enough to achieve Mundell's (1957) tariff-induced equilibrium, involving incomplete specialization with no home imports of commodities and with no divergence between domestic and foreign prices. In present terminology, the net inflow-impact in this case is positive. Effect (2) is now augmented to incorporate the familiar gains due to the disappearance of distortions in production and consumption, as domestic prices become equal to international prices. Under these circumstances, however, clearly the net inflow-impact is exactly offset by effect (1), since Mundell's (1957) tariff-induced (post-inflow) equilibrium yields precisely the same level of host-country welfare as does his free-trade (pre-inflow) situation. Therefore, this case does not provide an argument in favor of using tariffs to attract capital from abroad.

If the capital inflow then proceeds even further, initially it has no additional consequences for home welfare, by reasoning similar to Mundell's (1957), as long as specialization remains incomplete. Eventually, however, the inflow leads to extra host-country gains, by reasoning similar to MacDougall's (1960) [cited also by Hamada (1974)] or Minabe's (1974), once specialization becomes complete in the capital-intensive good. Although such further inflows of capital would not be induced by the original tariff (imposed selectively on the good no longer imported), they could be exogenously determined.

The analysis of the present paper may be summarized in figure 2. The free-trade pre-inflow position is at point F. The distance FT represents the welfare loss due to imposing a tariff in the absence of capital inflows from abroad. Given the tariff, the welfare effects of (untaxed) capital inflows are illustrated by the curve $TAMM'D$ (whose lowest point is A), assuming that home importables are capital-intensive along FT. Segment TA shows the type of welfare loss analyzed in the previous diagram. Segment AM (in figure 2) shows the welfare path to the Mundell (1957) equilibrium at point M, which has the same height as F.[2] The home coun-

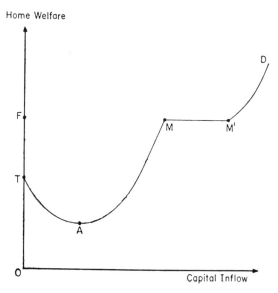

Figure 2

try remains incompletely specialized with no capital-intensive imports along the horizontal segment MM', until complete specialization in capital-intensive goods is reached at point M'. This pattern of specialization with home imports of labor-intensive goods is maintained throughout the segment $M'D$, which represents the region in which MacDougall's (1960) reasoning applies. Alternatively, if home importables were labor-intensive (instead of capital-intensive) along FT, $TAMM'D$ would be replaced by a continuously upward-sloping curve (not drawn) through T, according to a similar line of argument.

The authors are grateful to Jagdish N. Bhagwati, Christopher J. Heady and Vahid F. Nowshirvani for helpful comments. The authors alone are responsible for any remaining errors or shortcomings. Carlos F. Díaz Alejandro thanks the National Science Foundation for financially supporting his research under NSF grant SOC 75–04518.

After this research was completed for the case of capital inflows not large enough to extinguish host-country imports or achieve complete specialization in production, the editor of this journal drew the authors' attention to independent work by Hamada (1974) and Minabe (1974), who present (among other things) analysis similar to that offered here and who cite a related contribution by Uzawa (1969). This literature also considers cases with zero imports or complete specialization, which subsequently were taken into account here as well, by including some additional discussion below.

References

Bertrand, T. J. and F. Flatters, 1971, Tariffs, capital accumulation, and immiserizing growth, *Journal of International Economics* 1, 453–460.

Bhagwati, Jagdish N., 1973, The theory of immiserizing growth: Further applications, in: Michael B. Connolly and Alexander K. Swoboda, eds., *International Trade and Money* (University of Toronto Press) 45–54.

Hamada, Koichi, 1974, An economic analysis of the duty-free zone, *Journal of International Economics* 4, 225–241.

Johnson, Harry G., 1967, The possibility of income losses from increased efficiency or factor accumulation in the presence of tariffs, *Economic Journal* 77, 151–154.

MacDougall, G. D. A., 1960, The benefits and costs of private investment from abroad: A theoretical approach, *Economic Record* 36, 13–35.

Minabe, Nobuo, 1974, Capital and technology movements and economic welfare, *American Economic Review* 64, 1088–1100.

Mundell, Robert A., 1957, International trade and factor mobility, *American Economic Review* 47, 321–335.

Tan, Augustine H. H., 1969, Immiserizing tariff-induced capital accumulation and technical change, *Malayan Economic Review* 13, 1–7.

Uzawa, H., 1969, Shihon Jiyuka to Kokumin Keizai (Liberalization of foreign investments and the national economy), *Economisuto* 23, 106–122 (in Japanese).

24

National Welfare in
an Open Economy
in the Presence of
Foreign-Owned Factors
of Production

Jagdish N. Bhagwati
and Richard A. Brecher

I Introduction

In the presence of foreign-owned factors of production in an economy, the traditional conclusions regarding the effects of exogenous parametric changes or policy changes on national welfare need to be modified. Thus, in an open economy, the absence of the usual foreign and domestic distortions *a la* Bhagwati (1971) and Johnson (1965) will not ensure that an exogenous term-of-trade improvement or a policy shift from autarky to free trade will improve national welfare.[1]

For example, take the traditional 2 × 2 model of trade theory and assume that the importable good is labour-intensive, labour is wholly national and capital is wholly foreign. A shift from autarky to free trade will then, by lowering the relative domestic price of the importable good, lower the real wage of labour *a la* Stolper-Samuelson (1941) and thereby result in national immiserization from the shift to free trade. Free trade therefore worsens rather than improves welfare, given the presence of foreign capital in this example.

Bhagwati and Tironi (1978) formulated the original problem as relevant to analyzing the widespread concerns of Latin American policymakers, who feared that regional trade liberalization would benefit foreign investors and could harm the Latin American nations themselves in consequence. In addressing this particular problem recently for the 2 × 2 model, the Bhagwati-Tironi analysis allows the tariff to vary by policy, but assumes that each of the two factors of production is wholly foreign or wholly national. This latter assumption permits them to adapt readily to their problem the well-known results on income distribution by factor class, originating from Stolper-Samuelson (1941) and developed in Bhagwati (1959), Johnson (1959, 1960) and Rao (1971).

This paper was originally published in *Journal of International Economics* 10, no. 1 (February 1980).

Unfortunately, the real world does not permit us to divide all factors exclusively into the national or the foreign category. Capital flows to countries that cannot be assumed to have no capital of their own, and labour moves into countries that surely have native populations. Thus, it is necessary for this reason alone to examine the problem at hand by permitting the factors of production to be both national and foreign, as we do presently.

More importantly, while it is clear that a redistributive effect resulting from changing goods price-ratio could lead to paradoxical outcomes for national welfare, we are able to demonstrate a stronger proposition in this paper. Namely, the paradox of national immiserization following improvement in the country's external terms of trade will arise *if and only if* the redistributive effect against nationals goes so far as to result in the *Differential-Trade-Pattern* phenomemon, as defined below.

Our geometric analysis, moreover, has the added advantage of using familiar trade-geometric techniques to simplify and resolve what appears to be a potentially complex problem. Furthermore, although the explicit focus of this paper is the national-foreign distinction, the two-group analysis presented here applies equally well to a broad spectrum of alternative domestic distinctions (e.g., those based on race, ethnicity or sex).[2] Moreover, the analysis is just as readily applicable, as we demonstrate later, to the theory of customs unions.

In section II we trace the effects of variation in the goods price-ratio on the income accruing to national factors, thus defining their "income line" at alternative price-ratios. In section III, we relate this perfectly general analysis first to exogenously-induced changes in external terms of trade, assuming free trade, and therewith discuss the effects on national welfare that would follow from such changes. We also relate the analysis next to effects of tariff variation on national welfare. Section IV offers some concluding observations.

II National Income Variations as Goods Price-Ratio is Varied

The first problem that we analyze relates to the behavior of the national "income line" as the prevailing price-ratio for goods is varied.

The model has two factors of production, K (for capital) and L (for labour). The overall factor endowment is $\bar{K}$ and $\bar{L}$, while the national (i.e., domestically-owned) factor endowment is $\bar{K}_n$ and $\bar{L}_n$. The two traded goods are X and Y.

With the usual restrictions on the linear homogeneous production functions for the two goods, and assuming the absence of factor-intensity reversals for the rest of our analysis, we can define an aggregate production possibility curve, $T_x'T_y'$ in figure 1 for the aggregate factor endowments $(\bar{K}, \bar{L})$. For the usual trade-theoretic analysis, with well-behaved social utility curves, a goods price-ratio AB will be defined for autarky and the utility index U^G would rise monotonically as P_x/P_y (the relative price of X in terms of Y) was varied up from A to T_x' or down from A to T_y' (with reversed pattern of trade). (For simplicity of exposition, we assume that all income earned by factors from abroad is consumed locally, to avoid having to show repatriation of such income in figure 1.) This relationship between P_y/P_x and U^G, as illustrated in figure 2, follows from deriving *first* the implication of the goods price-ratio variation for the aggregate budget line and *then* deducing the welfare level (U^G) achieved in figure 1.

For *national* welfare, however, we need to define these two steps for domestically-owned factors *alone*. First, as in this section, we must derive the national budget line, as defined by the domestic goods price-ratio. Next, as in the following section, we must deduce the national welfare level (U^N) reached in consequence.

The natural way to proceed with the analysis then would appear to be to draw onto figure 1 the national production possibility curve, T_xT_y, defined by the domestically-owned endowments $\bar{K}_n$ and $\bar{L}_n$. One may then be tempted to draw the goods price-ratio tangent to it, as to $T_x'T_y'$, and to treat the resulting income line as the *national* budget line.

But, except for a range of possible cases, this cannot be done. To see why, and to state the correct and complete analysis of the problem, let us turn to the familiar Samuelson diagram in figure 3—which relates the goods price-ratio (P_y/P_x), the factor-price (rental-wage) ratio P_K/P_L, and the sectoral capital-labour ratios K_x/L_x (for good X) and K_y/L_y (for good Y). Assume, without loss of generality, that $\bar{K}_n/\bar{L}_n < \bar{K}/\bar{L}$; that is, the foreign-owned endowment is capital intensive (as would be the case if foreign capital alone had come into the country *a la* Bhagwati and Tironi, 1978).

There are two cases that can arise then: *either* there is a range of factor price-ratios at which incomplete specialization will obtain on *both* T_xT_y and $T_x'T_y'$ *or* there is no such range. Figure 3 illustrates the former, more interesting case; the latter, which corresponds incidentally to the Bhagwati-Tironi restrictive case, will be analyzed subsequently and related to the former.

The analysis then must distinguish among three zones of goods price-ratios: Zone I, where they lead to incomplete specialization in production

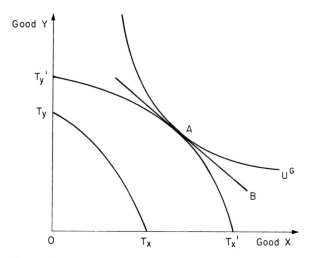

Figure 1

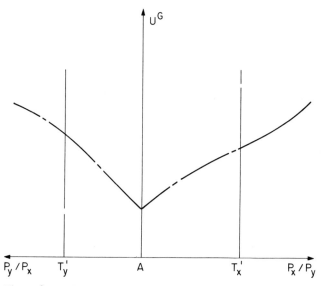

Figure 2

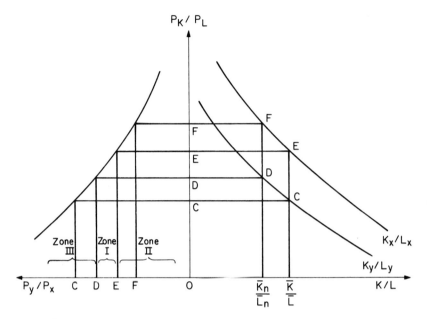

Figure 3

for both the production possibility curves T_xT_y and $T'_xT'_y$; Zone II, where complete specialization on the capital-intensive good X occurs on $T'_xT'_y$ before it does on the national curve T_xT_y; and Zone III, where complete specialization on the labour-intensive good Y occurs on T_xT_y before it occurs on the aggregate curve $T'_xT'_y$. Take each, in turn.

Zone I   For the aggregate endowment ratio, $\bar{K}/\bar{L}$, the range of factor price-ratios for incomplete specialization is clearly CE (i.e., OC to OE) on the vertical axis of figure 3. For the national endowment ratio, $\bar{K}_n/\bar{L}_n$, the range for incomplete specialization is DF. Therefore, DE represents along the vertical axis the range of factor prices over which *both* T_xT_y and $T'_xT'_y$ will show incomplete specialization. Consequently, for any goods price-ratio in the range DE (i.e., OD to OE) along the left-hand horizontal axis, it is evident that the choice of capital-labour ratios in X and Y will be *identical* for T_xT_y and for $T'_xT'_y$, and hence there will be a unique set of real factor prices (P_K/P_i and P_L/P_i, i = x, y) along both of these production possibility curves.[3] Given this uniqueness, the value of national income ($\bar{L}_nP_L/P_i + \bar{K}_nP_K/P_i$, i = x, y) can be represented by the goods price-ratio tangent to T_xT_y, for the same reason that the value of aggregate income ($\bar{L}P_L/P_i + \bar{K}P_K/P_i$, i = x, y) is representable by the goods price-ratio tangent to $T'_xT'_y$. Thus, even though T_xT_y is only a hypothetical

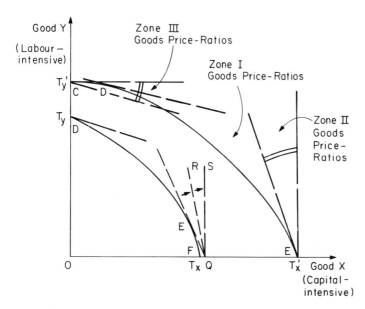

Figure 4

construct and national factors combine with foreign factors to produce at common techniques throughtout the economy along $T_x'T_y'$, we can see immediately that the foregoing procedure for deriving the national budget line (by putting the goods price-ratio tangent to T_xT_y) will be valid as long as P_y/P_x is in the range DE.

Therefore, for this overlapping range (DE) of incomplete specialization, we can indeed proceed in figure 4 to place the goods price-ratio tangent to T_xT_y to derive the national income line. Besides, a movement from E to D along T_xT_y and $T_x'T_y'$ will imply—given the resulting rise in the wage-rental ratio and the condition $\bar{K}_n/\bar{L}_n < \bar{K}/\bar{L}$—a rise in the share of aggregate income going to domestically-owned factors.

Zone II   But vary now the goods price-ratio P_y/P_x down from OE in figure 3. It is evident that there will be complete specialization on good X on $T_x'T_y'$, while on T_xT_y we would get incomplete specialization in production until the goods price-ratio becomes OF (figure 3). Since the returns to domestically-owned factors must reflect what happens on $T_x'T_y'$, however, it follows that the relative rewards of K and L will remain fixed at $P_K/P_L = OE$ in figure 3 for all changes in the goods price-ratio from OE to OF *and* further.

Therefore, the share of national in aggregate income will also remain constant, for such variations in the goods price-ratio, at OQ/OE. The national income line therefore will become EQ in figure 4 for the goods price-ratio OE in figure 3 and will shift on its anchor Q thereafter to QS through QR as P_y/P_x falls steadily from OE to zero in figure 3.

Clearly, therefore, the stretch EF on T_xT_y is not relevant to the determination of the national income line. The diminishing wage-rental ratio that it reflects as K/L ratios change with a varying goods price-ratio are, in fact, arrested because of the opportunity to combine with the foreign factors. The gain that such an opportunity represents for national factors is measured by the distance between (1) the income line produced by tangency of a goods price-ratio along EF in figure 4; and (2) the parallel income line (anchored on Q) that actually obtains, thanks to interaction with the foreign factors and the consequent anchoring of the techniques and factor rewards at E on $T_x'T_y'$.

Zone III   Varying the goods price-ratio in the opposite direction, from OD upwards toward OC and beyond in figure 3, then defines the remaining set of possible variations in the goods price-ratio.

At goods price-ratio OD, T_xT_y shows specialization on good Y and $T_x'T_y'$ shows incomplete specialization, in figure 4. If factor prices were constant as P_y/P_x rises, T_xT_y would have led to continuous improvement in the national budget line, each successive budget line being anchored on D and rotating upwards. However, P_K/P_L is *not* fixed, but will continue to fall as the aggregate economy moves along $T_x'T_y'$ from D to C. Therefore, given the associated increase in the wage-rental ratio and the condition $\bar{K}_n/\bar{L}_n < \bar{K}/\bar{L}$, the share of national in aggregate income will rise with the move from D towards C on $T_x'T_y'$. However, the move to C from D is also accompanied by a declining intercept of the aggregate income line with the vertical axis. Therefore, while the former effect works to raise the national income line, the latter effect works to lower it.

It is possible to establish, however, that the combination of these two effects yields an unambiguously upward shift in the national income line, according to the following reasoning. The real value of national income in terms of good Y is given by $Q_y = \bar{L}_nP_L/P_y + \bar{K}_nP_K/P_y$. By differentiation of this equation, $dQ_y/d(P_L/P_y) = [\bar{L}_n/\bar{K}_n + d(P_K/P_y)/d(P_L/P_y)]\bar{K}_n$. Since the first-order conditions for profit maximization can be manipulated easily to show that $d(P_K/P_y)/d(P_L/P_y) = -L_y/K_y$, then $dQ_y/d(P_L/P_y) = (\bar{L}_n/\bar{K}_n - L_y/K_y)\bar{K}_n$. Thus, $dQ_y/d(P_L/P_y) \geqq 0$ because $\bar{L}_n/\bar{K}_n \geqq L_y/K_y$ within Zone III, with the strict equality holding only for the borderline case of goods price-ratio OD. Consequently, as P_L/P_y increases continuously with P_y/P_x (*a la* Stolper-Samuelson) within Zone III, Q_y rises correspondingly, and hence the national income line shifts upwards while becoming flatter.[4] Once the goods price-ratio reaches OC in figure 4, however, and specialization on good Y ensures at T_y' for the aggregate economy, successive increases in P_y/P_x will not change the share of national in aggregate income and the national income line will rotate upwards (along with P_y/P_x) from a fixed anchor on the vertical axis in figure 4.

What happens in the goods price-ratio range from OD to OC is that the presence of foreign factors introduces diminishing wage-rental ratios, which would have been avoided if national factors had operated in isolation (at D in figure 4). At the same time, *a la* Stolper-Samuelson, an "income-redistribution" phenomenon works to labour's and hence to national advantage. Apparently, however, the net impact on the national income line is unambiguously favourable in the general case for the sub-range of goods-price ratios OD $\leqslant P_y/P_x \leqslant$ OC. For price-ratios in the sub-range $P_y/P_x >$ OC, there is, of course, only a favourable rotation of the national income line as P_y/P_x improves and the economy is specialized on good Y. These two sub-ranges together define all the possibilities in Zone III.

In concluding this section, note that the T_xT_y curve clearly would be of little use if $\bar{K}_n/\bar{L}_n$ were so much below $\bar{K}/\bar{L}$ that Zone I did not exist.[5] In this case, we can see immediately that the situation can be described fully by the foregoing analysis of Zones II and III. Of course, it is clear that this case, where there is no Zone I, is implied by the Bhagwati-Tironi analysis where capital is wholly foreign and labour is wholly domestic. For, in this case, where the Stolper-Samuelson-Bhagwati-Johnson-Rao analysis can be applied directly, the overall factor endowment ratio is $\bar{K}/\bar{L}_n$ and the national endowment ratio is $\bar{K}_n/\bar{L}_n = 0$. Indeed, in this case, it is evident that national income in units of Y (Q_y) *and* of X (Q_x) will unambiguously rise as the real wage of labour rises in terms of *both* Y and X with the rise of P_y/P_x, *a la* Stolper-Samuelson.

III Welfare Implications in an Open Economy

The preceding analysis can be readily grafted onto two familiar problems of the theory of trade and welfare: (1) the welfare effects of exogenously-induced changes in the external terms of trade (as a result of some type of parametric shift abroad) under free trade, and (2) the welfare comparison of free trade and autarky. The critical role of the *Differential-Trade-*

Pattern phenomenon emerges from our analysis. The discussion holds equally well for both the large-country and small-country cases, even though the magnitude of adjustment in the equilibrium value of international prices could depend upon the economy's degree of monopoly power in world trade.

Exogenously-Induced Changes in the Terms of Trade
As noted above, in the context of figure 2, the conventional result, with a standard social utility function, is that improvements in the terms of trade monotonically improve welfare under free trade, given the pattern of trade. This result, however, does not hold necessarily in the presence of foreign factors of production. To see this, consider terms of trade variations *within* the three zones distinguished in section II for the general case where Zone I also obtains. The analysis can be readily extended by the reader to terms of trade changes *between* the zones.

Changes within Zone I   Within Zone I, the domestic price-ratio (which is identical to the external terms of trade under free trade) can be put tangent to T_xT_y to derive the national income line, as shown in section II. It follows therefore that terms-of-trade improvement within Zone I ought to increase national welfare.

It should be observed, however, that a given change in P_y/P_x may mean both an improvement in the terms of trade for the economy as an aggregate and a simultaneous terms-of-trade deterioration from the national point of view. This apparent paradox is easily seen and quickly resolved, by noting simply that the equilibrium value of P_y/P_x may differ between aggregate autarky (along the actual production possibility curve $T'_xT'_y$) and national autarky (along the hypothetical curve T_xT_y), so that the aggregate (actual) pattern of trade may differ from the national (hypothetical) pattern of trade. For this reason, although national welfare improves monotonically with the national terms of trade, aggregate terms-of-trade improvement will not imply an increase in national welfare unless the aggregate and national patterns of trade happen to be the same.

This is illustrated in figure 5, where the $T'_xT'_y$ curve has been omitted, to avoid cluttering the diagram. The aggregate-autarky price-ratio (determined along the omitted curve $T'_xT'_y$) is drawn tangent to T_xT_y at A'. The national-autarky price-ratio is tangent to T_xT_y at A. (To have ray OA' steeper than ray OA as drawn, a sufficient but not necessary condition is a unique set of homothetic indifference curves corresponding to both U^G and U^N, in view of the well-known Rybczynski Theorem.) For any reductions in P_y/P_x from A', U^G would have improved. However, for all such changes between A' and A, within the autarkic price-ratios cone

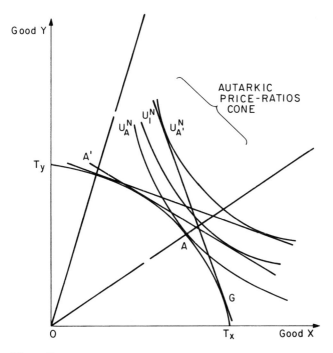

Figure 5

AOA', U^N obviously declines because for national factors the aggregate terms-of-trade improvement is a terms-of-trade derterioration. Therefore, U^N declines steadily from U_A^N, through U_I^N to U_A^N. However, further declines in P_y/P_x will start improving U^N and figure 5 shows the P_y/P_x at G which raises U^N back to the level A' consistent with the aggregate-autarky price-ratio. Obviously, then, still further decline in P_y/P_x would have raised U^N above the level at A'.

It follows that the net result of terms-of-trade improvements for the aggregate economy may be to raise, lower or leave national welfare unchanged. This general result still would hold if ray OA' were flatter than ray OA. Only if the two rays coincided would aggregate terms-of-trade improvement necessarily imply an increase in national welfare. We have thus shown that, in Zone I, the paradox of conflicting movements in aggregate and national welfare will arise when there is a difference between the national and aggregate patterns-of-trade. This *Differential-Trade-Pattern* phenomenon will now be discussed in the context of the other two zones.

Changes within Zone II Within Zone II, there is (aggregate) specialization on good X along $T_x'T_y'$ in figure 4. It is evident then that any improve-

25

ments in the aggregate terms of trade will imply corresponding improvements in the national terms of trade since both the national and aggregate patterns trade will necessarily involve excess supply of good X. Successive rotations outwards of the national income line, anchored on Q, will produce increasing national welfare, U^N. Therefore, changes in U^G may be used to infer the direction of change of U^N; there is no complication as in Zone I, since the *Differential-Trade-Pattern* phenomenon cannot arise here.

Changes within Zone III   Within Zone III, however, the possibility of *Differential-Trade-Pattern* phenomenon re-emerges. In the aggregate, there is first the range of incomplete specialization (up to C from D on $T_x'T_y'$ in figure 4) and then complete specialization on good Y. For variations in the aggregate terms of trade within the incomplete-specialization range, our earlier analysis shows that the national income line must rise with P_y/P_x. By the same token, U^N must also rise with P_y/P_x. Thus, when P_y/P_x rises, U^N and U^G will move together or in opposite directions according as the economy (in aggregate) exports good Y or X respectively.

However, beyond the point of specialization on good Y, the aggregate terms-of-trade improvement (resulting from a rise in P_y/P_x) must also increase national income and therefore U^N. The net effect of terms-of-trade improvements in Zone III therefore may be to *lower* or increase national welfare when there is incomplete specialization along $T_x'T_y'$, but must be to raise national welfare when aggregate specialization is complete on good Y.

Note, moreover, that the contrary behaviour of U^N and U^G, possible in the case of incomplete specialization, does require that the aggregate pattern of trade be different from the national pattern of trade; for, such a possibility will arise if and only if the aggregate trade pattern involves the export of good X^6 and the national trade pattern (owing to complete specialization on good Y, necessarily in Zone III) involves the export of good Y instead.

It is evident therefore that directional changes in national welfare generally cannot be inferred from the direction of changes in the terms of trade in the aggregate if the economy is in Zones I and III. Interestingly, for both of these zones, the paradoxical behaviour of national welfare arises simply because the aggregate pattern of trade masks a contrary pattern of trade for the domestically-owned, national factors of production. If only we could draw aside the veil imposed by the presence of foreign factors, and see directly the national (hypothetical) equilibrium production and consumption, the paradox would have disappeared.[7] Therefore, we may describe the paradox of Zones I and III as arising from the *Differential-Trade-Pattern phenomenon*. The redistribution of income *a la* Stolper-Samuelson does indeed take place in both Zones I and III; but it might not be sufficiently strong to create the paradox of deterioration (improvement) in national welfare when the economy's terms of trade improve (deteriorate). Sufficient strength, moreover, is here synonymous with a difference between the national and aggregate patterns of trade.

Autarky versus Free Trade
Since neither free trade nor autarky creates tariff revenue, the analysis of this paper can be readily used also to rank these two trade policies in the presence of foreign-owned factors of production.

It is seen immediately that, in Zones I and III, the *Differential-Trade-Pattern* phenomenon may arise and thus lead to autarky (in the aggregate) being better for national welfare than free trade. (Zone II can be ignored at this stage in the discussion, since aggregate autarky cannot occur when only good X is produced along $T'_x T'_y$, assuming that aggregate consumption is always positive for each good). Thus, the conventional welfare ranking (of free trade being superior to autarky) may be reversed in the presence of foreign-owned factors of production within an economy.

IV Concluding Remarks

In conclusion, a few words should be said about the meaning of the term "autarky," as used by us in this paper. By general convention in practical parlance, autarky refers to the absence of trade across national borders. At the same time, evidently "autarky" does not exclude domestic "trade" between resident citizens of different countries. The national and foreign factors in our analysis are indeed engaged in domestic trade,[8] even in the absence of international (i.e. trans-border) trade. The analytical problem is therefore identical to that which would arise in the case of customs unions. For, once a customs union is formed with common external tariff and free internal trade *and* factor mobility, changes in individual member countries' welfare as external conditions change for the union as a whole are evidently analyzable in precisely the same fashion as changes in national welfare in the presence of foreign factors of production.

Thanks are due to the National Science Foundation Grants No. SOC77–07188 and SOC79–07541 for financial support of the research underlying this paper. The comments of John Black, Alan Deardorff, Murray Kemp and Alasdair Smith have led to improvements.

References

Bhagwati, Jagdish N. 1959. "Protection, Real Wages and Real Incomes." *Economic Journal*, December.

———. 1971. "The Generalized Theory of Distortions and Welfare," in Jagdish Bhagwati *et al.* (eds.), *Trade, Balance of Payments and Growth: Essays in Honor of Charles P. Kindleberger* (North-Holland).

———, and Ernesto Tironi. 1978. "Tariff Change, Foreign Capital and Immiserization: A Theoretical Analysis." MIT, mimeographed, August; *Journal of Development Economics* (forthcoming).

Johnson, Harry G. 1959. "International Trade, Income Distribution and the Offer Curve." *Manchester School* 27: 241–260.

———. 1960. "Income Distribution, the Offer Curve and the Effects of Tariffs." *Manchester School* 28: 215–242.

———. 1965. "Optimal Trade Intervention in the Presence of Domestic Distortions," in Robert E. Baldwin *et al.* (eds.), *Trade, Growth and the Balance of Payments: Essays in Honor of Gottfried Haberler* (Rand McNally).

Rao, V. S. 1971. "Tariffs and Welfare of Factor Owners: A Normative Extension of the Stolper-Samuelson Theorem." *Journal of International Economics* 1: 401–416.

Stolper, Wolfgang, and Paul Samuelson. 1941. "Protection and Real Wages." *Review of Economic Studies* 9, November.

25

Capital Accumulation in the Open Two-Sector Economy

M. Alasdair M. Smith

I. The Basic Model

The model is the standard two-sector model, with one of the outputs being a pure investment good, the other being a pure consumption good.

Production levels of the goods are respectively Q_I and Q_C; and I and C denote domestic absorption levels. The investment good is taken as the numeraire, and the price of the consumption good is p. The capital and labour inputs available are K and L; the rental rate on capital is r and the wage rate is w.

A full-employment, perfectly competitive open economy with balanced trade satisfies the following relations:

$$K = a_{KI}Q_I + a_{KC}Q_C, \tag{1}$$

$$L = a_{LI}Q_I + a_{LC}Q_C, \tag{2}$$

$$1 \leqslant r a_{KI} + w a_{LI} \tag{3}$$

with equality if $Q_I > 0$,

$$p \leqslant r a_{KC} + w a_{LC} \tag{4}$$

with equality if $Q_C > 0$,

$$p(C - Q_C) + I - Q_I = 0. \tag{5}$$

Equations (1) and (2) are full-employment conditions; perfect competition requires (3) and (4); and (5) is the statement of balance-of-trade equilibrium. The coefficients a_{MN} measure the amount of input M required in the production of one unit of output Q_N. They are chosen so as to minimise the cost of production, that is they minimise $r a_{KN} + w a_{LN}$ subject to

This paper was originally published in *The Economic Journal* 87, no. 346 (June 1977): 273–282.

$f^N(a_{KN}, a_{LN}) = 1$, where f^N is the constant-returns-to-scale production function of Q_N. Optimal choice of technique is easily shown to give rise to the equations

$$0 = rda_{KN} + wda_{LN} \ (N = I, C) \tag{6}$$

(which hold trivially in the case of no choice of technique), so that changes in p, r and w must satisfy

$$0 = dra_{KI} + dwa_{LI} \tag{7}$$

if $Q_I > 0$, and

$$dp = dra_{KC} + dwa_{LC} \tag{8}$$

if $Q_C > 0$; these equations being obtained from the total differentiation of (3) and (4) and from (6).

The value of national income is

$$Y = I + pC \tag{9}$$

$$= Q_I + pQ_C \tag{10}$$

$$= rK + wL, \tag{11}$$

where (10) follows from (5), and (11) from (1)–(4). The labour force grows exogenously at the rate n, so steady state requires investment at a level which makes the capital stock grow at the rate n also:

$$I = nK, \tag{12}$$

and from (9), (11) and (12) we have

$$pC = (r - n)K + wL. \tag{13}$$

Taking the total differential of (13) with L constant enables us to compare steady states with different saving rates and different relative prices. (1), (2), (7) and (8) allow the elimination of the input prices:

$$dpC + pdC = (r - n)dK + drK + dwL \tag{14}$$

$$= (r - n)dK + dpQ_C, \tag{15}$$

which implies

$$pdC = (r - n)dK + dp(Q_C - C). \tag{16}$$

This equation plays a central role throughout the paper.

In a closed economy $Q_C = C$, and in an open economy which is so small as to have no influence on its terms of trade $dp/dK = 0$. In either case, (16) implies that across steady states dC/dK has the sign of $(r - n)$, which is the standard "golden rule" result on the effect of capital accumulation on steady state consumption.

In a large open economy, however, a rise in K will lead to an increased net export of the more capital-intensive product, implying an endogenous change in p, so that dC/dK depends not only on $(r - n)$ but also on the "terms of trade effect" $(Q_C - C)dp/dK$.

This fact seems first to have been noted by Bertrand (1975). It may seem paradoxical, for the golden rule is accepted as a result of complete generality. There is, however, an interpretation of the apparent paradox as a standard second-best proposition. Free trade is not the optimal trade policy for a large country. If the optimal trading rule is not applied, there is no reason to suppose that the usual rule for optimal savings will continue to be valid. (Negishi (1972, pp. 174–7) has demonstrated in the case of a small country the converse proposition that in the absence of optimal savings, the free-trade rule for optimal trade no longer holds.) What we should expect, however, is that with an optimum tariff, the standard relationship between consumption and capital accumulation will be restored.

The formal argument is as follows. (The derivation of the optimum tariff follows the lines of the analysis in Caves and Jones (1973, pp. 244–7).) Let net exports of the consumption good be $E_C = Q_C - C$, and let the domestic price of the consumption good be π, which will, in general, be different from the world price p. Relationships (1), (2), (3), (5), (6) and (7) continue to apply, but (4) and (8) hold with p replaced by π, which modified relationships are denoted by (4′) and (8′) below. The value of national income at domestic prices is

$$Y = I + \pi C \tag{17}$$

$$= Q_I + \pi Q_C + (p - \pi) E_C \tag{18}$$

$$= rK + wL + (p - \pi) E_C, \tag{19}$$

using (5), (3), (4′), (1) and (2). Taking differentials for constant K and L and using (7), (8′), (1) and (2) gives

$$dI + \pi dC = -d\pi C + drK + dwL + (dp - d\pi) E_C + (p - \pi) dE_C \tag{20}$$

$$= -d\pi C + d\pi Q_C + (dp - d\pi) E_C + (p - \pi) dE_C \tag{21}$$

$$= dp E_C + (p - \pi) dE_C. \tag{22}$$

The tariff is at its optimal level if the value of income is maximised at domestic prices, which implies $dI + \pi dC = 0$, so that

$$dpE_C + (p - \pi)dE_C = 0, \tag{23}$$

an optimum tariff formula which may be more familiar in the form

$$\pi = p + E_C \frac{dp}{dE_C} = \frac{d(pE_C)}{dE_C}, \tag{24}$$

showing the equality of the domestic price ratio and the slope of the foreign offer curve.

In steady state (12) continues to hold but (17) and (19) imply that (13) is replaced by

$$\pi C = (r - n)K + wL + (p - \pi)E_C \tag{25}$$

so that across steady states

$$\pi dC = -d\pi C + drK + dwL + dpE_C - d\pi E_C + (r - n)dK$$
$$+ (p - \pi)dE_C \tag{26}$$
$$= (r - n)dK \tag{27}$$

from (21), (22) and (23).

Recalling that the optimum tariff in a small economy is zero, (27) allows us to state a general result that in the comparison of steady states in an open economy *imposing an optimum tariff*, dC/dK has the sign of $(r - n)$.

II. Comparative Dynamics: Capital-Labour Ratio Constant

The equation (16) can form the basis of an analysis of the effects of trade in a two-sector economy under alternative assumptions about capital accumulation. In this section I assume that the capital-labour ratio is the same in trade as in autarky.

In the short run, the inputs K and L are in fixed supply. It is a standard proposition of the two-sector model of production that a rise in the relative price of one good induces an increase in its production. This is usually shown as a shift along the transformation curve. A formal proof uses (1)–(4) and the fact that input coefficients are chosen to minimise costs to establish the inequality

$$(p^1 - p^2)(Q_C^1 - Q_C^2) \geqslant 0, \tag{28}$$

which is the desired result, where 1 denotes the situation before and 2 the situation after the relative price change.

Let the world price of the consumption good be p^T and the autarky price be p^A. If initially $p^T > p^A$, so the country has a comparative advantage in the consumption good, then Q_C rises above Q_C^A and Q_I falls below Q_I^A. But if we wish the economy to remain in steady state with the same K/L ratio, (12) requires that I remains the same, so that $Q_I - I$ becomes negative and $Q_C - C$ positive, from (5). Hence (16) with $dK = 0$ shows that as p rises from p^A to p^T, if the economy invests just enough to remain in steady state, then consumption is increased by trade. This case is illustrated in figure 1.

The same is true, a fortiori, if the economy were to impose an optimum tariff. For, if π^0 and p^0 are the domestic and foreign prices when the optimum tariff is imposed, then if the country is a net exporter of consumption goods, it must be the case that $p^0 > \pi^0 > p^A$, as illustrated in figure 2. (26) implies that with K and L constant

$$\pi dC = dpE_C + (p - \pi)dE_C \qquad (29)$$

and in the movement from autarky to the optimum tariff equilibrium p rises, E_C rises, and $p - \pi$ becomes positive, so that the economy attains steady state with a permanently increased level of consumption.

The fact that these new equilibria, attainable immediately as a result of trade, are steady states and therefore sustainable into the future is a clear indication of the existence of gains from trade. Consumption at every point in time will be higher than on the autarky steady state path.

The alternative case in which $p^T < p^A$ can be analysed similarly. The comparative advantage in the investment good leads Q_C to fall below Q_C^A and Q_I to rise above Q_I^A. $Q_C - C$ becomes negative because $Q_I - I$ becomes positive. Again, equation (16) with $dK = 0$ shows that if the economy is to remain in steady state, consumption will rise; and, again, consumption rises also in the case of an optimum tariff being imposed. These two cases are shown in figures 3 and 4.

III. Comparative Dynamics: Saving Rate Constant

The effect of trade on steady state consumption if the saving rate is the same in trade as in autarky is easy to deduce from the results of the previous section. Again equation (16) is the key, though now it is used in a different way. What I do here is make more precise the argument sketched out in Smith (1976, section 7), and extend it to the case of a large economy. The first step is to compare the steady state analysed in the previous section with the steady state with the same saving rate as the autarky equilibrium.

In contrast with the previous section, the direction of comparative

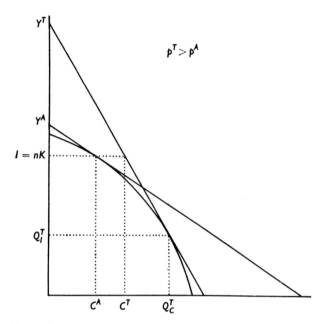

Figure 1

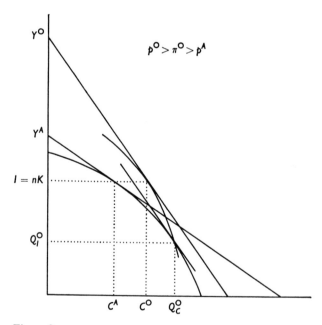

Figure 2

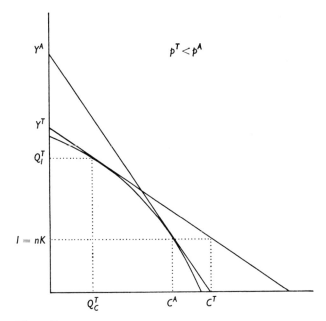

Figure 3

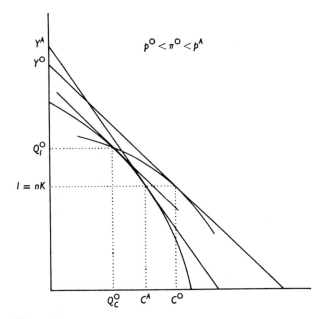

Figure 4

advantage is important. If $p^T > p^A$, then, in the obvious notation, for fixed K and L

$$Y^A = I^A + p^A C^A < I^A + p^T C^A < r^T K + w^T L = I^T + p^T C^T = Y^T,$$

(30)

where (30) follows from the same type of argument as establishes (28). The fact that $Y^A < Y^T$ means that if, as in section II, I were to be held constant, the saving rate would be reduced from $s = I^A/Y^A = nK^A/Y^A$ to $s' = nK^A/Y^T$. The free trade steady state with the same capital-labour ratio as the autarky steady state has a lower saving rate.

If, therefore, when trade opens up the saving rate is kept at s, capital will accumulate faster than the labour growth rate. The economy will move towards a steady state with a higher value of K/L than the steady state of section II.

When an optimum tariff is imposed, $(p^O - \pi^O)E_C$ is positive. If $\pi^O > p^A$, (17)–(19), and the type of argument used to establish (30) imply, in the obvious notation, that

$$Y^A < I^A + \pi^O C^A < r^O K + w^O L < r^O K + w^O L + (p^O - \pi^O)E_C = Y^O.$$

(31)

Now, equation (16) (or in the case of the optimum tariff, equation (27)) can be used to compare the open steady state with saving rate s' with the open steady state with saving rate s. Accumulation will raise consumption if r exceeds n, in a small economy or in a large economy imposing an optimum tariff. Consumption falls if r is less than n.

In a large open economy with free trade, there is a terms-of-trade effect that must be taken into account, and its sign will depend on which good is the more capital-intensive.

Conversely, if $p^T < p^A$, $Y^T < Y^A$ in the short run and there will be decumulation, which in a small country, equation (16) tells us, will lower or raise consumption as $(r - n)$ is positive or negative. In a large free trade economy, there is again a terms-of-trade effect to be taken additionally into account.

In a large economy imposing an optimum tariff for which $\pi^O < p^A$, Y^O may be larger or smaller than Y^A. The gain from the tariff may outweigh the effect on the value of income of the shift along the transformation curve. Then, (27) shows that dC/dK depends only on $(r - n)$, but we cannot tell whether K will rise or fall.

Figures 1–4 show the effect of trade on the value of income under the assumption about saving made in section II. The corresponding diagrams for the case of fixed saving rates would be slightly different but would show qualitatively similar changes in Y.

What I have done so far is to compare the steady state with the same saving rate as in autarky and the steady state with the same capital-labour ratio as in autarky. To compare the autarky steady state with saving rate s and the trade steady state with the same saving rate, we have to put the above argument together with the analysis of section II.

Before listing the results, one more observation must be made. The terms of trade effect may obviously outweigh the effect of capital accumulation or decumulation, especially if $(r - n)$ is close to zero. But it cannot outweigh the effect, analysed in section II, of the initial opening up of trade. This is because, as Deardorff (1974) has shown, if the autarky steady state is stable (a necessary condition for this type of comparative dynamics to be meaningful), then the direction of comparative advantage will not be reversed by capital accumulation or decumulation. Equation (16) implies that when we compare p^A and the *final* value of p^T the second term must be positive.

Thus we obtain the following results:

(i) In a small economy with initial comparative advantage in the consumption good, the initial gain in consumption represented by the possibility of immediately attaining steady state with saving rate s' is reinforced by the subsequent effects of capital accumulation if r exceeds n throughout the transition towards the asymptotic steady state.

(ii) In a small economy with initial comparative advantage in the investment good, the initial consumption gain may, if r exceeds n, be counteracted by the effects of capital decumulation.

(iii) In a large free trade economy, the effects of terms of trade changes may reinforce or counteract the effects of capital accumulation or decumulation, but, if the autarky steady state was stable, the total effect is as in (i) or (ii) above.

(iv) In a large open economy imposing an optimum tariff, with initial comparative advantage in the consumption good, the effects are as in (i) above.

(v) In a large open economy imposing an optimum tariff, with initial comparative advantage in the investment good, the initial consumption gain may be followed by either capital accumulation or decumulation, the effects of this depending on the sign of $(r - n)$.

These results extend somewhat the results of Johnson (1971), Vanek (1971), Deardorff (1973), Togan (1975), and Bertrand (1975).

IV Comparative Dynamics: Profit Rate Constant

I turn now to the final comparison: of trade and autarky steady states which have the same profit rate. One special feature of this case is that, because of the factor price equalisation theorem, complete specialisation is likely to occur, but the basic relations of the model, we have seen, continue to apply.

Suppose that when trade opens up the country has a comparative advantage in the more capital-intensive product. (I assume no factor intensity reversals.) We have seen that one short-run effect is to change the value of income, but there will also be a change in factor prices: the profit rate will rise and the wage rate fall. This is the Stolper-Samuelson theorem, which is easily confirmed from (7) and (8). To move from this steady state to a steady state with the lower, autarky, profit rate, a rise in the capital-labour ratio is required. If the country is small so that the world price is given, the Rybczynski theorem (which follows from (1) and (2)) implies that there will be increased production of the more capital-intensive good (and it is clear from (3) and (4) that there will be complete specialisation if the rest of the world has the same technology).

If the country is large and does not impose an optimum tariff, the eventual equilibrium price will be different from the initial world price, but the direction of comparative advantage must be the same and the above argument still holds.

The final effect on consumption levels is deduced by using (16) to compare the autarky steady state and the free trade steady state with the same profit rate. The second term in (16) must be positive: it encompasses the initial effect of the opening-up of trade and the terms of trade effect, if any. The first term has the sign of $(r - n)$.

The optimum tariff case is rather like the small-country case. From (29) we have seen that the opening-up of trade with the imposition of an optimum tariff raises the level of C. If the domestic price π^0 is such as to induce increased production of the capital-intensive product, then, as above, there will be capital accumulation and, from (27), its effect has the sign of $(r - n)$.

Thus, if the target profit rate satisfies $r \geqslant n$, both the free trade steady state and the optimum tariff steady state have higher consumption levels than the autarky steady state with the same profit rate. If $r < n$, the total effect on consumption is ambiguous.

A similar argument applies to the case where the country has its comparative advantage in the more labour-intensive product, but now trade leads to decumulation so that it is when $r \leqslant n$ that trade leads to increased steady state consumption, while if $r > n$, the total effect is of ambiguous sign.

In Smith (1976, section 6), I drew a distinction between the "static" and "intertemporal" effects of trade: the "static" effects being the effects associated with the price changes between autarky and trade, the "intertemporal" effects being the effects of changes in the capital stock. In the model presented here, this distinction is neatly illustrated in equation (16) where the first term is the "intertemporal" effect, the second is the "static" effect. This model also shows the possibility of an alternative dichotomy, between the short-run effect analysed in Section II and the capital accumulation effects analysed above.

V. Two Comments

(a) Since at several points in sections III and IV the possibility arises of trade reducing steady state consumption, even when $r \geqslant n$ and when trade policy is optimal, it should be emphasised that this is not to be taken as contradicting the usual gains from trade propositions. Section II has shown us that trade always implies a potential Pareto improvement in the sense that consumption at each point in time is increased. Sections III and IV show that, depending on the saving objective, actual consumption may be unequally distributed over time. It is easy to confirm that when $r \geqslant n$, trade can reduce steady state consumption only by boosting consumption in the short run. We have the usual result that trade benefits some and harms others: here the "some" are the early time periods of the open economy, the "others" are the later time periods.

(b) The basic model of section I is easy to generalise to more than two sectors, and the result of section II is also clearly a general result, but the comparative dynamics results of sections III and IV do not generalise. (In Smith (1976) I have shown how some fundamental aspects of this model carry over to input–output and vintage technologies, but how, similarly, only the simplest forms of such technologies give determinate comparative dynamic results.) The model is therefore to be taken as providing illustrative and, perhaps, instructive examples of how trade may affect the intertemporal allocation of consumption rather than precise predictions about the real world.

VI. Conclusions

A glance at sections III and IV will show the impossibility of giving a brief summary of results, and even there a complete list of possible cases is not given. The fact is that there is, in a way typical of trade theory, a range of different cases to be considered. My aim here has not been to attempt to present a simple and memorable taxonomy of results. It has been to present methods by which results can be obtained and thereby make the theory of trade and growth more accessible. There are several features of those methods worth recalling in conclusion.

(i) The equation (16) is a crucial relationship, allowing one to discuss the effects of price changes, both exogenous and endogenous, and of capital accumulation, under alternative saving assumptions.

(ii) The steady state which is immediately attainable on the opening up of trade is an important benchmark in the analysis.

(iii) Although the terms of trade effect of capital accumulation in large economies seems at first likely to complicate the analysis, it turns out that this effect is always dominated by the effects of the initial price change resulting from the opening up of trade, and also that the analysis is easily extended to the case of the imposition of an optimum tariff, in which case the terms of trade effect is eliminated.

I am grateful for helpful comments on an earlier version of this paper from John Black and John Martin.

References

Bertrand, T. J. (1975). "The Gains from Trade: an Analysis of Steady State Solutions in an Open Economy." *Quarterly Journal of Economics*, vol. 89 (4), pp. 556–68.

Caves, R. E. and Jones, R. W. (1973). *World Trade and Payments*. Boston: Little Brown and Company.

Deardorff, A. V. (1973). "The Gains from Trade in and out of Steady-state Growth." *Oxford Economic Papers*, N.S. vol. 25 (2), pp. 173–91.

Deardorff, A. V. (1974). "Trade Reversals and Growth Stability." *Journal of International Economics*, vol. 4 (1), pp. 83–90.

Johnson, H. G. (1971). "Trade and Growth: a Geometrical Exposition." *Journal of International Economics*, vol. 1 (1), pp. 83–102.

Jones, R. W. (1965). "The Structure of Simple General Equilibrium Models." *Journal of Political Economy*, vol. 73 (6), pp. 557–72.

Negishi, T. (1972). *General Equilibrium Theory and International Trade*. Amsterdam: North Holland.

Smith, M.A.M. (1976). "Trade, Growth and Consumption in Alternative Models of Capital Accumulation." *Journal of International Economics*, vol. 6 (4), pp. 371–84.

Togan, S. (1975). "The Gains from International Trade in the Context of a Growing Economy." *Journal of International Economics*, vol. 5 (3), pp. 229–38.

Vanek, J. (1971). "Economic Growth and International Trade in Pure Theory." *Quarterly Journal of Economics*, vol. 85 (3), pp. 377–90.

26

Foreign Exchange Constraints in Economic Development and Efficient Aid Allocation

Ronald I. McKinnon

Two recent works by authors actively participating in development programming, H. B. Chenery and M. Bruno (3) for Israel and A. Manne (9) for Mexico, suggest a dual role for the state of the foreign exchange balance as it affects economic growth. We have the classical view that foreign aid or investment only has the effect of supplementing domestic saving in the receiving country. On the other hand, we have the modern view stressed by (3) and (9) that many goods have strategic importance in efficient industrial growth but cannot be produced domestically in the early stages of industrial development, or after a war. Foreign aid or private investment can have a large favourable impact on the growth rate when such a bottle-neck constraint is binding, even though these transfers are a small fraction of available domestic saving. For example, Manne (9) found that optimal use of a relatively small increase ($75 million) in foreign exchange available to Mexican authorities would increase the annual growth of the industrial sector from 5.5 to 8.0 per cent, if one takes a literal and probably overly optimistic interpretation of his results. He found the constraint imposed by domestic saving not to be binding in this range.

The modern view involving bottlenecks is undoubtedly an extreme form of the idea of comparative advantage associated directly with the growth process. Export expansion and production for import substitution, as well as foreign aid, might be used to relieve such bottlenecks, but like savings rates, the possibilities for export themselves depend on the level

This paper was originally published in *The Economic Journal* 74 (1964): 388–409. Also published in Jagdish Bhagwati, editor, *International Trade: Selected Readings*, Penguin Books, 1969. The version published here omits a portion of section I and all of sections II–IV.

of economic development. Exports of the primary products of many underdeveloped countries are now very much tied down by worldwide marketing arrangements, so that additional quantities cannot be sold even if the seller were willing to accept very unfavourable terms of trade. Even producers of "primitive" industrial goods such as textiles face limited market outlets and administrative restrictions. However, exporters of the more advanced industrial goods face relatively few direct barriers to trade and favourable terms of trade so that countries like Japan have managed to grow out of the bottleneck difficulties that face less developed countries. In addition, the idea of a bottleneck is largely associated with very different levels of economic development among countries so that advanced countries can potentially send complex industrial capital goods to underdeveloped areas. The same conditions would not apply so strongly to Britain in the initial stages of her industrial development, as there were no other advanced countries on which she could draw. Natural resource endowments and the need for imported raw materials might also contribute· to bottleneck effects, apart from the problem of buying advanced capital equipment.

The purpose of this paper is to construct a growth model of the Harrod-Domar type which incorporates in a crude way the effects of international trade on the growth of newly developing countries, given the modern economic environment discussed above. In particular, the ideas of separate savings and bottleneck constraints are illustrated, and maximum potential exports and savings are made to depend on the level of income (capacity). The result is best viewed as a planning model reflecting the potentialities of a developing economy, since there are no behavioural equations to simulate actual behaviour. The model differs from that of H. G. Johnson (8, chapter 5) in that foreign capital goods directly affect the productive capacity of the economy and exports do not passively react to foreign demand conditions, but are directly related to domestic economic growth. In many ways the model can be viewed as a simpler general exposition of several ideas given by Chenery and Bruno for the case of Israel. Hopefully, the simpler methods of aggregation (possibly less useful for actual planning models) used here clarify and extend our understanding of how marginal and average propensities to save and to export affect development possibilities. In particular, a general framework is given for evaluating the "pay-off" in terms of economic growth of foreign transfers under different values of these savings and export parameters.

I. A Simple Model with Constant Average Propensities to Save, Import and Export

In order to show the impact of foreign trade on the aggregate productive capacity of the economy, it is necessary to specify that foreign goods enter as inputs into the domestic production function. In section 1 below a simple modification of the basic Harrod-Domar production function is used to show domestic needs for foreign capital goods. Following this, in section 2, additional provision is made for the current account use of materials (intermediate products) that must be imported. Throughout the paper, potential and actual domestic savings, total imports, and potential and actual exports are specified in various ways to depend on the level of income and capacity of the developing economy. From these relationships it is possible to derive the effects of foreign capital transfers on the growth rate.

Capital Goods Only Are Imported

Consider a simple fixed coefficient production function of the Leontief type:

$$P = \min (\alpha K_d, \beta K_f), \qquad \alpha > 0, \beta > 0. \tag{1.1}$$

P is the potential output capacity of the economy. K_d and K_f represent domestically produced and foreign-produced capital goods. Units for K_d and K_f are chosen so that one unit of output P can be used to construct one unit of K_d or buy at the current terms of trade—considered fixed—one unit of K_f.

Suppose there exists a fixed maximum average propensity to save out of income such that

$$\max S = sY, \qquad 0 < s < 1, \tag{1.2}$$

where Y is *domestically* generated income (returns to the domestic factors of production) resulting from the use of domestic output capacity P. Since we are not primarily concerned with the problems of a mature economy, we can assume (perhaps for planning purposes) that $Y = P$. The idea of a maximum saving rate reflects (a) the institutional problem of appropriating domestic savings for capital formation,[1] and (b) if other bottlenecks exist, maximum potential domestic savings will not be fully used.

The total amount of investment at any time, t, equals domestic savings S_t plus a foreign capital transfer F_t (if any), i.e. $I_t = S_t + F_t$. Investment expenditures will be distributed between foreign and domestic capital goods. Initially, we assume that foreign capital transfers are zero, but domestic production can be freely exported to obtain foreign capital goods. Thus, there are no constraints on growth other than domestic savings, i.e. $S_t = \max S_t$. From (1.1) and (1.2) we derive the Harrod-Domar equilibrium growth path. Domestic income has been assumed to accommodate itself to maximum capacity such that

$$\frac{dY}{dt} = \frac{dP}{dt}.$$

Now we know $\dfrac{dP}{dt}$, the change in output capacity, depends on the level of net investment. From (1.1) we have that one new unit of capacity, P, needs $\dfrac{1}{\alpha}$ units of K_d and $\dfrac{1}{\beta}$ units of K_f, requiring $\dfrac{1}{\alpha} + \dfrac{1}{\beta}$ units of domestic output for new investment. Thus

$$\frac{dP}{dt} = \frac{1}{\dfrac{1}{\alpha} + \dfrac{1}{\beta}} I = \frac{1}{\dfrac{1}{\alpha} + \dfrac{1}{\beta}} sY.$$

Let

$$\sigma = \frac{1}{\dfrac{1}{\alpha} + \dfrac{1}{\beta}},$$

where σ corresponds to the output-capital ratio in the original Harrod-Domar model.

Thus

$$\frac{dP}{dt} = \frac{dY}{dt} = \sigma s Y$$

and

$$Y_t = Y_0 \, e^{\sigma s t} \quad \text{or} \quad Pt = P_0 \, e^{\sigma s t}. \tag{1.3}$$

σs will be the growth rate, as in the original Domar model (4), if there are unlimited export possibilities to obtain foreign capital goods at the given terms of trade. If $\beta \to \infty$, then $\sigma \to \alpha$ and we get the original Domar production function, but this is not necessary to achieve the σs growth rate.

In the Introduction the hypothesis was put forward that export capabilities of developing countries were dependent upon the growth of output capacity which is associated with industrialization. Suppose

$$\max E = \varepsilon P, \qquad 0 < \varepsilon < 1, \tag{1.4}$$

where exports, E, are measured in the same units as P, K_d and K_f under the assumption of a rigid price system. If ε is too small so that exports are not sufficiently great to finance needed imports of foreign capital goods, then the growth rate σs will not be achievable and a bottleneck will exist. More precisely, if $I_{ft} = \dot{K}_{ft}$ is the level of investment in foreign capital goods a certain level of I_{ft} will be required to sustain a growth rate of σs. To avoid a bottleneck, I_{ft} must be less than max. E_t for a growth rate σs. From (1.2) and (1.3) we have

$$I_{ft} = \frac{1}{\beta}\, \dot{P}_t = \frac{\sigma s}{\beta} P_0\, e^{\sigma s t} = \frac{\sigma s}{\beta} P_t. \tag{1.5}$$

From (1.4) and (1.5), $I_{ft} < \max E_t$, requires

$$\beta\varepsilon > \sigma s, \text{ which implies } S_t = \max S_t \text{ and } E_t < \max E_t \tag{1.6}$$

to avoid a bottleneck. This result is in accord with our intuition, as a large β (small requirements for foreign capital goods) or a large ε (export capabilities) will cause (1.6) to hold.

Now suppose $\beta\varepsilon < \sigma s$ so that a bottleneck exists, i.e. $E_t = \max E_t$ and $S_t < \max S_t$, what will be the growth rate for output? Since $I_{ft} = \max E_t$, from (1.5) we have

$$I_{ft} = \frac{1}{\beta}\, \dot{P}_t = \varepsilon P.$$

Thus, solving the differential equation,

$$P_t = P_0\, e^{\beta \varepsilon t} \tag{1.7}$$

and the bottleneck growth rate is $\beta\varepsilon$, which, of course, is less than σs. Figure 1 can be used to visualize this result by looking at the effects of a foreign capital transfer (foreign aid or investment) on the growth rate. Let $f = F/Y$ be the foreign transfer as a fraction of national income and let ω be the growth rate. f would have the effect of increasing ε if the bottleneck exists, i.e. increasing purchases of foreign capital goods. f would have the effect of increasing s if the savings constraint exists, i.e. increasing the effective level of total investment in both domestic and foreign capital goods. More precisely, the rate of income growth is

$$\omega = \beta(\varepsilon + f) \text{ if } \beta(\varepsilon + f) < \sigma(s + f) \qquad \text{(bottleneck)} \tag{1.8}$$

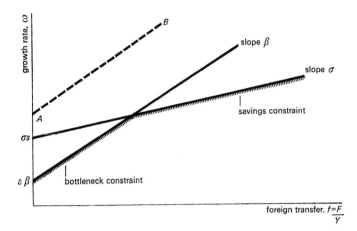

Figure 1. Effects of foreign transfer growth rate.

and

$$\omega = \sigma(s + f) \text{ if } \beta(\varepsilon + f) > \sigma(s + f) \qquad \text{(savings constraint).} \qquad (1.9)$$

We note that

$$\beta > \sigma = \frac{1}{\dfrac{1}{\alpha} + \dfrac{1}{\beta}} \qquad \text{for } \alpha > 0, \beta > 0.$$

Thus when the bottleneck constraint holds, foreign-aid transfers will always have a proportionately greater effect on the growth rate than if the savings constraint holds. This result is easily rationalized intuitively, as expenditures for foreign capital goods will form only a fraction of domestic capital formation. Thus foreign-aid transfers will always have a proportionately greater effect on the bottleneck constraint than on the savings constraint. The impact of foreign-aid transfers on growth rates will be very large under the bottleneck constraint if β is large, i.e. foreign capital-goods requirements are small. For these reasons, if $\varepsilon\beta > \sigma s$, i.e. the bottleneck constraint does not hold when $f = 0$, then the bottleneck constraint will never hold—see dotted line AB in figure 1. Only the savings constraint will be binding for any given foreign transfer in this case.

The author is indebted to Hollis Chenery for suggestions and ideas appearing in his own paper, "Foreign Assistance and Economic Development," presented to the Econometric Society, Boston, December 1963.

References

1. K. J. Arrow, H. B. Chenery, B. S. Minhas and R. M. Solow, "Capital-labor substitution and economic efficiency", *Review of Economics and Statistics*, vol. 63 (1961), pp. 225–50.

2. H. B. Chenery, "Comparative advantage and development policy", *American Economic Review*, vol. 51 (1961), pp. 18–51.

3. H. B. Chenery and M. Bruno, "Development alternatives in an open economy: the case of Israel", *Economic Journal*, vol. 57 (1962), pp. 79–103.

4. E. Domar, *Essays in the Theory of Economic Growth*, Oxford University Press, 1957.

5. R. F Findlay, "Capital theory and development planning", *Review of Economic Studies*, vol. 29 (1962).

6. M. Frankel, "The production function in allocation and growth: a synthesis", *American Economic Review*, vol. 52 (1962), pp. 995–1022.

7. R. Harrod, *Towards a Dynamic Economics*, Macmillan, 1948.

8. H. G. Johnson, *International Trade and Economic Growth*, Allen and Unwin, 1958.

9. A. Manne, "Key sectors of the Mexican economy, 1960–1970", A. Manne and H. M. Markowitz, eds., *Studies in Process Analysis*, monograph 18, Cowles Foundation for Research in Economics at Yale University, John Wiley, 1963.

10. R. Nurkse, *Patterns of Trade and Development*, Blackwell, 1961.

11. F. P. Ramsay, "A mathematical theory of saving", *Economic Journal*, vol. 38 (1928), pp. 543–59.

27
Three Alternative Concepts of Foreign Exchange Difficulties in Centrally Planned Economies

Padma Desai and
Jagdish N. Bhagwati

I Introduction

The recent entry of the Soviet economy into the world economy, in regard to trade, credit, and technology, has prompted much popular and some scientific discussion of the foreign exchange problems confronting the Soviet Union.[1] However, the analysts of these problems have deployed, and the generalist discussions have occasionally confused, what are quite distinct concepts of the foreign exchange problems.

It is necessary, therefore, to distinguish among three alternative concepts, which are in reality quite different from one another. These are (1) Foreign Exchange Bottleneck; (2) Open Payments Deficit; and (3) Suppressed Payments Deficit. These are considered in sections II–IV, respectively.

II Foreign Exchange Bottleneck

The concept of a foreign exchange bottleneck is a simple *ex ante* planning concept and has no intrinsic relationship (as we will shortly demonstrate) to the *ex post* payments deficit concepts. As developed in the planning literature, it essentially amounts to arguing that, given the objective function and domestic resources-cum-technology of the planners, their inability to transform available into demanded goods is the effective constraint on increasing the value of this objective function.

The classic statement of a foreign exchange bottleneck is in a simple corn-tractor model. The economy produces corn, saves and exports corn to import tractors which constitute investment and produce the corn. In this economy, let the current objective be to increase investment. This means buying more tractors from abroad. Now, if the finance minister

This paper was originally published in *Oxford Economic Papers*, November 1979.

cannot tax the economy into saving more corn, to purchase more tractors by exporting this corn, then the economy has a *savings* bottleneck. However, if the economy can be coaxed or taxed into more saving, but the economy faces a unitary price elasticity of demand in the world markets for its corn, foreign exchange receipts will not increase. Tractor imports and therefore investment will not increase; we then have a transformation or *foreign exchange* bottleneck.[2]

It will be evident to the reader that a necessary, though not sufficient condition for a foreign exchange bottleneck to exist is the absence of the economy's ability to transform goods into one another in world markets at the initial world prices. That is, a "small" country, which is atomistic in world markets, cannot have a foreign exchange bottleneck. (It follows equally that, compared to the free trade situation, such an economy will, for a more general class of objective functions (than merely maximizing the volume of investment), do *better* by *restricting* its trade, as is well known from the theory of optimal tariff in the presence of monopoly power in trade.)

In the Soviet context it can be argued that the foreign exchange bottleneck operates *not* with respect to growth of income, but rather with respect to a shift towards greater availability of consumer goods in total and in composition.

This argument of foreign resource inflow being a contraint on the growth and diversification of consumption .levels is best illustrated by reference to the classical and idealized demonstration of the foreign exchange bottleneck for developing countries in figure 1.

Assume there that the economy, at the relevant point of time, has a production possibility vector, $\bar{P}$, that is, resources cannot be transferred from one sector to another.[3] Let the two sectors be producing capital and consumer goods respectively *a la* the standard two-sector model. For the developing countries traditionally, the argument of the developmental planners during the 1950s and 1960s was that a foreign exchange bottleneck existed for raising investment (that is, availability of capital goods) and growth of income. For, starting from $\bar{P}$, the foreign offer curve facing them was $\bar{P}QR$ and if the developing countries could save more than $\bar{P}W$, say $\bar{P}N$, the incremental *ex ante* savings worth NW would not yield any incremental imports of capital goods and hence there would be no increase in *ex post* investment. NW worth of consumer goods, saved by the developing countries, would only accure to foreigners *via* terms of trade loss from $\bar{P}Q$ to $\bar{P}V$.[4]

The Soviet Union's present situation, on the other hand, may be

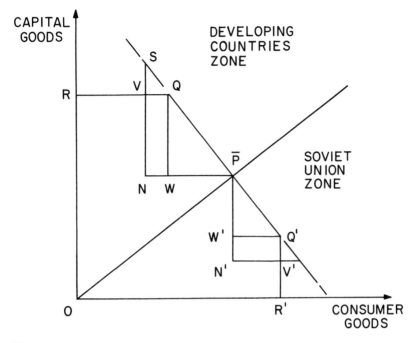

Figure 1

idealized in this illustration by turning the dilemma on its head. With its objective of shifting availabilities in favor of consumer goods, the foreign exchange constraint for the Soviet Union would seem to imply a willingness, but not the ability (beyond $\bar{P}W'$ of capital goods), to transform capital goods[5] into consumer goods through foreign exchange earnings with foreign offer curve $\bar{P}Q'R'$. The foreign exchange constraint of the Soviet Union, therefore, is indeed, as with developing countries, on shifting the availabilities between investment and consumption through trade. However, in the case of the developing countries, this is translated into a constraint on growth of income; in the case of the Soviet Union, it amounts rather to a constraint on the composition of the growing income.[6]

III Open Payments Deficit

In constrast to the *ex ante* planning concept of the foreign exchange bottleneck, the payments deficit concepts relate to the *ex post* macroeconomic situation.

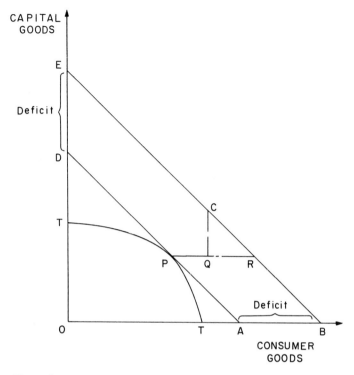

Figure 2

For "flow" current-account deficits, it is evident that an open payments deficit means that imports exceed exports *ex post*. Therefore we can amend the illustration in figure 1 to portray an open deficit simply as in figure 2. There, the production possibility curve is TT; production is at P; the world price line, identical with the domestic price line, is APD; the domestic expenditure line is BCE and the national income line is APD, so that the open deficit is AB (if measured in units of consumer goods) or equivalently DE (if measured in units of capital goods).[7] With the consumption vector chosen at C, the deficit is "absorbed" as PQ of consumer goods and CQ of capital goods.

Note two things. First, unlike the foreign exchange bottleneck concept which hinges critically on the assumption of monopoly power in trade, an open payments deficit can arise obviously regardless of whether the country is atomistic in world markets. Second, it is possible for such an open payments deficit to arise in several alternative ways. Holzman's (1978) interesting recent paper in fact argues that CPEs have a built-in tendency to get into payments difficulties because they systematically

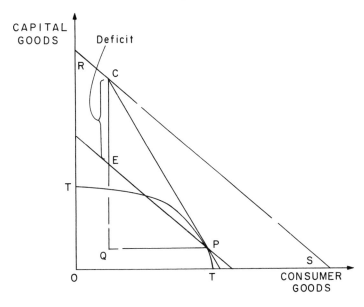

Figure 3a

either overestimate export earnings or overestimate production/income. Drawing on these two ideas, we will illustrate precisely some (but by no means all) of the ways in which CPEs may actually experience open payments deficits.

Demand-Determined Open Deficit
First, consider cases where the CPE overestimates export performance, not because of supply difficulties but because of unduly optimistic assessment of world demand for its exports, but sticks to its import targets instead of revising them downwards. The resulting (world-) demand-determined open deficit may be illustrated for two polar cases: (i) where the export quantity is forecast accurately but the price is overestimated; and (ii) where the export price is forecast accurately, but the quantity is overestimated.

In figure 3a, the first case is illustrated. The CPE plans *ex ante* for PQ exports in exchange for QC imports. However, the terms of trade turn out to be PE instead of PC. Thus the planned and actual exports PQ pay for only QE imports. With planned imports sticky at QC, the CPE then has to run an open payments deficit of CE. The effective social budget line then is RCS and exceeds the income line PE by the deficit.

Note that the "adjustment mechanism" postulated here allows for the

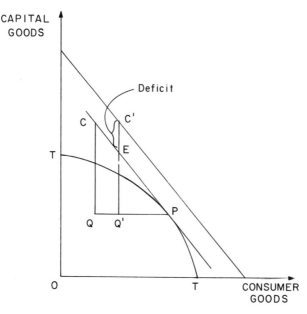

Figure 3b

disequilibrium resulting from the *ex post* deterioration in export prices relative to *ex ante* expectations to be eliminated by external borrowing or running down of reserves *and* without permitting reallocation of consumption and production decisions so as to maximize some objective function subject to the constraints constituted by domestic transformation and *ex post* foreign transformation possibilities and borrowing stipulated at CE.[8]

In figure 3b, we illustrate the other polar case where the quantity of exports is overestimated and falls short of PQ by QQ', whereas their price and hence the terms of trade are correctly anticipated as PEC. Exporting PQ' however will pay only for Q'E imports, thus leaving a payments deficit of C'E to pay for the planned and actual imports CQ = C'Q'.[9]

Supply-Determined Open Deficit

Consider next a situation where the failure in export performance comes from an overly optimistic assessment of production of exportables.

Then, assuming that the CPE is atomistic in world markets and can trade as much as it wants to, let P_e be the *expected* production vector and P_a the actual *ex post* production vector, so that $P_a P_e$ measures the shortfall in exportable production. $P_e Q$ and QS represent the planned exports and

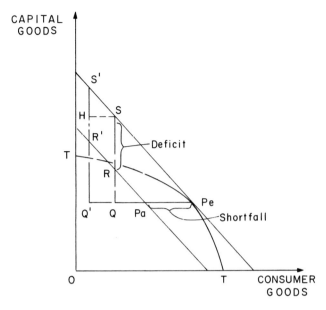

Figure 4

imports respectively. If expenditure is not revised downwards *a la* Holzman (1978), expenditure and income will diverge by SR, which will constitute the open deficit. However, depending on what the planners choose to export in face of the production shortfall, the import level (but not the deficit) will vary; and it can differ from the *ex ante* level QS. In figure 4, if the shortfall in exportable production leads the planners to a fully offsetting reduction in (total) exports from P_eQ to P_aQ, the CPE will wind up importing altogether SQ, the planned level of imports. On the other hand, if part of the shortfall in exportable production is accommodated through reduced *domestic* availability, exports will not be reduced as much. Thus, if they fall, not to P_aQ but to P_aQ', the payments deficit will remain the same (for it equals the postulated excess of expenditure over income) but the actual import level will rise to $Q'S'$ ($> QS$).

But we can tell an altogether different story, reflecting a different "adjustment mechanism". So far, we have argued with Holzman (1978) that the excess of expenditure over income is fixed by the assumption that anticipated expenditure is necessarily *ex post* expenditure while *ex post* income falls below anticipated income, and therefore that the trade decisions must accommodate to yield consistency with this. Rather, assume now that it is domestic expenditure that will adjust to accommodate the trade decisions.

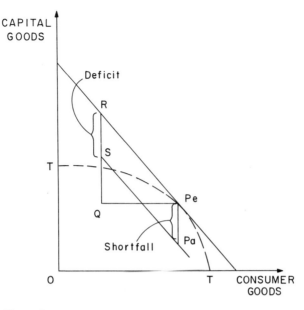

Figure 5

Thus, in figure 4, assume that the planners react to the shortfall in exportable production by reducing exports from $P_e Q$ to $P_a Q'$. The planned level of imports is sticky at SQ. Then R'H is clearly the level of imports that cannot be financed from export earnings. These imports then imply a corresponding, open payments deficit, a deficit in this instance that is smaller than under the Holzman (1978) assumptions: HR' < S'R' (= SR).

In conclusion, note that the supply-determined open payments deficit can equally arise from shortfall in importable production. Thus the planned exports QP_e, when effected, will yield in figure 5 the anticipated imports QR. But $P_e P_a$, the shortfall in importable production, implies a shortfall then in domestic availability of RS importables which may lead to an open payments deficit of identical magnitude to eliminate this shortfall.

IV Suppressed Payments Deficit

In contrast to the open payments deficit, no matter what precise circumstances cause and shape it, the suppressed payments deficit characterizes a situation where these same circumstances are not permitted to "spill over" into the balance of payments in the shape of an excess of imports over exports.

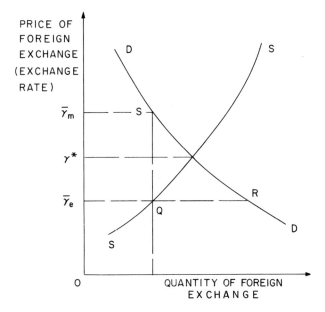

Figure 6

In the case of market economies, this distinction between open and suppressed payments deficits is quite important for analytical purposes. For, a suppressed deficit implies essentially that, instead of maintaining the balance between expenditure and income by a suitable mix of macroeconomic policies which preserves unified exchange rates, and similarly in contrast to the open deficit situation which also permits the preservation of unified exchange rates, the suppressed deficit situation typically implies differential, effective exchange rates on foreign transactions. This is seen in the traditional foreign-exchange-market diagram in figure 6. There, the exchange rate r* corresponds to an equilibrium, unified exchange rate that clears the market. The exchange rate $\bar{r}_e$ leads to an excess demand for foreign exchange that could be met by an open deficit, financed by borrowing or use of reserves, of amount QR; this situation also yields identical, unified exchange rates for export and import transactions (which underlie the supply and demand curves respectively). However, when the open deficit is suppressed, the exchange rate $\bar{r}_e$ generates supply of foreign exchange $\bar{r}_e Q$ which is cleared in the market at the "premium-inclusive" price, or effective exchange rate, $\bar{r}_m$; and therefore the effective exchange rates on exports ($\bar{r}_e$) and on imports ($\bar{r}_m$) are unequal in this suppressed-deficit situation.

The general-equilibrium "real" counterpart of these distinctions in the traditional two-sector model of trade theory is usually demonstrated as the free-trade solution for the equilibrium unified exchange rate, the free-trade-with-transfer (equal to the deficit) solution for the open deficit case, and a tariff (implying a higher effective exchange rate on imports than on exports) solution for the suppressed deficit case.

The "suppressed deficit" concept therefore permits us to examine explicitly the allocational implications of managing the balance of payments, not by adjusting the exchange rate (and therewith the domestic and foreign residents' transactions), but by pegging the exchange rate and using exchange controls to equate import payments to exchange earnings.

Thus, aside from the obvious fact that an open payments deficit and a suppressed deficit differ because the open deficit implies increased current availability of resources to the economy, the open deficit also is characterized by an adjustment mechanism that ensures, *ceteris paribus*, unified exchange rates whereas the suppressed deficit does not. For CPEs, however, the latter distinction is not particularly relevant in view of the general delinking of the foreign payments situation from domestic production and consumption decisions. Thus, for the case illustrated in figure 3a, the open deficit situation was not based on either steady-state optimality or even short-run optimality (given the production decision). The corresponding suppressed deficit situation again, if shown by winding up at E (implying that the imports take the entire adjustment burden), would not generally represent an optimal situation either. The distinction between open and suppressed deficits is therefore unlikely to be of the same significance for CPEs as it is regarded for the analysis of market economies: the welfare implications for resource allocation of these alternative situations are not as clear for the CPEs as they are for the market economies.[10,11]

Thanks are due to the National Science Foundation Grants No. SOC77–07254 and No. SOC77–07188 for financial support of the first and second authors, respectively, in writing this paper. Thanks are due to Franklyn Holzman and Peter Neary for extremely helpful comments on an earlier draft of this paper.

References

1. Bhagwati, Jagdish N. 1978. *The Anatomy and Consequences of Exchange Control Regimes*. Cambridge, Massachusetts: NBER, Ballinger and Co.

2. Bhagwati, Jagdish N. "The Nature of Balance of Payments Difficulties in Developing Countries." In *Measures for Trade Expansion of Developing Countries*, October 1966. Japan Economic Research Center, Center Paper No. 5.

3. Chenery, Hollis, and Michael Bruno. 1962. "Development Alternatives for an Open Economy: The Case of Israel," *Economic Journal*, volume 72.

4. Desai, Padma. 1978. "The Productivity of Foreign Resource Inflow to Soviet Economy," *Harvard Russian Research Center*, 1978. Paper presented at the *American Economic Association* Meetings, Chicago (1978). Also in *American Economic Review*, May 1979.

5. Findlay, Ronald. 1971. "The Foreign Exchange Gap and Growth in Developing Economies." In J. Bhagwati et al., editors, *Trade, Balance of Payments and Growth*. Amsterdam: North Holland Co.

6. Holzman, Franklyn, 1978, "Foreign Exchange Problems of Centrally Planned Economies," *American Review*, May 1979. Paper presented at the *AEA* Meetings, Chicago.

28

**Investment,
the Two-Sector Model,
and Trade in Debt and
Capital Goods**

Stanley Fischer and
Jacob A. Frenkel

Introduction

The two-sector model of economic growth has frequently been used to
analyse the growth process of an open economy. Two different sets of
assumptions have been made about the structure of trade. One specification allows for trade in both consumption and investment goods (e.g.
Oniki and Uzawa (1965) and Johnson (1971)). The alternative specification allows for the existence of international financial markets and
assumes that there is trade in consumption goods and securities, but not
in investment goods themselves (e.g. Frenkel and Fischer (1972) and
Fischer and Frenkel (1974a, 1974b)).

The main difficulty in modeling trade in both investment goods *and*
securities using a two-sector model of an economy for which the terms of
trade are fixed is that if a country can trade in both securities and investment goods, then it is a matter of indifference what its capital stock is. Its
income will be the same at all times—so long as it is not specialized—
whether it acquires income streams from abroad by buying securities or
whether it owns physical capital.

This paper presents a two-sector model of a small growing economy
that trades in both investment goods and securities as well as consumption goods. The key innovation is the specification of a demand function
for investment goods, based on an adjustment cost formulation in which
more rapid rates of investment reduce the rate of return to capital. The
introduction of the investment demand function not only allows for
simultaneous trade in investment goods and securities but also breaks

Reprinted with some condensation from the *Journal of International Economics*
2 (August 1972): 211–233. The present version includes a shorter introduction
and omits section 6 of the original article, which analyses the composition of the
trade account.

the familiar link between the stability of the model and relative factor intensities in production: the model introduced here is not unstable even if investment goods are more capital intensive in production than consumption goods.

The model is used to study the dynamics of capital accumulation and the various balance of payments accounts. Particular stress is laid on the interaction of foreign borrowing, debt service, and domestic capital accumulation.

The relationship we posit between the rate of investment and the production possibilities of the economy is introduced informally in section 1. In section 2 we discuss the production technology and derive the demand function for investment goods; the complete model is presented in section 3; the steady state of the system is considered in section 4; the dynamics of the capital stock and trade accounts are discussed in section 5, with concluding remarks in section 6.

1. Investment and the Transformation Frontier

The basic innovation of this paper is the positing of a relationship between the rate of investment at each instant and the position of the production possibility frontier at that instant. Since the nature of this relationship is not immediately obvious from our formulation of the production functions for the two sectors (in section 2), we provide an informal discussion of it in this section.

We distinguish between investment—the installation of capital goods —and the production of investment goods. Denote gross investment per capita by $(\dot{k} + nk)$, the production of investment goods by Q_1, and that of consumption goods by Q_c. Given the capital stock at any moment of time, and neoclassical production functions in each sector, we obtain a concave-to-the origin production possibility frontier (PPF), such as any of the frontiers shown in figure 1.

We assume that the position of the PPF in figure 1 depends on the rate of gross investment per capita in the economy. In particular, let $T_0 T_0$ be the frontier, at a given level of the capital stock, at which there is zero gross investment. At any higher level of investment, the PPF will lie inside $T_0 T_0$, and the more rapid is investment, the closer to the origin is the PPF assumed to be. The basic notion these shifts reflect is that the process of investment disturbs the regular production processes.[1]

Our formulation is, however, specific: the PPF map, as a function of the rate of investment, is assumed to be homothetic. That is, as between any rates of investment, corresponding to, say, $T_0 T_0$ and $T_1 T_1$, the ratio

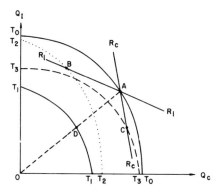

Figure 1

of the distance of the two frontiers from the origin along every ray through the origin, is assumed to be the same. For obvious reasons, we call this "Hicks neutral adjustment costs." [2]

2. The Rate of Return on Capital and the Demand for Investment Goods

The production functions in the two sectors are

$$Q_c = \alpha F_c(K_c, L_c),$$ (1)

$$Q_1 = \alpha F_1(K_1, L_1),$$ (2)

where K_i and L_i are the inputs of capital and labor in each sector, and α is an efficiency factor, which determines the shrinking of the PPF. The production function is linearly homogeneous in its arguments, with diminishing marginal returns to each factor. The same production functions, with $\alpha = 1$, exist in the rest of the world, although in fact nothing substantive in the paper depends on having the same production functions.

In per capita terms,

$$q_c = \alpha \frac{k - k_1}{k_c - k_1} f_c(k_c),$$ (3)

$$q_1 = \alpha \frac{k_c - k}{k_c - k_1} f_1(k_1),$$ (4)

where $q_i \equiv Q_i/L$, $k_i \equiv K_i/L_i$, $k \equiv K/L$ and $f_i \equiv F_i/L_i$. The small country assumption implies that p_k, the relative price of capital goods, is given to this economy, as is i, the world interest rate. This interest rate is taken to be the return on equities issued abroad, and is equal to the world rental rate on capital, $r(p_k)$, divided by p_k. The rental rate on capital is determined by the world production technology, which is given by (3) and (4) with $\alpha = 1$.

We consider now the rate of return on capital in the domestic economy, ρ, as a function of α, the efficiency factor, and k, the per capita capital stock, leaving aside for the moment the consequences of any differences between the domestic and world rates of return. The relationship between ρ, α, and k depends on whether the economy is producing both goods or whether it is specialized in the production of only one of the goods. In the nonspecialized region, we shall compare a situation where α is greater than unity (in the domestic economy) with a situation where α is equal to unity (in the world economy). The higher is α, the greater the *effective* amounts of capital and labor in the economy though the overall capital—labor ratio is unaffected by changes in α. Thus capital—labor ratios in each industry will be the same as they are in the world economy, and factor payments per *effective* unit of capital and labor will be the same as they are in the world economy. However, the rental rate per *physical* unit of capital and the wage rate per *physical* unit of labor will be higher in the domestic than in the world economy. Accordingly, the rental rate per physical unit of capital will be higher the greater is α. The return to be obtained by investing domestically one unit of capital, costing p_k in the world market, will be an increasing function of α and will exceed i, the world interest rate, so long as α exceeds unity.

Thus ρ is an increasing function of α in the nonspecialized region; it is also clear that ρ does not depend on k, so long as the economy is not specialized, since the economy is free to adjust the scale of operation of the two sectors by moving along a Rybczynski line.

The relationship between ρ, α and k is slightly different in regions of specialization. Suppose that only the investment good is being produced. Then the per capita output of the investment good is

$$q_1 = \alpha f_1(k) \tag{5}$$

with the rate of return on physical capital

$$\frac{\partial q_1}{\partial k} = \alpha f_1'(k). \tag{6}$$

By differentiating (6) with respect to α and k we obtain the effects of changes in these variables on the rate of return:

$$\frac{\partial^2 q_1}{\partial k \partial \alpha} = f_1'(k) > 0, \tag{7}$$

$$\frac{\partial^2 q_1}{\partial k^2} = \alpha f''_1(k) < 0. \tag{8}$$

Thus increases in the efficiency factor increase the rate of return on physical capital while increases in the capital stock reduce the return. Similar relationships hold where only the consumption good is produced.

Summarizing the above discussion, we have the domestic rate of return on physical capital, ρ, as a function of α and k:

$$\rho = \rho(\alpha, k) \quad \rho_1 > 0 \quad \rho_2 = 0 \quad \underline{k} \leqslant k \leqslant \bar{k},$$

$$\rho_1 > 0 \quad \rho_2 < 0 \quad \text{otherwise,} \tag{9}$$

where ρ_i is the partial derivative of $\rho(\ )$ with respect to its ith argument and $\underline{k}$ and $\bar{k}$ are the lower and upper specialization points respectively.

Further, in the nonspecialized region, when $\alpha = 1$ and accordingly the efficiency of domestic and foreign factors is the same, equation (10) must be satisfied:

$$\rho(1, k) = i, \quad \underline{k} \leqslant k \leqslant \bar{k}. \tag{10}$$

As discussed in section 1 above, the efficiency factor, α, is assumed to be a decreasing function of the per capita rate of gross investment

$$\alpha = \alpha(\dot{k} + nk), \quad \alpha' < 0. \tag{11}$$

We assume further that there are positive values of per capita investment at which α exceeds unity.

The demand for investment goods is now readily derived. So long as the domestic rate of return on capital exceeds the world interest rate, i, there will be an incentive to borrow to finance purchase and installation of investment goods. At each instant, investment will be desired at that rate which makes the domestic return on capital equal to the world return. In the nonspecialized region this will be achieved when α is unity (from (10)). In general, we have

$$\rho(\alpha(\dot{k} + nk), k) = i \tag{12}$$

so that the demand for gross investment per capita—which, given access to the world securities market, is assumed always to be satisfied—is

$$\dot{k} + nk = \phi(k, i); \quad \phi_1 = 0 \quad \phi_2 < 0 \quad \underline{k} \leqslant k \leqslant \bar{k}, \tag{13}$$

$$\phi_1 < 0 \quad \phi_2 < 0 \quad \text{otherwise,}$$

where ϕ_i is the partial derivative of $\phi(\ )$ with respect to its ith argument.

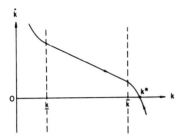

Figure 2

From the gross investment demand function we obtain the equation describing the behavior of the capital stock through time:

$$\dot{k} = \phi(k, i) - nk. \tag{14}$$

This function is illustrated in figure 2. Within the nonspecialized region, α is constant at unity and the locus relating $\dot{k}$ to k is linear with a slope of $(-n)$. Outside this region the locus is steeper as diminishing returns on capital force continuous increases in α, the efficiency factor, to maintain the rate of return on capital constant. We have indicated k^*, the steady state capital stock, as being in the region $k > \bar{k}$ purely for expositional reasons—there is no reason why k^* should not lie in either of the other regions.

Notice that the differential equation for $\dot{k}$, (14), is qualitatively a special case of the differential equation for $\dot{k}$ in the closed two-sector model with consumption goods more capital intensive (or the open two-sector model with no trade in capital goods and the usual factor intensity assumption)— but the link between investment and the output of investment goods has been broken. In particular, the derivative $\partial \dot{k}/\partial k$, so crucial to stability, does not depend on the factor intensity assumption.

3. The Model

We now set out the supply and demand functions and the balance of payments accounts for this economy. The production and supply relations depend on the capital stock, on α, and on the (fixed) relative price of capital.

Given that α is unity in the nonspecialized region, the per capita supply functions in that region can be written as they are in the standard two-sector model:

$$q_c = q_c(k, p_k), \ (k_c - k_1)\frac{\partial q_c}{\partial k} > 0, \quad \frac{\partial q_c}{\partial p_k} < 0 \Bigg\} \tag{15}$$

$$\underline{k} \leqslant k \leqslant \bar{k}.$$

$$q_1 = q_1(k, p_k), \ (k_c - k_1)\frac{\partial q_1}{\partial k} < 0, \quad \frac{\partial q_1}{\partial p_k} > 0 \Bigg\rfloor \tag{16}$$

The effects of increases in the capital stock on the outputs of the two sectors depend on the factor intensities (the Rybczynski theorem).

In the specialized regions, the supply functions are

$$q_c = \alpha f_c(k) if (k_c - k_1)(k - \bar{k}) > 0, \tag{17}$$
$$= 0 \qquad if (k_c - k_1)(k - \bar{k}) < 0,$$

$$q_1 = \alpha f_1(k) if (k_1 - k_c)(k - \bar{k}) > 0, \tag{18}$$
$$= 0 \qquad if (k_1 - k_c)(k - \bar{k}) < 0,$$

subject to

$$\frac{\partial q_c}{\partial k} = \alpha f'_c(k) = r \quad \text{if } q_c > 0 \text{ and } q_1 = 0, \tag{19}$$

$$\frac{\partial q_1}{\partial k} = \alpha f'_1(k) = i \quad \text{if } q_1 > 0 \text{ and } q_c = 0, \tag{20}$$

so that

$$q_c = \frac{p_k i}{f'_c(k)} f_c(k) \quad \text{if } q_c > 0 \text{ and } q_1 = 0, \tag{21}$$

$$q_1 = \frac{i}{f'_1(k)} f_1(k) \quad \text{if } q_1 > 0 \text{ and } q_c = 0. \tag{22}$$

The expressions on the right-hand side of (17) and (18) indicate that when the overall capital labor ratio is below $\underline{k}$, the entire capital stock is employed in whichever sector has the lower capital intensity, and similarly when $k > \bar{k}$, the capital stock is employed in the industry with the greater capital intensity. Equations (19) and (20) provide a relationship between α and k which must be satisfied if there is specialization—it is the requirement that the domestic rate of return on capital be the same as the world return—and substitution into (17) and (18) gives the "reduced form" production functions (21)-(22) in the specialized regions.

Our basic production and supply relations are thus (15) and (16) in the nonspecialized region and (21) and (22) in the specialized regions.[3]

The wage is the residual of output per capita after payments to capital.

It is clear from (21) and (22) that as capital increases over time and α is appropriately adjusted through investment behavior, the output of the good produced increases. In addition, the wage rate in the specialized region, which is

$$v = p_j\alpha[f_j(k) - kf'_j(k)], \quad j = I, c, \tag{23}$$
$$p_I = p_k, p_c = 1,$$

is an increasing function of k. Thus outside the nonspecialized region, in which the wage rate is constant at the world rate, the real wage increases with the capital stock.

On the demand side we assume, for convenience, a constant savings ratio:

$$c^d = (1 - s)y, \tag{24}$$

where y is per capita income. Investment demand is given by (13), repeated here:

$$(\dot{k} + nk)^d = \phi(k, i). \tag{13}$$

Income in turn consists of payments to factors located in the economy, plus interest payments (in terms of the consumption good) on net ownership of foreign securities, iz:

$$y = rk + v(k) + iz, \tag{25}$$

where r is the rental rate on capital and v is the wage rate.

Savings is equal to the value of the accumulation of assets per capita, so that

$$sy = p_k(\dot{k} + nk)^d + (\dot{z} + nz)^d, \tag{26}$$

where $\dot{z} + nz = \dot{Z}/L$ is the rate of accumulation of foreign securities, per capita. It is assumed that all demands are satisfied at each instant. The trade balance surplus per capita, b_T, is given by

$$b_T = q_c - c^d + p_k(q_1 - (\dot{k} + nk)) \tag{27}$$
$$= q_c + p_k q_1 - (c + p_k(\dot{k} + nk)).$$

It is the difference between the value of domestic output and the value of domestic demand for commodities (consumption plus investment).

The service account surplus, b_s, is earnings on net holdings of foreign securities:

$$b_s = iz. \tag{28}$$

The capital account deficit, b_c, must be equal to the surplus in the current account, and is accordingly

$$b_c = b_T + b_s$$
$$= q_c + p_k q_1 + iz - (c + p_k(\dot{k} + nk))$$
$$= sy - p_k(\dot{k} + nk),$$

so, using (26),

$$b_c = \dot{z} + nz. \tag{29}$$

That is, the capital account deficit is the difference between saving and investment, and is equal to net imports of foreign securities

4. The Steady State

In the steady state the capital stock is constant at a level k^*, determined by investment behavior (equation (14)). Corresponding to that level of the capital stock is the steady state wage rate. If the steady state capital stock is within the nonspecialized region, the wage rate will be the same as the world wage rate. Outside the nonspecialized region the steady state wage rate is given by (23).

In the steady state, savings is just sufficient to maintain the stock of nonhuman assets per capita constant. Thus, from (26),

$$s[rk^* + v(k^*) + iz^*] = n[p_k k^* + z^*],$$

$$p_k k^* + z^* = \frac{sv(k^*)}{n - is}. \tag{30}$$

Thus a necessary and sufficient condition for steady state wealth and income to be positive is that $n - is > 0$.

The steady state level of net holdings of foreign securities, in turn, is

$$z^* = \frac{sv(k^*)}{n - is} - p_k k^*$$

or

$$z^* = \frac{s[v(k^*) + rk^*] - np_k k^*}{n - is}. \tag{31}$$

Thus, if savings out of steady state *output* exceed steady state investment, net holdings of foreign securities will be positive, and conversely.

In the steady state the capital account deficit is nz^* and the service account surplus is iz^*. The trade account surplus is, therefore, $(n - i)z^*$.

Accordingly, whether the capital account will be in deficit or surplus (and the service account correspondingly in surplus or deficit) in the steady state depends solely on whether savings out of steady state *output* exceed or fall short of steady state investment. If, in the steady state, the savings out of domestic output exceed domestic investment, the country will be a net creditor with a capital account deficit and service account surplus. If the country is a creditor, then the steady state of the trade account depends on the relationship between i and n; if, as we assume henceforth, $i > n$, a creditor country will have a deficit on trade account.

5. Dynamics of the Capital Stock and International Accounts

Figure 3 is the basic diagram used in analysing the behavior of the trade account, the service account, the capital account, and the balance of indebtness through time. In figure 3 we show the loci in (z, k) space along which the various accounts balance.

5.1. The Net Creditor Position
From equations (13), (25), and (26) we derive equation (32) for the change in per capita holdings of foreign securities:

$$\dot{z} = s(rk + v) - p_k\phi(k, i) - (n - is)z. \tag{32}$$

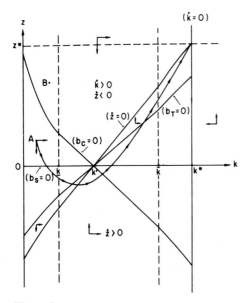

Figure 3

The rate of change of holdings of securities, per capita, $(\dot{Z}/L)$ is equal to savings minus investment; (32) follows by recognizing that $(\dot{Z}/L = \dot{z} + nz)$. Since, given p_k and i, $\dot{z}$ is a function only of z and k we can draw the locus on which $(\dot{z} = 0)$—per capita holdings of foreign securities are constant—in figure 3. The slope of that locus is

$$\frac{dz}{dk}\bigg|_{\dot{z}\,=\,0} = -\frac{\partial \dot{z}/\partial k}{\partial \dot{z}/\partial z} = \frac{s(r + (dv/dk)) - p_k(\partial\phi/\partial k)}{n - is} > 0. \tag{33}$$

This slope is positive, since dv/dk and $(-\partial\phi/\partial k)$ are both nonnegative, while the existence of a steady state implies $n - is > 0$.

Note that in the nonspecialized region both dv/dk and $\partial\phi/\partial k$ are zero and thus, the $(\dot{z} = 0)$ locus is linear with a slope of $sr/(n - is)$. From (32) it is seen that the intersection of the $(\dot{z} = 0)$ locus with the k axis occurs at that k—call it k'—for which $s(rk' + v) = p_k\phi(k', i)$. At any point above the $(\dot{z} = 0)$ locus, $\dot{z} < 0$ and below the $(\dot{z} = 0)$ locus, $\dot{z} > 0$. Note that k' is not necessarily in the nonspecialized region.

5.2. The Trade Account

The trade account is balanced when the value of output $(rk + v)$ equals the sum of consumption demand $((1 - s)y)$ and investment demand $(p_k\phi)$. Thus (using (25)) the condition for a balanced trade account is

$$(1 - s)iz = s(rk + v) - p_k\phi(k, i). \tag{34}$$

Accordingly, the slope of the $(b_T = 0)$ locus—the locus on which the trade account is balanced—is

$$\frac{dz}{dk}\bigg|_{b_T\,=\,0} = \frac{s(r + (dv/dk)) - p_k(\partial\phi/\partial k)}{(1 - s)i} > 0. \tag{35}$$

By considerations similar to those involved in the discussion of the $(\dot{z} = 0)$ locus, the $(b_T = 0)$ locus is linear in the nonspecialized region with a slope of $sr/(1 - s)i > 0$. Under the assumption that $i > n$, the $(b_T = 0)$ locus is flatter than the $(\dot{z} = 0)$ locus. Note also that its intersection with the k axis occurs at the same value of k $(k = k')$ for which the $(\dot{z} = 0)$ locus intersects the k axis. Since in the specialized regions dv/dk and $(-(\partial\phi/\partial k))$ are positive, both the $(\dot{z} = 0)$ and $(b_T = 0)$ loci are steeper in those regions than they are in the nonspecialized region.

At any point above the trade balance locus $(b_T = 0)$ income is higher than it is on the locus and consumption demand is increased, causing a trade balance deficit. Thus above the $(b_T = 0)$ locus $b_T < 0$, and below that locus $b_T > 0$.

While the path of the balance of trade does not depend on the relative factor intensities in production, the *composition* of the trade account as between consumption and investment goods does depend on the relative factor intensities. [For details see Fischer and Frenkel (1972, section 6)].

5.3. The Capital Account

The deficit in the capital account is the excess of savings over investment. The capital account accordingly balances when

$$s(rk + v + iz) - p_k\phi(k, i) = 0. \tag{36}$$

We can now show the locus on which there is balance in the capital account in figure 3. It has the slope

$$\frac{dz}{dk}\bigg|_{b_c = 0} = -\frac{s(r + (dv/dk)) - p_k(\partial\phi/\partial k)}{is} < 0. \tag{37}$$

This locus has a negative slope because increases in the capital stock tend to increase the excess of savings over investment; decreases in z are required to reduce savings to maintain balance in the capital account when k rises.

In the nonspecialized region the ($b_c = 0$) locus is linear with a slope of $-r/i = -p_k$; its slope is steeper in the specialized regions. Its intersection with the k axis also occurs at the point k'. For any point above the ($b_c = 0$) locus, savings exceed investment and there is a capital account deficit, while below the locus, $b_c < 0$.

5.4. The Service Account

The surplus in the service account is simply iz, and thus the ($b_s = 0$) locus is the k axis along which $z = 0$. Obviously there is a service account surplus above the k axis and a deficit below it.

5.5. The Accumulation of Capital

We have already discussed the $\dot{k}$ equation (14). There is a unique value of k, k^*, at which the per capita capital stock is stationary. In terms of figure 3, k^* may be anywhere on the k axis—in particular it could be either less than or greater than k'. If k^* exceeds k'—which is the case we study—the country will be a net creditor in the steady state.

Since, from (14) and (32), $\partial\dot{k}/\partial k < 0$ and $\partial\dot{z}/\partial z < 0$, (and also $\partial\dot{k}/\partial z = 0$) the system is stable in k and z. Hence, the directions of the arrows in figure 3.

Consider now a time path for the economy starting from initial con-

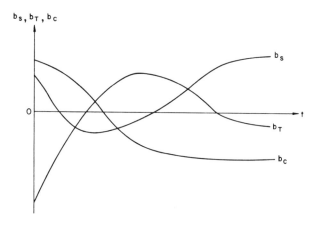

Figure 4

ditions A. At point A, the economy is a net creditor, the trade account is in deficit, and the capital and service accounts are in surplus. Savings fall short of investment so that the economy exports securities, reaching a point where its net creditor position is zero. At that point of time, the service account is balanced and the surplus in the capital account equals the deficit in the trade account. As the process continues, the economy becomes a net debtor. The cumulative debt increases and the deficit in the trade account decreases monotonically. When the trade account balances, the deficit in the service account equals the surplus in the capital account and the country's net debtor position continues to rise until it reaches its maximum—the point in time at which $\dot{z} = 0$—and the deficit in the service account also reaches a maximum.[4] From then onward the capital account surplus decreases and eventually (in the case shown) becomes a deficit. Similarly, the service account eventually switches back to, and remains in, surplus.

In the path starting at A the trade account is shown switching only twice, and the economy reaches a steady state with a trade account deficit. In general, although the trade account cannot switch more than twice in the nonspecialized region, it may switch from surplus to deficit and vice versa several times in the specialized regions, unless there are restrictions on the production functions and the $\alpha(\quad)$ function.[5] For example, given Cobb-Douglas production functions and $\alpha'' \geq 0$ (see equation (11)) there can in fact be no more than two switches, as in path A. Figure 4 describes the time path of the various accounts as implied by path A of figure 3.

6. Concluding Remarks

The purpose of the present paper has been to construct a simple model of a small open two-sector economy which includes, on the one hand, trade in both consumption and investment goods, and, on the other, trade in securities. Models including trade in both consumption and investment goods but not in securities exist (see, for example, Oniki and Uzawa (1965) and Johnson (1971)), as do models with trade in consumption goods and securities, (see Frenkel (1971), Frenkel and Fischer (1972) and Fischer and Frenkel (1974a) (1974b)).

The basic difficulty in constructing a model with trade in both types of goods and securities arises from the indeterminacy of the rate of investment, and consequently the capital stock, in the usual two-sector small country model when there is access to a world securities market. The model becomes determinate once a demand for investment goods is introduced. This demand is derived, in the present paper, from considerations of the effects of the rate of investment on the efficiency of production.

Given our formulation of the investment demand function, the stability of the model and the time pattern of the major international accounts do not depend on factor intensities. The time pattern of the major accounts depends on saving and the demand for investment and not on details of the technology; under reasonable specifications of the behavioral functions, these accounts behave in a manner consistent with the well-known stages-of-development hypothesis (e.g., Kindleberger (1968), p. 484). The only economic variable in the small economy which depends crucially on factor intensities is the composition of the trade account. Our formulation also permits an analysis of the behavior of the economy in specialized regions which is symmetric with the analysis for the nonspecialized region.

In principle, the demand for investment goods could be derived from portfolio considerations without appealing to technological factors such as adjustment costs. In the absence of uncertainty, however, appeals to xenophobia or national pride are necessary to generate determinate portfolio demand functions in a model as simple as the two-sector small country model (see Bardhan (1967)).

The model developed can, of course, be used to investigate the effects of various policy measures on the steady state values of endogenous variables and on their time paths. Such policy measures would include taxes and/or subsidies on production, on consumption, on factor markets, on trade in goods, or on trade in securities.

Finally, the analysis is confined to a barter economy. It could be extended to a monetary economy by adding portfolio relationships determining the demands for money and other assets; part of the flow of savings manifests itself as a flow demand for money while the behavior of the monetary authority determines the flow supply. The essentials of the analysis are, however, unaffected.

We are indebted to Harry G. Johnson for providing much of the stimulus for this paper and for his subsequent comments. Thanks are also due to Rudiger Dornbusch and other members of the International Economics Workshop at the University of Chicago.

References

Bardhan, Pranab K. (1967) "Optimum Foreign Borrowing." in K. Shell, editor, *Essays on the Theory of Optimal Growth*, pp. 117–128. Cambridge, Mass.: MIT Press.

Fischer, Stanley, and Frenkel, Jacob A. (1972) "Investment, the Two-Sector Model and Trade in Debt and Capital Goods." *Journal of International Economics* 2 (August 1972): 211–233.

Fischer, Stanley, and Frenkel, Jacob A. (1974a) "Economic Growth and Stages of the Balance of Payments: A Theoretical Model." in G; Horwich and P. A. Samuelson, editors, *Trade Stability and Macroeconomics: Essays in Honor of Lloyd A. Metzler*, pp. 503–521. New York: Academic Press.

Fischer, Stanley, and Frenkel, Jacob A. (1974b) "Interest Rate Equalization, Patterns of Production, Trade and Consumption in a Two-Country Growth Model." *Economic Record* 50 (December 1974b): 555–580; and "Errata." *Economic Record* 51 (September 1975).

Frenkel, Jacob A. (1971) "A Theory of Money, Trade and the Balance of Payments in a Model of Accumulation." *Journal of International Economics* 1, 2, pp. 159–187.

Frenkel, Jacob A., and Fischer, Stanley. (1972) "International Capital Movements along Balanced Growth Paths: Comments and Extensions." *Economic Record* 48 (June 1972): 266–271.

Johnson, Harry G. (1971) "Trade and Growth: A Geometrical Exposition." *Journal of International Economics* 1, 1, pp. 83–101.

Kindelberger, Charles P., (1968) *International Economics*, 4th ed. Homewood, Ill.: Irwin.

Oniki, H., and Uzawa, H. (1965) "Patterns of Trade and Investment in a Dynamic Model of International Trade." *Review of Economic Studies* XXXII(1), 89, pp. 15–38.

Notes

Chapter 1

1. "International Trade and the Equalisation of Factor Prices," *Economic Journal*, vol. LVIII, June, 1948, pp. 163–184. I learn from Professor Lionel Robbins that A. P. Lerner, while a student at L.S.E., dealt with this problem. I have had a chance to look over Lerner's mimeographed report, dated December 1933, and it is a masterly, definitive treatment of the question, difficulties and all.

2. Actually we may admit the limiting case of "incipient specialisation," where nothing is being produced of one of the commodities, but where it is a matter of indifference whether an infinitesimal amount is or is not being produced, so that price and marginal costs are equal.

3. I am indebted for this line of reasoning to my colleague at M.I.T., Professor Robert L. Bishop, who for some years has been using it on beginning students in economics, with no noticeable disastrous effects. This proof is suggestive only, but it could easily be made rigorous.

4. Some readers may find it paradoxical that—with a fixed ratio of total labour to total land—we nevertheless lower the ratio of labour to land *in both industries* as a result of producing more of the labour-intensive good and less of the other. Such readers find it hard to believe that men's wages and women's wages can both go up at the same time that average wages are going down. They forget that there is an inevitable shift in the industries' weights used to compute the average-factor ratio. Really to understand all this the reader must be referred to the Edgeworth box-diagram depicted in W. F. Stolper and P. A. Samuelson, "Protection and Real Wages," *Review of Economic Studies*, vol. IX (1941), pp. 58–73.

5. The representative firm concept is in the case of homogeneous production functions not subject to the usual difficulties associated with the Marshallian concept; in this case, it should be added, the "scale" of the firm is indeterminate and, fortunately, irrelevant.

6. The left-hand curve is drawn in a qualitatively correct fashion. Actually its exact quantitative shape is determined by the two right-hand curves; but the chart is *not* exact in its quantitative details.

We may easily illustrate the importance of point (5) of our hypothesis, which insists on differences in factor intensities. Consider the depicted pathological

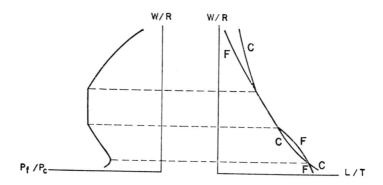

case which does not meet the requirements of our hypothesis, and in which factor intensities are for a range identical, and in still other regions food becomes the labour-intensive good. The resulting pattern of commodity prices does *not* necessarily result in factor-price equalisation. Compare p. 175, n. 1 of my earlier article.

7. J. B. Clark recognised in his *Distribution of Wealth* that the "upper triangle" of his labour-marginal-productivity diagram must correspond to the "rectangle" of his other-factors diagram. But his draughtsman did *not* draw the curve accordingly! This is a mistake that Philip Wicksteed in his *Co-ordination of the Laws of Distribution* (London School of Economics Reprint) could not have made. Clark, a believer in Providence, was unaware of the blessing—in the form of Euler's theorem on homogeneous functions—that made his theory possible. Wicksteed, a man of the cloth, appreciated and interpreted the generosity of Nature. Compare also F. H. Knight, *Risk, Uncertainty and Profit*, ch. IV, for a partial treatment of these reciprocal relations. G. J. Stigler, *Production and Distribution Theories: the Formative Period*, gives a valuable treatment of Wicksteed's theory as exposited by Flux and others.

8. In terms of our earlier $a, b, \ldots, \alpha, \beta, \ldots$, these equations are of the form

$$\frac{P_f}{P_c} a = c, \frac{P_f}{P_c} b = d, \text{ etc.}$$

9. The Implicit Function Theorem tells us that two suitably continuous equations of the form $W_1(y_1, y_2) = 0 = W_2(y_1, y_2)$, possessing a solution (y_1^0, y_2^0), cannot have any other solution provided

$$\Delta = \begin{vmatrix} \dfrac{\partial W_1}{\partial y_1} & \dfrac{\partial W_1}{\partial y_2} \\[2mm] \dfrac{\partial W_2}{\partial y_1} & \dfrac{\partial W_2}{\partial y_2} \end{vmatrix} \neq 0.$$

In this case, where $y_1 = L_f/T_f$, etc., it is easy to show that

$$\Delta = \begin{vmatrix} \dfrac{P_f}{P_c} f'' & -c'' \\[3mm] -\dfrac{P_f}{P_c} \dfrac{L_f}{T_f} f'' & +\dfrac{L_c}{T_c} c'' \end{vmatrix} = \frac{P_f}{P_c} f'' c'' \left[\frac{L_c}{T_c} - \frac{L_f}{T_f} \right]$$

By hypothesis of diminishing returns f''' and c'' are negative, and the term in brackets (representing the respective labour intensities in food and clothing) cannot be equal to zero. Hence, the equilibrium is unique. As developed earlier, if the factor intensities become equal, or reverse themselves, the one-to-one relation between commodity and factor prices *must* be ruptured.

10. The real wage of every resource must be the same in every place that it is used, when expressed in a common denominator. This gives us $r(n - 1)$ independent equations involving the $(n - 1)$ commodity-prices ratios and the $n(r - 1)$ factor proportions. If $n = r$, we have a determinate system once the goods price ratios are given. If $n > r$, we have the same result, but now the international price ratios cannot be presented arbitrarily as there are constant-cost paths on the production-possibility locus, with one blade of Marshall's scissors doing most of the cutting, so to speak. If $n < r$, it is quite possible for free commodity trade to exist alongside continuing factor-price differentials. It is never enough simply to count equations and unknowns. In addition we must make sure that there are not multiple solutions: that factor intensities in the different commodities and the laws of returns are such as to lead to a one-to-one relationship between commodity prices and factor prices.

11. The reader may be referred to the earlier paper's discussion of figures 1 and 2, with respect to "step-like formations" and overlap.

12. Statical increasing returns is related to, but analytically distinct from, these irreversible cost economies induced by expansion and experimentation and which provide the justification for "infant industry" protection. Statical increasing returns might justify permanent judicious protection but not protection all around, since our purpose in bringing about large-scale production is to achieve profitable trade and consumption.

One other point needs stressing. For very small outputs, increasing returns to scale may take place without affecting the above analysis provided that total demand is large enough to carry production into the realm of constant returns to scale. Increasing the "extent of the market" not only increases specialisation, it also increases the possibility of viable pure competition.

13. A "Pythagorean" production function of the form $F = \sqrt{L^2 + T^2}$ is an example of such a homogeneous function with increasing marginal productivity. So long as neither factor is to have a negative marginal productivity, *average* product must not be rising; but this is quite another thing. Surprisingly enough, the production possibility curve may still be convex with increasing marginal productivity. I have been asked whether any essential difference would be introduced by the assumption that one of the commodities, such as clothing, uses no land at all, or negligible land. Diminishing returns would still affect food as more of the transferable factor is added to the now specific factor of land; but no essential modifications in our conclusions are introduced.

Chapter 2

1. This proposition is implied in Ohlin ([81], chap. 9), Iversen ([28], chap. 2), and Meade ([55], chaps. 21 and 22).

2. For the necessity of these assumptions and a fairly complete list of references to the literature on factor-price equalization see Samuelson [92].

3. It is assumed that capitalists in their role as consuming units do not move with their capital.

4. It will become evident later that the terms of trade and factor prices do not change even when this assumption is dropped.

5. Actually, under the assumed conditions any tariff is prohibitive, as will eventuallly become clear.

6. Compare Stolper and Samuelson [99].

7. The proof is easily demonstrated in figure 2. At unchanged prices equilibrium must lie along OP-extended. With the larger endowment of capital, $O''P'$ must be shorter than OP. Since these lines have the same slope and constant returns to scale apply, output of cotton at P' must be less than at P. A paper by R. Jones written at the Massachusetts Institute of Technology in the spring of 1955 contained a similar proof.

8. SP' must equal in value the marginal product of the capital inflow at constant prices. In figure 4–1, PP' is the change in output associated with the increase in capital; steel output increases by RS but cotton output decreases by PW. The marginal product of the capital inflow is the value of RS minus the value of PW, which, in terms of cotton, is $P'S$.

9. The R lines in figures 3a and 3b must be parallel when output expands at the same price ratio in each country, and they must be straight since production changes are compensating.

10. One qualification to the argument must be noted which is not necessary when the other country is very large. A condition for the marginal product of capital in A to rise as a result of the tariff is that the price of steel rise relative to the price of cotton. It is possible, if the foreign offer curve is very inelastic, that the improvement in A's terms of trade in raising the relative price of exports (cotton) will more than offset the effect of the tariff in raising the relative price of imports (steel). The condition that the "normal" case is satisfied requires that the sum of the foreign elasticity of demand and the domestic marginal propensity to import be greater than unity (the marginal propensity to import is relevant because the improvement in the terms of trade increases income). This is Metzler's qualification to the Stolper-Samuelson tariff argument (see Metzler [63]). If this criterion is less than unity a tariff imposed by a labor-abundant country would stimulate foreign investment rather than attract capital—a result, it should be noted, based on the static assumptions of this model; if dynamic elements were involved, the direction of the capital movement would depend on whether the effects of the tariff on production preceded or followed the effects on the terms of trade.

11. If trade were a perfect substitute for factor movements in the absence of trade impediments, a rough idea of the cost of trade impediments could be acquired by calculating the increase in world income which could take place if capital were redistributed from capital-rich to capital-poor countries until its marginal product throughout the world was equalized. Alternatively, this could be con-

sidered the cost of capital immobility. This statement would have to be qualified in the many-factor case.

12. We make this assumption so that the change in the terms of trade resulting from A's tariff is small. In passing, however, it should be noted that the more mobile is capital, the smaller is the change in the terms of trade resulting from a tariff; this means that the optimum tariff will be smaller with, than without, capital mobility; and in the limiting case where capital is perfectly mobile, discussed earlier, the optimum tariff is zero.

Also, in what follows I neglect to discuss the tariff proceeds which are implicitly assumed to be redistributed in such a way as to leave A's indifference map unchanged. Alternatively, to abstract both from changes in the terms of trade and the tariff proceeds, it could be assumed that the tariff is prohibitive.

13. However, interest rates must be the same! Because capital goods—call them machines—can move costlessly from one country to the other, the price of machines in money terms will be the same in both countries; and since machines will move to A until marginal products in money terms are equal, interest rates (the return to a machine as a proportion of the price of a machine) must be the same in both countries. The interest rate, of course, is not commensurable with the marginal product of capital unless the latter is defined as a proportion of the price of machines; in the new equilibrium the two are equal when the marginal product of capital is so defined.

14. It is true that B's national has increased, since the effect of A's tariff is to raise B-wages and stimulate capital investment in A, where B-capitalists receive a higher rate of return than at home; but it cannot be said that B-capitalists are better off, since, *ex hypothesi*, they are indifferent between investment at home and an investment in A in which the rate of return is 10 per cent higher. In any case, the purpose of policy makers in A is to raise A's, not B's, income.

15. It may be possible to rescue the argument in other ways by assuming irrational, although possibly not implausible, behavior. For example, after B-capitalists have begun investing in A, they may acquire more confidence and be willing to accept a smaller interest differential. In this case, after the capital movement the marginal product of labor may be higher, and the marginal product of capital lower, than before the tariff, thereby increasing A's national income. Or, whereas some (relatively) capital-scarce countries may fear "exploitation" from foreign investment, others may view the increase in productive capacity resulting from it as desirable in itself (perhaps with the intent of future expropriation!)—in which case this factor would have to be balanced against the reduction in national income.

16. It is sometimes overlooked that internal economies of scale do not constitute an argument for a tariff. An industry must not only be able to compete some years after the tariff; it must also earn a sufficient return to repay the economy for the loss of income resulting from the tariff in the period of the industry's infancy. The investment will them be worthwhile only if future output is sufficient to earn for the firm the current rate of interest on the capital involved. But when economies to scale are internal, the investment will be profitable for private enterprise. Only when divergences between private and social costs due to *external* economies of scale are present is the case for government intervention valid.

17. But if the same nonlinearities of scale exist in B the argument is weakened; economies of scale in A-importables will cause the marginal product of capital to fall at a slower rate than in their absence, but in this case the marginal product of capital in B will rise at a much faster rate as capital is exported. Similar economies of scale in B, then, may cancel out the effect of economies in A in inducing a larger capital movement, although this effect could be neglected if B were the rest of the world and A were a small country.

18. A possible extension of the model to allow for many goods could be made as follows: All goods could be ordered in terms of their capital intensities (that is, the ratios of capital to labor at any given price ratio). B would export those goods that are most capital-intensive and A those goods which are most labor-intensive. In the absence of trade impediments, one of the intermediate commodities would be produced in common, establishing the ratio of factor returns in much the same way as goods produced in common establish the ratio of international values in a Graham model. The effect of a tariff in A (as of any impediment) is to increase the relative price of capital-intensive goods in A and to lower them in B, thus raising in A and lowering in B the marginal product of capital. Thus, not one commodity but a whole series of commodities would be produced in common, A's exports comprising only the most labor-intensive and B's exports only the most capital-intensive goods. In A new capital-intensive industries, and in B new labor-intensive industries, would be created. If some capital were not allowed to move to A, the margin of comparative advantage would be extended to capital-intensive industries in A, thus increasing the number of goods produced in common in both countries.

Chapter 3

1. As an example in each field see Kemp [14] and Meade [15].

2. These basic relationships are usually presented as inequalities to allow for the existence of resource(s) in excess supply even at a zero price or for the possibility that losses would be incurred in certain industries if production were positive. I assume throughout that resources are fully employed, and production at zero profits with positive factor and commodity prices is possible. For a discussion of the inequalities see, for example, Dorfman et al. [5] or Hicks [9].

3. This is the procedure used by Meade [15]. The λ and θ notation has been used by Amano [1]. Expressing small changes in relative or percentage terms is a natural procedure when technology exhibits constant returns to scale.

4. Let P and W represent the diagonal matrices,

$$\begin{pmatrix} p_M & 0 \\ 0 & p_F \end{pmatrix} \text{ and } \begin{pmatrix} w & 0 \\ 0 & r \end{pmatrix},$$

respectively, and E and X represent the diagonal matrices of factor endowments and commodity outputs. Then $\lambda = E^{-1}AX$ and $\theta = P^{-1}A'W$. Since $|A| > 0$ and the determinants of the four diagonal matrices are all positive, $|\lambda|$ and $|\theta|$ must be positive. This relation among the signs of $|\lambda|$, $|\theta|$, and $|A|$ is proved by Amano [1] and Takayama [22].

5. For another example of the Wong-Viner theorem, for changes in real income along a transformation schedule, see Jones [13].

6. Factor endowments come into their own in influencing factor prices if complete specialization is allowed (or if the number of factors exceeds the number of commodities). See Samuelson [18] for a detailed discussion of this issue.

7. The reciprocal relationship between the effect of a rise in the price of commodity i on the return to factor j and the effect of an increase in the endowment of factor j on the output of commodity i is discussed briefly by Samuelson [18].

8. The solutions, of course, are given by the elements of λ^{-1} and θ^{-1}. If M is labor-intensive, the diagonal elements of λ^{-1} and θ^{-1} are positive and exceed unity, while off-diagonal elements are negative.

9. A graphical analysis of the dual relationship between the Rybczynski theorem and the Stolper-Samuelson theorem is presented in chapter 5 of Jones, R. W., *International Trade: Essays in Theory*, Series in International Trade, vol. 4, North-Holland Publishing Company, 1979.

10. I restrict the discussion to the case of excise subsidies because of the resemblance it bears to some aspects of technological change, which I discuss later. later. In the case of taxes, $s_i = 1/(1 + t_i)$, where t_i represents the *ad valorem* rate of excise tax.

11. I have bypassed the solution for $\hat{M}$ and $\hat{F}$ separately given from (1b) and (2b). After substituting for the factor-price ratio in terms of the commodity-price ratio the expression for $\hat{M}$ could be written as

$$\hat{M} = \frac{1}{|\lambda|}[\lambda_{TF}\hat{L} - \lambda_{LF}\hat{T}] + e_M(\hat{p}_M - \hat{p}_F),$$

where, e_M, the shorthand expression for $\{1/|\lambda|\,|\theta|\}(\lambda_{TF}\delta_L + \lambda_{LF}\delta_T)$, shows the percentage change in M that would be associated with a 1% rise in M's relative price along a given transformation schedule. It is a "general equilibrium elasticity of supply," as discussed in Jones [13]. It is readily seen that $\sigma_S = e_M + e_F$. Furthermore, $\theta_M e_M = \theta_F e_F$, where θ_M and θ_F denote the share of each good in the national income.

12. For previous uses see Amano [2] and Drandakis [6].

13. See Shinkai [19] for a discussion of the fixed-coefficients case. At constant commodity prices the impact of endowment changes on the composition of output is the same regardless of elasticities of substitution in production. Thus, a necessary and sufficient condition in Shinkai's case is the factor-intensity condition. For the variable coefficients case the factor-intensity condition was first discussed by Uzawa [24].

14. The two requirements are equivalent if $\theta_F = \theta_L$, i.e. if total consumption $(p_F F)$ is matched exactly by the total wages (wL). This equality is made a basic assumption as to savings behavior in some models where laborers consume all and capitalists save all. For example, see Uzawa [24].

15. A condition similar to (16a), with the assumption that $\sigma_D = 1$, is presented by Amano [3].

16. For a more complete discussion of savings behavior as related to the rate of profit, see Uzawa [25] and Inada [10].

17. The suggestion that a change in technology in a particular industry has both "factor-saving" and "cost-reducing" aspects has been made before. See, for example, Bhagwati and Johnson [4] and Meier [16]. Contrary to what is usually implied, I point out that a Hicksian "neutral" technology change in one or more industries has, nonetheless, a "factor-saving" or "differential factor" effect. The problem of technological change has been analyzed in numerous articles; perhaps those by Johnson [11] and Findlay and Grubert [7] should especially be mentioned.

18. Strictly speaking, I want to allow for the possibility that one or both effects are zero. Thus, technological change is "regular" if and only if $(\pi_L - \pi_T)(\pi_M - \pi_F) \geqq 0$.

19. Note that Q_M and Q_F are the same weights as those defined in section 6. The analogy between the composition of σ and that of $(\pi_L - \pi_T)$ becomes more apparent if $|\lambda|(\pi_M - \pi_F)$ is rewritten as $Q_D\{(\pi_M - \pi_F)/|\theta|\}$. The differential factor effect is weighted average of the Hicksian factor biases in each industry and a magnified $(1/|\theta|)$ differential industry effect.

20. Q_L equals $(\lambda_{LF}\theta_{LM} + \lambda_{LM}\theta_{LF})$, and Q_T is $(\lambda_{TF}\theta_{TM} + \lambda_{TM}\theta_{TF})$. Note that $Q_L + Q_T$ equals $Q_M + Q_F$.

21. These relationships involve the *difference* between π_L and π_T on the one hand and π_M and π_F on the other. Another relationship involving *sums* of these terms is suggested by the national income relationship, as discussed in section 7. With technical progress, $\theta_M\pi_M + \theta_F\pi_F$ equals $\theta_L\pi_L + \theta_T\pi_T$.

22. Recalling n. 19, consider the following question: If the elasticity of substitution between factors is unity in every sector, will a change in the ratio of factor endowments result in an equal percentage change in the factor price ratio? From section 6 it is seen that this result can be expected only if σ_D is unity.

23. See Johnson [12] and the extensive bibliography there listed. The most complete treatment of the effects of various differences in production conditions on positions of comparative advantage is given by Amano [2] who also discusses special cases of Harrod neutrality. For a recent analysis of the impact of endowment and technology changes on the terms of trade see Takayama [23].

24. Account must be taken, however, of the fact that with trade the quantities of M and F produced differ from the amounts consumed by the quantity of exports and imports.

Chapter 4

1. See Shepard (1953) and McFadden et al. (1975) for a general discussion concept of the dual of a production function and its application. See Amano (1963) and Jones (1965) for the application of this general concept to the two-sector model.

2. The phenomenon of negative shadow prices and its relationship to various peculiarities of highly distorted economies are investigated in recent papers by Srinivasan and Bhagwati (1978) and Bhagwati, Srinivasan and Wan (1978).

3. Burgess (1976) develops a similar diagram in his analysis of the effects of tariffs. The present diagram was developed while commenting on a paper by Neary and is used in the final version of that paper [see Neary (1978)]. The application of this diagram to the exposition of many of the properties of the two-sector model was developed independently by Woodland (1977).

4. The equation that defines the tangent to the $\tilde{P}_X = P_X^0$ curve is given by $a_{LX} W + a_{KX} R = P_X^0$ where a_{LX} and a_{KX} are the amounts of labor and capital, respectively, that are used in producing a unit of X, at the factor price combination indicated by the corresponding point on the isoprice curve.

5. For the case of zero elasticity of substitution between labor and capital, the isoprice curve is a straight line. For the case of infinite elasticity of substitution, the isoprice curve is a right angle.

6. The disposal of tax revenue and the finance of subsidies are neglected in this discussion. The effects of taxes and subsidies on factor owners refer to the effects on them in their role as factor owners, not as general taxpayers or transfer recipients.

7. The concept of shadow prices of factors of production and the application of this concept to diverse issues in international trade theory and in project evaluation has been pursued in a number of recent papers. In particular, see Diamond and Mirrlees (1976), Findlay and Wellisz (1976), and Srinivasan and Bhagwati (1978).

8. This application of shadow prices to project evaluation is consistent with the general principles recommended by Little and Mirrlees (1969). It should be noted that some care is needed in applying this principle to "large" projects, for a large project might well alter the structure of rewards. This is particularly a problem in the context of the standard two-factor model since in this model the introduction of a new output is likely to lead to the cessation of production of one of the economy's existing outputs.

9. Johnson (1966) and later Herberg and Kemp (1971) and Bhagwati and Srinivasan (1971) analyze the effect of factor market distortions on the shape of the transformation curve. It is also generally recognized that factor market distortions lead to a situation in which the tangent to the transformation curve does not necessarily correspond to the product price ratio.

10. Jones (1971) and Magee (1973) note that a number of peculiarities of highly distorted economies are associated with a divergence between relative intensities measured by physical factor ratios and relative factor intensities measured by value shares. For the case illustrated in figure 4 the negative shadow rental rate for capital is associated with such a divergence between the two measures of relative factor intensity. More generally, if only wage rates are distorted, or only rental rates are distorted, then a negative shadow price will be associated with a divergence between the two measures of relative factor intensity. However, if both wage rates and rental rates are distorted, there is no necessary relationship between a negative shadow price for one factor of production and a divergence between the two measures of relative factor intensity.

11. It has been recognized for some time that factor market distortions can lead

to a situation in which growth in the supplies of factors of production is immiserizing; see Bhagwati (1968) and Bertrand and Flatters (1971). Recently, it has been recognized that this possibility is related to the phenomenon of a negative shadow price for a factor of production; see Bhagwati, Srinivasan and Wan (1978).

Chapter 6

1. Actually, it is difficult to be sure exactly what Travis was saying. He has never, to my knowledge, provided an example of a tariff that reverses the pattern of trade, though such an example is possible, as I show in section 5. Nor is it clear whether Travis meant his remarks to be valid in a model of only two primary factors. In his (1972) article, he used and vigorously defended the two-factor assumption, but concluded that, if tariffs are high enough, the bulk of trade will be in goods requiring other primary factors.

2. To see this, let t be a vector of ad valorem tariffs cum transport costs for each industry. Given technology, tastes, and factor endowments, the difference between the two countries' factor-price ratios, $\Omega = \omega^A - \omega^B$, must be a continuous function of $t, \Omega(t)$. Let t^0 be a particular vector of non-negative trade impediments, let t^a be a vector that would prevent trade entirely, and suppose that $\Omega(t^0) > 0$ (as in figure 1) yet $\Omega(t^a) < 0$. Then by continuity there exists $t' > 0$ such that $\Omega(t') = 0$ and such that trade takes place. But if $\Omega = 0$, then factor prices are equal and so are commodity prices, and it is impossible for trade to take place over positive trade impediments, $t' > 0$. From this contradiction it follows that $\Omega(t^a) \geqq 0$. Since $\Omega(t^a) = 0$ can also be ruled out as implying that $\Omega(t) = 0$ for all t, it follows that $\Omega(t^0) > 0$ implies of $\Omega(t^a) > 0$.

3. Unequal factor prices do not, of course, ensure that the two isocost lines will intersect, as drawn, since one could lie wholly outside the other. In that case, as the analysis below indicates, the chain proposition holds trivially since all goods will be exported by the same country. Were balanced trade assumed, such a situation would of course be excluded.

4. See footnote 2.

5. Rather remarkably, no assumption has been needed about demand or about relative factor prices in autarky. However, if demand were so biased as to make the autarky relative wage in A less than the autarky relative wage in B, then factor prices would have to be equalized by free trade and the factor prices assumed in figure 1 could not arise. This also follows from the argument given in footnote 2.

6. In another context I have called this the assumption of "natural" trade [see Deardorff (1980)]. This formulation is consistent with any of a variety of explicit assumptions about the nature of transport costs, so long as these costs are non-negative. However, the reader may prefer to think of a more explicit assumption, such as that of Samuelson (1954), who let a certain fraction of each good be used up in transport.

7. Note that if trade impediments were positive for all goods, then the qualification that factor prices be unequal would be unnecessary. For equal factor prices would mean equal commodity prices and thus no trade.

8. I have called this a conjecture because I do not regard the argument provided by Bhagwati (1972) to be a proof, though naturally when a proposition is valid there can be some disagreement as to what constitutes proof. Bhagwati (p. 1054) argued that "... while a commodity in the middle of a chain of exportables may be priced out of the export market into being a nontraded good by high transportation costs, it is impossible for it to be turned into an imported good." Now it is certainly true that the cost of transporting a given exportable cannot cause *it* to be imported. But I see no a priori reason why the cost of transporting some other good might not cause this to happen. Suppose, for example, that the cost of importing eggs were to raise their price so high as to cause substitution away from both bacon and eggs towards oatmeal. Then oatmeal could become imported and bacon exported, even if the reverse would be true if eggs could be imported cheaply. The proof in the text shows that this cannot happen in a two-factor model (where chickens and pigs—or the farmers that raise them—could be employed planting oats), but I see nothing in Bhagwati's remarks to rule this out.

9. Note that, since V_i is defined in nominal terms, we do not encounter the problem of defining either a natural unit for value added or a "price" of value added, which has been a source of difficulty in the effective protection literature. In particular, our construction does not require the separability assumption that has been stressed by Bruno (1973) and by Bhagwati and Srinivasan (1973). It should also be mentioned that V_i, as functions of K_i and L_i, possess the same homogeneity and concavity properties that are assumed of the production functions, F_i. See Diewert's (1973) discussion of variable profit functions.

10. In the special case, often assumed, of fixed coefficients between intermediate inputs and final output (so that $X_{ji} = a_{ji}X_i$) the function

$$V_i = \left(p_i - \sum_{j=1}^{n} p_j a_{ji} \right) F^i(K_i, L_i).$$

The isoquants of V_i are then identical to the isoquants of F^i, and the unit-value-added isoquant is that for which

$$X_i = 1 \left/ \left(p_i - \sum_{j=1}^{n} p_j a_{ji} \right) \right. .$$

11. This may sound like a description of producers who take a loss on every unit but "make it up in volume". This need not be the case since there was initially a positive margin for value added, and hence a small enough input price increase will leave that margin positive. But it does point up the possibility that unit-value-added isoquants may not just move, but may disappear when input prices increase. This is particularly true when there is no possibility of substitution away from intermediate inputs, as in the fixed coefficients case of the preceding footnote. This possibility makes a counterexample even easier to obtain, however, since it means that a tariff increase can shift all production to good 2.

12. It is essential for the counterexample that the isoquant, $V'_1 = 1$, lie outside the line CC', which is tangent to the $V_2 = 1$ isoquant where it crosses the K^A/L^A ray. In the figure, this requires a substantial movement of the V_1 isoquant, but this need not be the case. If good 2 were only slightly more labor-intensive than

good 1, CC' would lie very close to AA' and a small movement of the V_1 isoquant would suffice.

13. I am indebted to Jagdish Bhagwati for suggesting this construction of the counterexample, which is more direct than was used in an earlier version of this paper. The earlier construction drew upon a result of Batra and Casas (1973) who showed that a nontraded intermediate good of extreme factor intensity can cause the Heckscher-Ohlin theorem to be violated. Thus, if we begin, as in this example, with the theorem holding under free trade, a prohibitive tariff on an intermediate good can reverse the pattern of trade.

14. Note that direct-plus-indirect capital intensities do not work either. For when the intermediate good in our example was traded freely, then good 2 was imported even though it may be the most capital intensive on the direct-plus-indirect basis.

15. Melvin (1968) also stated this proposition for the two-factor case. Vanek's demonstration, which has been generalized to bilateral trade by Horiba (1974), allows for any number of factors.

16. Baldwin (1971, p. 130) states in a footnote that "tariffs can weaken the pattern of indirect factor trade in a Heckscher-Ohlin model but cannot alone produce paradoxical results." It is unclear from the context, however, just what model he has in mind and thus whether this is any more than a statement of the (later) Bhagwati-Jones proposition that was proved above in section 3.

Chapter 7

1. Authors who allow for increasing returns in trade by assuming that scale economies are external to firm include Chacoliades (1970), Melvin (1969), and Kemp (1964), and Negishi (1969).

2. A Chamberlinian approach to international trade is suggested by Gray (1973). Negishi (1972) develops a full general-equilibrium model of scale economies, monopolistic competition, and trade which is similar in spirit to this paper, though far more complex. Scale economies and product differentiation are also suggested as causes of trade by Barker (1977) and Grubel (1970).

3. The results in this section bear some resemblance to some nontheoretical accounts of the emergence of backward regions. We might propose the following modification of the model: suppose that the population of each region is divided into a mobile group and an immobile group. Migration would then move all the mobile people to one region, leaving behind an immiserized 'Appalachia' of immobile people whose standard of living is depressed by the smallness of the market.

Chapter 8

1. I am informed by the editor [Jagdish Bhagwati, for *Journal of International Economics*] that R. Gordon, in an unpublished manuscript, arrived independently at similar conclusions to those of McCulloch and Johnson regarding equivalence in the presence of U.S. oil-type quotas.

2. That quotas and tariffs would be non-equivalent under uncertainty seems to be a corollary to the general view that, while a quota may be equivalent to a tariff at one point in time, the equivalence does not hold if supply and demand conditions change; unless, of course, the quota is changed continually to its equivalent tariff value. But, the frequency with which quotas and tariffs can be changed in any economic regime are rarely identical; tariffs frequently can be changed only over a much longer period. Also note that, as Bhagwati (1965) pointed out, industries in some developing countries prefer to have both tariffs and quotas, instead of relying on the latter; the uncertainty of being protected by quotas is rather greater than the uncertainty of holding onto tariff protection, since quotas are also addressed to the balance of payments situation and may well lose their protective effect if the payments situation is improved.

Chapter 9

1. Barber's article represents the pioneering contribution on this subject. It is perhaps not surprising that the main idea can be found, treated briefly, in J. E. Meade (1955), pp. 162–3

2. A recent Australian official committee has made some calculations of effective protective rates and has given the concept some prominence in Australia. See Committee of Economic Enquiry (1965).

3. Even when the protective-rate structure consists wholly of positive nominal tariffs, it is not inevitable that excess demand for non-traded goods (and hence exchange-rate appreciation) results. For the tariff structure may have yielded some negative effective rates; these draw resources from tradables into non-tradables and create a tendency toward excess supply of non-tradables. But, unless consumption-substitution elasticities are zero, positive nominal tariffs on final goods must lead at least to some shift in the demand pattern toward non-tradables. It is possible that the extra supply of non-tradables just happens to equal the extra demand, so that no exchange-rate adjustment is required.

4. If there are traded inputs in those non-traded goods which are themselves inputs in traded-goods industries, the matter becomes more complicated. Only that part of the value of the input which is value added by primary factors directly and indirectly (that is, via non-traded inputs into these non-traded inputs, and so on) should be treated like a primary factor and so included in value added in the protected industry. In other words, ideally one should go down the input-output structure until one reaches a traded input; and, to obtain value added for our formula, all direct contributions by primary factors should be summed with all indirect contributions by primary factors through non-traded inputs. In the summation process, tradable inputs (even though they may actually be produced domestically) should be treated as leakages.

5. This is so well known that detailed substantiation is hardly needed. But see the papers by Balassa (1965) and Basevi (1966) cited earlier, and in particular W. P. Travis (1964), pp. 187–225. The subject is discussed thoroughly by Johnson (1965), but the distinction made in the present section of this paper under point (ii) below is not made by him.

6. The effects of the multiple system on the capital account are ignored here. In fact, the method can readily embrace all current and capital account items.

7. This may be a defense of those discussions of the effects of the Canadian tariff which set up as the alternative to the Canadian tariff, not unilateral free trade but rather world free trade or a free-trade area with the United States, and which ignore the exchange-rate adjustment. See Young (1957).

8. Apart from his actual statisical work, Basevi's highly original contribution is this concept of the effective protective rate for labor. He does not deal with the difficulties discussed here—that is, he ignores tariffs on capital goods and the possibility of non-traded capital goods.

9. This is my original formula. See Corden (1963), p. 197 n.

10. Balassa (1965), in making calculations for the United States, United Kingdom, E.E.C., Sweden, and Japan has 'relied largely on the input-output tables for Belgium and the Netherlands.'

Chapter 10

1. At U itself the frontiers coincide. Thus, if there were some distribution of income which brought us under autarky to U rather than D, opening up trade would at that point (1) in fact be followed by no international transactions taking place, and hence would (2) represent the limiting case where trade neither helps nor hurts us. (If individuals' tastes and endowments happen to be much alike at home there might be no redistribution of income that would, *under autarky*, get us to U. In such a case we would know that the *cum*-trade utility frontier of figure 4 does lie uniformly outside the autarky utility frontier. On the other hand, if U is a possible autarky point the *cum*-trade frontier will touch the autarky utility frontier at one or more points; but it must always lie north-east of the autarky point corresponding to D—as we shall see.)

2. See Baldwin (1948 and 1952) and Kenen (1957). Given more than two goods, we need modify the exposition only trivially.

3. It may help the reader to imagine the offer curve as being cut out from figure 2 with scissors and then being carefully transposed over to figure 3 so as to trace out the envelope of its outlying tangents. At a point like W not only is the offer curve tangential to the envelope but in addition if we go back to the corresponding pivot point O' the slope of the production possibility schedule there will also necessarily be the same. This follows from the geometrical properties of an envelope and has the important economic interpretation that at an optimal point production substitution ratios must be equal to trading substitution ratios (as well as to consumption substitution ratios).

4. If the autarky point D will in fact become outmoded by the opening of trade, then D and U cannot coincide and we know that—by going north-east from D—everyone can be made better off than they were under autarky.

5. Pareto's economics would have been better understood had he explicitly used the utility-frontier concept. I may refer the reader to Samuelson (1947, ch. 8;

1950, p. 6; 1956). As Graaff points out (1957, ch. 4) Professor M. Allais of Paris also developed this social utility-frontier concept.

6. As mentioned in footnote 1 *ef* might touch *pq* at one or more points (indeed in the limiting case where trade is always indifferent, at all points). It would be wrong, though, to think that *ef must* somewhere touch *pq*: as already indicated, the point *u* corresponding to *U might* never touch the *pq* frontier; and in that case *ef* would lie everywhere north-east of *pq*. If *ef* refers to a country large enough to affect its terms of trade, we can define a new frontier midway, so to speak, between the autarky frontier *pq* and the optimum-tariff frontier *ef*. I refer to the free-trade frontier that results from zero tariffs but with different lump-sum redistributions of income. This new frontier can never loop inside *pq* or outside *ef*. It corresponds to a free-trade locus that could be pencilled into figure 3 midway between *PQ* and *EF*.

7. See Baldwin (1953–54) p. 160 for a defence of my 1939 argument against an Olsen-like criticism.

8. See Scitovsky (1941–42). See, too, Samuelson (1956) for a discussion of how these concepts all fit together.

9. Since convexity of *PQ* makes the *EF* envelope convex too, I believe the argument could be extended to the general case.

10. I have changed my 1939 notation and am neglecting changes in factor supplies.

11. Perhaps some situation very near to autarky, but involving a little trade, could be proved to give points north-east of *d*. This is suggested by the fact that small redistributions will usually involve small deadweight distortions of a higher order of infinitesimals. For the theory of feasibility—sometimes called the theory of the second best—still in its infancy, see Boiteux (1956), Lipsey and Lancaster (1956–57), Graaff (1957, ch. 5), Little (1957, app. 4), Ramsey (1927) and Samuelson (1950, pp. 18–19).

12. See Samuelson (1938), for a discussion of these issues and for what appears to be the first of the modern rediscoveries of the Mill-Bickerdike theorem that some tariff is optimal.

13. Other devices, such as perfect planning or perfect discrimination, might accomplish the same result.

Chapter 11

1. Hagen (1958, p. 496, n. 2) traces the origins of the argument to Jacob Viner's review of M. Manoilesco's *The Theory of Protection and International Trade*, (P. S. King, 1931), in the *Journal of Political Economy*, vol. 40 (1932), pp. 121–5.

2. For an analysis of the protective incidence of a particular tariff structure, see Johnson (1963).

3. It should perhaps be emphasized that the welfare being maximized is the national welfare, and the distortions in question are distortions only from the national point of view. Also, tariff retaliation by other countries does not necessarily prevent a country from gaining by the imposition of an optimum tariff structure; see Johnson (1953–54).

4. MRS symbolizes marginal rate of substitution in domestic consumption, MRT_d marginal rate of transformation in domestic production, MRT_f marginal rate of transformation in foreign trade; all of these are defined in terms of the amount of the export good given up in exchange for a unit increment of the import good.

5. It should be noted that, for analysis with the techniques of trade theory, factor prices must be assumed to be rigid in real terms; if factor prices are rigid in money terms ("money illusion" of the Keynesian type is present), full employment can always be secured by devaluation coupled with an appropriate domestic fiscal-monetary policy. This point is not made explicit in Haberler's analysis; see Haberler (1950), pp. 227–31.

6. Bhagwati and Ramaswami (1963, p. 49) use this demonstration to show that Hagen's analysis errs in concluding that self-sufficiency is necessarily better than free trade in this case.

7. Bhagwati and Ramaswami (1963, p. 47) use this demonstration to show that Haberler was wrong to recommend an export or import subsidy in this case.

8. Bhagwati and Ramaswami (1963) list eight reasons for the existence of a wage differential between the rural and urban sectors, of which four are economic and four (one of which is Hagen's) may involve genuine distortions. They agree with the earlier analysis of Fishlow and David (1961) in regarding Hagen's 'dynamic' argument for the existence of a distortion as an illegitimate superimposition of dynamic considerations on static analysis. The same point has been made by Kenen (1963). Fishlow and David's other reasons correspond approximately with those discussed here, although they introduce the interesting case of factory legislation preventing the younger members of the family from working; they do not, however, raise the possibility that there may be a distortion of investment in migration of human capital.

9. The analysis here is incomplete, since in certain circumstances competition would lead to the workers bearing the cost of the nonspecific part of the training received on the job through lower initial wages. On this point see Becker (1962).

10. This paragraph was prompted by the existence of an apparent conflict in the literature on protection. W. M. Corden (1957) shows that the most efficient (least-cost) method of protection is by a subsidy (when the terms of trade are fixed) or by an optimum tariff and a production subsidy (when the terms of trade are variable). J. H. Young (1957) shows that protection by tariff costs less than protection by subsidy. As shown below, both are right. The explanation is that Corden takes the object of protection to be to increased domestic production, whereas Young takes the object to be to replace imports by domestic production.

Chapter 12

1. I assume here that the wage differential is "distortionary" and cannot be attributed to legitimate economic grounds, such as disutility in occupations where the higher wage is charged. For a detailed discussion, see Fishlow and David [13] and Bhagwati and Ramaswami [2].

2. See Kemp [21], Chapter 11, for a fuller discussion of alternative types of produc-

tion externalities. I have in mind here the case of a "pure" production externality of the Meade variety, as set out in footnote 9 later.

3. Instead of a consumption externality, one could assume a situation in which sellers charge a uniform premium on a commodity's import and production price.

4. The precise sense in which monopoly power in trade represents a market imperfection, in the trade sector, is that foreign prices will not equal the marginal, foreign rate of transformation (as discussed later in the text).

5. Since the production tax-cum-subsidy policy is equivalent to a tax-cum-subsidy given to *all* factors (used in production) of an equivalent and uniform magnitude, the factor tax-cum-subsidy policy referred to in this paper relates to a tax-cum-subsidy policy that applies in a *discriminatory* fashion between or among factors.

6. The classic proof of this proposition is in Samuelson [28]. For later treatments, see Samuelson [29], Kemp [22] and Bhagwati [4] and [5].

7. The phenomenon of diminishing marginal cost of transformation can arise either because of increasing returns [21, Ch. 8] (which is a purely technological phenomenon) or because of factor market imperfection in the shape of a wage differential [2] [13] [20]. The phenomenon has to be ruled out so as to eliminate certain well-known difficulties that it raises (requiring in particular the distinction between global and local maxima [30] and attention to second-order conditions and possibilities of inefficient specialization [27]).

8. Equalities have been used in stating the first-order conditions, for each pair of commodities, so as to preserve simplicity; they imply, of course, incomplete specialization in production and consumption. Inequalities can be introduced easily, but nothing essential would be gained by way of additional insights. The simplifying assumption of a two-commodity system will also be used through the rest of the paper; this does not critically affect the analysis, although problems associated with devising optimum policy *structures* (e.g., the optimal tariff structure [14] in the case of monopoly power in trade) are naturally not raised in consequence.

9. This externality can be formally stated as follows [21, p. 128]: For linearly homogeneous production functions $x = x(K_x, L_x)$, $y = y(K_y, L_y, x)$ it can be shown that, with y entrepreneurs not having to pay for their "input" of x, the economy will be characterised by Distortion 2.

10. A constant wage differential will also lead to Distortion 2; in this instance, we have a case of two distortions occurring at the same time. In fact, the wage differential case leads also to the possibility of a nonconvex production possibility set, as we have already noted; furthermore, as Bhagwati and Srinivasan [11] have shown, the response of production to relative commodity price change also becomes unpredictable, a question, however, of no welfare significance in the context of this paper.

11. A constant rate of factor tax-cum-subsidy will also produce Distortion 2, as in the case of a constant wage differential. However, as we shall see later, a variable factor tax-cum-subsidy policy can be devised which produces *only* Distortion 4.

12. Unlike the case of a *constant wage* differential, which also leads to Distortion 2 in addition to Distortion 4, we can devise [7] a variable tax-cum-subsidy that satisfies the constraint on factor employment while creating *only* Distortion 4.

13. Their argument is summarised as follows: They use the notation [8]: C_i, X_i denote the consumption and domestic output respectively of commodity i, where $i = 1, 2$. Also, P_c denotes the ratio of the price of the first to that of the second commodity confronting consumers (DRS); P_t denotes DRT $= dX_2/dX_1$; and P_f denotes the ratio of the world price of the first commodity to that of the second commodity, i.e., the *average* terms of trade. The marginal terms of trade FRT $= P_f$ only in the special case in which national monopoly power does not exist.

The welfare function $U(C_1, C_2)$ and the production functions are assumed to be differentiable as required. The U_i denotes the marginal utility of commodity $i(i = 1, 2)$. It is assumed throughout the analysis that under laissez-faire there is nonspecialisation in consumption and production, and that some trade takes place. Then, the following expression, for the change in welfare when there is an infinitesimal movement away from laissez-faire equilibrium, is derived:

$$dU = U_2[dX_1(P_f - P_t) + (X_1 - C_1)dP_f + (P_c - P_f)dC_1].$$

If one uses this expression, the different distortions are easily analyzed for alternate policy rankings. Thus, in the case in which DRT $\neq$ FRT $=$ DRS, which is Distortion 2 in the text just following, the expression reduces to $dU = U_2[dX_1(P_f - P_t)]$ because $P_c = P_f$, $dP_f = 0$ and $P_f \neq P_t$. It follows that either a tariff (trade subsidy) or a factor tax-cum-subsidy that increases (reduces) X_1, if $P_f > P_t(P_f < P_t)$, will increase welfare.

14. For finite tax-cum-subsidies, however, the production tax-cum-subsidy will be superior to the factor tax-cum-subsidy.

15. This conclusion holds for infinitesimal tax-cum-subsidy. A finite consumption tax-cum-subsidy will actually be worse than laissez-faire in this instance, as it will impose a "consumption loss" on the economy, over and above the loss it is already suffering from the endogenous Distortion 2.

16. This conclusion again holds only for infinitesimal tax-cum-subsidies on production or factor use. For finite tax-cum-susidies, these policies will necessarily be worse than laissez-faire (unless inferior goods are present).

17. Again, this conclusion concerning the consumption tax-cum-subsidy must be read in the same sense as in note 15.

18. For finite tax-cum-subsidies, however, the factor tax-cum-subsidy policy will be inferior to the production tax-cum-subsidy policy, as Bhagwati and Srinivasan [7] have demonstrated.

19. This statement must again be read in the same sense as in note 15 and note 17 earlier.

20. I am indebted to Dr. Alan Martina for correcting my original error where I argued that a production of factor tax-cum-subsidy would "not help." It *may*, owing to the income effect on consumption as income declines with the use of either of these policy instruments.

21. This statement must be interpreted again in the same sense as in notes 15, 17, and 19 earlier.

22. For phenomena of immiserizing growth arising from reasons other than distortions, see Melvin [25] and Bhagwati [9].

23. On this, see Bhagwati [4], Kemp [23], and Bhagwati–Kemp [10].

24. For the consumption tax-cum-subsidy, the complication arising from inferior goods is not relevant.

25. Note again the *caveat* regarding inferior goods. This will not apply, however, where the consumption distortion is reduced.

26. These conclusions can also be derived by reference to the Bhagwati-Ramaswami-Srinivasan [8] formula, in note 13, which reduces for this case to $dU = U_2[dX_1(P_f - P_t) + (P_c - P_f)dC_1]$.

27. This is seen again by examining the Bhagwati-Ramaswami-Srinivasan formula which reduces, in this instance, to $dU = U_2[dX_1(P_f - P_t) + (P_c - P_f)dC_1]$. It is clear then that a reduction in the tariff, by affecting both X_1 and C_1 may worsen rather than improve welfare; and that the welfare effect of successive tariff changes need not be unidirectional.

Chapter 13

1. This polarity has been pointed out by Srinivasan and Bhagwati (1973) who consider a third closely related type.

2. Lefeber (1971) has also explored this case in a model with one consumer good and one investment good, instead of the two consumer goods of the traditional model.

3. Rigidity of the nominal (instead of the real) wage need not lead to unemployment in the standard barter model of international trade, as pointed out by Johnson (1965).

4. As shown by Brecher (1971), the following analysis could be extended readily for a minimum wage specified in terms of either the first good or a constant-utility combination of both goods.

5. The minimum wage is treated here as a "fact of life" which, for social or political reasons, government and unions are unable or unwilling to alter within the time period considered in this paper. (This assumption does not rule out the longer-run possibility—not discussed in this paper—of varying the minimum wage by government action or by union response to the level of unemployment.) Consequently, for the welfare maximizations of section 3, the government treats the wage as a policy constraint rather than a policy tool. Admittedly, this type of constrained government also might be unable or unwilling to impose the labor subsidy required by the first-best solution, which is a reason for considering the other policy packages in the ranking.

6. It is assumed that $f_i(0) = 0$, $\lim_{k_i \to \infty} f'_i(k_i) = 0$ and $\lim_{k_i \to 0} f'_i(k_i) = \infty$ for $i = 1, 2$, where f'_i is the derivative of f_i with respect to k_i.

7. This result follows from the fact that full employment of both factors is consistent only with $k_2 \leqq \bar{K}/\bar{L} \leqq k_1$, as implied by the identity $K/L \equiv k_1 L_1/L + k_2 L_2/L$.

8. Whether or not factor intensities reverse at some disequilibrium $\omega(\neq \bar{\omega})$ is of no concern in this paper.

9. For further discussion of the minimum-wage transformation curve, including the regions of complete specialization, see Brecher (1974) who shows the following two results. First, for all $p > \bar{p}$, production occurs at R_2. Second, for all $p < \bar{p}$, production occurs on $R_1 T_1$, with output (and employment) rising as p decreases.

10. These assumptions imply that the foreign elasticity of imports with respect to (relative) price is always greater than one in absolute value. If regions of inelastic foreign demand (with $g' < 0$) were allowed, the analysis would be more complicated algebraically (not geometrically), but there would be no change in any of the main policy results reported below. This invariance of conclusions has to do with the fact that an elastic foreign demand (with $g' > 0$) still would be necessary condition at any of the optimal positions considered below.

11. As shown by Bhagwati and Srinivasan (1969), welfare can be allowed to depend also upon non-consumption variables. In the present context, social welfare could be made to depend upon total employment in addition to aggregate consumption. For example, it could be assumed that social welfare is a concave function $W[U(C_1, C_2), L]$ of U and L; where $\partial W/\partial U > 0$ and $\partial W/\partial L > 0$, if U and L are both finite. The analysis of section 3 could be reworked by maximizing W subject to the constraints of the system, in much the same way that U is maximized below. For the three alternate policy combinations considered in this paper, their W-welfare ranking (in the case of W-maximization) would be the same as their U-welfare ranking (in the case of U-maximization performed below). Unsurprisingly, however, W-maximization would yield a smaller U and a larger L than does U-maximization—except under the first-best policy which would give the same U and the same $L(\bar{L})$ under either maximization.

12. Use of community indifference curves may require socially optimal lump-sum transfers that depress employed labor's income below $\bar{w}_2$. If so, it is assumed that unions—which may be sufficiently powerful to force the producer to pay $\bar{w}_2$—are not strong enough to set a floor to labor's after-tax income. In other words, this paper is concerned with a (pre-tax) minimum-wage constraint, and not with a (post-tax) minimum-income constraint.

13. For an illustration of the entire consumption-possibility frontier, including the non-linear parts corresponding to complete specialization in production, see Brecher (1971).

14. In fact, imposing an optimal trade tax will decrease employment when the home country exports the labor-intensive good as explained by Brecher (1974).

15. Tax-cum-subsidies on production, instead of consumption, could be used to achieve the same welfare levels discussed below.

16. An ad valorem consumption tax of τ_2, imposed on the second good, would imply $\text{MPL}_2 = \bar{w}_2(1 + \tau_2)$. Thus, variations in τ_2 would alter the equilibrium MPL_2, the equilibrium k_2 (which depends only on MPL_2 under constant returns

to scale), and the minimum-wage transformation curve [which depends on k_2 as shown by equation (6)]. This complication is ruled out by assuming $\tau_2 = 0$. More generally, this complication would arise whenever the domestic consumer and the domestic producer faced different money prices for the (second) good which defines the minimum wage—not the case under simply a trade tax or trade subsidy.

17. However, if $\bar{t} > 0$, imposing $\bar{t}$ together with $\bar{\tau}$ may reduce employment below the free-trade level when the home country exports the labor-intensive good, as suggested by footnote 14.

18. The value of t^* would be zero if the home country had no monopoly power in trade, as in the case considered by Bhagwati (1968, pp. 20–22). Thus, as he argued, only a labor subsidy would be needed then.

Chapter 14

1. Since this paper was written, my attention has been drawn to two interesting papers, by Wolfgang Mayer (1974a) and by Murray C. Kemp, Yoshio Kimura, and Koji Okuguchi, which study adjustment mechanisms similar to those considered here. However both of these papers are exclusively concerned with a small open economy, and do not discuss the question of factor-market distortions.

2. The term long run is to be understood in the Marshallian sense, as a period long enough for each sector to have adopted a scale of production which is (privately) optimal in the light of its external environment. A corollary of this is that factors have been allocated such that they earn the same net return in each sector. Since throughout this paper I assume that total factor supplies are fixed, it is clear that this long run may be relatively short in comparison with the time periods usually considered in the theory of economic growth. The sense in which the appellation "Marshallian" is appropriate should become clear in section IV below.

3. Most writers in the enormous literature on factor-market distortions deal exclusively with the long-run, two mobile factors, case. (See especially Arnold C. Harberger and Jones (1971a).) Exceptions include: Charles E. McLure, Jr. who uses a model where labor is sector specific but capital instantaneously mobile; Magee (1976, pp. 85–86) who briefly discusses the adjustment process, citing unpublished work by J. Marquez-Ruarte; and the author (1978b), who examines the consequences of a particular factor-market distortion in both mobile and immobile capital models, but without examining the adjustment process.

4. The notation used is that of Jones (1965): λ_{ij} is the proportion of the fixed stock of factor i used in sector j; θ_{ij} is the share of gross payments to factor i in the value of output of sector j; and σ_j is the elasticity of substitution between capital and labor in sector j.

5. This point has been noted by Jones (1975, p. 13). However in his model there are no long-run factor-market distortions. Hence a difference between the physical and value factor-intensity rankings can obtain only during the transition period and *not* in a state of long-run equilibrium.

6. One difficulty with this assumption arises if either factor is "inessential" in the production function of either sector (in the sense that the isoquants of the function intersect the axis corresponding to that factor). In such cases the assumption of complete factor-price flexibility implies that the return of the relevant factor in the sector concerned may be zero during part of the adjustment period. This situation is logically consistent, provided it is assumed that the inessential factor is maintained above subsistence level by lump sum transfers where necessary. However, it is not a very appealing situation, and where it is likely to occur a different adjustment mechanism, similar to those mentioned in note 12, may be preferred to that of the present section.

7. The only previous writer to discuss these loci appears to be Magee, who considered only one of the two loci, calling it first a "distortion equilibrium locus" (1971, p. 630), and later, following Marquez-Ruarte, an "iso-price locus" (Magee, 1976, pp. 28, 86). The latter term is inappropriate in the present context, however, since with both factor markets in disequilibrium, *any* point in the production box is a feasible short-run equilibrium for a given relative goods price. For a geometric derivation of the *LMEL*, see Neary (1978a).

8. For example if a differential is paid by the import-competing sector, free trade may be inferior to no trade (see Batra, p. 264); if it is paid by the export sector, an increase in the terms of trade may reduce welfare (Batra, pp. 268–70); and growth may be immiserizing even when the terms of trade are constant and there are no impediments to trade (Batra, pp. 272–73). As Jagdish N. Bhagwati has pointed out, most if not all of these paradoxes may be viewed as special cases of the general phenomenon of immiserizing growth.

9. In discussing their principal equation, Johnson and Mieszkowski (p. 550) invoke stability considerations in order to establish the sign of the denominator (which may be shown to be a simple multiple of σ). However they do not specify a dynamic adjustment process, and other writers on tax incidence in the presence of nonzero initial taxes have ignored this issue (see, for example, Adolf L. Vandendorpe and Ann F. Friedlaender, p 219).

10. The parallel with growth theory is not exact however, since I am comparing a static model exhibiting short-run factor specificity with a dynamic model where capital is instantaneously transferable between sectors. For studies of two-sector growth models with capital specificity, see Ken-Ichi Inada and Antonio Bosch, Andreu Mas-Colell, and Assaf Razin.

11. The implicit assumption made by Jones is that the commodity market is cleared by a tâtonnement price adjustment mechanism, but that factor markets adjust completely to each suggested price announced by the hypothetical auctioneer. But in this bizarre situation, the model would be unstable whenever the aggregate supply schedule were downward sloping, since factor markets would be adjusting in the face of fixed commodity prices (even though no trading was actually taking place) and so the stability analysis of section II would be appropriate.

12. It may be shown that the stability conditions of this paper continue to apply under alternative adjustment mechanisms, which allow for short-run labor market segmentation and sluggish adjustment of wage levels in response to excess labor supply.

13. Among the least satisfactory assumptions of the present model that may be mentioned are the absence of any explicit costs to factor reallocation, the assumption that elasticities of substitution in production are no greater in the long run than in the short run, and the lack of consideration given to monetary factors. Moreover, it may be questioned whether the process of capital reallocation can be distinguished even conceptually from that of capital accumulation.

Chapter 15

1. This method of introducing market disruption presupposes that the QR-level is prespecified but that the probability of its being imposed will be a function of how deeply the market is penetrated in the importing country and therefore how effective the import-competing industry's pressure for protection will be vis-à-vis the importing country's government. The effect of modifying this simplifying assumption so as to allow for varying levels of a quota is noted later in this section.

2. Instead of assuming that the fixed quota of $\bar{E}$ will be imposed with probability $P(E)$, one could assume that a quota of $\bar{E}$ will be imposed with probability density $P(\bar{E}, E)$. In other words, the quota level $\bar{E}$ is variable and the probability of imposition depends both on the level $\bar{E}$ and on the quantum of exports E in the first period. Let $f(\bar{E})$ denote the maximum of $U(C_1, C_2)$ subject to $F(X_1, X_2) = 0$ and $E_1 \leq \bar{E}$, where $C_1 = (X_1 - E_1)$ and $C_2 = (X_2 + \pi E_1)$. Then the expected welfare in period 2, given the export level E in the first period, is $\int f(\bar{E}) P(\bar{E}, E) \, d\bar{E}$. Let us denote this by $h(E)$. Thus the maximand ϕ now becomes $U[X_1 - E, X_2 + \pi E] + \rho h(E)$ and condition (3') becomes $U_1/U_2 = \pi + \pi' E + \rho h'(E)/U_2$. Now $h'(E)$ is the change in expected welfare in period 2 due to an additional unit of export in period 1 and this has to be added to the marginal terms of trade $\pi + \pi' E$. Nothing substantive therefore changes. Note however that if we allow for *many* exporting countries and if the *share* in the overall quota level granted in period 2 to *one* exporting country will increase with the export level achieved by that country in period 1, this would produce an incentive to *increase*, rather than decrease, the export level in period 1, *ceteris paribus*. Hence, our analysis based on one exporting country would need to be modified correspondingly.

3. However, we cannot assert that $\phi^L_{NQ} > \phi_Q^{OPT}$ except in the case of a small country with no influence on the terms of trade; this follows from the fact that ϕ^L_{NQ} is no longer the first-best policy in the presence of monopoly power in trade, so that U^* may well exceed $\bar{U}$ in table 1.

4. Needless to say, for a country with no monopoly power, it is not meaningful to think of market-disruption leading to QR's: if the country is indeed atomistic in foreign markets, its exports surely will not cause market disruption. Our analysis, of course, allows for monopoly power; only figure 1 illustrates the simple case of a small country.

5. It should be pointed out that atomistic firms in period 1 are assumed to respond to that period's prices only. This assumption can be justified on the ground that they are likely to assume that these prices will carry over into the next period, since there is no other, obvious mechanism by which they can anticipate the 'true' period 2 prices.

6. *In addition*, of course, to the usual optimal tariff if there is also monopoly power in trade.

7. The underbar and the overbar refer to the quota and no-quota values, respectively.

8. The economic rationale for this assumption is that the probability of the exporter invoking an export embargo may be a function of the "import dependence" of the importer.

Chapter 16

1. See the clarification of this point in Bhagwati and Hansen (1974).

2. In fact, Bhagwati and Hansen, in their forthcoming article (1974) which came to my attention only after this paper's first draft was completed, have shown that quite a few different models of smuggling can be constructed including the one considered in this paper. They also point out the possibility of obtaining results contrary to those they obtained in their 1973 paper. Also see the Introduction in Bhagwati (1974).

3. For a discussion of this point see Musgrave (1959) and Melvin (1970).

4. These are the only two costs included in the analysis. The very act of smuggling as compared to legal trade may be considered morally wrong, thus smuggling activity as such may directly enter in the consumers' utility functions, whereas our welfare function ignores this by making welfare a function of the consumption of the two commodities. Smuggling may also affect the general attitude of the population towards other laws of the land, like payment of taxes, and may also lead to undermining the public's confidence in the government, if the government fails to take action against smuggling. If people lose confidence in the government, it may also affect their behaviour towards work, thus affecting production. These problems are ignored in our simplified model.

5. In the Bhagwati-Hansen Model (1973), real costs are reflected in less favourable terms of trade through smuggling. Thus in the presence of smuggling the country faces two terms of trade, one in legal trade and the other in smuggling. Furthermore, they implicitly assume that smuggling is a completely riskless affair. For further discussion, see Bhagwati and Hansen (1974).

6. For a detailed discussion on the derivation of the production possibility surface in such a model, see Melvin (1968).

7. For a proof of this, see Melvin (1968) and Batra and Casas (1973).

8. To maintain the assumption of perfect competition in the smuggling industry, we assume that the smugglers have a knowledge of the risk costs in terms of goods confiscated, fines and punishment levied. A smuggler takes these costs as given to him and can smuggle any amount of the imported good without affecting these costs. These costs are assumed to be increasing due to intra-industrial, inter-firm diseconomies of scale in smuggling (i.e., there are increasing risk costs if everyone tries to smuggle more; a single smuggler is unimportant to affect these costs).

9. We are here assuming that the smuggler can sell his good at the domestic price of the legally imported good. Thus we are implicitly assuming that the consumers are willing to pay the same price for the smuggled good as for the legally imported good, which further means that consumers face no risks in, and have no aversion to, using the smuggled good.

10. By this we mean that the risk of smuggling, a unit of a commodity in terms of confiscation of goods, fine, punishment, etc., increases as the total amount of smuggling increases.

11. Our assumption of increasing risk costs is crucial in enabling us to get a determinate solution to the problem of distribution of imports between legal and smuggled since it generates a positively sloped supply curve AB.

12. At the level of smuggling given by D in figure 3, AG is equal to the per unit risk cost in smuggling in terms of X, and as the smuggler is a price taker, he takes this cost as given, as indicated in note 8. Then it is obvious that there are no pure profits in smuggling at the level of smuggling given by D, a condition for the existence of perfect competition.

13. Bhagwati (1968) has explained this phenomenon as yet another instance of the generalized theory of immiserising growth: that, if growth occurs subject to a distortion, it may be immiserising because the loss caused by the distortion may be accentuated and this incremental loss may outweigh the gain that would accrue if growth occurred under optimal policies instead.

14. Because the introduction of smuggling does not change W, the k_i remain unchanged. Hence in equation (2), we have the same unchanged capital-labour ratio as in (1).

15. This follows directly from the constancy of capital-labour ratios and reduction of labour input in the production of X and M.

16. The determination of welfare level in the presence of smuggling from a production point like F' exactly follows the procedure of determining welfare level in the non-smuggling situation. Draw the terms of trade line from F' and the community indifference curve on this line tangent to the price ratio parallel to the tangent at F' gives the welfare level.

17. Bhagwati and Hansen (1973) have concluded that smuggling must always decrease welfare in legal trade is not completely eliminated. We have shown above that this may not always be true.

18. The analysis can readily be modified to include a shifting ABB' supply curve of illegal imports, with C_T changing. We merely choose a case where, for simplicity, this is ruled out.

19. For the spelling-out of the necessary caveats (e.g., problems arising from inferior goods) in this proposition, see Bhagwati (1968) and Vanek (1965).

20. We may also note that, once the tariff rate becomes redundant in the presence of smuggling, there are no further changes in the level of smuggling for tariff changes, indicating that there is a maximum limit to the amount of M which is smuggled, and hence a maximum inward shift of the transformation curve.

Chapter 17

1. See Bhagwati and Ramaswami (1963); Johnson (1965); Bhagwati, Ramaswami and Srinivasan (1969); Bhagwati (1971); and the numerous writings of Kemp, Findlay, Corden, Magee, Brecher, and several trade theorists.

2. Very early and pioneering analyses by Joshi (1972) and Lal (1974) attempting to examine the Little-Mirrlees (1969) *Manual* rules along trade-theoretic lines must also be mentioned. Corden (1974) also has a discussion of these rules.

3. For a historical review of the antecedents of the DRC concept, especially in Israel, see Bruno (1972). The use of ERP as a project criterion appears, on the other hand, to have been the subject of internal World Bank memoranda during the mid-1960s stemming presumably from the notion that, in some sense, they reflected "comparative advantage."

4. Provided that inferior goods are ruled out, there is of course a monotonic relationship between welfare and the distance of the availability locus (at international prices) from the origin, given a well-behaved social utility function. Thus, provided the degree of protection, and hence the degree of consumption distortion, remains unchanged over the entire economy before and after the acceptance of the project, one can disregard without error the fact that trade distortions will also distort consumption. It follows immediately, of course, that if one is dealing with a quota restriction, rather than an ad valorem tariff, so that we have essentially a *variable* (degree of) distortion, the aforementioned monotonic relationship between welfare and the distance of the availability locus (at international prices) will break down. More on this is to be found in Bhagwati and Wan (1977).

5. The notation $\hat{w}*$, $\hat{\gamma}*$ is used here because the circumflex refers to the distorted situation and the asterisk to the evaluation of output change at international prices.

6. This is also the procedure suggested for deriving shadow factor prices by Diamond and Mirrlees (1976) in their analysis of a similar problem. It may be noted here that, in the case where the trade distortion is not ad valorem but, say, a specific tariff (or subsidy) or a quantitative restriction, the coefficients $\hat{l}_1$, $\hat{k}_1$, $\hat{l}_2$, and $\hat{k}_2$ will change with the withdrawal of factors even for a "small" project and one cannot use this procedure for estimating shadow factor prices. Moreover, note also that, if the number of factors differs from the number of goods, then shadow factor prices may not be uniquely defined for small changes and/or may be nonstationary for large changes. On all this, see Bhagwati and Wan (1977).

7. Compare Bhagwati (1968); Johnson (1967) who deals with the precise distortion in our model here; and Bhagwati (1971) who states the general theory of immiserizing growth that explains and ties together the different instances of immiserizing growth. The phenomenon of negative shadow factor prices, in turn, is related to the empirically important phenomenon of value subtraction at international prices: the latter requires, but does not necessarily follow from, the former; see Bhagwati, Srinivasan, and Wan (1977).

8. An alternative analysis of the inappropriateness of the Findlay-Wellisz procedure, in programming terms, is available from the authors, on request.

9. We could also, in principle, have distinguished between "gross" and "net" values, as explained in the text presently. However, there is no evidence that gross measures have been computed so that we confine ourselves in the text to only the net measures.

10. While the DRCs are conceptually stated below for the project X_3, they can be readily adapted for the existing activities as well.

11. For complexities that arise in this regard, however, when the number of primary factors is less than the number of traded goods, see Bhagwati and Wan (1977).

12. For an interesting analysis of the problem as to when a project accepted (rejected) by the incorrect use of first-best factor prices would be rejected (accepted) by the correct use of second-best factor prices, see Findlay-Wellisz (1976).

13. Of course, the choice of a project on the basis of ERP rankings may nonetheless, in specific cases, be a correct choice. In fact, the interested reader may well analyze the conditions under which this will be the case, just as Findlay-Wellisz (1976) have analyzed elegantly the conditions under which the use of first-best shadow factor prices à la Bacha-Taylor (1971) will nonetheless result in a correct choice/rejection of a project.

14. Such a rule (or variations thereof) can be found in the context of import-substituting industrialization in many less developed countries. See Bhagwati and Desai (1970) and Bhagwati and Srinivasan (1975) for India, and Bhagwati (1977) for more extended discussion of such rules and the associated policies of "automatic" protection. An early and correct analysis of the implications of such a rule on cost-benefit analysis is in Little-Mirrlees (1969). In fact, Bruno (1962, pp. 112–13, 147) appears to have had the earliest analysis of this "fabric-garment" example!

15. This distortion was brought into analytical discussion by Harris and Todaro (1970); the "sector specificity" and its critical importance were noted and analyzed in Bhagwati and Srinivasan (1974) and in Srinivasan and Bhagwati (1975).

16. This is the distortion where the sticky, actual wage exceeds the shadow wage but the sticky wage applies universally across sectors. The major papers on this distortion, initially analyzed by Haberler (1950), are by Lefeber (1971) and Brecher (1974a, 1974b).

17. Among the principal positive analyses of the distortion when the same factor must be paid for differentially by different sectors are those by Hagen (1958), Johnson (1966), Bhagwati and Srinivasan (1971), Herberg and Kemp (1971), Jones (1971a), and Magee (1976); the welfare analyses are by Hagen (1958) and Bhagwati and Ramaswami (1963). Pearce and Mundlak have made valuable contributions also.

18. The model as set out in Harris and Todaro (1970) is misspecified on the demand side. See therefore the correct specification, as set out in Bhagwati and Srinivasan (1974) and followed here.

19. At points other than P on PQ, furthermore, the shadow rental of capital will be the *average* product of capital in X_2 at P along the curve APB, rather than its market value which will equal the marginal product.

20. At Q also, the shadow price of capital will continue to be the average product of capital in manufacturing at point P, since at Q only the manufactured good, X_2, is produced using all the available capital and the same technique as at P.

21. For these and other pathologies, see Bhagwati and Srinivasan (1971) and Magee's excellent survey (1976).

22. Jones (1971a) calls the differential-weighted intensities the "value" as against the Samuelsonian "physical" factor-intensities.

23. On the analysis of the possibility of such "stationarity" of the "marginal-variational" shadow factor prices, in more general models with many goods and factors, see Bhagwati and Wan (1977).

24. For example, the latter is done readily, using the Jones (1971b) model where each of two sectors has a specific factor. The project (X_3) can then be thought of as drawing one or both of these specific factors and/or the mobile, nonspecific factor(s) from the existing, distorted situation.

Chapter 18

1. Points (1) and (2) are clearly related, for the existence of (1) is a *necessary* condition for (2), but they are more conveniently treated as separate points, since (1) is not a *sufficient* condition for the existence of (2).

2. In everything that follows the "home country" will be labelled A, the "union partner" B and the rest of the world C.

3. This argument presumes that relative prices in each country reflect real rates of transformation. It follows that the resources used to produce a unit of X in country A could produce any other good to the value of 35s. and, since a unit of X can be had from B by exporting goods to the value of only 26s., there will be a surplus of goods valued at 9s. accruing to A from the transfer of resources out of X when trade is opened with country B.

4. The point may be made slightly more formally as follows: the conditions necessary for the maximizing of *any* function do not, in general, provide conditions sufficient for an increase in the value of the function when the maximum value is not to be obtained by the change.

5. One of the two countries might be an efficient producer of this commodity needing no tariff protection, in which case, *a fortiori*, there is gain.

6. Care must be taken to distinguish between complementarity and competitiveness in costs and in tastes, both being possible. In the Makower-Morton model these relations exist only on the cost side. An example of the confusion which may arise when this distinction is not made can be seen (Meyer, 1956). Meyer's definitions, if they are to mean anything, must refer to the demand side. Hence he is not entitled to contrast his results with those of Makower and Morton, or of Viner, all of whom were concerned with cost complementarity and competitiveness.

7. It is assumed throughout all the subsequent analysis that the tariff revenue collected by the Government is either returned to individuals by means of lump-

sum subsidies or spent by the Government on the same bundle of goods that consumers would have purchased.

8. Lipsey (1957), pp. 43–44. The changes made in the quotation are minor ones necessary to make the notation in the example comparable to the one used in the present text.

9. If we assume that consumers adjust their purchases to the relative prices ruling in their domestic markets, then the optimum conditions that rates of substitution in consumption should equal rates of transformation in trade can be stated in terms of equality between relative prices ruling in the domestic markets and those ruling in the international market.

10. The point of his taxonomy or of any taxonomy of this sort, it seems to me, must be merely to illustrate how the model works. Once one has mastered the analysis it is possible to work through any particular case that may arise, and there would seem to be no need to work out all possible cases beforehand.

11. For example, the same rate of tariff might not be charged on all imports. In this case it is only necessary to weight each dollar's increase or decrease in trade by the proportion of this value that is made up by tariff—the greater is the rate of tariff the greater is the gain or loss. It is also possible, if one wishes to make inter-country comparisons, to weight a dollar's trade in one direction by a different amount than a dollar's trade in some other direction. These complications, however, do not affect the essence of Meade's analysis, which is to make a *small change* in some tariffs and then to observe that the welfare consequences depend on the net change in the volume of trade and to continue the study in order to discover in what circumstances an increase or a decrease in the net volume of trade is likely.

12. A unique second-best level (i.e. the level which maximizes welfare subject to the existence and invariability of all the other taxes, tariffs, etc.) for any one variable factor can be shown to exist in a large number of cases (see, for example, Lipsey and Lancaster, 1956, sections V and VI), but cannot be proved to exist in general (ibid., section VIII).

13. This may be given a more formal statement. Consider the direction of the change—towards or away from the second-best optimum position—caused by the change in the tax. Moving away from the second-best optimum is a *sufficient*, but not a necessary, condition for a reduction in welfare. Moving towards the second-best optimum is a *necessary*, but not a sufficient, condition for an increase in welfare.

14. Note also that everything is assumed to be a substitute for everything else; there are no relations of complementarity.

15. Perhaps a more intuitively appealing argument as to why these estimates probably do not over estimate the order of magnitude of the gain is as follows. "Typical European tariffs on manufactured goods are in the order of 20 per cent. This means that industries from 1 to 20 per cent less efficient than foreign competitors will be protected by these tariffs. If the costs of different industries are spread out evenly, then some tariff-protected industries would be 20 per cent less efficient than foreign competitors, but others would be only 1 per cent less efficient,

and their average inefficiency would be in the order of half the tariff rate, which is 10 per cent less efficient than foreign competitors. Typically, not much more than 10 per cent of a country's resources would be devoted to producing behind tariff walls. This means that 10 per cent of a country's resources would be producing 10 per cent less efficiently than if there were no tariffs, which makes a reduction in national income of something in the order of 1 per cent." See Lipsey (1968), p. 772.

16. In singling out Professor Johnson, I do not wish to imply that he is alone in practising the sort of economics which I am criticizing. On the contrary, he is typical of a very large number of economists who have attempted to obtain quantitative conclusions from qualitative arguments.

17. See also Johnson (1958b) for a similar argument.

18. Milton Friedman's argument (1953) that survival of the fittest proves profit maximization notwithstanding. What seems to me to be a conclusive refutation of the Friedman argument is to be found in Archibald (1959).

I have since changed my mind in respect to this belief. See the more detailed arguments in Lipsey (1967), p. 12. The following quotation should indicate the nature of my present disagreement with the argument in the text. "Before you accept this argument which is usually thrown about quite uncritically ask yourself what the text books all say about the argument that a poor, low productivity country cannot trade profitably with a rich, high productivity one. "Nonsense," say the books, "it is comparative not absolute advantage that determines the flow of trade and the gains from it." Assume, for example, that everybody in Britain is absolutely 20 per cent less efficient than everybody on the Continent. If we go into the common market on an exchange rate which will yield an external balance, then there will be *no* effect on overall efficiency: some industries will have a comparative advantage, some will not, and payments will be balanced at the given levels of efficiency. The only way in which increased efficiency could be forced on Britain would be if we went in at an over-valued exchange rate. This means that very few industries would be able to export and that imports would flood in from the continent. We would then be hoping that the domestic level of efficiency would react so that the overall level of costs and prices would fall in Britain, *vis-à-vis* Europe, and that a balance of payments would be achieved at the formerly overvalued rate once the increase in efficiency had occurred. But there is no reason to think that a rise in efficiency with a constant price level which is the equivalent to a temporary increase in the rate of economic growth would improve the balance of payments. Certainly there is little in our recent history to suggest that it would cause a deflation. Probably the best we could hope for would be a parallel rise in wages and no change in the price level. Thus, even if the gain were realized, we would have to contemplate a subsequent devaluation of the pound. This in itself would be no disaster but it is not easy to devalue a single currency within the rules of the Common Market nor is there any evidence that the Six would contemplate allowing us to enter on an over-valued rate. We would also be taking the chance—in my opinion a very outside one in light of evidence of the 1920s—that an overvalued exchange rate would produce a rise in efficiency rather than a decline in employment and in national income."

Chapter 19

1. The proposition together with an indication of the lines along which a proof may be constructed, may be found in Kemp (1964, p. 176). A geometric proof for the canonical three-countries, two-commodities case has been furnished by Vanek (1965, pp. 160–165).

Chapter 20

1. Sir Donald MacDougall has noted the importance of considering the factor bias accompanying technical progress for international trade problems. See MacDougall (1957, p. 518).

2. The concept of factor intensity has been discussed extensively in the recent literature on international trade theory. See Samuelson (1948; 1949), Pearce and James (1951–52) and Jones (1956–57).

3. There is an extensive literature on this subject in classical, Marxian, and modern economics. The major modern references are Hicks (1935) and Robinson (1946). Since in our model the amounts of the factors remained fixed, the effect on relative factor shares is known once the shift in the factor price ratio has been determined.

Chapter 21

1. J. R. Hicks [3]. The following are of interest: H. G. Johnson [5]; E. J. Mishan [6]; and W. M. Corden [1].

2. Exception must be made, however, in the case of Professor Johnson [4] [5].

3. As distinguished from *importables*.

4. This argument obviously rests on the assumption of "well-behaved" (convex) indifference curves and (concave) transformation curves, concavity being defined with reference to the origin and *not* in the strict mathematical sense.

5. Rybczynski [7]. Linear homogeneity of the production functions and diminishing returns are *sufficient* conditions for the proposition to hold. The strong Samuelson notion of factor-intensity is not necessary.

6. Johnson [5]. Diminishing returns are *sufficient* for this proposition to hold. The proposition can be readily extended to more than two goods and factors.

7. The conditions under which this result will obtain have been investigated in a brilliant paper by Findlay and Grubert [2].

Chapter 22

1. For proof, see Harry G. Johnson, "International Trade and Economic Growth —A Supplementary Analysis," *Arthaniti*, Vol. V, 1–13. The same result will follow from non-neutral technical progress in the protected industry, unless it is

sufficiently strongly biased towards saving the factor used intensively in the export industry.

2. Jagdish Bhagwati, "Immiserizing Growth: A Geometrical Note," *Review of Economic Studies*, Vol. XXV, No. 3, June 1958, 201–5.

Chapter 23

1. If foreign profits were repatriated in terms of home importables (instead of exportables), the host country would be left with bundle Z' (instead of Z), and home consumption would be at point C'_2 (instead of C_2); where point Z' (on line DD') lies directly below P_1, line $Z'C'_2$ (not drawn) has a slope given by the world price ratio, and C'_2 (like C_2) lies necessarily southwest of C_0. In general, if foreign profits were repatriated in terms of both goods, the host country would be left with a bundle on line segment ZZ', and home consumption would be at the corresponding point on line segment $C_2C'_2$. A particular case of interest would arise if foreign profits were repatriated by withdrawing the two goods in the proportion given by the slope of line OO', since this case is analytically similar to having these profits consumed in the host country by the foreigners according to the home pattern of demand.

2. Point A corresponds to the capital inflow just large enough to extinguish home imports, because Mundell's (1957) analysis shows that a tariff-imposing country with zero imports gains from a capital inflow as the domestic product-price ratio approaches the international ratio of commodity prices.

Chapter 24

1. The term "autarky" in the present context is taken to mean the absence of trade across national *borders*, in conformity with conventional terminology of economic policy discussions. More elaboration of this point is provided in section IV below.

2. Thus, our general-equilibrium analysis can throw light on the conditions under which parametric changes at the national level may lead to conflicting outcomes for differently-endowed racial, ethnic, sexual and other differentiated groups within the nation.

3. For ease of identification, figure 3 is marked, both for P_K/P_L and for P_y/P_x, with identical lettering: C, D, E, and F. Thus, the factor price-ratio range DE corresponds to the goods price-ratio range DE. Similarly, the positioning of the letters C, D, E and F on the K_x/L_x and K_y/L_y schedules indicates, as noted in the text, corresponding points of specialization in production on T_xT_y and $T'_xT'_y$. Again, the lettering on T_xT_y and $T'_xT'_y$ in figure 4 will correspond to the lettering in figure 3 to facilitate grasp of the relationship between the two illustrations.

4. Of course, $dQ_x/d(P_L/P_x) \geqslant 0$ also because $\bar{L}_n/\bar{K}_n \geqslant L_x/K_x$. Except for the borderline case of goods price-ratio OD, it is evident that $\bar{L}_n/\bar{K}_n$ exceeds both L_x/K_x and L_y/K_y as P_y/P_x varies from D to C and therefore *both* Q_y and Q_x will improve unambiguously with increase of P_y/P_x.

5. If, as in the Bhagwati-Tironi analysis, there is only labour in the national endowment, and capital is essential for production, T_xT_y would shrink to the origin! Otherwise, in their model, it would have a Ricardian shape if capital is dispensable.

6. This is, in fact, the paradoxical case considered in Bhagwati and Tironi (1978), section II, but without the underlying explanation and argumentation *a la* the national production possibility curve, as set out in this paper.

7. Of course, this does not mean that the paradox cannot arise if national and foreign tastes are homothetic. For, it is the difference in the trade pattern, as determined by the production and consumption choices at the specified goods price-ratio, that is the critical variable in creating the paradox in both Zones. Nor should the reader forget that the hypothetical national equilibrium production will reflect, in Zone III (as also Zone II, for that matter), the interaction with foreign factors: the national income line cannot simply be drawn by reference to T_xT_y alone by tangency of the goods price-ratio with it. In Zone I, however, the presence of foreign factors does nothing to affect the correctness of such a procedure.

8. This intra-national trade might be *either* goods for goods (in Zone I where trade in factor services is not necessary to equalize marginal products) *or* goods for factor services (in Zones II and III where marginal products would otherwise remain unequal).

Chapter 26

1. In this connexion, R. F. Findlay (5) shows that a high proportion of consumer goods may have to be produced in order to draw labour into the industrial sector.

Chapter 27

1. Two examples of the latter are Holzman (1978), who analyzes why the CPEs run into payment deficits, and Desai (1978), who constructs and estimates a simple Swan-Solow model of the Soviet Union to calculate the social productivity of foreign credits to the Soviet Union, while considering conceptually also the foreign exchange bottleneck that is discussed in the text above. We have profited greatly from reading Holzman (1978), in writing this paper.

2. An early analysis of the foreign exchange bottleneck concept, and its differences from the concepts of payments deficits, is in Bhagwati (1966). An elegant treatment of the concept in a more elaborate framework is in Findlay (1971). In computable planning models, the concept has been used often by Hollis Chenery and his associates: e.g. Chenery and Bruno (1962).

3. That is, the "clay" assumption applies to all factors of production.

4. The super-imposition of the foreign offer curve $\bar{P}QR$ on the production point $\bar{P}$ is, of course, the technique due to Baldwin. The stretch QR represents unitary foreign elasticity of demand for the developing countries' exports of consumer goods.

5. The idealized treatment of the Soviet economy in figure 1 may appear unrealistic to the reader who knows that the Soviet Union exports mainly raw materials such as ores, timber, oil and gas, and chemicals such as potash and ammonia. This worry can be laid to rest by thinking of exports at the *margin*, as in fact we need to do here; and then it is readily seen that figure 1 is close enough to reality. Thus, recall that Soviet machinery exports are widely referred to in the Sovietological literature as "soft exports" whereas exports of raw materials beyond current levels appear infeasible owing to supply, rather than demand, difficulties.

6. We may note explicitly that the argument in the text assumes that wage goods availability will not constrain the growth of Soviet income.

7. The equivalence of world and domestic prices, and the tangency of the latter with TT, are simplifying assumptions and can be relaxed without affecting anything essential in the argument in the text, of course.

8. Thus, subject to these constraints, the maximization of a standard social utility function would evidently result in a different *ex post* equilibrium.

9. Again, note that our depiction of the payments deficit with consumption at C' does not necessarily reflect an optimal *ex post* equilibrium. For, if we were to maximize a social utility function subject to TT, maximal exports of PQ' at terms of trade PE, and a deficit of C'E, we could wind up with consumption at a point other than C'. In addition, there is no reason, of course, to expect that a deficit equal to C'E is itself necessarily optimal.

10. The resource allocational implications for market economies when the adjustment mechanism consists of exchange controls, in place of actual or simulated exchange rate adjustment, can also be rich and complex, depending on how the scarce foreign exchange is actually allocated by the authorities. For a detailed analysis of the "anatomy" of exchange control regimes and their economic consequences, see Bhagwati (1978).

11. Moreover, as Neary has reminded us, this raises the possibility of a suppressed deficit actually yielding a higher welfare level than the corresponding open deficit (which was itself sub-optimal), because of second-best considerations.

Chapter 28

1. Although we do not, in this paper, consider situations in which there is gross disinvestment, it would seem appropriate to assume that increases in the rate of disinvestment also move the PPF toward the origin. We note that our specification of the per capita rate of gross investment as the determinant of the shrinkage of the PPF is only one possibility; for example, others are the rate of gross investment per unit of output or per unit of capital. Each of these has different consequences for the stability of the system; our specification is—as we repeat later—chosen in large part for its simplicity.

2. In principle, other assumptions about the nature of the shifts are, of course, possible. For example, if the adjustment costs of investment affect only the efficiency of labor ("Harrod neutral adjustment costs"), and the production of consumption goods is labor intensive, then investment would shift $T_0 T_0$ to $T_2 T_2$

and the new production point—at the given terms of trade—would be at point B on the Rybczynski line $(R_1 R_1)$. Similarly, in the case of "Solow neutral adjustment costs," where only the efficiency of capital is affected, the transformation frontier shifts to $T_3 T_3$ and the new production point would be at C on the Rybczynski line $(R_c R_c)$. Our specification is motivated by the desire to present the argument in its most simplified form.

3. It will be found, differentiating (21)-(22) with respect to k, that the value of the "marginal product" of k so obtained exceeds r, the rental rate on capital. This is because there is a relationship between α and k which is satisfied at every instant as a result of aggregate investment behavior. It is, however, assumed that the economy is made up of numerous investors, each of whom takes α as given, and that accordingly capital receives the world rental rate, r. This corresponds to an assumption of competition in the rental and investment markets. The discrepancy between the private and social returns to capital entails a distortion—similar to those arising in models of learning by doing—which could be corrected by taxing investment.

4. At the point for which the deficit in the service account equals the surplus in the capital account, $iz = \dot{z} + nz$. Since $z < 0$, $\dot{z} = (i - n)z < 0$ (since $i > n$) and thus the net debtor position rises.

5. The slope of the growth path increases monotonically with k; since the $(b_T = 0)$ locus is linear in the nonspecialized region, there cannot be more than two intersections (at one of which the path has a negative slope) between them in the nonspecialized region. In the specialized regions, the behavior of the slope of the $(b_T = 0)$ locus depends on elasticities of substitution and also α''.

Index